## DATE DUE

# The USA and
the New Europe

# The USA and the New Europe
# 1945–1993

*Peter Duignan and L. H. Gann*

BLACKWELL
*Oxford UK & Cambridge USA*

First published 1994

Blackwell Publishers
238 Main Street
Cambridge, Massachusetts 02142
USA

108 Cowley Road
Oxford OX4 1JF
UK

*Library of Congress Cataloging-in-Publication Data*

Duignan, Peter.
    The USA and the New Europe, 1945–1993 / Peter Duignan and
L. H. Gann.
        p.    cm.
    Includes index.
    ISBN 1–55786–518–3. – ISBN 1–55786–519–1 (pbk.)
    1. Europe – Foreign relations – United States. 2. United States –
Foreign relations – Europe. 3. Europe – Politics and government – 1989–
4. Europe – Economic conditions – 1989– 5. Europe – Foreign relations
– 1989– 6. Europe – Defenses. I. Gann, Lewis H., 1924–. II. Title.
D1065.U5D86 1994
327.7304–dc20                                                        93–17859
                                                                                CIP

*British Library Cataloguing in Publication Data*

A CIP catalogue record for this book is available from the British Library.

Typeset in 10 on 12 pt Erhardt
by Pure Tech Corporation, Pondicherry, India
Printed in Great Britain by Page Bros. Norwich.
This book is printed on acid-free paper

# Contents

# List of Figures

# Preface

"The British Empire and the United States will have to be somewhat mixed up together in some of their affairs for mutual and general advantage," Winston Churchill explained in a wartime broadcast. The process was unstoppable and, "like the Mississippi, it just keeps rolling along." Churchill's remarks applied with equal force to relations between the United States and postwar Europe. The Atlantic partnership born of World War II has since shaped the modern world. It was this partnership which created peace and prosperity for Western Europe and North America alike, after many years of turmoil and bloodshed. It was this partnership which defeated the Soviet challenge and ended the Cold War. It is this partnership which the newly independent countries of East-Central Europe wish to join in some form. It is this partnership which has created innumerable linkages, official and non-official, uniting the North Atlantic states – the most successful alliance in modern history.

The present study seeks to analyze the reciprocal relationships between the United States and Europe in their various aspects – social, political, economic, cultural. We have dealt at some length with the historical origins indispensable for a proper understanding both of the movement from 1945 to unite Europe, and of Euro-American relations in general. We have discussed both formal organizations such as the European Community (EC), the North Atlantic Treaty Organization (NATO), and the "Single Market of 1992." Thereafter we have discussed the breakup of the Soviet empire, the emergence of a new order in what was once the Soviet domain, and the future of American policy regarding Europe. As the European states tighten their existing links, the United States will meet many new challenges. We have tried to explain what they are, and how American policy-makers should respond.

We are unashamedly "Atlanticist" by conviction; we hold no brief for the neo-isolationism that has begun to gather strength among "inward-looking" politicians on both the right and on the left of the American political spectrum. We have tried to look at the world through both American and European spectacles. But we remain convinced that, despite numerous disagreements, European and American interests coincide in the long run. Our work is intended to contribute to transatlantic understanding; hopefully it will appeal alike to undergraduates and general readers interested in world affairs.

We should like to thank the Hoover Institution for permitting us to use much extended and updated versions of articles which have previously appeared in the Hoover Essays series. And our debts are many to Hoover Director John Raisian for the steady support for and generous underwriting of this book.

We are indebted to the following who have kindly read individual chapters: Samuel Barnes, Director of the German Center at Georgetown University; James McAdam, Department of Political Science, Notre Dame University; Norman Naimark, History Department, Stanford University; and at the Hoover Institution, Dennis L. Bark, Angelo Codavilla, Robert Hessen, A. F. Peterson, Henry Rowen, Thomas Sowell, Richard F. Staar and Marcia Weigel. We should also like to express our gratitude to our secretary, research assistant and friend, Theory Berger, for her unwearying help.

The authors take full responsibility for any errors or omissions that remain; the opinions and judgments expressed here are theirs alone.

# 1

# Introduction

Most Americans have always regarded Europe as the "mother continent" from which they traced their ancestry. As the American historian Daniel J. Boorstin put it, "our roots were European; we got our religion, common-law, constitutionalism and political ideals of liberty, justice and equality from Europe." Americans equally derived from Europe their fears of aristocrats, feudalism, and monopoly. The vast size and wealth of their continent and their pioneering history tended to make them more confident, self-reliant, and individualistic than Europeans. European travelers traditionally stressed the American's untoward bumptiousness. But at the same time, Americans had a sense of insecurity and of cultural inferiority toward Europe. Despite their reputation for national exuberance, Americans have periodically experienced moods of national despondency. These were even profounder in the nineteenth than in the twentieth century. As a diarist put it just before the outbreak of the Civil War: "We are a weak, divided, disgraced people, unable to maintain our national existence . . . It's a pity we ever renounced our allegiance to the British Crown."[1] Despite periodic recurrences of national melancholy, the achievements of World War II in general brought about a major change of attitudes; Americans thereafter were more confident in their experiment. They wanted to export the advantages of their system to the world at large, and increasingly believed, at least until the Vietnam War, in the worth, even the superiority of US culture, political and economic systems, science and technology.[2]

The US began as an outgrowth of Europe – more specifically as a British colony. The first Englishmen to settle permanently on this side of the Atlantic arrived at Jamestown in 1607. British sovereignty thereafter extended over what later became the Thirteen Colonies – a loose chain of territories wedged between the Atlantic Ocean and the Allegheny

Mountains. British America would stay under the British Crown for more than a century and a half, for as long a time as elapsed between the enunciation of the Monroe Doctrine in 1823 and the present day. A brilliant lexicographer such as Noah Webster might later stress the peculiarity of the American language (in his *American Dictionary*, 1828); but in fact American English never diverged from British English as Afrikaans would diverge from High Dutch; Britain, her empire, and the US remained linked by a common tongue and culture which would become strongly influenced by American usage.

The mutual impact was profound. The Americans accepted from Britain not only folkways, language, and culture, but also a legal system based on the Common Law, a variant of British parliamentary institutions and of British local government. The Founding Fathers had all been born British subjects; they discussed politics according to the norms familiar to educated Englishmen of a liberal disposition. Well-schooled Americans of the period had read Shakespeare and Milton; they were familiar with the King James Bible and the *Book of Common Prayer* which deeply influenced American as well as British thought and speech. American lawyers had read great British jurists such as Sir William Blackstone. Literate Americans were familiar with the philosophy of Locke and Hume. Americans and British people read the same folk tales and the same nursery rhymes, sang the same tunes, had the same tradition of voluntarism and the same religious diversity. When the Americans took up arms against the British Crown, they fought in defense of what they considered the liberties due to True-Born Englishmen, liberties previously secured by the English parliament against the English king during the seventeenth century.

Anglo-America would come to dominate most of North America. An intelligent observer living in 1750 would have found such a forecast surprising. Two hundred fifty years ago, a prophet might well have predicted that the heirs of Spain, dominant in most of South America, Central America, and what is now the American South-West, would win the struggle for continental supremacy. Alternatively, a gambler might have bet on the French, who occupied a huge belt of territory stretching from Canada along the Mississippi Valley down to New Orleans and the Gulf of Mexico. But it was the English-speaking peoples who won out in the course of extended conflicts; it was English traditions of constitutional government that prevailed rather than royal absolutism or that trust in centralized government which had characterized France and Spain.

But though the bulk of North America remained English-speaking, great differences arose between America and the Motherland. Britain was a monarchy supported by a hereditary aristocracy and an Established Church. The American colonists rejected all these institutions. Within the United

Kingdom, as constituted at the time of the War of Independence, there were few immigrants, and slavery was outlawed. The US, by contrast, had substantial foreign minorities (especially Germans), and a small African-American population, mostly enslaved. From the very beginnings of American settler society, American relations with Britain, and indeed with Europe as a whole, were marked by profound ambivalence.

The American War of Independence was indeed the first American civil war. In the Thirteen Colonies, all those who would not or could not fit into the American political culture and middle-class society – including many of the rich and well-born at the top, as well as outsiders such as Indian tribesmen, Scottish Highlanders, poverty-stricken tenant farmers, some of the blacks – sided with the king, as against those colonists who backed the Continental Congress and General Washington. European opinion was likewise split. All those who accounted themselves as pro-gressives, as *philosophes*, or as moderate reformers were apt to see the future with the United States. By contrast, it was "Church and King" mobs which burned the houses of pro-American sympathizers in England.

George Washington's "Farewell Address" (1796) warned against "pas-sionate attachments" to specific countries; it did not set the United States on an isolationist course, however. It was Thomas Jefferson in his first inaugural address (1801) who emphasized no "entangling alliances" with foreign governments. The war of 1812 with Britain reinforced American distrust and determination to resist foreign interference in the Western Hemisphere – hence the Monroe Doctrine (1823). The US even refused to take part in the anti-slave trade campaign after 1807 because of the bitter memories of British seizure and search tactics. In fact it was the British claim to the right of search of suspected slave ships which was a major cause of the war of 1812. The US refused to let the British Navy stop and search American ships; the Stars and Stripes in effect came to protect slavers. It was not until the Webster-Ashburton Treaty of 1842 that the issue was solved by assigning an American African Squadron to stop American ships suspected of carrying slaves. Thus began again American cooperation with European powers and a weakening of the isolationist spirit in the US.

The United States has not so much pursued an isolationist foreign policy as it has avoided entangling alliances while pursuing its national interests. These interests have caused American presidents and Congress to be actively engaged with foreign states throughout the history of the US. American foreign policy aimed to keep the US one nation, whole and indivisible, to protect its borders and frontiers, to keep hostile, foreign powers out of North America, and to ensure American commerce access to markets and resources worldwide.[3]

A free-trading America from its beginning sought to buy and sell throughout the world. Commodore Matthew C. Perry "opened up" Japan to American commerce after 1854, and at the Berlin Conference of 1884–5, the US insisted that the Congo region be a free trade area. Then in 1899, Secretary of State John Hay proclaimed an open door policy for trade with China. In World Wars I and II the Americans returned to Europe to fight alongside of the democracies. After World War II, the US fought for global trade liberalization through the General Agreement on Tariffs and Trade (GATT). The US, in other words, has never been a truly isolationist nation.

## EUROPEAN VIEWS OF AMERICA

Despite numerous diplomatic disputes between Britain and the US, a special relationship developed from the late nineteenth century between the two countries, much closer than, say, the relationship between Spain and the Argentine, France and Quebec. Upper-class Americans widely took the British upper class as their model; Harvard and Yale prided themselves on their affinity to Oxford and Cambridge. Americans have always drawn heavily on British books; many a rich American in the late nineteenth century boasted of marrying his daughter to a British aristocrat with a splendid title and an empty purse. The US-Canadian frontier remained unfortified; there was indeed an intimate connection between US and Canadian expansion to the West, as settlers crossed and recrossed the frontier without hindrance.

But ambivalence dominated Euro-American relations from the beginning. Many Europeans admired, even idealized America. Goethe, greatest of German poets, apostrophized the US at the beginning of the last century in a poem entitled *Amerika, du hast es besser*: America, you are better off than we are; may God preserve you in future from Europe's mournful legacy, from romantic ruins, from tales of bandits, knights, and ghosts. America, Alexis de Tocqueville had written admiringly (1834–40), may justly boast of "a marvellous combination . . . the spirit of religion and the spirit of freedom." Religion supplies to freedom "the divine source of its right." Freedom also stands indebted to those many newcomers "who came in waves to plant themselves on the shores of the New World . . . When the immigrants left their motherland, they had no idea of any superiority of some over others. It is not the happy or the powerful who go into exile, and poverty with misfortune is the best-known guarantee of equality among men."[4]

Tocqueville may have somewhat romanticized America. But he was rarely wrong. Religion affected American political culture in a direct and even more in an indirect way. Pastors and church elders left their imprint, both in promoting moral idealism and often in giving to American politics a peculiar touch of self-righteousness. Equally important, as Tocqueville had stressed, was the role of the immigrants. These men and women had come to the US for economic, political, religious, or racial reasons; they had crossed the ocean to escape from the authority of noblemen, kings, religious authorities, landlords, and more recently, commissars. (Anti-communism in America was strengthened by successive waves of refugees from Eastern Europe, China, Cuba, and Vietnam.) Generally speaking, these newcomers were ambivalent in their attitude toward their respective countries of origin; but they were self-consciously patriotic toward the land of their adoption. Americans – on the whole – were accustomed to self-help, and more respectful toward the self-made man or woman than most Europeans. Americans were for self-improvement, informed, active in self-government and voluntarism. J. S. Mill and Tocqueville said Americans were self-reliant, individualistic, practical men; they were also joiners and pluralists with many different cultures and suspicious of state churches. Not that there was full social equality in the United States: Americans were used to striking differences of wealth, and familiar with ethnic and religious prejudice. But the country was too vast and varied to permit the emergence of a nationally recognized upper class. An old family in Boston counted for nothing in Los Angeles, where its very name might be unknown. The higher ranks in the civil service and the armed forces did not carry the same prestige as they did in Europe. The average Texan or Nevadan might not even recognize the names of eastern prestige schools such as Philips Exeter Academy in New Hampshire, or Hotchkiss School in Connecticut.

It was a system that made for a surprising degree of stability – given the enormous disparities that divided US society. Until recently, Americans voted more often, in national, state, and local elections, than the citizens of any other country. There was a great army of unpaid activists. (During the 1960 presidential elections, for instance, some 4,000,000 volunteers were busy organizing rallies, ringing doorbells, mailing envelopes, and so on.) Each presidential, each gubernatorial candidate had to create or rebuild a personal organization – in a country where people moved often, and over enormous distances. The American system accommodated flux in a way which no European system could rival. It gave temporary places of prominence to an extraordinarily large number of people and provided for political alliances of the strangest kind, even alliances that might cut across ideological divisions. Kipling, the bard of empire, had puzzled over the American Spirit's strange shifts of mood:

That bids him flout the Law he makes,
That bids him make the Law he flouts
Till, dazed by many doubts, he wakes
The drumming guns that have no doubts[5]

But even Kipling had no doubts that the American Spirit would find salvation at last.

Lord Bryce, in *The American Commonwealth* (1888), wanted the US to be a world power and its democratic system to spread to Europe. Israel Zangwill, an Anglo-Jewish writer, at the end of the century, called America God's crucible, the great melting pot which would fuse and reform the European peoples. Even less doubtful were the countless immigrants who flocked to the US from Europe during the nineteenth and the twentieth centuries. The America of fact did not always turn out to be the America of fiction, the *goldene medinah*, the golden state of the Jews, or the *Land der unbegrenzten Möglichkeiten*, the land of unlimited opportunities of the Germans. Nevertheless, they came by the millions – Germans, Scandinavians, Irish; later, people from Eastern and Southern Europe including Poles, Russians, Jews, Italians, Greeks, and many others. From the turn of the century, there was also a massive increase in the number of Spanish-speaking people (not so much Spaniards from Europe as Mexicans, and after World War II Puerto Ricans and Cubans), as well as newcomers from the Far East.

The precise ethnic makeup of the American people is hard to disentangle, because of intermarriage and because ethnic and racial boundaries remain murky. By the time of the 1980 Census, 50 million persons reported themselves to be of English origin, the largest single group – but more than half of those also listed other ethnic origins as well. The same applied to the 49 million who put down "German," and to those who described themselves as Scottish or Welsh by descent. Three-quarters of the 40 million Americans who categorized themselves as Irish also reported other ancestries; the same went for 4 million Swedes, and for a majority of 31/2 million Norwegians. Twelve million said that they were of Italian origin – but of those only 7 million indicated exclusively Italian ancestry. A majority of the 8 million who claimed to be of Polish ancestry also reported forebears of other nationalities.[6] But despite massive recent immigration from Latin America and Asia, something like four-fifths of the US population remains of European origin (including that large proportion of Hispanics who describe themselves as "white" on the census forms). These boundaries moreover remain tenuous. No matter what their nationality, Americans would marry whom they pleased, but usually before World War II within the same religious cohort.

Despite the diversity of their ethnic roots, the great majority stayed in the land of their adoption. They took up citizenship, and came to feel at home in a country whose people were not expected to know their place, but would rather make their place. Immigration created ethnic lobbies of a specifically American kind. Naturalized citizens would use their political influence to help the cause of their kinsmen in Europe: Irish Americans supported the cause of Irish independence against Britain; Polish Americans agitated against the rule of the Russian Czars, and Czechs against the Hapsburgs. Immigration in and of itself also acted as a spur to further immigration, as newcomers would commonly help other relatives and friends to make the long journey across the Atlantic. Indeed, the immigrants' letters to friends and relatives at home provided information about the US much more accurate and relevant than a great many academic tomes on the subject. The US thus always seemed a land of opportunity to foreigners and immigrants seeking the "American dream." The US was the first great nation to achieve modernization in the sense of eliminating hereditary class distinction, reducing class barriers, seeking equal opportunity, and creating a mass consumer society.

Of critics there were of course many. From the early beginnings of their country Americans were derided as uncouth and lawless; later they were widely equated with the *nouveaux riches* – more so even than those wealthy Argentinians or Creoles who were satirized in the light comedies of nine-teenth-century France. Americans were supposedly materialistic, brash, Philistine. Their society was said to be artificial, without organic links, lacking both a traditional peasantry and an aristocracy rooted in the soil. Americans were eternally restless, always willing to move. Americans were reportedly greedy, crude, devoid of tragic imagination. They had no respect for their betters. Heinrich Heine, the romantic revolutionary, could not stand America, and neither could Jakob Burckhardt, an imaginative conservative. "When good Americans die, they go to Paris," Oscar Wilde scoffed in *A Woman of No Importance*. "Indeed? And where do bad Americans go? Oh, they go to America!" Americans had other supposed failings. They were insufferable in their moral pretentiousness, a characteristic that they were thought to share with their English cousins. "Corruption, Immorality, Irreligion, and above all, Self Interest" ruled the US, argued an aristocratic British diplomat at the beginning of the nineteenth century. "There is no faith and no knowledge of the Lord amongst most of our brethren; in the US the younger generation inherit nothing from their parents except what is needed to make their way in this world," echoed an Orthodox Jewish visitor from Eastern Europe at the end of the century.[7]

In theory, the British should have been the most pro-American among Europeans – Britons and Americans were supposedly "cousins." Many

Americans were indeed Anglophiles, especially upper-class people from the East Coast. But their sentiments were not necessarily reciprocated in Britain. The traditional British Establishment in Britain was indeed apt to look down on Americans as brash and uncultured. (Some old-fashioned Tories, for example, would criticize Winston Churchill on the grounds that he was half-American.) Qualities regarded as virtuous in the US – enthusiasm, an evident dedication to hard work, openness, and lack of class consciousness – seemed vices to a great many old-fashioned British upper-class people, though not to the bulk of British workers.

Views hostile to the US were widespread in Europe at large – there was indeed a curious continuity in European critiques concerning America and the Americans. Long before the Thirteen Colonies attained their independence, Swiss immigrants found that *alles ist ganz anders hier*, everything is quite different here. Many liked the change – freedom from caste distinctions, higher living standards, personal freedom. "In this country anyone who gains riches, gold and silver, is esteemed like a lord in Europe." "I shall never return to Switzerland as long as I live, for I have come to a goodly land." "Evidently I have done well by my children in having left my fatherland, and for this I thank God eternally. We live under a goodly and gentle government. Provisions are plentiful; there are no tithes and no labor services; speech is free."

But there was another side to America. Woe betide those who did not make good, who missed their families in the Old Country, or who longed for security and accepted custom.

In this country there are innumerable religions – Reformed, Sabbatarians, Tumblers, Quakers, Atheists who have no religion, no churches and no schools, who believe neither in God nor the Devil, in Heaven or Hell. There are also countless tongues here English, Swedish, Gaelic, High German, Low German, Dutch . . . this is a refuge for exiled sectarians, an asylum for all manner of evil-doers from Europe, a confusing Babel, a refuge for unclean spirits, a homestead for Satan, in truth a new Sodom.[8]

Sir Charles Dilke, an English Radical who toured the US during the 1860s, described Americans in terms normally associated with "post-industrial" America. Americans were foolishly permissive toward their children, who "never dream of work out of school hours, or of solid reading that is not compulsory," and as a rule, turn out to be "forward, ill mannered, and immoral."[9] American women were too independent; crime was rife in America; American courts combined excessive legalism with excessive leniency; there were too many foreign immigrants not likely to be absorbed in the general population. Americans were addicted to strange cults that appealed, not just to the poor and the ignorant, but also to solid citizens who ought to know better. Americans were too soft to fight. (At the outbreak of the Mexican-American War in 1846, European military opinion thus widely predicted an American defeat, as did the London *Times*.) America was offensive, above all, to the rich and the well-born. As Charles Francis Adams, the US minister in London, explained during the US Civil War, "the great body of the aristocracy and the commercial classes are anxious to see the United States go to pieces while the middle and lower classes sympathize with us."[10]

From the end of the nineteenth century, there were two new twists to anti-American sentiment. Americans intervened in countries where they were not wanted. "To whom do I owe the displeasure of this intrusion," Dame Europe coldly asks Uncle Sam (according to a British cartoon of the Cuban War of 1898). "My name is Uncle Sam" goes the reply. "Any relation of the late Colonel Monroe?" [President James Monroe, framer of the Monroe Doctrine] Dame Europe chillingly answers.[11] Above all, there was the new attack from the left. Marx had still admired the US. According to Marx, the American colonization of California (taken forcibly from Mexico), the occupation of Australia, and the opening of China and Japan, were alike progressive developments, part of the historic task incumbent on the bourgeoisie to establish a world market and a global system of production.[12] Thereafter self-styled progressive opinion in Europe underwent a decisive shift. European socialists debated at considerable lengths the contradictions of US monopoly capitalism. They also puzzled why an advanced capitalist country such as the US failed to develop a great revolutionary movement, or at least a solidly proletarian party, among the disinherited mass of immigrants. Few of these critics accepted the commonsense explanation that the great majority of immigrants liked what they found, and had no wish to make fundamental political changes. The real or assumed deficiencies of the American working class were explained in terms of a false consciousness imposed upon them by their masters. The American – like the Jew – was equated with the city slicker, the huckster, the rootless cosmopolitan. By the end of the nineteenth century, the entire ideology and vocabulary of anti-Americanism was already well in place.

## AMERICAN VIEWS OF EUROPE

The Americans were as ambivalent about Europe as Europeans were about America. Americans were immigrants. Immigrants from whatever country are apt to look on their own or their ancestor's homeland with some degree of nostalgia. But immigrants also leave home for some good cause – whether poverty, persecution, or mere boredom. The old country may be remembered also with dislike, at time with blank hatred. Europe at its best was respected for culture, aristocratic elegance, and social prestige. By the end of the last century, Britain, to a lesser extent France, became the Mecca of American artists, literati, social climbers, millionaires who married their daughters to the sons of aristocratic families. London was associated with the best of men's tailoring; Paris with feminine elegance and *avant garde* art; Berlin and Göttingen with scholarship. (Later, in American movies, foreign accents were *de rigueur* for wicked countesses, pastry cooks, psychiatrists, and vampires.) On a more serious note, Americans owed a profound debt to European science, art, and scholarship, and also industrial skills, business enterprise, and investment. Throughout the nineteenth century, the US remained a massive importer of European, especially British, capital.

From their country's beginning, Americans had seen themselves as a new nation, with new laws, and a new and freer polity. The French observer Crèvecoeur had long ago insisted in his *Letters from an American Farmer* (1782) that America had transformed Europeans into new men unburdened by respect for dukes, counts or bishops, and churches. Yet a great many American intellectuals did not share his optimism. They felt they lived in a cultural wilderness that lacked Europe's great past. For culture and tradition, educated Americans had long looked to Europe and thousands had crossed the Atlantic to find inspiration or training there and a more sophisticated way of life. Indeed, it was not until after World War II that American culture became self-confident and assertive – in part a reflection of US military and economic power.

There was, however, also another side to the coin. Europe was also regarded as a potential menace. Sophisticated and supercilious European diplomatists were suspected of wishing to involve innocent Americans in foreign wars not of their making. Popery, libertinism, and unbelief were associated at various times with Europe by frightened Nativists – but also subversion and revolt. Indeed Europe might corrupt America, supposedly intended by God (claimed John Winthrop) as a "city built upon a hill, the eyes of all people are upon us." Above all, Americans, themselves descended from immigrants, have always felt ambivalent about each generation of new immigrants – usually poorer and less skilled than the old-timers.

> Wide open and unguarded stand our gates
> And through them presses a wild and motley throng –
> Men from the Volga and the Tartar steppes,
> Featureless figures from the Hoang-ho,
> Malayan, Scythian, Teuton, Celt, and Slav
> Fleeing the Old World's poverty and scorn.

Thomas Bailey Aldrich's poem, written a century ago, struck an answering chord among many of his countrymen who dreaded the strange-looking newcomers from Europe and elsewhere. The immigrants were feared on many grounds – as competitors willing to depress the American workers' living standards by working for lower wages, and also as potential subversives, "hyphenated Americans," with no loyalty to their country of adoption. In fact, these suspicions were misconceived. Militants among the immigrants formed a small minority. The great majority had no intention of overthrowing the republic that had given them refuge; they looked for personal advancement through individual effort, not to a revolutionary transformation of society. Nevertheless, stereotypes concerning subversion, libertinism, and unbelief were at various times associated with Europe by Nativist opinion – as was "Popery," or Catholicism.

Throughout American history, ethnic preferences have shifted in time, with the most recent arrivals usually being the most unpopular. By the end of the last century, for example, Scandinavians had found acceptance; jokes about "dumb Swedes" were replaced by taunts at "stupid" Poles or Italians (who by then did much of the unskilled work previously associated with Northern European immigrants); there were now likewise jeers at Jews who were moving into the textile and other light industries. The foreigners least distrusted by the end of the nineteenth century were the British. This would have surprised Americans who had lived through the Revolutionary War or the Anglo-American War of 1812, at which time patriotic propaganda had described the British as brutal, supercilious, and hypocritical. (Indeed, many British immigrants, disliking their native country's class structure, were just as vocal in their criticism.) Anti-British sentiments found reinforcement later during the nineteenth century by Irish newcomers full of hatred for their homeland's British oppressors. There was more trouble during the US Civil War when the British upper class (as distinct from the workers) was apt to side with the South, while John Bull was denounced in the US as

> Ever victorious
> Haughty, vainglorious
> Snobbish, censorious,
> Great John Bull[13]

But throughout the nineteenth century British immigrants kept coming to the US – farmers, professional people, artisans, and skilled workers. (Indeed, far more people migrated to the US from the United Kingdom after the US had attained independence than before.) The British immigrants' occupational structure resembled the Americans' more than the occupational structure of Eastern or Southern European newcomers. The British people who arrived in the US did not regard themselves as a minority; their presence in the US was regarded by the American Wasp (White Anglo-Saxon Protestant) Establishment as a welcome counter-weight to assorted foreigners (mostly Catholic) from Eastern and Southern Europe, slightingly referred to as "dirty whites." The British immigrants helped to offset the anti-British sentiment occasioned by the Civil War in the North, and also by a variety of lesser disputes between Britain and the US over the Canadian boundary, fishery rights, and such like.

But Wasp culture dominated the United States from the seventeenth century on. The Wasps established the American character, according to Richard Brookhiser in *The Way of the Wasp* (1991). No immigrant group has yet been able to establish "a rival way of life." The Wasps had political power, economic dominance and social prestige. Their institutions were Ivy League schools, the Episcopal Church, Wall Street, and the State Department. Although elitist, Wasps allowed people of character and intelligence to join. Wasp values, claims Brookhiser, made America great, wealthy and independent. The most important values were: success due to hard work, civic-mindedness, anti-sensuality and "conscience watching over everything. . . ." Immigrants to America were expected to adopt these values; they mostly did, and the country flourished as a result. The white Protestant establishment weakened after World War II and in the 1980s staggered under attacks from multiculturalism – a most unpleasant altern-ative to the Wasps' culture.

The US was from its beginnings the immigrants' refuge *par excellence*. In this capacity the US was far more significant than any other country, be it Australia, Brazil, Canada, or the Argentine. By contrast, few Amer-icans ever sought permanent homes for themselves abroad, except for a handful of blacks who went to Liberia, Finnish-Americans who migrated to the Soviet Union, and a small number of American Jews who settled in Israel. But Americans of whatever race, color, or creed very rarely changed their US nationality. Overwhelmingly they preferred real or alleged domestic ills to the putative advantages of foreign lands.

There were, of course, some exceptions. Not all foreign-born immig-rants to the US remained in America; some went back, especially to countries such as Britain where there was no religious or racial persecution to deter homesick people from returning to the land of their birth. The role of the returned American immigrant – British, German, Italian, Greek, etc. – remains to be studied. Very frequently he or she came back with new ideas and some accumulated savings that enabled the returnee to rise both socially and economically. In addition, American entrepren-eurs, from the end of the last century, began to set up affiliates in Europe, especially in Britain where US firms such as Singer and Ford, discount stores such as Woolworth, found no language barriers to impede their work. From Britain, American trusts would often extend their operations to the British colonies and the European continent.

## AMERICA IN THE GLOBAL ARENA

Relations between Britain and the US improved in other ways, too. By the end of the last century, the British government stood resolved to avoid conflicts with its so-called American cousins at almost any cost. To Britain, imperial Germany with its great High Seas Fleet seemed an immeasurably greater menace than the US. Hence the British generally sympathized with the US during the Spanish-American War of 1898. (Kipling's much misquoted poem "Take Up the White Man's Burden" was written to encourage Americans in their imperial venture.) The Spanish-American War formed another watershed in US relations with foreign countries. Earlier wars fought by the US had been confined to the North American landmass, and had not involved transmaritime expansion. All of America's earlier wars, moreover, had widened existing rifts within the US electorate, pitting practitioners of American *realpolitik* against those who considered themselves godly. (For example, the Mexican-American War, 1846–1848, had been popular in the slave states, unpopular in New England.)

The Spanish-American War, by contrast, had more enthusiastic and united support from Americans than all previous and most subsequent wars engaging the US. Chauvinists determined to teach a lesson to objectionable Latins suddenly found themselves in thorough agreement with humanitarians determined to end Spanish imperialist oppression in Cuba. (There was, moreover, no Spanish ethnic lobby in the US. Spaniards were more likely to emigrate to Latin America than to the US, while Spanish-Americans, including Mexican-Americans, were more apt to side against Spain than with Spain.) While the postwar annexation of the Philippines created bitter divisions, the campaign to expel the Spaniards from the New World met with almost universal approbation. America now stepped into the global arena, with imperial ambitions, and one of the world's major navies. The Spanish-American War thus inaugurated a revolutionary change in world affairs.

Fear of foreign entanglements was also weakened by the subsequent war in the Philippine Islands and American participation in the Boxer Relief Expedition to Peking, China (1900) – actions unthinkable as late as 1884 when the US Senate opposed sending observers to the Berlin Conference to discuss African affairs, even though Americans were important traders and explorers in the region. When Theodore Roosevelt became president in 1901, he was determined that the US should play a greater role in world affairs. And he did. Roosevelt was the most activist president in US history until Woodrow Wilson. For example, in 1904 Roosevelt called a peace conference to end the Russo-Japanese War in order to maintain a power equilibrium in Asia. (The desire to maintain a balance of power then became the principle reason for US intervention against Germany in World War I and II.) At the Algeciras Conference called in 1906 to discuss Germany and France's quarrel over Morocco, Roosevelt even got the German Kaiser to compromise.

Even more striking was the US's economic impact overseas. From the 1870s onward American farmers in the Middle West sent overseas cargoes of grain and meat; improved shipping and improved methods of refrigeration cheapened the costs of transport. European producers, including British aristocrats and Prussian junkers, found increasing difficulties in meeting American (and also Argentinian and Australian) competition. The US began to overshadow the major European countries as a manufacturing nation, and as a producer of vital raw materials such as coal, iron, and steel. (By 1914 the US, already turned out nearly five times as much steel as Britain and more than twice as much as the German Empire. The US produced nearly three times as much pig iron as Britain and twice as much as Germany.)[14] The US no longer fitted into the accepted framework of European great power relationships, a fact as yet unrecognized by most policy-makers and theoreticians on both sides of the Atlantic. Yet, American economic influence was already beginning to be apparent, especially in Britain. A British journalist complained, with much exaggeration:

> The average citizen wakes in the morning at the sound of an American alarm clock; rises from his New England sheets, and shaves with his New York soap, and Yankee safety razor. He pulls on a pair of Boston boots over his socks from West Carolina [sic], fastens his Connecticut braces, slips his Waterbury watch into his pocket and sits down to breakfast. . . . Rising from his breakfast table the citizen rushes out, catches an electric tram made in New York, to Shepherds Bush, where he gets into a Yankee elevator, which takes him on to the American-fitted railway to the city. At his office of course everything is American. . . . [15]

How would Americans use this enormous might? When World War I started, the answer seemed clear; the Americans would not use this power at all, but would stay clear of European entanglements. European affairs no longer seemed the business of a people whose forebears had left their native shores for good reasons and bad – to escape religious persecution, to avoid the draft, to escape from poverty, to evade the unwelcome attention of tax-gatherers, rent collectors, or wronged maidens. Public opinion regarding the war was moreover divided along cleavages of class and ethnicity that remained characteristic of American politics. British Americans naturally sympathized with Britain's cause. So did the US Eastern Establishment, linked to the British upper class through ties of trade, education, sometimes marriage – receptive, moreover, to the claim that Britain represented the cause of parliamentary democracy and of small nations. Danes and Norwegians tended to support the Western Allies, as did Italians, Serbs, Czechs, and Romanians, the latter generally hostile to the Hapsburg empire allied to Germany.

But there was also substantial support for Germany. Swedes were often Germanophile (unlike Danes and Norwegians). Subsequent Nazi stereotypes to the contrary notwithstanding, Jews were apt to regard the German cause with sympathy. German Jews would side with their former countrymen. Yiddish-speakers from Eastern Europe found the pogrom-ridden Czarist monarchy infinitely more objectionable than the German empire, which did not persecute Jews, and whose citizens spoke High German, a tongue closely linked to Yiddish. The Irish (about 4.5 million people) likewise formed a major bloc. To most of the Irish, any foe of Britain's seemed a friend. Moreover, the Irish – like the Italians and the Jews – had mainly settled in big cities along the Eastern seaboard. They formed an influential lobby, powerful especially in municipal politics.

Above all, there was a substantial German minority; more than 8 million of America's 105 million people at the time had been born in Germany, or had at least one German parent. The Germans concentrated especially in the Middle West. Most of them had long settled in the US (one-tenth of the Union forces during the Civil War had consisted of Germans). Germans as a group had done well in the US. The German cultural influence, moreover, had been considerable. The US was heavily indebted to German models for the structure of postgraduate training, for experts and expertise in a variety of academic disciplines: an estimated 9,000–10,000 Americans went to German universities between 1815 to 1914. Germans were reputed to be thorough, hard-working, and sentimental. It was a time when loanwords from the German language consisted only of friendly-sounding words such as *Lieder, Kindergarten* and *Oktoberfest* – *Gestapo, Panzer*, and *Endlösung* were as yet unknown.

Given the strength of isolationist sentiment in the US, the country at first stayed neutral. But when Imperial Germany began to conduct unrestricted warfare against Great Britain, the US was drawn in. American lives were lost; American ships went to the bottom of the sea. To make matters worse, British intelligence caught Germans in a plot (revealed in the Zimmermann Note) proposing an alliance between Germany, Mexico, and Japan in case the US went to war. Mexico would then recover the lost territory in Texas, New Mexico and Arizona which the US had taken after winning the Mexican-American War. Ironically, Imperial Germany's military victory over Russia – a feat never repeated by the Third Reich – worsened Germany's political condition. Once the Romanov dynasty disintegrated, the Western Allies' cause was no longer tainted by association with Czarist absolutism; their claim to be defending democracy seemed more credible than ever before, not only to people of Anglo-Saxon stock, but also to Jews, Poles, Balts, Finns, and other reluctant subjects of the former Czars.

In 1917, the US entered World War I. In military terms alone, the US contribution was not as impressive as Britain's or France's. In economic and diplomatic terms, however, the changes were unmistakable. President Woodrow Wilson issued his "Fourteen Points" unilaterally; the US had become the world's most productive economy. From being an importer of capital, the US switched to being an exporter. Without American financial support, Britain could not have continued the war effectively. By 1917 her gold reserves were virtually exhausted; most of her American assets had been sold. Even though Britain in 1918 commanded the world's largest navy, the largest air force, the greatest number of tanks, and the greatest colonial empire, it was American power that underpinned the Alliance.

The global balance of power thereby underwent a decisive shift – one which German planners had been too slow to understand. For all the efficiency of their staff work, the Germans failed to grasp that the US's economic potential now heavily outclassed that of any European power. Germany's priority should have been to keep the US out of the war at any cost. Instead, the Germans gravely underestimated the Americans, a mistake that would continue to be made for generations to come. World War I also carried other lessons. Despite its internal divisions, the American Republic rested on much more solid foundations than its critics imagined. There was social unrest. But there was never, at any time, the slightest chance of a social revolution. Moreover, despite its multi-ethnic character, the US developed none of the ethnic fissures that plagued alike the Czarist and the Hapsburg, and later also the Soviet, empires.

True enough, the US involvement in World War I led to an outbreak of anti-German hysteria, with vandalism, the public burning of German books, the renaming of towns, and even of foods (frankfurters became hot dogs; German cabbage became liberty cabbage). The Germans in the US may indeed have encountered particular animosity for a time, for Germans were the only non-English-speaking immigrants who widely looked on their native country as an alternative model, as successful industrially, militarily, and culturally as the US. The German lobby, moreover, was badly divided – split into Protestants and Catholics; "church Germans" and secularists; progressives (such as Governor John Peter Altgeld of Illinois) and conservatives. However, once the US entered the war, German-Americans remained overwhelming loyal to their adopted country, and in time anti-German sentiment abated. Whatever the political strength of an ethnic lobby in the US, such a lobby would never be used as a Fifth Column on behalf of a foreign country engaged in war against the US.

## RETREAT FROM EUROPE

Having played a decisive part in war, the US might have been expected to dominate the peace. Instead America once more retreated from Europe, disillusioned with "the war to end all wars." The US would not join the League of Nations pioneered by President Wilson. His "Fourteen Points" were forgotten. ("Fourteen Points," scoffed Georges Clemenceau, the great French war leader, "Ten were enough for the Almighty.") The US refused to commit itself to future help for Europe; for instance, no guarantees were given to France against future German aggression. There was contempt in Congress for those European countries (except Finland) which defaulted on their war debts wholly or in part.

Isolationism found expression in restrictions on immigration. (These included a quota system, elaborated in 1924, which was designed to favor Northern Europeans as against assorted Slavs, Latins, Greeks, Jews, and Turks. Chinese and Japanese were excluded altogether.) Isolationism also went with high tariffs (popular in particular with Republicans, and embodied in legislation such as the Emergency Tariff Act of 1921). There was bitter hostility to all those suspected of having "gotten us into war." Critics derived from every part of the American political spectrum – Mid-Western Republicans who denounced "Wall Street," the "City" (London's financial center), and an international cohort of arms manufacturers, the so-called merchants of death. It became accepted almost as a truism that the US had gone to war to save the bankers and merchants who had strained themselves to the utmost to supply Britain and France with credit and arms. Isolationism was also reflected in US defense policies. With its huge economic potential, the US could easily have become the world's premier naval power. Instead, the US, at the Washington Naval Conference (1922), settled for parity with Britain; the US air force remained puny; the US army was reduced to a size in which it could not have confronted even a minor European army, such as Belgium's or Switzerland's.

There was no effective political cooperation between the US and its former allies after the war, or during the Great Depression, or during the rise of Nazism. Despite American isolationism, however, US cultural influence on Europe grew apace. Americans continued to come to Europe as tourists, performers, merchants, and students. American artists crossed the Atlantic; so did American prize fighters, and American entertainers, especially black artists. Hollywood movies conquered the world – neither German UFA nor Sovfilm could compete on the world market with American studios. The mass-produced car, cheap enough for ordinary people to buy, seemed peculiarly American. (In Europe, by contrast, the automobile long remained the chosen vehicle of the rich.) Jazz was the Americans' music *par excellence*, no matter how loudly traditionalists objected; jazz triumphed in the dance halls, and even affected classical music (as in Ernst Krenek's jazz opera (*Jonny spielt auf*). American performers scored brilliant successes in the European capitals (even the Nazis, who denounced jazz as the decadent production of Negro and Jewish *Untermenschen*, had to make concessions by permitting modified forms of jazz at their own receptions). Americans saw themselves as harbingers of modernity, mass culture, mass production, and mass consumption. Many European intellectuals shared these assumptions. "Skyscrapers," Jean Paul Sartre reflected, "were the architecture of the future, just as the cinema was the art and the jazz the music of the future."[16] Meanwhile, American intellectuals bemoaned the fact that the US had produced few great artists, musicians or writers, and depreciated America's cultural achievements. Not until the 1930s did some Americans begin to appreciate the richness of American culture. But it was the achievements of World War II that produced confidence, optimism and a sense of America's greatness.

Then as now, of course, the traffic in ideas went both ways. Americans went to Europe to study, for example, Russian studies, management methods, nuclear physics, linguistics, and engineering in Germany; art in France; banking and maritime technology in Britain, as well as being Rhodes Scholars. Americans remained profoundly indebted to European pioneers in every field, from architecture to zoology. In music, even the saxophone, that quintessentially modern American jazz instrument, had been invented in Paris by Adolphe Sax, a contemporary of Richard Wagner. All the same, the American contribution was in some ways unique, and so was American economic power. Already by the mid-1920s, by which time the world economy had temporarily recovered from World War I, the US had become the world's largest exporters, and the principal source of new, as opposed to existing, capital investments. Roughly half of America's new investments went to Europe, particularly Germany, where US private investors for a time helped to pay for reparations and for the funding of the Weimar Republic's welfare state. (Most of the war debt was never repaid). It was a time when even the communists, with all their dislike of "Wall Street," had a soft spot for "Fordism," that specifically American combination of mass production methods and high wages.

Equally important later on was the impact of the "New Deal." Despite pessimistic forecasts to the contrary, American capitalism did not collapse as a result of the Great Depression; communism did not develop into a mass movement; Fascism did not take root among Americans. (Most Italian-Americans stood aloof from Fascism; the great majority of German-Americans had no sympathy for Hitler, whose followers in the US, organized in the German-American Bund, never amounted to an influential body.) The "New Deal" aroused widespread admiration in Europe among moderates, conservatives, Social Democrats, and Labour Party supporters alike – America provided public works such as highways, dams, electrical projects, even mural art, but without the militarism that accompanied such projects in totalitarian countries.

Europeans also had other reasons for looking with favor at the US. For all its restrictions on immigration, the US remained by far the most open country in the world for people seeking refuge from Nazi, Fascist, and later communist oppression. The newcomers during the 1930s, many of them Jewish, or linked to Jews by ties of friendship or marriage, included famous scientists, actors, poets, novelists, film makers, physicians, historians, in one of the great intellectual migrations of European history. A goodly number came from Britain, but the bulk of them derived from German-speaking Central Europe, Poland, and the lands of the former Austro-Hungarian empire.

The US was now coming into its own in every sphere of intellectual endeavor. Up to 1933, when Hitler took over in Germany, it was Germany that had always produced the largest number of Nobel Prize winners in medicine and the sciences. From then onward the balance of power irreversibly shifted; henceforth the US always headed the list. US predominance continued even after the European refugee scholars of the 1930s had begun to retire from their positions at US universities. (Between 1957 and 1990 the US gained 113 Nobel Prizes in the sciences and economics, as against 53 won by all the EC countries, and 2 by Japan.) Not all the newcomers, of course, liked the US or remained permanently: for example, Thomas Mann and Bertold Brecht returned to Europe after World War II. Nevertheless, the great migration strengthened existing intellectual ties between Europe and North America. American science, technology, business methods and organizations by now had clearly reached world stature.

The US also became involved in Europe's ideological struggles. To millions of Americans, the Spanish Civil War (1936–1939) in particular became a conflict between Good and Evil. No other foreign civil strife had ever aroused similar passions in America. The supporters of the Spanish Republic included not merely active communists, a small but relatively influential group, but a broad alliance of moderate socialists, liberals, and self-styled progressive conservatives. To them, the war meant a crucial struggle against Fascism worldwide – a view popularized not only by Ernest Hemingway and leftist intellectuals but also, later, by popular movie personalities such as Ingrid Bergman in *For Whom the Bell Tolls*. Franco supporters were much less numerous, but also influential. They derived, not so much from declared Fascists, but from militant anti-communists, and Catholics aghast at the persecution of nuns and priests at the "Reds' " behest. Several thousand Americans departed to fight in Spain with the Loyalists in the Abraham Lincoln Brigade; to most of the American intellectual community the Spanish Civil War henceforth provided a mirror in which world events would continue to be reflected – with progress forever arrayed against reaction, vice against virtue, capitalism against socialism.

Nevertheless, the bulk of the American people remained isolationist. However much professors and journalists might argue about the Spanish Civil War, or Nazism in Germany, or Stalinism in Russia, the mass of the US population wished to remain uninvolved. Once World War II started in Europe, however, the Allied cause aroused sympathy among the great majority of Americans. But despite President Roosevelt's endeavors (e.g. the Lend-Lease Act of 1941), despite the Anglophilia of the old East Coast Establishment, the US would probably not have entered all-out war but for Japan's attack on Pearl Harbor on December 7, 1941, and Germany's declaration of war against the US.

## RETURN TO EUROPE

Yet once having stepped into the arena, the Americans meant to win – with a resolve never grasped by either German or Japanese policy-makers. The US rejected an "Asia First" strategy advocated by traditional isolationists, and instead concentrated its main efforts against Hitler, who was correctly perceived as the main enemy. The immense resources of the US proved decisive in the winning of the war. After Pearl Harbor, there was in the US a political unanimity not witnessed again until the Gulf War 50 years later. American society, though ethnically mixed, displayed its accustomed cohesion. German-Americans, Italian-Americans, Japanese-

Americans overwhelmingly proved loyal. The American way of life made a strong appeal even to German prisoners-of-war in the US. (There were something like 400,000 of them, as against only 50,000 Italians; of a selected sample of those returning to Germany, 74 percent left with friendly feelings towards the US. They included men of subsequent prominence in the Federal Republic of Germany.)

American private enterprise, though controlled and restricted by extensive governmental regulation, staged a miracle of mobilization of a kind never previously seen in world history. Big science came into its own, financed with huge public grants, linked to the universities and to a massive industrial complex. The American fleet became the world's mightiest – as if Pearl Harbor had never occurred. The US air force came to dominate the skies. No one who ever saw the giant air armadas that filled the sky during the invasion of Normandy will ever forget the sight, a shattering display of American, or (American-subsidized) British air power. The US deployed the greatest army ever sent overseas in world history. The GIs were better dressed, better paid, and more expensively equipped than any European soldiers. In the European imagination the olive-uniformed Yanks – tall, gangling, gum-chewing – appeared astonishing in their self-confidence. British soldiers might resent the Yanks' superior pay and their reputation for unfairly courting British women with perfume and silk stockings unavailable in British shops; but though he might scoff at the Americans, Tommy Atkins [Britain's GI Joe] was glad at heart that the Yanks had come. The US, as the "arsenal of democracy," in four and a half years of war produced 6,500 naval vessels, 294,400 airplanes, 86,300 tanks, 64,546 landing craft, 3,500,000 jeeps, trucks, and personnel carriers, 53,000,000 tons of cargo vessels, 12,000,000 rifles, carbines, and machine guns, and 47,000,000 artillery shells, and put 12 million men into the armed services.

The American army, moreover, seemed more democratic than European armies. (There were no separate sergeants' messes in the US army, as there were in the British army; proportionately more enlisted men became officers than in the British Army.) Americans performed impressively, especially at tasks requiring engineering skills, or complex organization of the kind involved in seaborne landings. Germans soldiers might taunt the Americans for their initial inexperience, or lack of discipline. But members of the Wehrmacht who encountered Americans were impressed by the massive weight of firepower that Americans could deploy, and their ability to learn fast from previous errors. Every German soldier would infinitely sooner be taken prisoner by the Americans than by the Russians (or even the French); to be sent to a prisoner-of-war camp in the US was accounted a first prize in the Wehrmacht's lottery of defeat. Above all, once the fighting stopped, Germans without exception would much rather dwell in the American than the Soviet zone of occupation.

The Americans also consolidated their economic supremacy. Whereas much of Europe suffered devastation on an unparalleled scale, the American homeland remained untouched by war; on the contrary, war had witnessed an extraordinary growth of American industrial productivity and an unprecedented rise in the gross national product (from $ 11.0 billion, in 1929 prices, in 1939 to $ 180.9 billion in 1945). For many Americans, war – despite its hardships and dangers – turned into a positive experience. War created an almost universal labor shortage. Wages rose; formerly unemployed workmen had money to spend on luxuries as well as necessities. Millions of black Americans migrated north and found jobs in industry, jobs that had formerly been denied to them. Hostility, education and job discrimination against Catholics and Jews diminished. Millions of women moved into the labor force; many of them stayed in their new-found posts after the war, with the result that by 1946 five million more women were in paid employment than in 1941. In the US, at war's end prosperity created new expectations, and overall a new sense of optimism and well-being.

By their joint exertions, the US and Britain between them restored the prestige of democratic government, badly tarnished during the 1930s when Nazism and Fascism had widely appeared to be the model of the future. But it was American society and the American economy that obviously worked. The international "demonstration effect" of the US (and British) democracy was enormous. Unlike Hitler, Mussolini, and Stalin, neither Roosevelt nor Churchill feared plots from their generals. American society – based on a modified free enterprise principle – created a productive miracle that would have appeared improbable even to writers of science fiction. The American and British alone had a credible record of maintaining civil liberty. (The internment of Japanese Americans in the US and of many German Jewish refugees in Great Britain was a regrettable departure from the Allies' high standards; all the same, civilian prisoners in every other belligerent country – Germany, Japan, France, the Soviet Union – would have gladly traded places with those in Anglo-American hands).

World War II was likewise decisive in shaping future relations between the US and its Western Allies. President Roosevelt's great design (the Atlantic Charter) of course differed much from what transpired later. Roosevelt believed that there could be a permanent partnership between the US and the Soviet Union. Treated with consideration, granted their rightful sphere of influence in Eastern Europe, the Soviet Union would collaborate with Western capitalism in a new world order. This would be run through the United Nations, but would be essentially based on a partnership between the "Big Four" – the United States, the Soviet Union, China, and Britain. Relations with Britain would be friendly, but the British, as well as the French and the Dutch, would have to surrender their ill-gotten empires in the cause of world peace.

In fact there was already friction between the US and the Soviet Union while the war still went on. By contrast, US ties with Britain (and also with the so-called "white Dominions," of Canada, Australia, New Zealand, South Africa), were infinitely tighter than US links with any other country. US and British diplomatists might disagree over Soviet ambitions or the future of the British empire; US and British strategists might quarrel over the impending invasion of the European continent; US and British sailors would customarily get into fights when going ashore in the same port. But US and British economic and defense policies were much more closely coordinated than those of any sovereign allies. This "special relationship" remained just as real 40 years later.[17]

Relations with France, by contrast, were much worse – and remained so for years to come. Roosevelt personally disliked Charles de Gaulle, France's wartime leader. Indeed, the two stood worlds apart. De Gaulle was a proud and touchy soldier, a believer in *realpolitik*, intensely preoccupied with his country's prestige, sure that he alone embodied his country's glory and *esprit*. Roosevelt, intensely civilian in his ethos, never awed by martial splendor, was convinced that the US should guide the world into a new moral order that would supersede Old World power politics. Roosevelt refused to regard de Gaulle as France's only legitimate representative. Roosevelt, moreover, always projected domestic politics on the foreign screen; there was no French voting lobby in the US, as there was a Polish, an Irish, and a Jewish lobby. French interests thus were held of small account.

US relations with Italy, oddly enough, would turn out to be much easier. The German alliance was unpopular in Italy; Mussolini's much heralded "Pact of Steel" with Hitler would never have survived a popular referendum. Once the Allies were firmly entrenched in Italy, and Germany's defeat seemed certain, Mussolini fell; Italy switched sides; the Italians cooperated with the Allies; and the US began to render massive aid to its former enemy, a policy welcomed with special enthusiasm by Italian-Americans, by Catholics of all ethnic backgrounds, and by other enemies of Stalinism who feared the challenge posed by the powerful Italian Communist Party.

US opinion regarding Germany was much more complex. After World War I ended, there had arisen a feeling of guilt among many intellectuals, a sense that Germany had been victimized by Allied rapacity in the Treaty

of Versailles (1919). There was no such pro-Germanism after World War
II – the Nazis, with their murder campaign and death camps had too
grossly besmirched their country's reputation. Indeed, it was intellectually
fashionable to be hostile to Germany; sophisticates who would have
blanched at expressing the slightest hostility to Jews or blacks could
indulge in anti-German remarks to their heart's content. Nevertheless,
anti-Germanism in the US never became anything like as powerful as it
did for a time in Britain during World War II, where leading intellectuals
such as A.J.P. Taylor, Sir Lewis Namier, and Hugh Dalton all became
vigorous proponents of anti-Germanism. The US, by contrast, had never
felt in mortal danger of Germany; about one-fifth of the US population
traced their descent wholly or partly to Germany; German names such as
Eisenhower, Spaatz, and Nimitz were conspicuous among the list of the
US's greatest commanders; the German impact was profound on the
Lutheran churches, and to a lesser extent, on the Catholic Church. Once
the war had ended and the Morgenthau Plan to reduce Germany to a
"potato patch" was seen to be a blunder, there was little doubt that a
reformed and repentant Germany would work its passage back into
American esteem as West Germany came to be seen as the dynamo for
restructuring Europe and as the shield, with US help, against Soviet
might.

World War II was also fraught with other far-reaching consequences.
Americans widely became convinced that only a united Europe free of
economic nationalism, trade wars, and customs duties would prevent future
European wars; the US should constitute a model for Europeans to follow.
A political federation, however, would only work if sustained by a prosperous and expanding economy. Hence US policy-makers had became
convinced, already during wartime, that the US must provide financial
aid, and that the New Deal should be exported to Europe. The Atlantic
Charter, the Four Freedoms, Lend-Lease all reflected the Americans' new
spirit of humanitarian interventionism.

By contrast, there was in Europe, when the war ended, a pervasive
pessimism, expressed in gloomy philosophies such as existentialism. Entire
cities lay in ruins, millions of people had lost their lives in battle, in
bombing, or in death camps. To return even to prewar "normalcy" seemed
for many Europeans an unattainable fantasy. Compared with the Europeans' pessimism, the Americans had a healthy optimism. Their belief in
economic growth, in a dynamic society sustained by mass production, mass
consumption, and social equality, provided that element of hope which
would prove essential for the postwar recovery of Europe.[18]

America also continued to deeply influence Europe's popular culture.
Jazz remained a major contribution, and US popular music derived

inspiration from the traditional strains of the American West (themselves influenced by Mexican *corridos* or ballads), and from tunes brought across the Atlantic by European immigrants – English, Irish, German, Jewish, Italian, and others. American music in turn spread through the remotest parts of the globe; musicians such as Bing Crosby and Louis Armstrong were acclaimed abroad as much as at home. So were American movies, some of which were fantasies that in fact also contributed to spreading disinformation concerning the real America. American movies and musical comedies similarly supplied much of Europe's entertainment; all modern fairy tale characters – *Superman, Donald Duck, Bambi, the Wizard of Oz,* the heroic Cowboy – came from America. To the old-style European liberal, the US was the bastion of freedom. To the refugee scientist of the 1930s the US provided new academic opportunities as well as a shelter. To social reformers (including British Labourites such as Ernest Bevin or Harold Laski) the US was the land of the New Deal. To the efficiency expert, the US was the country that had pioneered mass production methods. America was also the land in which a person might redeem failure in the "Old Country." Alternatively, the "rich uncle from America" would appear in melodrama as a *deux ex machina*, ready to help an ambitious young man to a career. (This theme returned in as recent a production as *Heimat*, an enormously popular German TV series in the 1980s.) And even critics of the US such as Bertrand Russell or Arnold Toynbee never hesitated privately to make money in a country that they denigrated in public.

The US dominated not only Europe, but the world. The US held a temporary monopoly of nuclear arms. It stood supreme in the natural and physical sciences. In religious terms regarding the number of practising believers, in terms of trained manpower and financial resources, the US was at once the world's largest Protestant, Catholic, and Jewish country. America contributed more to international charity than the rest of the world combined: terms such as "Joint" and "Care" packages entered the international vocabulary. Even international bodies such as UNRRA (United Nations Relief and Rehabilitation Administration) were largely financed with the American taxpayers' money.

Overall, American English came to be what Latin had been to the literate classes of medieval Europe – the principle language of international communications as well as a prestige symbol. (The use of English spread through textbooks, teacher exchanges, student travel, tourism, imported films, TV programs and jazz, and through English terminology in international organizations, banking, aviation, maritime communications, and the military. English also dominated in the social sciences, and scientific and technological publications.) The role of English became particularly important in smaller countries such as Sweden and Holland; neither French nor German could equal the importance of English throughout Europe and the world at large. American broadcasts also had tremendous political influence. Few Americans at the time realized the enormous impact that the Voice of America, Radio Free Europe, and Radio Liberty (beamed to the Soviet Union) made on the Soviet satellites.[19]

The US, moreover, enjoyed special advantages with regard to its civic culture. The US constitution of 1787 is the world's oldest written constitution. Its success has helped to make the US one of the most politically stable countries in the world. (Even during the stormy 1960s, hardly any revolutionary professed willingness to abolish the constitution, however much he or she expressed hostility to the hated "System" in general.) The American constitution was studied with interest by the founding fathers of the German Federal Republic and the Italian Republic after World War II, and later by scholars and politicians during the Soviet Union's demise. The *Federalist Papers* would remain relevant when the works of Lenin and Stalin were moldering in the attic. American federalism, the system of checks and balances, of the separation of powers, has been modified, but has endured and remained a strength of American democracy. No Marxist-inspired constitution could make a similar claim. And in 1991 European Community members spoke of a federal union of nations to form a United States of Europe.

At the same time the US enjoyed a high level of interest in politics, media attention to political affairs, pride in the country, sense of civic duty, and trust in political institutions. American constitutionalism helped to integrate wave after wave of immigrants into the US political culture. Up to the late 1960s, US respondents in public opinion polls thought more highly about their own political system, and displayed more participatory and supportive attitudes than non-Americans. Americans, on the whole, also felt more certain of their ability to influence governmental action than most Europeans. Not surprisingly, the US after World War II saw itself as the major actor in world history. The US assigned to itself the political, economic, moral, and military responsibility of reviving the world economy, or preventing the future expansion of world communism, and possibly even turning back the tide. Isolationism and non-involvement were in full retreat.

The partial Americanization of Europe had begun in wartime and continued after 1945. The US as the "arsenal of democracy" had equipped its allies, and provided the majority of forces for the war in the West and in the Pacific. Millions of troops had been stationed first in Britain, then in occupied Western Europe. Americans brought new habits, attitudes and diets to Europeans. Mores and morals became more open and friendly, and less class-biased. Thousands of GI brides linked families across the Atlantic. Sexual liaisons numbered in the millions. The GIs brought new ambition and appetites to help break down national stereotypes. Military governments ruled West Germany, Austria and Italy, reshaped their governments, and helped to liberalize their education systems and economies. Later the Marshall Plan (1947–51) was to revitalize Western Europe, and NATO was to defend the region against the threats of communism and of Germany. The US had truly come into its own; as Churchill noted at war's end, "America stands at this moment at the summit of the world."

## ATTITUDES WITHIN THE ATLANTIC COMMUNITY AFTER 1945

What of the dominant attitudes within the Atlantic Community, as it evolved between the end of World War II and the 1980s? On both sides of the Atlantic there remained a good deal of ambivalence. Anti-Americanism continued to be influential – much of it reactionary and anti-modern. Americans were resented for their political and economic power, their bragging and their riches. America was identified with the real or imagined evils of urbanism and free enterprise alike. Some Europeans were envious and resentful of the US. The British Labour Party, according to Anthony Crosland, resented the US because it took over leadership from the British, and because of the success of capitalism over socialism. Certain British and European conservatives were anti-American because of the US role in encouraging decolonization. (The Suez Crisis in 1956 was the most serious clash between European colonialism and American anti-colonialism.)[20] Western Europe's dependency on the US was another source of anguish and resentment. The US not only helped Europe recover, but also defended it against the Soviet Union. Dependency hurt some Europeans' pride, but helped push them into working toward a United States of Europe to stand as a third force between the US and the USSR.

The partial Americanization of Europe was somewhat balanced by the increasing influence of Europe on America. The ordinary immigrant from Western Europe was no longer an unskilled or semi-skilled worker or a farmer, as he or she had been in the olden days. The bulk of European newcomers were highly skilled technicians or professionals. More European professors lectured at US universities; more European scientists worked at US institutes. European investors played a major part in US economic life. In terms of acquiring business assets in the US, British, German, French, and Dutch investors between them played a much more important role than the much-discussed Japanese. There was ever-increasing cooperation between major corporations in the US and Europe. For example, Daimler-Benz, a German giant, collaborated with US corporations such as Westinghouse in manufacturing machinery required for mass transit, including engines for subways and automated train control components. Daimler subsidiaries manufactured heavy-duty trucks in the US, or turned out medical equipment. Indeed, Daimler's activities in the US became so complex that the company had to open an office in Washington DC just to handle relations with the US government. As Daimler's chairman put it "collaboration *sans frontières* is more and more becoming an indispensable prerequisite for one's own economic and technological success."[21]

Europe also influenced day-to-day living in the US – this to an extent not understood by professional anti-Americans who believed that cultural influence went along a one-way street. An American executive might wake up to the buzz of a German-made Braun alarm clock, prepare an Italian espresso in a German-manufactured Krups coffee maker, eat a croissant from the French-owned Vie de France bakery chain, spread butter supplied by the Anglo-Dutch Lever Group, purchased at a Giant supermarket owned by the Dutch Alber Hejn Group. Thus refreshed, the executive might have a hot shower with the new deodorant Lever 2,000 soap, shave with a Norelco shaver from Philips, then slip into an Italian-made suit from Giorgio Armani. Thereafter he might ride to the office in a Swedish Volvo filled with gas at a BP (British Petroleum) station, then pick up a Spanish business associate at the Watergate Hotel (owned by the British Trusthouse Forte Company) and discuss a new best seller published by Doubleday (just acquired by the German firm of Bertelsmann). *C'est la vie*. The US and Europe also came to resemble one another in more fundamental ways. American life became much more bureaucratized than in the olden days; US bureaucracies rivalled their European counterparts in arrogance and complexity. At the same time, the US intelligentsia assumed a much more prominent place in US life than two generations earlier – a development familiar already to Europeans.

Still, to nationalists in Europe, the US was the dominant player in world politics, and the Europeans had to depend on the Americans for their military defense until the collapse of the Warsaw Pact in 1989. After 1992 the Europeans may become the world's economic leaders, but they have yet to prove they have military and political power equal to the US or indeed that they can act forcefully as a political unit.[22] Charges of economic imperialism were hurled at the US throughout the postwar decades. Although the US saw itself as an anti-colonial power, leftists defined the US as imperialistic because of its economic penetration of world markets.

Lenin (*Imperialism*, 1917) defined imperialism as the last stage of capitalism; he thus made the US appear an imperialist power even though the US had no colonies. West German leftist youths claimed the US had colonized Germany. The French had long preached against the American challenge. The British left also widely accepted the Marxist definition of the US as a neocolonialist power. Opposition to American economic takeovers therefore was widespread in Europe from 1945 on; the EEC adopted a partially protectionist policy from 1958, and American multinationals who set up plans in Europe were perceived by Jean Louis Servan-Schreiber as embodiments of *The American Challenge* (first published in French in 1967).

American self-criticism was the source of much of this anti-Americanism in Europe. The attacks on American society by American liberal-left academics and journalists focused on the failures of capitalism, of the industrial-military complex, of civil rights abuses and of the policy of containment. Critics such as Vance Packard, Herbert Marcuse, Paul Baran, Noam Chomsky, and Susan Sontag helped convince many Europeans of America's evil. Naive actresses such as Jane Fonda and Shirley MacLaine or Communist Party functionaries such as Angela Davis were believed when they fantasized about American society. American newspaper columnists were among the worst America-bashers. Walter Lippmann kept saying the Cold War was America's fault. Anthony Lewis claimed the US was the most dangerous and destructive power in the world; and Tom Wicker claimed that the American system did not work – this at a time of the greatest prosperity and military power in the country's history.[23]

Much anti-Americanism in postwar Europe was therefore reinforced by American critics and by American movies, television, drama and popular music – for these all too often display only the worst aspects of American society: its criminality, racism, violence, the supposed materialism, emptiness, and crassness of life in the United States. Nevertheless, it was hard for many Americans to understand why they, who had saved Europe from self-destruction in World Wars I and II at great loss of American lives, and who had then helped to rebuild that region after World War II, were resented and treated with distrust.

Given the murderous history of communism, objectively there could be no justification for treating the US and the USSR as moral equivalents. Nevertheless, many European and US intellectuals seldom stopped criticizing the US, while excusing communism's failures. Some churchmen even claimed that communism was morally superior to capitalism. Luckily, anti-Americanism never forced the US to retreat into isolation or a "Fortress America" mentality. The US remained committed to NATO and to globally containing communist expansion – not always with success.

Until the Vietnam War, the majority of Europeans liked the United States, and believed it was seriously committed to their security. Thereafter European distrust of US leadership and judgment increased. Public opinion polls in Western Europe from 1954 to 1982 were generally more favorable than unfavorable to the US, but nevertheless suspicious of US political judgment. Although the Europeans had relied on the US nuclear umbrella to defend them, the peace movement spread fear of a nuclear war in West Europe because of so-called American brinkmanship.

In the late 1980s the debate about the US revolved around President Reagan's rearming and his hard-nosed attitudes toward the Soviet "evil empire." There was also concern by scholars such as Paul Kennedy (*The Rise and Fall of Great Powers*, 1987) about US commitment to be the world's policeman and US ability to sustain its military status as a superpower. The US had supposedly overreached itself by spending too much on defense at a time when the US economy suffered from slow growth, a loss of technical superiority in many fields, national budget deficits, a trade deficit, and the poor education obtained by so many American high school students. In addition, peace movements and the Greens bitterly censured the US policy of nuclear deterrence, and may thereby have weakened US military policies in Europe vis-à-vis the Soviet Union. The Greens and anti-nuclear advocates opposed Presidents Carter's and Reagan's arms buildup and Reagan's confrontational posture towards the Soviet Union, especially after the coming to power of Gorbachev (1985) and his policies of *glasnost* and *perestroika*. Stephen Haseler has best summed up the nature of European anti-Americanism as not just opposition to US policies, but resentment of US power and material success and the feeling of dependency on this superpower.[24]

In the postwar period, Europe's elites wrongly believed that American democracy was without real culture and was excessively individualistic. The US incurred censure at the same time for being vulgar and elitist, bellicose and soft, materialistic yet preachy. Anti-Americanism appealed to those who equated the US with modernity in its worst aspects – with the destruction of customary family and religious ties. But the US was also blamed for failing to "develop" the Third World in an adequate manner, for hogging too many of the world's resources. Anti-Americanism pleased nationalists of every description who denigrated the US as a collection of rootless cosmopolitans drawn from every nation on earth. But the US was also lambasted for its real or assumed chauvinism. Anti-Americanism frequently went with hostility to the Americans' capitalist ruthlessness; yet US capitalists were also denounced for their alleged inability to compete on the world market against the Japanese and Germans.

Anti-Americanism appealed in particular to social elites – not so much the traditional upper classes, but to leftist television producers, journalists, academics, clergymen. They took pride, not merely in their assumed superior intellectual ability, but also in their social and aesthetic chic. Hence they widely enjoyed sneering at President Reagan as a former B-movie actor and at Prime Minister Thatcher for being a grocer's daughter from Grantham who bought her clothes at Marks and Spencer's (the British equivalent of Macy's). An American variant of this creed particularly blamed the Wasps. Thus Charles Reich's *The Greening of America* (1970) claimed that Americans found work empty, pointless, and enslaving, the Wasps being lampooned with special severity. The political traditions of the American bourgeoisie were widely regarded with contempt; political freedom, personal liberty, limited government were exposed to ridicule; by contrast, now-discredited revolutionaries such as Fidel Castro and Che Guevara were held up for emulation.

Anti-Americanism in this era had its roots in US power, wealth, and consumerism. But it was capitalism and US foreign policies which drew the most criticism, especially from the left. The US was conceived to be obsessed with communism. American policies in Vietnam and Central America were attacked; US support for juntas and authoritarian rightists was condemned. Fear of a nuclear war fed movements in Europe against American nuclear weapons, but rarely against Soviet weaponry. The Vietnam War was the nadir for the United States in the eyes of Europe's elites. But President Reagan, from 1981 onward, restored American confidence and that of the US's allies by re-arming and projecting American power in an effort to contain communism.

The US, being the world's greatest capitalist power and the sworn opponent of socialism, was consistently under communist attack. From the beginnings of Soviet rule in 1917, Soviet communists had predicted the total collapse of capitalism, a collapse only temporarily delayed (according to Lenin) by imperialism. When imperialism and colonialism was ended, communists had to invent another excuse for capitalism's continued vitality, neocolonialism became the explanation. Communists insisted that communism was morally superior to capitalism. By the late 1970s, however, the intellectual configuration of the Western world had greatly changed. Only fellow travellers and a handful of "revolutionary theologians" by now believed in communism's superior morality or efficiency. The prestige of communism and, to a lesser extent, of socialism, further diminished as the Warsaw Pact collapsed, and as the Soviet Union subsequently disintegrated.

These changes did not put an end to anti-American feelings in Europe, however. The US did have a much worse crime problem than any Western

European country; but the TV screen created the image of a US with murder and mayhem round every street corner. There was the anti-Americanism of those Europeans who feared foreign immigration, and dreaded the US as the land of multiculturalism run amok. There was also, from the 1980s onward, a new form of anti-Americanism inconceivable 30 years earlier – the anti-Americanism of those who equated the US with inefficient management, shoddy workmanship, and economic decline à la anglaise. Exaggerated as these impressions might be, they derived in part from genuine deficiencies, and also from grave errors in public relations. (It was surely one of President Bush's major errors to take on an official trip to Japan 21 corporate executives – including a senior official from General Motors who had just announced the layoff of 74,000 workers, the closing of numerous plants, and, into the bargain, an $ 80 million compensation package for the upper echelon of management.)[25]

Above all there was anti-Americanism home-made. Few foreigners ever denounced the US with the same passion as Paul Fussell, an American writer, to whom the US was BAD, in capital letters, and hell was other Americans.[26] Such sentiments widely appealed to a moral coalition whose members drew their inspiration from three separate traditions: religious (particularly Quakers, Unitarians, Episcopalians, Jews); secular humanist (both Marxist and non-Marxist); and bohemian (including outsiders of every kind who gloried in their own alienation from society). Overwhelmingly they rejected the doctrine of Original Sin; they repudiated the past, and put their trust into a glorious future. Whatever their philosophical antecedents, they regarded themselves – like seventeenth-century Puritans – as a Chosen band, a moral vanguard, destined to lead the oppressed masses from present-day America, a new Egypt, to a Promised Land of the vanguard's own creation.

The impact of anti-Americanism, however, should not be exaggerated. The history of the Atlantic Community since the end of 1945 had, after all, been an extraordinary success story, at least for that part of Western Europe which, as the British *Economist* put it, had been "lucky enough to have been liberated (or defeated) by the Americans." Whereas the first part of the present century had been a time of disaster, the second had seen a period of peace unmatched since the post-Napoleonic era. "The average West European's income (at 1990 prices) has risen more than 300 percent from $ 4,860 a year in 1950 to $ 20,880 in 1990. Life expectancy for West Europeans went up in that time from 67 to 76 years."[27]

True enough, both Western Europe and the US suffered from serious social problems. In Western Europe there were, for example, new ethnic tensions, as Western Europe itself became a magnet for immigrants rivalling the US. By 1992 the share of foreign-born people in many

Western European countries was indeed higher than in the US, the world's classic country of refuge. (In 1991 the share of foreign-born persons amounted to about 17 percent in Switzerland, 11 percent in France, 9 percent in Belgium, 7.5 percent in Germany, 6.3 percent in Britain – as against 6 percent in the US.) Of course no European country could compare with the US as regards ethnic diversity. The US in particular continued to suffer from bitter racial rivalries, as expressed, for example, in the 1992 riots in Los Angeles. Nevertheless, the US's problems seem manageable when compared with those of other multi-ethnic countries such as Russia, Romania, Yugoslavia, and many others. Europeans widely appreciated America's relative tranquillity. Within the US the moral coalition proved unexpectedly fissiparous as militant feminists, ecologists, gays, and minority advocates increasingly pursued divergent aims. The moral coalition could not easily gain a mass following in a country whose citizens, in public opinion polls, overwhelmingly expressed satisfaction with their own lives. (The same generalization applies to Western Europe.)

The breakdown of communism in the former Warsaw Pact countries weakened anti-Americanism both directly and indirectly. The enormous propaganda campaign directed and financed by the Soviet Union and its allies suddenly ceased. Marxists of every kind were suddenly put on the defensive. Why had they failed to foresee communism's impending disaster? Why had they so widely failed to understand the demographic, moral, and economic ravages experienced by every country that had ever been under communist rule? Moreover, by the 1980s, even before the breakup of the Soviet Union, some of the old-fashioned anti-Americanism of the French left had already lost its sting. In France, where Jean-Paul Sartre was once the country's most influential intellectual, and anti-Americanism was *de rigueur* among the smart set, attitudes changed. From the 1980s onward it became perfectly acceptable among literati to talk of *la France qui gagne* (France which makes money), to appear preppy – *bon chic, bon genre* – and even to praise wines from California. As Richard Bernstein put it, "the noisome, Sartrean, fashionably leftist jargon that treated the United States as a bourgeois and therefore philistine tyranny, an 'imperialist' menace posing a threat at least as grave as the one posed by the Soviet Union has become *ringard*" (fusty, old-fashioned in French youth jargon).[28]

For decades, the left appeared psychologically unable to rid itself of its anti-Americanism. But when the Cold War ended and Marxist-Leninist dictatorships collapsed, anti-American sentiments weakened in Europe. By an odd twist of fortune, it was precisely in the formerly communist states of Europe that the US continued to be most widely admired by ordinary people. It was a mighty change for the better!

# 2

# An Expanding Alliance
# 1945–1987

When World War II ended, the US emerged as the world's leader and North America as a continent of prosperity. While postwar Europe was anxious and fearful, Americans were full of confidence and optimism in themselves and in their country. Americans rejoiced in their federal constitutional system (and wanted to give it to Europe as a model for new democratic states). Americans were proud of capitalism and its wartime performance as the arsenal of democracy. The left in Europe feared and hated American capitalism and its economic imperialism. Wall Street was much distrusted, as was the US economic history of boom and bust. Although Europeans were depressed by past failures of democracy and the past dominance of fascism, they still felt culturally superior to the US.

In 1949 (and in later years) the Vatican newspaper *Osservatore Romano* claimed that communism was not as inimical to Christianity as capitalism. Many Protestant churchmen thought that capitalism was incompatible with Christianity. For example, the Archbishop of Canterbury, William Temple, attacked capitalism's self-interest and concern with money and materialism. The Archbishop opined that Europe's leaders had turned their back on capitalism and were not interested in whether America was going to reform that evil system.

Many of postwar Europe's leaders felt inferior in face of America's wealth and power, its egalitarianism and democracy. While Americans were staunchly individualistic and anti-socialist, the European left was pro-socialist. Yet workers in the supposedly reactionary free enterprise system were the most productive in the world; their output was higher, and they shared more in the wealth they created than did European workers. There was less social envy and class hostility in the US than in Europe. American workers felt they had more opportunities than did the workers of Europe. Furthermore, there was no social stigma attached to being in the working class.

Even during the late 1950s, by which time Western Europe had fully recovered, and had indeed become much richer than in prewar days, the US remained the world's economic giant. It led by far in the ownership of cars, television sets, telephones, in energy production, steel output, and a multitude of other economic indicators. The Americans' per capita income of $2,572 was more than twice Great Britain's, about three times Western Germany's, five times Italy's. The US dominated the world's currencies. But the greatest American miracle was the growth of population. Within a single decade, from 1950 to 1960, the US population grew from 150,100,000 to 179,390,000 people: the greatest percentage jump – 18 percent – for any decennial period in 50 years. The numerical increase amounted to 28,000,000 people, almost as many as had dwelled in the entire US at the outbreak of the Civil War. Some 41,000,000 Americans were born during the decade, nearly as many people as lived in the whole of England in 1961 (43,460,000).[1] The US was the world's leading power.

## COLD WAR AND MARSHALL PLAN

The only serious challenge to America's unsought postwar supremacy derived from the Soviet Union. To a substantial minority of Europeans, the Soviet Union as yet appeared the land of the future. The Soviet hosts had won glory in World War II; they outnumbered the Western armies. Poland, East Germany, Czechoslovakia, Yugoslavia, Albania, Romania, and Bulgaria all passed under communist domination. The pace and pattern of the takeover varied, but in the end the result was similar: a privileged *nomenklatura* exercised power; all overt opposition was eliminated; and the ruling power attempted to control every aspect of society.

In organizational terms, the Eastern European countries were linked militarily to the Soviet Union through the Warsaw Treaty Organization (the Warsaw Pact, formed in 1955). In economic terms, Moscow's satellites were tied to the Soviet Union through the Council for Mutual Economic Aid (Comecon, set up in 1949). Moscow's control was not total. In 1948 Yugoslavia, under the leadership of Josip Broz Tito, succeeded in extricating itself from the Soviet alliance; so did Albania in 1960. (Unlike the remaining countries of Eastern Europe, both Yugoslavia and Albania had escaped direct Soviet military occupation.) But the bulk of the Eastern European countries remained Soviet dependencies. Their leaders echoed Soviet phraseology, and, at least in public, pretended to regard the Soviet Union as a model for humanity ("to learn from the Soviet Union means to win," the East German communists put it.) Throughout Eastern Europe, ordinary people had to get used to the "double truth" (one for public usage, the other for private consumption). As Churchill put it in his 1946 address at Westminister College, Fulton, Missouri, an "Iron Curtain" had descended across the continent. Like it or not, a substantial minority of Europeans came to look upon Soviet power as irresistible and communism as the political system of the future.

Soviet influence was by no means confined only to Eastern Europe. By 1945, Greece was involved in a bitter civil war that pitted the communists against the rest. The Soviet Union supplied indirect help to the Greek insurgents. Had they won, Soviet influence would have extended to the Eastern Mediterranean. Soviet influence was powerful also in France and Italy, whose communist parties followed Stalin's lead in every major issue of policy. The Italian and French communist parties had turned into mass organizations, led by disciplined cadres, supported by great trade union movements, and millions of voters. The Italian and French parties commanded experts of every kind, from engineers, publishers, and economists to shop stewards and professional street fighters. Both parties had become powerful patronage machines, wielding great overt influence, able to provide advantages for the most unlikely people – not necessarily communists – who were willing to oblige the leadership over particular issues.

The communists also played a leading part in the battle of ideas. It is difficult to recall in the 1990s the degree to which intellectuals such as Louis Aragon, Jean-Paul Sartre, Pablo Neruda, Berthold Brecht, Sean O'Casey, G. B. Shaw, and Lord Russell were willing at one time to praise communism, to deny or to exculpate Stalin's atrocities, and to abase themselves before communism. The sociologist Paul Hollander has told in detail the story of these "Political Pilgrims," and analyzed their motives. There was among self-styled progressive intellectuals a widespread feeling of both cultural and personal guilt; there were great hopes for a magnificent future in which mankind would be freed from capitalism and exploitation and from sin, hopes which linked to confront unpleasant present realities in conflict with the intellectuals' vision. Such views were fueled by the communists' success in using the "anti-Fascist" appeal: in communist phraseology, even the Berlin Wall became known as the "anti-Fascist protection wall," *der anti-faschistische Schutzwall*). Whatever the reasons, many fellow travellers degraded themselves in apostrophizing Soviet tyranny in verse such as the following:

> One day all Germans will praise Stalin's name
> Each German city will proclaim his fame
> He will be loved 'midst vineyards on the Rhine.
> In Bonn a student vows "his cause is mine."[2]

Thus scribbled Johannes Becher, once a respectable poet in Weimar Germany, who later wrote the national anthem of the German Democratic Republic. Charity forbids us from translating the rest of the poem.

The Soviets soon engaged in an all-out propaganda offensive against the Western powers, whose assumed capitalist overlords were accused of every crime under the sun. The Soviet Union and its allies created a vast array of fronts and publicity organizations throughout the world, coordinated by the Cominform (Communist Information Bureau, set up in 1947 as the successor of the Comintern or Communist International). Most of these bodies sought to influence specific groups; they accordingly included organizations such as the World Federation of Trade Unions; the World Federation of Democratic Youth; the International Students; the Women's International Democratic Federation; the International Organization of Journalists; the International Association of Democratic Lawyers; the International Radio and Television Organization. Other fronts appealed to the public to promote causes such as peace, nuclear disarmament and national liberation for Third World countries.

In addition, each Soviet satellite state maintained its own network of friendship societies and such like organizations. Attempts were made even to influence emigrés, either by threats to relatives, or by favors of visas (a field in which communist Czechoslovakia in particular excelled). For all their variety, these fronts shared common features. They were coordinated with Soviet intelligence. They deliberately appealed to non-communists of the liberal left. The fronts tried to avoid being labeled communist, but all key positions remained under communist control. The fronts invariably praised communism and the Soviet Union, vilified capitalism and the US, and twisted the meaning of terms such as "peace," "liberation," and "democracy" in such a way as to conform to the Communist Party line.

Moreover, communist propaganda made an immense effort to elucidate theory (a practise copied by Third World statesmen such as Kwame Nkrumah). Under Stalin, the regnant doctrine asserted that the world was divided into two camps: capitalists on one side of the great divide, socialists on the other. Peaceful coexistence between the two opposing systems was said to be impossible in the long run; sooner or later the two camps would clash in a cataclysmic confrontation that would decide humanity's future. And in their international disinformation campaign, the communists could rely on a great number of scholars and journalists in the West inclined to echo communist propaganda over certain issues. A few examples must suffice. According to Ralf Dahrendorf, one of the most distinguished of German sociologists, later knighted in Britain, the German Democratic Republic had created "equal opportunity, permanent discussion, privileged free access to elite positions," "a mentality of upward mobility and achievements, confidence in the state and plan, not market rationality." The German Democratic Republic, according to Sir Ralf, had established for itself public legitimacy "on the part of its citizens." Hence the GDR constituted "the first modern society on German soil."[3] Equally gullible was Paul Samuelson, a Nobel Prize winner in economics, and author of one of the most widely used textbooks in the United States. "It is a vulgar mistake to think that most people in Eastern Europe are miserable," Samuelson wrote in the tenth edition of his textbook, this after the suppression of the East German uprising of 1953, the 1956 Hungarian rising, and the Soviet invasion of Czechoslovakia in 1968. (In the Eleventh Edition, Samuelson took out the word "vulgar.")

Such distortions went with bitter denunciations of those academics willing to paint the Soviet Union and its allies in their true colors. In happier times, many years later, the governing mayor of St Petersburg (Leningrad), for example, explained how "the seventy-years social experiment [in the Soviet Union] proved a continuation of the worst sides of the Russian autocracy and the Russian bureaucratic machine. Communism on our Russian soil made people's lives utter madness: reality became absurd, and the human being in it absurd."[4] During the Vietnam imbroglio and its troubled aftermath, however, it had taken a bold professor to say as much at a public rally on any campus in the US.

Given these internal and external challenges to the West, given Stalin's assumption that permanent coexistence between capitalism and socialism was impossible, American intervention proved decisive in redressing the world balance of power. Not that the Americans had initially sought a permanent stake in Europe. When World War II ended, the US rapidly, and with very little friction, demobilized an armed force amounting to a total of some 12,500,000 men and women. (By 1949, the Americans had no more than two divisions in the whole of Europe, and the bulk of the US forces were fit only for constabulary duty. The Soviet Union's armed forces at the time comprised more than five million men, organized into 175 divisions of varying strength and effectiveness. An estimated one million men, one-fifth of the total divisional strength, was deployed in Eastern Europe.) The American people, however, were tired of war and foreign entanglements. "Bring the Boys Home" was a most popular slogan, and the US government had no choice but to comply.

Neither was there at first much enthusiasm in the US for providing economic assistance to foreigners, whether ex-allies or ex-enemies. Wartime aid extended to Britain ended abruptly. Britain received substantial postwar loans – but only on arduous conditions. There was indeed almost no precedent for financing even a friendly foreign country in peacetime, much less subsidizing a former enemy. Rather than pay for the rehabilitation of defeated countries, victorious states in the past had been wont to exact reparations from the vanquished. The Marshall Plan constituted a total departure from past European practice; the Plan indeed formed the greatest voluntary transfer of resources from one country to another known to history. Technically known as the European Recovery Program, the Plan passed by the US Congress with a decisive majority, and was signed by President Truman on April 3, 1948 – just in time to influence the Italian election in that year.

The Marshall Plan did not, in and of itself, cause Western European economic recovery. (Indeed, there was little direct correlation between the amount of US aid received, and the speed of economic recovery in the various recipient countries. France and Britain obtained much more aid per capita than West Germany, which nevertheless progressed more quickly than either.) But the Marshall Plan (guided by the European Cooperation Administration, ECA) helped to tide Western Europe over a dangerous period; the Plan provided new confidence to Western Europe. The Plan furnished money, food, fuel, machinery, at a time when the Western European economies were all in disarray. Marshall Plan experts argued in favor of free trade, decentralized management, of breaking up cartels, of the elimination of quotas and customs, and of labor-saving technologies. The Americans also delivered know-how. For example, at the Doboelman soap works in Holland, American experts showed the Dutch how to cut processing time from five days to two hours with new machinery. In Norway, fishermen used a new type of net made from yarn spun in Italy. In Offenbach in West Germany, Marshall Plan leather revived the handbag industry; in Lille, Marshall Plan coal kept a steel factory in business; and in Roubaix, Marshall Plan wood maintained one of the world's largest textile mills. In 1945 only 25,000 tractors were in use on French farms, four years later Marshall Plan aid had put another 200,000 tractors in the field. Overall, American investment in Western Europe grew apace, and more and more US patents found customers abroad. Americans had good reason for talking about "the American century."

A host of US technical experts, consultants, and managers also contributed their experience to Western Europe. But there was also a reverse flow of Europeans to the US. As William James Adams, an economist, puts it with regard to France:

Under the Marshall Plan, France dispatched large numbers of business executives, trade unionists, civil servants to the United States with an eye toward absorption of American productivity. They returned not only with . . . butch haircuts and wineless lunches, but also with an appreciation of how business was conducted in a relatively dynamic, seemingly dis-organized setting.[5]

The Plan likewise represented an immense US political commitment. It was not for nothing that George C. Marshall, a professional soldier, received the Nobel Peace Prize for his efforts. In a more intangible sense, Europeans benefited from the American sense of optimism and the American premise that peace, labor productivity, consumerism, welfare and profits went hand in hand – this at a time when gloomy Existentialist philosophies were in high fashion among European intellectuals. America produced cheaper coal (coal miners struck in Europe's coldest winter, 1946) and sent food to tide the Europeans over and then the means to quickly revive their economies through the Marshall Plan. The Marshall Plan, like NATO, created an intricate network of intra-European and transatlantic contacts among businessmen, civil servants, and trade unionists.

Above all, the Marshall Plan was designed to push Europeans toward political and economic cooperation – a major objective of US policy-makers. Paul G. Hoffman, who headed the ECA, predicted European unification through a common market. Aid was administered through the OEEC (Organization for European Economic Cooperation created in 1948, replaced in 1961 by the OECD, Organization for Economic Cooperation and Development). In terms of a narrowly-conceived *realpolitik*, the Americans might have benefited from dealing separately with their European allies in a strictly bilateral fashion. In practice, the Americans looked toward a new Western European economic association. The US was both a lobbyist for a united Europe, and also a role model. Surely, European federalists argued, the US could not have developed into the world's greatest economic power, had the 50 states remained divided by customs barriers, and if a New Yorker visiting California were obliged to show his passport every time he or she crossed the border of a state. The OEEC created a network of transnational bodies and transnational committees to deal with specialized questions. (These included the European Payments Union (EPU), set up in 1950, essentially a central bank and clearing house for intra-European trade and payments. By 1959 the European currencies had largely become convertible, and the EPU was replaced by the European Monetary Agreement.)

Yet the Marshall Plan was only passed against heavy US domestic opposition. American isolationists resented having to spend the American taxpayer's money on foreign countries that had already defaulted on their previous debts from World War I. Businessmen didn't want to reconstruct competitor European industries. Congressmen only wanted to give food, not loans. The Soviet Union and its allies all the world over denounced the Plan for strengthening the hold of US capitalism on Western Europe; hence the Soviet Union would not become a beneficiary of the Plan, neither would Moscow permit any of its satellites to participate. Even pro-American Europeans were bound to feel uneasy. It was hard to ask a foreign country for aid; harder still to ask aid from a donor whom visiting European dignitaries had traditionally described in unflattering terms. A handful of purists also complained at the Plan because of its Keynesian connotations, its refusal to leave European recovery to the free market alone.

Nevertheless, the Plan worked. It succeeded in part because it gained widespread political acceptance within the US itself – a remarkable political achievement. The Plan represented a new welfare capitalism – confident, committed to raising productivity, raising wages, expanding markets, and establishing good labor relations by depoliticizing trade unionism. The Marshall planners were convinced that only a prosperous Europe would resist communism, and that only a prosperous Europe would provide expanding markets for US as well as European producers. Some of the overseas representatives of the Marshall Plan, as well as Paul G. Hoffman, the Plan's chief administrator, were businessmen, "regular guys," invulnerable to the deadly charge of being "do-gooders" and "one-worlders." Some were also Keynesians, but they were less effective than the bankers and military who ran West Germany. On the whole, the Plan was well administered; there were no scandals, no massive diversion of funds into the pockets of political and bureaucratic racketeers. Yet the expenditure involved was astronomical by the standards of the time. The Marshall Plan and other forms of foreign assistance between them cost the US $ 17.6 billion (or $ 120 billion in current value for the Marshall Plan alone) – the largest voluntary transfer of resources in history. Ten years after the end of the greatest war in history, Western Europe had not only fully recovered, but had become far more prosperous and productive than before.

Economic cooperation went with the liberalization of trade. In prewar days, the various European countries had tried to protect themselves against the effects of the slump by bilateral barter deals and an elaborate game of "beggar-my-neighbor." Tariffs, import controls, and similar devices had multiplied. After World War II the Western Allies switched direction. At the Bretton Woods Conference in 1944, the Allied powers, chief among them the US, agreed to set up the International Monetary Fund (IMF). This fund was designed to make gold and scarce currencies (in effect dollars) available to its members, and thus to facilitate international trade. The same conference set up the Bank for Reconstruction and Development (the "World Bank"), for the purpose of making development loans. In 1947, the General Agreement on Tariffs and Trade (GATT) succeeded in reducing tariffs below the level of prewar years both in the US and in Europe.

Transatlantic ties tightened in many other respects. For instance, there was the impact of military occupation in Italy, and above all, in Germany. The US example affected de-Nazification, constitution-making, economic recovery, and also education in West Germany. General Lucius D. Clay, Military Governor in the US Zone of Occupation during the critical years of 1947 to 1949, had a major personal impact; indeed, he has a perfectly good claim to be remembered as one of the unofficial Fathers of the German Federal Republic. In Italy, the influence of American Catholics, the public aid given the US through the Marshall Plan, and private assistance given by Italian Americans played a part in keeping the Italian Communist Party from sharing power.

## NATO AND WESTERN DEFENSE

When World War II ended, there was at first little commitment to a continued American military presence in Europe. President Roosevelt expected to withdraw all American soldiers within two years; isolationism remained strong, especially in the Mid-West. It was not merely left-wingers who wanted to "bring the boys home," but also conservatives with the most impeccable credentials, men such as ex-president Herbert Hoover. It was Stalinist intransigence which re-created the Western Alliance. Contrary to Soviet and pro-Soviet propaganda, moreover, it was not bellicose Americans who had inveigled peace-loving Europeans into an aggressive alliance. It was, above all, pressure from the British (and to a much lesser extent from the Canadian) government which had finally persuaded the US to join the alliance and to return to Europe militarily. (The formation in 1949 of the North Atlantic Treaty Organization, NATO, had been preceded by the communist takeover in Prague in 1948, the Berlin blockade initiated in 1948, and the creation in the preceding year of the Cominform, the Comintern's successor.) In the words of Lord Ismay, a British general, NATO was formed to keep Germany down, the Soviets out, and the Americans in.

US support for NATO was at first only tentative. There was, indeed, European criticism of America's alleged resolve to fight "to the last European." The decisive shift came with North Korea's assault on South Korea in 1950. This act of aggression, openly supported by Stalin with propaganda and arms shipments, was instrumental in getting the US to embark on massive rearmament. The Korean War, moreover, confirmed Americans in their fear that the Soviet Union might try on a large scale in Western

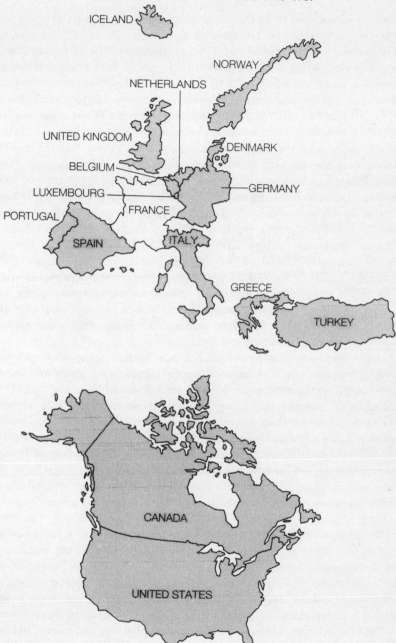

*Figure 2.1* NATO member countries at 1992 (France was a military member 1949–66, and remains a political member).

Europe what the North Koreans had attempted on a small scale in South Korea – the pursuit of revolution by military means. By dint of its sacrifices in the Korean War, the US had demonstrated its willingness to support a threatened ally. Henceforth there would be no more talk about America's being willing to fight to the last Allied soldier.

Not that NATO was without problems. Europe's military needs led to the rearmament of West Germany, which joined NATO as a full partner in 1954. German rearmament occasioned bitter disagreement within Western Europe, and also within West Germany itself. (It was only from 1959 onward that the German Social Democratic Party fully accepted West Germany's role.) European statesmen and military leaders remained only too aware how far they depended on the upstart power of the US both in the economic and military field. Nevertheless, NATO worked effectively both as a military and a political alliance. In both capacities, NATO created a great array of new links between the US and Western Europe. English became NATO's military lingua franca, just as it became the standard language of air and sea communications. The US provided much of NATO's conventional, and most of its nuclear weaponry; the US supplied NATO's supreme commanders; the US provided much of the military technology and equipment. Many European officers and technicians were trained by Americans.

NATO also served as a channel for new ideas – sometimes with unintended consequences. (For instance, the Portuguese army which rose against the country's dictatorship in 1974 had been influenced by ties to NATO as well as by the experience of a lengthy and unpopular colonial war. General Francisco da Costa Gomes, one of the leaders of the revolution, had earlier served as a senior liaison officer with NATO.) NATO also influenced the US. Several hundred thousand Americans came to be stationed in Europe at any one time. Larger still was the number of American dependents, the wives and children of servicemen and civil officials who, between them, created permanent American enclaves and intensified reciprocal relations between Western Europe and North America.

The Allies had to coordinate policies and strategy through a supranational organization. To meet these problems, the Allies set up an organization of considerable complexity. The Council served as the supreme organ of the Alliance, with permanent representation from each member government. The Council was responsible for implementing the provisions of the treaty; its work was organized by the secretary-general who directed its secretariat and its five divisions: political affairs, defense planning and policy, defense support, infrastructure, logistics, scientific affairs. The Council's chief administrative officer was the secretary-general. The first incumbent was Lord Ismay, who had made his reputation as chief of staff to the British minister of defence during World War II; Ismay held the post until 1957, when he was succeeded by the former prime minister (and foreign minister) of Belgium Paul-Henri Spaak, like Eisenhower, a chairman to the manner born.

The Council was assisted by a host of specialized committees and agencies that dealt with matters as diverse as the press services and economics. NATO's military direction lay with the military committee composed of the chief-of-staff of each member state. Subordinate to the military committee were the major commands and planning groups Supreme Command Europe (SACEUR); Supreme Allied Commander Atlantic (SACLANT); Allied Commander-in-Chief Channel (CINCHAN); Canada-US Regional Planning Group (CUSRPG); and a number of other military agencies. Supreme headquarters were in Paris, and later shifted to Brussels. (Here NATO's impact, however, was much smaller than the EEC's. By 1990 there were still fewer than 2,300 NATO officials in Brussels, as opposed to 14,000 EC Eurocrats.) Subordinate agencies were located in Paris, Bonn and Rome.

NATO was, above all, more than a military alliance. It developed an extensive system of committees dealing with subjects as varied as political collaboration; the settlement of intra-alliance disputes; consultation on foreign policy; economic, scientific, technical, social, and cultural coopera-tion. The Secretary-General of NATO, who headed its international staff, became almost as powerful a man as the SACEUR. The Alliance united policy-makers and executives of many different nationalities in a common task. No other alliance in history had comprised such a diversity of partners or cooperated on such a broad range of subjects, nor lasted as long. (By the early 1980s, NATO comprised Belgium, Canada, Denmark, France, Greece, Iceland, Italy, Luxembourg, the Netherlands, Norway, Portugal, Spain, Turkey, the United Kingdom, the United States, and West Germany – enlarged in 1990 by the accession of East Germany, though with a special status within NATO.) No doubt NATO had its troubles. But these were kept in bounds and NATO worked. Contrary to all previous predictions and previous precedents, German, French, British, Dutch, Italian, and American military men cooperated successfully. NATO remained an alliance whose members had joined freely; they were not simply satellites such as the Soviet Union's Warsaw Pact partners.

NATO remained an association of sovereign nation-states; its members could leave the alliance as they pleased. (In 1966 France withdrew from NATO's military command, though France continued to cooperate with the Alliance.) Individual members remained free to decide the percentage of the GNP or the size and composition of the forces to be contributed to the Alliance. NATO's sphere of action remained confined to Western Europe and its strategic role remained defensive. Threats to the Alliance that might emerge elsewhere, in Africa, the Middle East or Caribbean, would still have to be dealt with by its individual members – an arrangement initially welcomed and later regretted by the Americans. NATO possessed no coordinated intelligence service; the intelligence services of the individual countries would continue to operate in an uneasy, and often mutually hostile, fraternity.

NATO also lacked a propaganda organization capable of rivalling the Soviet propaganda machine in Western Europe. NATO likewise wanted for an agency for political warfare. In this regard, the Allies differed among themselves, and even individual member states – including the US – pursued no consistent policy. For example, John Foster Dulles, Eisenhower's secretary of state designate, talked at length about the need to liberate Eastern Europe. But when the Hungarians revolted in 1956, the US would not even withdraw diplomatic recognition from the resultant Hungarian puppet regime, much less recognize a Hungarian government-in-exile. The absence of a coordinated political strategy became all the more obvious from the later 1950s onwards, when the Soviets became more skillful in their foreign policy, increasingly used "peace" slogans for their own purposes, and resolved to make their weight felt in the Third World.

NATO also had many technical problems. NATO proved much less adept at standardizing its equipment than the Warsaw Pact. NATO's command structure was so complex as to be certain of being superseded in the event of war. Reliance on nuclear deterrents created difficult, probably insoluble problems, as the Soviet Union perfected its own nuclear arsenal. NATO consistently underestimated its own capacity for conventional defense. Benumbed by headcounts, Western planners were apt to overrate the value of non-Soviet divisions within the Warsaw Pact, most of which might have proved highly unreliable in the event of a conflict. Hence, as William Park, a British student of strategy, put it, "NATO was born with an inferiority complex regarding its conventional force capabilities, unwarranted even in the early years."[6]

NATO's sense of inferiority vis-à-vis the Red Army was hardly justified. By the late 1950s, after West Germany had put in place a substantial new force, the Bundeswehr, the Western Allies were already in fairly good shape, despite the Soviet Union's numerical superiority.[7] The NATO forces, moreover, kept experimenting to improve their fighting capability. During the early 1980s, NATO developed a new strategy – FOFA, "Follow on Forces Attack." This provided for a flexible defense in depth, with rapid strikes on the enemy's lines of communications and headquarters, designed to smash the aggressor's infrastructure. Nobody knows how it would have worked, but given the inflexibility of the Soviet forces, the allies would surely have done well in the event of a Soviet attack – despite the opposition of German "Greens" and pacifists to a land strategy mistakenly equated with the former Wehrmacht's.

Even more contentious was the proposed use of nuclear weapons both on the tactical and the strategic level. It was NATO's sense of numerical inferiority which had first impelled NATO to build tactical nuclear arms. The reason for this numerical imbalance was budgetary. None of the Western Allies were willing to match the Warsaw Pact armies in terms of manpower, tanks and guns. Initially NATO relied on its superiority in atomic weapons and on the qualitative superiority of its equipment. But these advantages evaporated as the Soviets improved their own armaments. During the 1950s, therefore, NATO began to deploy a great array of tactical nuclear weapons for direct battlefield support. (The French and British built their own nuclear deterrents – not so much to intimidate the Soviets but to assert French and British power within the Western counsels. Existing treaty obligations forbade the Germans to do likewise.)

Of all the major Western powers, it was West Germany which relied most heavily on the US nuclear guarantee, and which housed the largest number of nuclear projectiles on its soil. This dependency created its own psychological problems and its own peculiar ambivalence. The Germans wanted the US to deploy nuclear weapons on German soil so as to provide the maximum deterrent; the Germans looked to a "forward" defense entailing an Allied stand on the Elbe rather than the Rhine. But at the same time German opinion – particularly left-wing opinion – dreaded the enormous concentration of atomic weapons on German soil which would turn Germany into a nuclear battle field, and thereby spell *finis Germaniae*, an end to Germany.

Allied military policy was far from clear with regard to nuclear weapons, which could not be tested in maneuvers, and which were certain to turn any battlefield into shambles. By about 1957 NATO had deployed about 7,000 tactical nuclear weapons in Europe.[8] They included nuclear land mines, mortar rounds, recoilless rifle charges, air-dropped nuclear bombs, and nuclear artillery shells. Later, intermediate range nuclear force missiles were added – at the Europeans' request, but nevertheless against bitter anti-US opposition, especially from German, British, and Dutch pacifists and ecologists. Missiles were introduced and withdrawn (Jupiter, Thor), and reintroduced with modifications as Pershing II, as well as ground-launched cruise missiles (GLCM). The US – like the Soviets – also deployed shorter-range surface-to-surface missiles (SSMs) of increasing accuracy and mobility. No one, of course, can be sure what actually would have happened had these weapons been used in combat – no doubt they would have occasioned numerous nuclear Verduns and wiped out the bulk of the opposing forces.

Equally contentious were the problems concerned with strategic nuclear weapons, that is to say inter-continental ballistic missiles (ICBMs). Initially, only the US had the capacity to attack the Soviet Union with nuclear bombs and destroy its main cities. As the Soviets improved their own weaponry, US nuclear strategy was modified during the 1960s when Robert McNamara was secretary of defense. Deterrence of nuclear war rested on the country's assumed ability to absorb a nuclear strike and still destroy the Soviet Union. The Soviet Union, however, soon caught up to the US. Hence by the late 1960s, US planners reconciled themselves to a doctrine aptly named MAD (for mutual assured destruction.) According to prevailing orthodoxy, any effort to upset this balance was considered destabilizing. As Stanley Kober, an arms expert, put it, "it was this logic that impelled McNamara passionately to oppose the construction of anti-ballistic missiles (ABMs)."[9] The Americans thereafter tried to limit the construction of ABMs through instruments such as the 1972 Strategic Arms Limitation Talks (SALT I). But the Kremlin never accepted the US strategic assumptions; the Soviets continued to work on ABM technology; as Soviet Marshal Nikolai Orarkov maintained, every weapon in history had always produced a counter-weapon – and this generalization also applied to nuclear-missile weaponry.

The MAD doctrine had far-reaching political consequences. The NATO Allies all relied on the US deterrent; yet they also had understandable doubts whether the Americans were truly willing to sacrifice New York for London, Paris, or Hamburg. Would the Soviets and Americans not be tempted to abstain from using strategic nuclear weapons, preserving their respective homelands as nuclear sanctuaries, while destroying Europe with tactical nuclear weapons? It was this predicament which led President Ronald Reagan in 1983 to propose his Strategic Defense Initiative (SDI) to counter missile attacks by developing a new technology. To discuss the pros and cons of SDI (misnamed "Star Wars" by its opponents) would go beyond the scope of this chapter. We shall limit ourselves to pointing out one major inconsistency in the argument put forward by Reagan's critics. SDI was censured on two opposing grounds. It would not work, and would merely prove a money waster. Alternatively, SDI would indeed work, at least to a point, and thereby "destabilize" the global balance of power. Reagan's supporters, for their part, argued that SDI would add to the US deterrent power, even if only partially successful; SDI would assure US defense against a threatened missile attack by a minor power run by a Hitler-like madman; SDI, moreover, would reassure the NATO Allies if it could be made to work, and if the new technology were to be made available to the Europeans. Even the Soviet Union might find reassurance, once the counter-missile strategy were universally adopted.

These problems seemed impossible to resolve. So did a variety of other contentious issues, including constant quarrels over the NATO Allies' say in grand strategy and their respective contributions to the Alliance. (For instance, the Cuban missile crisis of 1961 had essentially involved the US and the Soviet Union alone; there was little consultation between Washington and the Western European capitals; Western Europe might have been plunged into a war of annihilation without having any say in the matter.) Even more controversial, from the Europeans' standpoint, was the Vietnam War. To the NATO allies, the US campaign in South-east Asia represented a dangerous diversion of resources from the strategic center to the periphery. The Vietnam War worsened German-American relations in particular. The most experienced officers and non-commissioned officers departed from Europe to the Far East. Discontent, drug usage, and alcoholism spread among US soldiers stationed in Germany; crime increased; morale declined, a process accelerated as US inflation diminished the purchasing power of the US serviceman's paypacket. Morale and efficiency were later rebuilt – but the GI would never again appear ten feet tall, as he had done during the end and immediate aftermath of World War II.[10]

In addition, there were – from NATO's early beginnings – constant quarrels concerning the Allies' respective contribution to the Alliance. The Americans especially felt that the Europeans did not fully pull their weight. This assumption rested on comparative statistics for defense expenditure. (By 1986 for example, the US provided 6.5 percent of its GNP for defense, more than any of its allies. The US accounted for 69 percent of the Alliance's total defense spending.) Nevertheless, such comparisons could be misleading. The definition of defense spending included the costs of non-NATO defense commitments. Hence US spending totals were biased by including the cost of maintaining US forces in areas where the NATO allies had no treaty commitments. Comparisons concerning comparative costs were apt also to take inadequate account of cost differentials; it was more expensive to maintain an American regular than a Bundeswehr conscript. In terms of troops provided and weapons placed in arsenals, the Allies made a massive contribution. Within Western Europe itself, the NATO Allies always supplied the bulk of the land forces – between 80 and 90 percent.

Disputes about burden sharing did not end the list of troubles that beset NATO. There were serious divisions both within the ranks of NATO's European partners, and between Europeans and Americans. Two subsequent allies – Greece and Turkey – almost came to blows over Cyprus. Even long-standing allies such as Britain and France at times addressed one another in terms more suited for enemies than allies. Nevertheless, NATO remained operational. The ties between North America and Western

Europe tightened; no transatlantic endeavor in history achieved greater success. As John Keegan, one of Britain's leading military historians, puts it, the development of Western Europe's armies during the last 40 years constitutes a record in which the citizens of the states involved may well take collective pride. A new German army was built – without damaging West German democracy. Four West European armies – the Spanish, French, Greek, and Portuguese – all intervened in the respective policies of their respective countries; but all of them ceased to do so in the end, and future military interference is unlikely to recur. The British army remained a remarkably effective institution throughout, despite the troubles of decolonization; NATO's smaller members, in Scandinavia and the Low Countries, built their forces from virtual non-existence to a level where each was able to make a respectable contribution to European defense; Italy's forces greatly increased their professional competence. "The standards of decency maintained and efficiency achieved by Western armies since 1945 are part of the record of the European renaissance."[11] Toward this achievement, the US made an indispensable contribution, not merely in terms of hardware, but also of management, organization, and democratic ethos.

In wider geo-strategic terms, NATO's success will not become apparent until the Soviet archives are opened to researchers. It seems, however, certain that NATO effectively deterred the Soviet Union from blackmailing the Western European countries. Without US backing, the various continental states of Western Europe could hardly have stood up to Soviet pressure at a time when the communist parties were particularly powerful in France and Italy. The Soviets of course tried to influence Western Europe through a variety of propagandistic and diplomatic means. But except for a brief moment in 1974 when the existing Portuguese dictatorship toppled, and the Portuguese Communist Party briefly hoped to gain power, Western Europe remained immune to communist takeovers.

Diverted from Western Europe, the Soviet Union thereafter intensified its endeavors along what might be called the outer periphery of the Western world. By the early 1970s, the Vietnam War and the domestic unrest of the 1960s had weakened American self-confidence. America's financial stability was threatened by inflation. By an act of deliberate abnegation, the US had conceded to the Soviet Union an apparent superiority in missiles as well as conventional arms. In addition, the Soviets during the 1960s and 1970s built a great navy, the world's second largest fleet. From the Soviet standpoint, Soviet military might would aid Soviet diplomacy, Soviet scholarship, and Soviet revolutionary expertise alike in promoting Third World "national wars of liberation"; these in turn would form stepping stones on the road to world-wide victory for Marxism-Leninism. Soviet propagandists in the West might laud "peaceful coexistence." But peaceful coexistence, according to Soviet theoreticians, could only exist between rival state systems. There could be no peaceful coexistence between opposing social systems; conflict was inevitable, and socialism Soviet-style was bound to win.

During the 1970s, the Soviets thus made substantial advances. Angola and Mozambique, formerly Portuguese colonies, emerged (1974) from colonial control as Marxist-Leninist republics, led by self-styled "vanguard parties." Indochina (South Vietnam, Cambodia and Laos) and Ethiopia likewise fell under Marxist-Leninist governance, as did South Yemen. The Marxist-Leninist cause was sustained by a large Cuban expeditionary force (mainly deployed in Angola), by a direct Soviet invasion of Afghanistan (1979), and by attempts to set up a Marxist-Leninist government in Nicaragua with Cuban support. This huge effort looked impressive enough on the map. But neither Angola nor Mozambique could be turned into effectively ruled dictatorships; on the contrary, armed oppositional groups continued to hold their own, massively supported by South Africa. The US successfully backed anti-Soviet guerrillas in Afghanistan and Ethiopia's imperial hegemony over Eritrea met with armed challenges. The Sandinistas failed to hold their own in Nicaragua, despite massive Cuban and Soviet support. Israel successfully defended itself in the so called Yom Kippur War of 1973, though only Portugal among the NATO allies would join the US in backing Tel Aviv. Throughout the Third World, self-styled Marxist-Leninist movements met with defeats. Being limited in its operations to Western Europe, NATO had no direct part in this remarkable counter-revolution. The Soviet Union's main opponent throughout the world was the US. But the US effectively cooperated with individual NATO partners such as Britain and France, and NATO provided a secure center in Europe.

Contrary to Soviet predictions, the Marxist-Leninist tide thus proved neither irresistible nor irreversible. NATO held firm; so did its individual components. Instead it was the Soviet empire which began to falter, exhausted by the immense effort involved in holding and subsidizing its Eastern European dependencies, maintaining military primacy on the European continent, securing a naval presence on every ocean, and sustaining revolutionary commitment in the Third World.

## UNIFICATION EFFORTS IN WESTERN EUROPE

Above all, the US took a vital part in promoting the economic and political unity of Western Europe after 1945. The first hesitant step came in 1947 when Britain concluded with France the Treaty of Dunkirk as a guarantee against possible German aggression. In 1948 Britain joined France and the

Benelux countries (Belgium, the Netherlands, Luxembourg) in the Brussels Treaty, which led to the creation of an organization known as the "Western European Union" (WEU), or "Brussels Treaty Organization." (This body was enlarged in 1954 through the accession of West Germany and Italy.) The WEU played a useful part in improving relations between its member states. For example, WEU had an important role in the negotiations that transferred the Saar region from French to West German control in 1955. But as a military and political instrument, WEU remained subject to serious limitations. NATO became the main defensive shield for Western Europe. The European Defence Community (EDC) was another moribund defense effort. Although negotiations for a EDC Treaty were started in 1951 and signed in May, 1952, the French National Assembly rejected the treaty in August, 1954.

Far more important was the Marshall Plan administered, as we have seen, through the Organization of European Economic Cooperation (OEEC). The Americans looked toward a new Western European association. OEEC created a complex network of transnational committees to deal with specialized questions. Most important of all, American encouragement, aid, and example promoted the creation of new agencies designed to promote closer union on a functional basis. These included, as noted earlier, the European Payments Union (EPU), set up in 1950.

Furthermore, in 1952, the main six Western European continental states (West Germany, France, Italy, Holland, Belgium, and Luxembourg) set up the European Coal and Steel Community (ECSC), operational in 1953 with Jean Monnet as the first president of the governing body, the High Authority. Further negotiations promoted by Monnet led to the creation of the European Economic Community (EEC, later known as European Community, EC). The EEC was set up in 1957, and began to function in 1958, designed to eliminate those economic barriers that still divided the members of the ECSC from one another. Given Europe's past and the commitment of most European states to protectionism, the EEC constituted a revolutionary departure on the road toward a genuine Common Market. Its creation was welcomed by the US, which had a direct stake both in the expansion of its trade with Europe and the well-being of the US subsidiaries in Europe as well as ensuring peace and cooperation in a customs union instead of economic rivalry as in the past.

The EEC formed a multiple compromise, between moderate Catholics such as Konrad Adenauer and Alcide de Gasperi on the one hand, and moderate socialists on the other. Similarly the EEC rested on an unstable agreement between free traders and interventionists such as Jacques Delors, a French socialist cast in Jean Monnet's mold, later president of the EC's governing Commission, who was determined to use the EC's machinery to promote an all-European economic and monetary union, a political union, and social policy. The EEC embodied a variety of other deals – between French and Germans; between advocates of a full European union and spokesmen for functional cooperation between sovereign states; between those who wanted to expand ("widen") the EEC and those who wished to consolidate ("deepen") the existing structures.

Overall the EEC proved a stunning success. Trade barriers diminished between the EEC members; (customs barriers finally ended in 1968). The EEC went a long way in assuring the free movement of workers within its boundaries. Labor unions as well as capitalists discovered the merits of transnational cooperation. Existing obstacles to the free transfer of capital diminished. The EEC set up a variety of transnational agencies. There was a striking expansion of commerce between the EEC's members, and also between the EEC as a whole and foreign countries, including the US. Living standards improved. The EEC states (with West Germany, France, Italy, and the three "Benelux" states as founder members) cooperated politically as well as economically. The idea of a new war between France and Germany, or France and Britain, or Britain and Germany, thereafter seemed inconceivable, a subject either for jokes or nightmares. It was an astonishing story, and the US could take some credit for having helped to turn a dream into a reality.

Not that all went well with the EEC. An association such as the EEC, built on innumerable compromises, could not escape constant conflict. Leaders such as de Gaulle and later Mrs Thatcher remained determined that the EEC should remain a loose association of sovereign states; their vision of the future was very different from the "Europeanists" strongly entrenched within the EEC's growing bureaucracy. There were innumerable problems which derived from the economic disparity between the industrial core states and the backward agricultural periphery. This disparity led to massive labor migration from countries such as Portugal, Spain, southern Italy, Yugoslavia, and Turkey, to the industrialized north. To cure these problems, EEC planners attempted to subsidize industrial development in backward regions, with dubious results. There were unresolved party issues between Christian Democrats and Socialists. Moreover, from the very start of the EEC, the German reunification issue loomed in the background. (In endorsing the EEC treaties, the West German Social Democratic Party (SPD) insisted that they would only accept the agreements on the assumption that these would not make more difficult the unification of Germany.) Above all, agricultural politics in Western Europe remained nationalistic and protectionist after 1957.

The EEC did not solve these difficulties. Whereas some countries (the Netherlands and Denmark) were aggressively for free trade, others

(Germany and France) were protectionist in agriculture. The Common Agricultural Policy (CAP) aimed at rationalizing agricultural policies. This proved a hard assignment, given the profound sociological differences between highly urbanized countries such as Britain, endowed with an efficient, highly mechanized farming industry, and countries such as France, West Germany, Italy, and Spain where small farmers remained numerous and influential in politics (especially in the Christian Democratic parties). Helped by protection, or by guaranteed prices much higher than those prevailing on the world markets, European farmers produced mountains of surplus grain, grapes, butter, and beef. Hence tension increased among the states of the EEC, and also with the US. The CAP promoted bureaucratic growth: 96 percent of EEC regulations came to deal with agriculture. The key weakness of the EEC's agricultural system was its price policy and subsidies which encouraged a massive rise in the production of unnecessary farm products. These problems of overproduction became even more acute after the 1960s. So did trade difficulties derived from the association of the "overseas territories" of EEC members with the Treaty of Rome, tackled only in part by the Treaty of Yaoundé in 1962.

More seriously, the EEC lacked broad popular support. Officials of the EEC would usually serve in Brussels for many years. They went home on holidays, but inclined to mix among their own kind. Their Brussels became almost a separate city, with something of Washington's or Canberra's rarefied atmosphere. Their supra-nationalism failed to catch on among their respective compatriots; it lacked the color, the sense of devotion that only traditional nationalism seemed to evoke. Football crowds went on cheering (or at times committing mayhem) for their national teams. Only a small portion of Western Europeans thought of themselves as Europeans first, British, French, or German second. There was indeed widespread though unfocused dislike for the new denationalized Europe, with its plate glass and concrete buildings, Eurospeak, Eurocrats, *Gastarbeiter*. Men and women might still be willing to die for Germany, for Britain or for France; none of them would risk his or her life for the EEC. Europe remained – as De Gaulle had both hoped and anticipated – *l'Europe des Etats*.

Businessmen, especially those running small firms, remained hostile to the EEC, as did of course communists and militant right-wingers of all stripes. The Community developed a large, privileged, impersonal bureaucracy of its own, accused by their respective national critics of "going native" in the new Euro-world. The agencies of the new Europe centered in cultural borderlands: Strasbourg, seat of the European parliament, and Luxembourg, where the Court of Justice met, were situated where German and French cultures fused; Brussels, where the Commission and Council

met, was the capital of a binational French and Flemish state. The doings
of international civil servants seemed remote, even incomprehensible, to
the man and the woman in the street.

There was also the British question. The British at first stayed out.
(Even after the Treaty of Rome had been signed in 1957, the Foreign
Office regarded the Common Market issue largely as a trade question, to
be left to the Treasury, and the treaty was not even properly translated
into English.) In 1961, the British at last began negotiations for admission
to the EEC. By this time, the British gross national product had fallen

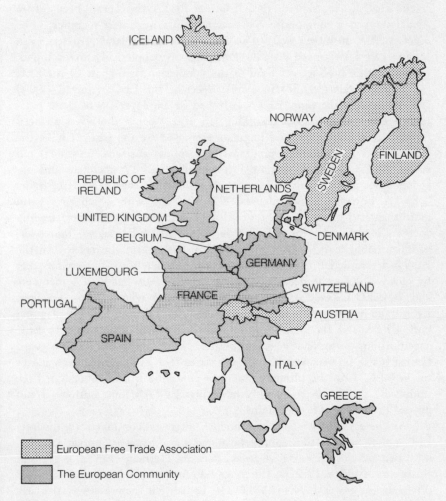

*Figure 2.2* The European Free Trade Association (EFTA) and the European
Community (EC), 1992.

much behind West Germany's and West Germany had replaced Britain as the US's main European partner in NATO. In 1967 the British withdrew from Aden, and a year later Britain announced that within three years, it would evacuate all military and naval bases east of Suez. De Gaulle, who had vetoed the original British application to the EEC, died in 1970. His demise signified the end of an era. In 1973 the British, who had joined a rival trade group, EFTA, finally secured membership of the EEC in a settlement achieved through personal talks between British premier Edward Heath, a Conservative, and French president Georges Pompidou, a Gaullist.

The British accession to the EEC left EFTA (European Free Trade Association) as a rump, with Switzerland as its wealthiest member. (The other EFTA members were Sweden, Norway, Finland, Austria, and Iceland.) EFTA received little publicity. Yet its people had a much higher gross domestic product per head of the population than those of the EEC ($11,750 as against $7,575 in 1985). Whereas the EEC required 17,000 civil servants at the time, EFTA only had 71 employees, 9 of them part-timers. English was EFTA's working language – hence there was no need for the 5,000 translators and linguists employed by the EEC. Unlike the EEC, EFTA had no costly programs on farming, customs, transport, and so on. EFTA lacked a common foreign policy; EFTA members did not abandon one iota of their sovereignty; they were held together by free trade.

EFTA, however, heavily depended on the EEC with which EFTA did more than half of its business. (EFTA became the EEC's largest trading partner, outstripping the US and Japan.) The EFTA states, moreover, had justifiable fears, after 1986, of being left out in the cold once the EEC had completed its arrangements for a completely free internal market by 1993. The free trade agreements concluded between EFTA members and the EEC covered only industrial goods, not agriculture or services. Even trade in industrial goods faced an array of technical barriers plaguing both EFTA and the EEC's own members – restrictions linked to EEC specifications on product size, composition, safety, and so forth. To guard against being side-tracked, the EFTA states thereby began to draw closer to the EEC, with the ultimate object of obtaining full membership. Free traders by conviction could only hope that EFTA's joint outlook would prevail in such an unequal union.[12]

Nevertheless, British and continental interests continued to diverge. EEC policy was in the main determined by a Franco-German entente, solidified by close personal relations between German chancellor Helmut Schmidt (in office 1972 to 1982), and French president Valéry Giscard d'Estaing (in power 1974 to 1981). The British felt themselves particularly aggrieved in the field of agriculture, where the British were among the most efficient producers, and resented having to pay excessively high prices for food so as to subsidize continental, especially French and German, farmers. Americans likewise criticized EEC farm policies, which discriminated against US agricultural exports. During the Falklands War, US public opinion and the US government staunchly backed Britain – much more so than any European country.

The EEC had other problems. There was the oil shock of 1973, and experts suddenly forecast an everlasting shortage of energy. The economics of Western Europe experienced a downturn; the "25 golden years" after World War II ended. The rise of mass unemployment led governments to give priority to national interests, at the EEC's expense. Traditional industries such as steel, textiles, and ship building declined; yet Europeans discovered that they were being outdone in high technology by the US and Japan. "Euro-pessimism" was in the air. Europe seemed to fall behind.

The 1970s, however, were not simply a barren epoch. In 1973 Denmark and Ireland as well as Britain joined the EEC. (Only Norway kept aloof, after a bitterly fought referendum in 1972; the second instance, after Britain, where EEC membership turned into a passionate political issue.) Parliamentary governance returned to Portugal and Spain after a long-lasting era of authoritarian rule, a peaceful change-over that facilitated the admission of these two countries to the EEC in 1986, following Greece's entry in 1981. In 1975 the EEC set up a Regional Development Fund and a Regional Development Committee to give assistance to the EEC's own "backward areas." More importantly perhaps, in 1978 Helmut Schmidt and Giscard d'Estaing created as their joint brainchild the European Monetary System (EMS), with its own currency, the ECU ("ECU" – both an acronym and the name of an ancient French gold coin). The EMS was designed in part to deal with the problems arising from the US decision to scrap the postwar system of fixed exchange rates and to replace it with floating rates. The EMS aimed at a tighter system, but in practice became "a Deutschmark zone." In 1979, as we have seen, the EEC was further strengthened by the first direct elections to the European Parliament.

In a more general sense, the late 1970s witnessed a general disenchantment with Keynesian policies, increasing distrust toward the regulatory state, state direction, and the real or assumed imperfections of the welfare state. (Even in Sweden, the very homeland of welfarism, the 44-year rule of the Social Democrats was temporarily broken in 1976 by a "bourgeois" coalition.) Free enterprise economics became intellectually respectable. In 1977 Milton Friedman received the Nobel Prize and in 1979 Margaret Thatcher became prime minister of Britain, determined to turn her country into an enterprise state. (She was re-elected in 1983 and 1987.) In the US Ronald Reagan moved into the White House (1981) replacing a Democrat, Jimmy Carter, and stayed for two terms, thereby continuing a period of

Republican domination over the US executive branch of government. In West Germany, Helmut Kohl stepped into the chancellor's office in 1982, heading a CDU-FDP coalition. In the same year, François Mitterrand assumed the presidency of France. Mitterrand was a socialist who had invigorated the Socialist Party. Nevertheless his election also signified a shift away from the extreme left, as the Socialists, in 1978 for the first time since 1936, had garnered more votes than the Communists.

The Atlantic economies (especially the US economy) began to recover; oil became plentiful. The winds of change were now blowing from the right. Even communist leaders (such as Santiago Carrillo in Spain and Enrico Berlinguer in Italy) were calling for ideological revision of their respective parties' doctrine – a remarkable reassessment that paralleled far-reaching shifts in the Soviet Union itself. The European economies did relatively well, despite widespread unemployment. The EMS performed more effectively than its critics had imagined. Even the British cooperated with the EMS, though they did not, for the time being, join the system. Moreover, in 1984, the Europeans reformed the CAP to make it less expensive (CAP had absorbed about 70 percent of the Community's budget), and to render CAP more acceptable to the British, and less wasteful. Priority was given to the reduction of those "wine lakes" and "butter mountains" whose existence consumers in socialist countries would have envied. In addition, the EEC, in 1985, set up an Integrated Mediterranean Program to help its backward southern periphery, and Italy, in particular, stressed its "Mediterranean vocation."

The extension of the EEC (known as the EC after 1986) went with a new challenge that none had considered at the time the EEC had been formed. Europe bought from Japan the most advanced industrial products available – cars, computers, videocassette recorders and their like. As Chalmers Johnson, an American scholar, put it, the movement toward unity in Europe entailed "a clearcut trade strategy aimed at recapturing competitive ability from Japan, and, to a lesser extent, the United States."[13] Nevertheless, the EEC turned out to be a stunning success. By 1984, 40 years after the Normandy invasion (and before Spain and Portugal joined), the EEC's gross domestic product amounted to about two-thirds of that of the US ($2,400.4 billion as against $3,627.9 billion). Its population was larger than that of the US (272 million as against 232 million), its exports were larger than those of the US ($227.2 billion as against $217.88 billion), and the EEC's members between them maintained as many men under arms as the US (2,109,000 as against 2,350,000).

Indisputably, moreover, the Western European states became more firmly integrated into a wider Atlantic community, and at the same time drew more closely together and lived peacefully. The EC became not merely a permanent fixture, but continued to expand. West Germany remained firmly cemented into the European community, linked to its Western neighbors by NATO, trade, tourism, and by a great variety of ties through civil servants, trade unionists, academics, and businessmen from different countries. The EC likewise created new bonds between politicians faced with new tasks that often transcended traditional divisions within their own countries. As a Belgian parliamentarian put it, "in all our countries religion is terribly important. It binds together every Catholic party in Europe, both leftists and conservatives, simply because they are Catholics. . . . In Europe people can sort themselves out on different lines."[14]

Europeans thereafter improved the machinery of economic cooperation. In 1968 the last customs barriers came down within the EEC. The EC went a long way in assuring the free movement of workers within its boundaries. The treaties guaranteed Community workers equality of treatment of terms of employment, wages, and other working conditions. The movement of capital was liberalized. The Community developed a comprehensive policy regarding research and technology. Moreover, the EC also profited again from strong leadership in the late 1980s. Jacques Delors, president of the EC Commission from 1985 on, had started life as a banker, later rose to be chief of social affairs in the *Plan Monnet*, a socialist Cabinet minister, and was wedded to that blend of Christian democracy and social reformism that had provided the community's original inspiration. Delors stood resolved both to improve the EC and extend its scope.

From June to December 1985, the Intergovernmental Conference (IGC) met to work out reforms of the EC treaties for the Luxembourg meeting of the European Council. The European Council thus led the drive for a unified internal market. In 1985 it asked the Commission to put forward a proposal for achieving a unified internal market by 1992. A few months later the Commission published a 93-page report with almost 300 specific suggestions to remove restrictions, with dates for council approval before December 1992. In 1986 the EC promulgated the "Single European Act" (entering into force on 1 July 1987 – a date that future generations of European school children will probably have to memorize for their history examinations).

The Single European Act (SEA) made many changes in legislative procedures, brought better political cooperation in foreign policy matters (European Political Cooperation, EPC) within the framework of the European communities, and most importantly worked for further economic and monetary union and extended policy areas of concern beyond the legal framework of the 1957 treaty. The Act formed a milestone toward the creation of a European superpower. The Treaty of Rome in 1957 had drawn its main inspiration from bureaucrats, intellectuals, politicians, and magnates of heavy industry. The program for "1992," the new target date, by contrast received support from corporate capitalists engaged in a broad range of enterprises which had already extended the scale of their operations through massive trans-frontier mergers. "1992" was backed likewise by professionals with transnational outlets for their respective skills, and by those who wanted a united Europe for its own sake; they were generally a confident lot. The EC had succeeded beyond its makers' most cheerful dreams.[15]

# 3

# The US and its Main Partners: Informal and Formal Links 1949–1985

When NATO came into being, Europe was mostly separated from America by a wall of ignorance. The US had a small staff of experts in the State Department, the armed services, in business, and academia familiar with Europe. The Europeans could draw on advice from emigrants to the US (rarely taken seriously by policy-makers) and on personal contacts – good or bad – with US soldiers, tourists and businessmen. Europeans could also rely on the series of a few gifted cultural interpreters such as Alistair Cooke, a Briton, and André Siegfried, a Frenchman. Nevertheless, Donald C. McKay, an American specialist concerned with France, could still maintain with perfect justice that "we Americans, for all the inadequacy of our knowledge, still know and understand Europe far better than Europe knows and understands us."[1]

Europe's relative ignorance of the US particularly affected the extreme left and the extreme right on the political spectrum. There was intense resentment amongst Marxists and *marxisants* in Europe with regard to the world's main bastion of capitalism. The US was likewise indicted for its racism, with race riots copiously displayed on newsreels and television screens. But the extreme right was scarcely less anti-American. The US supposedly corrupted traditional virtues through consumerism, through "nigger jazz" and "Jew-dominated" Hollywood. Fuel was added to anti-Americanism by decolonization. The US had begun its career as a nation in its war of independence from Britain. Numerous immigrants thereafter came to the US to escape from empires of one sort of another (especially Irish, Poles, and Jews). America defined itself as a bastion of democracy and an anti-colonial state.

Not surprisingly, therefore, Americans had a visceral sympathy for other anti-colonial movements. In this respect there was broad agreement between conservative presidents such as Eisenhower and liberal presidents such as Roosevelt and Kennedy. But American anti-colonialism was also tempered by *realpolitik* applied to the Cold War. American strategists fully understood the advantages available to the US in its confrontation with the Soviet Union from the dwindling imperial assets as yet under European control. US policy thus appeared at best inconsistent, at worst preachy and hypocritical – an attitude intensely disliked both by the US's allies and by neutrals. Eleanor Roosevelt (who survived her illustrious husband for many years, and continued to play an active part in politics) stood out as the archetypical representative of this US desire to shape the world in the image of the American middle class. As this jingle, found among her late husband's papers, put it in a joking fashion:

> And despite her global milling
> Of the voice there is no stilling.
> With its platitudes galore,
> As it gushes on advising.
> Criticizing and chastising
> Moralizing, patronizing.
> Paralyzing – evermore
> Advertising Eleanor.[2]

She found innumerable imitators, and they all caused equal resentment within Europe's traditional establishments.

On the other hand, Europe and America remained linked by innumerable ties. Trade and investment continued to expand. There was also the immense influence of what Europe found in America. There resided in the US far more Irish than in Ireland, far more Lithuanians than in Lithuania, far more Jews than in Israel. The number of Americans claiming at least partial British or German descent was respectively not much less than the number of British people in the United Kingdom or the number of Germans in the Federal Republic. Until the early 1970s, the US moreover remained a Mecca for European immigrants. (Between 1950 and 1970 more than 5.7 million legal immigrants came to the US, most of them from Europe, in addition to an unknown number of undocumented aliens.) In the olden days, a large proportion of newcomers had come as unskilled or semi-skilled workers; the new immigrants, by contrast, comprised many highly skilled men and women, professional people of the most varied background who belied traditional stereotypes even more than their predecessors had done.

The US began to attract students from abroad; it also acquired immense indirect cultural influence through the sheer quality of its academic institutions. As mentioned earlier, the US stood foremost in the number of Nobel Prizes gained and patents registered. The best of US universities and research institutes stood at the top of the world's academic league. Most of the world's best movies derived from the US. So did jazz, with its grounding in black American culture, the colorful musical, the modern movie and television industries. US painters, sculptors, writers, playwrights, and novelists acquired a new confidence after World War II and no longer felt obligated to judge their own work by the standards of Britain, France, and Germany. American literature, especially, gained international status. According to Martin Seymour Smith (*New Guide to Modern World Literature*, 1985), the Americans "were slow to recognize their own native geniuses." Yet the American self-discovery after World War II developed into a major world literature, and New York in time replaced London as the cultural capital of the English-speaking world.

Even the "new politics," with their anti-American connotation, owed a major debt to new American preoccupations with ecology (symbolized by Rachel Carson's 1962 book *Silent Spring*), feminism (expounded, for example, in Betty Friedan's *The Feminine Mystique* of 1963), and the black Americans' civil rights struggle.

American influence went even further. As Anthony Sampson, a British journalist, put it, the Americans' "real power, like that of the British in Victorian India, stems from their capacity to animate the natives. If you go into a German-American advertising agency, a French-American airline office, a British-American bank, it is not always easy to know which of the staff are Americans." There was a new community of transatlantic expatriates, Europeans willing to go anywhere, take new risks: "their released energy is not so unlike the energy of the Chinese in South-East Asia, of Indians in Nairobi, of Greeks in America"; their migration brought a new surge of energy and self-reliance which entailed success as well as trouble.[3]

American methods and thought continued to influence Europe, both in good times and in bad. After the disasters suffered by Europe in World War II, American confidence came as a tonic. Soviet successes such as their achievement in sending Sputnik into space (1957) might briefly dampen the sense of American superiority, but overall, there was striking, indeed naive faith – American courage, skill, ingenuity, and wealth could at the same time conquer space, stem the onslaught of communism, shoulder the main military burden of the West, cure poverty at home, rebuild Western Europe, and develop the so-called Third World. John F. Kennedy and Richard M. Nixon might differ on almost every conceivable political topic – but they shared the same faith in US ability to solve the world's problems, and their election techniques (particularly Kennedy's ability as a political performer on TV) were closely studied by the European establishments.

The American example also impressed European dissidents of every kind, feminists, ecologists and the "New Left" alike. The "Old Left" had taken its inspiration from Europeans – Marx, Engels, Lenin. The Old Left had regarded the working class as the savior of mankind. The "New Left," by contrast, centered on the campuses; they looked to an alliance between enlightened intellectuals and the world's underclass, in the slums at home and in the Third World. (The term "Third World" assumed that all the many nations comprised within this designation had much in common. The lack of realism entailed in this assumption makes the term fit for the trash can of history, together with "Third Reich," and "Third Rome" – the Russian Orthodox Church had once claimed that Moscow was destined to be the "Third Rome," following the Rome of the Popes and the Rome of the Caesars). The Old Left had prided itself on its assumed ability to understand and manipulate "objective" relations. "Concrete" was a favorite adjective in its public discourse. By contrast, the New Left, and also many intellectuals without a political program to their credit, instead emphasized the realm of subjective experience. Artistic creation, even religious quest, thus easily merged into self-exploration and the pursuit of novelty – both thoroughly American.

Since World War II, intellectual alienation in the United States has produced an adversarial culture that condemns American society root and branch. Its adherents see America as flawed and corrupt, imperialist and capitalist. Bruno Bettelheim found many of these people psychologically disturbed, estranged from the world they live in and angry at themselves, their parents and their society. Their alienation was projected against the American way of life. In general, radical critics have expected too much of Western, capitalist, societies and believed naively in the perfectibility of man and society. Since they then set unrealistically high standards for the US (but not the USSR), it was easy to attack America's social system.[4]

In their own way, the men and woman of the American New Left were, however, as Americanocentric as the most chauvinist of barroom patriots. The New Left, and not only the New Left, regarded "Amerika" as a new House of Bondage (an interpretation that went counter to the real immigrants' experience); the US became the world's new villain, the center of evil. Whereas the Old Left had welcomed industry, the New Left extolled those rural pursuits of which the militant campus youth had no first-hand experience. Blue jeans world-wide replaced the proletarian cloth cap; rock took the place of old-fashioned marching songs; the unstructured "demo" replaced the disciplined rallies of old.

The politics of youth (that is mainly white, middle-class youth) mingled with the black struggle for equality. During the 1950s and 1960s the legal barriers to black advancement in the US were all shattered – this against bitter Southern white resistance, broken only through the force employed by federal courts, federal administrators, and federal troops. The migration of black Southerners, mainly rural people, to the Northern cities accelerated – at this time the Northern industries still provided substantial employment for semi-skilled labor. The black middle class expanded, and its voice in US politics grew more influential. But at the same time the problems of big city slums worsened, crime grew and – contrary to the white liberals' optimistic hopes – white and black Americans failed to fuse. The politics of youth, however, were widely associated with the romantic idealization of the underclass. At the same time drugs were widely glamorized – not so much by the underclass but by middle-class intellectuals and pop singers who called on the public to "tune in, turn on, drop out." Above all, politicians of every stripe, left or right, increasingly came to depend on television, destined to be a dominant force in politics and recreation. In 1950, only about 11 percent of families in the US possessed a TV set. By 1960, the percentage had risen to 88 percent. Television watching had become the primary form of entertainment; thereafter Western Europe replicated the US experience.

## BRITAIN

As regards US relations with its individual European allies, Britain initially took first place. When World War II ended, Britain was still the world's third power. Its industrial output greatly exceeded that of West Germany and France, let alone of Italy and Japan. The British empire as yet remained intact; British bases circled the world, from Gibraltar, Aden, and Alexandria to Cape Town and Singapore. Britain still maintained conscription; her armed forces remained impressive. Britain also enjoyed more intangible advantages – a reputation for statesmanship, moderation, and democratic integrity that apparently destined Britain for Western Europe's political leadership.

There were close links between the British and the US – "the special relationship." It was Britain which had played the crucial role in the formation of NATO.[5] "Wasp" culture derived from Great Britain and dominated the folkways and customs of the United States from its beginning. There were also more intangible factors that benefited Britain. The Eastern establishment in the US remained anglophile. Harvard and Yale acknowledged the equality, if not the superiority, of Oxford and

Cambridge. British men's fashions continued to be prized amongst self-styled sophisticates, together with Dunhill pipes and Harris tweed jackets; so were upper-class British accents (particularly reserved in American movies for the use of English viscounts, Bengal lancers, and gigolos).

Moreover, British migration to the US (as well as Canada) continued. There were many other links between Britain and the US. A substantial number of British academics looked for jobs in the US, where they played an important part in a variety of academic disciplines, including archaeology, anthropology, geography, medicine, history and science. John Maynard Keynes, the British economist and government adviser, had a major impact on US academics: most economists were Keynesians; free marketeers, like Milton Friedman, were in a minority. Numerous British actors, physicians, engineers, and scientists made their homes in the US – indeed, the so-called "brain drain" from Britain became a subject of lively, though ill-informed, debate in Britain. Tory politicians such as Quintin Hogg fulminated against the world's richest country, which was supposedly plundering Western European brains. The emigrants themselves considered the matter in a very different light. The US offered not merely higher salaries, but also greater scope and higher occupational prestige. As a British aeronautical engineer, settled in the US, put it: "the poor image of the engineers [in Britain] results in poor pay . . . [but] an engineer is respected in America."[6] By its very existence, America modified customary attitudes in Europe.

Throughout the 1940s and the early 1950s, Britain remained the US's favorite ally, despite friction over the best policy to be adopted toward the People's Republic of China, British decolonization, the Suez invasion, or the creation of Britain's own atomic bomb (first tested in 1958). Despite constant disagreements, however, a British Commonwealth division served in the Korean War, and Britain constituted the US's chief base in Europe – an "unsinkable aircraft carrier." Relations between Britain and the US remained close – much to the distress of the French who resented the joint predominance of the "Anglo-Saxons."

However, Britain and the US perhaps understood one another much less well than they assumed, despite the link of a common language. Britain was a "tight little island," the US a subcontinent; Britain believed in the supremacy of Parliament, the US in the division of powers; Britain stood committed to the welfare state and massive state intervention in the economy; the US, at least in theory, remained wedded to private enterprise. Anti-Americanism in Britain was matched by certain anti-British sentiments in the US, especially among the Irish (who remembered Britain's record in "John Bull's Other Island") and Jews (who resented in particular the last phase of British governance in Palestine).

Americans complain about "uppity British," even though Americans are closer to the "Brits" than to any other people. Although many Americans are anglophiles, the feeling is not reciprocated by all the British; in fact many do not esteem "Yanks" very much. Officially, the US has a "special relationship" with the British, but many individuals don't see it that way. True, the majority of the people in Britain like Americans, and millions think so highly of the US that they have moved there. Some of the British middle and upper classes view Americans as commoners and America as an unsavory melting pot of different races and ethnic. The British think they are better educated, more cultured and refined than most Americans. Some of their anti-Americanism grows out of envy and jealousy. The British working class is apt to be more pro-American than the middle and upper classes, who widely believe they are superior, and scorn America's "lack of culture," egalitarianism, and bad manners. And although British cuisine is the blandest in the world, many Britons believe Americans only eat hamburgers and hot dogs!

The British ruling class, or what passes as such, commonly dislikes American power and energy, as well as the US's position as the leading power. American virtues – enthusiasm, openness, lack of class consciousness, hard work – often seem vices to the British establishment, though this generalization no longer applies to tough Tory politicians such as Margaret Thatcher and John Major. But even admirers of America commonly dislike the American penchant for universal improvement and global moralism.[7]

The first major break came with the Suez affair in 1956. Joint Anglo-French-Israeli action against Egypt split Britain from top to bottom; life-long friendships broke; political controversy attained an acrimony not seen in Britain since the 1930s. President Eisenhower regarded Anglo-French action as a betrayal; British hard-liners reciprocated such sentiments with regard to the US. Sir Anthony Eden was forced out of the prime minister's office, to be replaced by Harold Macmillan, who cautiously rebuilt the Anglo-American relationship. The British, for instance, received special US assistance in strengthening their nuclear deterrent, nominally independent of Washington, but in fact closely entwined with US strategy. But even Macmillan's aristocratic and avuncular charm, and his personal influence on President John F. Kennedy, could not restore Britain's former influence. Whereas Britain during the early 1950s could still boast of possessing the world's third strongest economy, it had declined by 1963 to fifth place, with West Germany third, and France fourth. In the early 1950s, Britain had still been the world's third military power, with a million men under arms. A decade later, the balance had shifted, and the West German *Bundeswehr* outnumbered the British forces.

During the late 1960s and the 1970s, immigration into the US from Europe diminished to a trickle. US immigration laws, passed in 1965, in practice, though not in intention, worked against Europeans. But much more importantly, conditions in Western Europe enormously improved. Hence immigrants from poorer countries such as Yugoslavia, Turkey, Spain, Portugal, Greece, and southern Italy increasingly sought work in well-to-do European countries such as France, Belgium, and Germany. The new immigrants to the US – especially Hispanics and Asians – lacked special ties to Europe (except new comers from India, Hong Kong and Singapore, who had learned British English at school). Within the US, there was a shift in the regional balance of power from the East and Northwest to the West and Southwest – geographically away from Britain. The traditional establishment itself began to change. Before World War II, as we have seen, the US establishment had mainly been of "Anglo-Saxon" Protestant stock, educated at boarding schools and Ivy League universities. The State Department, the most prestigious of US agencies, had largely been staffed by men brought up in the traditional way, apt to be anglophile in orientation. After the end of World War II, there were far-reaching changes. The State Department ceded numerous functions to young men and women from a more varied ethnic and geographical background. More specifically, the Foreign Service Act of 1947 broadened the social and geographical basis of recruitment to the State Department. By the late 1970s, the people accepted in the 1950s and the early 1960s were beginning to move into high positions, and to many of them Britain had ceased to be in any sense a cultural role model. Hyphenate Americans (Irish, Italian, Poles, Germans), thanks to the "GI Bill," had become more important; they were not necessarily pro-British, and they certainly did not admire upper-class Britain for its links to the US Eastern establishment.

As British prestige declined in the US, US prestige diminished in Britain. In 1975, South Vietnam finally fell to North Vietnamese assaults. The Soviet Union, in alliance with Cuba, expanded its influence in countries as far afield as Central America, Angola, Mozambique, Ethiopia, and South Yemen. In economic terms, the US share of world production and of exports fell, whereas the European's stake rose. (By 1970, for example, the EEC accounted for 29 percent of the world's exports, as against America's 14 percent.) The US's financial standing declined. (Its proportion of total international reserves fell from about 50 percent in 1950 to 16 percent two decades later.) The dollar became overvalued, and in 1971 President Nixon decided that the dollar could no longer be made freely convertible. Then came the Watergate crisis, and US prestige plummeted further. Not that there was an end to close personal relations between the White House and Number Ten Downing Street. For instance, President Jimmy Carter and James Callaghan (Harold Wilson's successor in the British prime ministership in 1976) got on extremely well. (On visiting Newcastle, England, Carter delighted a Northern English football crowd by shouting the local rallying cry "Haaway the Lads" in an excellent Newcastle accent.) Such personal successes could not, however, make up for a host of disagreements over economic issues, disarmament talks with the Soviet Union, and many other contentious points.

During the 1980s, however, estrangement gave way to a new rapproachment. In 1979 Margaret Thatcher became prime minister, the first woman to have held the office in British history. In 1981 Ronald Reagan assumed the US presidency. The two were natural allies. They spoke the same language in more senses than one. Both believed in private enterprise; both resented their respective countries' past humiliations at the hands of assorted foreigners from the Third World; both placed their trust in the traditional virtues; both regarded with dislike that leftish intelligentsia which had assumed such a major share in the politics of culture and the politics of welfare. Both considered big-spending governments and Keynesianism as public enemies; both denounced increased government spending – though to little avail. Both were subjected to that same snobbish hostility which dismissed Reagan as a B movie actor and Thatcher as a "grocer's daughter from Grantham." Both enjoyed a good deal of political good fortune, Mrs Thatcher in particular. Both successfully defied the traditional establishments entrenched in the trade unions on the one hand, in academia and the public services on the other. Indeed, Mrs Thatcher, the most radical of British postwar politicians, even went further than Reagan by defying also lawyers, churchmen, and elected officials in local government – worthies whom Reagan preferred to leave alone.

Reagan always remained aware of this special relationship, both between Britain and the US and between Thatcher and himself. British immigrants continued to come to the US, and Southern California in particular became home to what was in all probability the greatest concentration of British people outside the Commonwealth. Employed mainly in the high-tech industries, banking, the media, and academia, British people wielded influence beyond their numbers; moreover, they were not regarded as "hyphenated Americans" and blended easily into the social landscape. During the Falklands War in 1982 the US gave solid support to Britain against the Argentine – this contrary to the views of those who would have preferred the US to gain popularity with the Latin Americans. In exchange, Margaret Thatcher gave the US permission to use British bases to attack Libya, with the result that the American media praised Britain as America's only loyal ally. Thatcher's pro-American orientation was obvious also in her nuclear defense policy; her support for an American, rather than a European, takeover bid for Westland, Britain's only helicopter firm; and in British willingness to join President Reagan's Strategic Defense Initiative (SDI) project in 1985. Thatcher especially praised Reagan's rearmament program and his "get tough with communism" approach. The British prime minister even credited the US arms buildup and SDI with causing reform in the USSR: she believed that the Soviet economy simply could not stand up to the new arms race. For all the strains in the alliance, the "special relationship" revived, but it had to contend with the strong West German-US ties in politics, the military, and economics.

## CANADA

Among foreign countries, Canada claimed even closer ties to the US than Britain. Indeed many Americans, although they knew little about Canada, hardly regarded the English-speaking provinces of Canada as foreign; they were rather looked upon as honorary states of the Union. The US and English-speaking Canada shared the same values, talked the same language in almost indistinguishable accents; there was little difference in the appearance and life-style of British Columbia or New Brunswick on the one hand, the state of Washington or Maine on the other. From the origins of the two countries, people on both sides of the frontier had intermingled easily, and their expanding frontiers had intertwined. After the War of 1812, the US-Canadian frontier was unfortified, one of the earliest examples of bilateral disarmament in Western history. Canada was a NATO partner. US exports to Canada were larger than those to the entire EC, or those of the Asian continent and the African continent combined. With ratification of a free trade treaty in 1991, even closer economic ties should benefit both economies. In terms of public opinion polls, Canada consistently ranged first among countries for which American respondents expressed support or approval (followed, in that order, by Britain, France, Germany, and Israel).[8]

It is true that Americans thought they knew more about Canada than they did. Americans failed to grasp that Canada as a country had originated in opposition to the American Revolution and its form of democracy, that Canada derived much of its national identity from resistance to the US. Like English-speaking Canadians, Americans remained ignorant of French Canadian culture. Americans had little notion that Canadian membership in the Commonwealth was not a misfortune but an asset. Nevertheless, US-Canadian relations remained close, both in a diplomatic, economic, and a cultural sense; Canada formed a bridge to Britain and the English-speaking Commonwealth and over five million Canadians lived and worked in the US.[9]

## WEST GERMANY

The Federal Republic of Germany also claimed special ties to the US, similar in some ways to those with Britain. Germans had been among the earliest immigrants to the Thirteen Colonies; Germans had made a major contribution to building the US. (Between 1820 and 1980 an estimated 54,367,000 persons had migrated to the US, 36,876,000 of them from Europe. Germans had provided the largest contingent: 7,058,000. Italians came second with 5,346,000; newcomers from Great Britain third with 5,095,000; Ireland ranked fourth with 4,707,000.) But in other ways German-American relations differed strikingly from those existing between the US and Great Britain. An American soldier, tourist, or businessman in Britain did not have to learn a new language, as in Germany. The US and Germany had fought on opposite sides during two World Wars. The Third Reich blackened Germany's image throughout the US. Within Germany, the collapse of the Third Reich marked *die Stunde Null* (Zero Hour), a shattering and unprecedented break in German history. So did the creation of the Federal German Republic in 1949.

The new state depended wholly on American economic and military support; West Germany's founding fathers were fully aware of the fact – no matter whether they liked or disliked Americans. During its formative years, West Germany was ruled by the Christian Democratic Party (CDU). The CDU was a conservative party according to its own lights; in fact it was in many ways more revolutionary than its rival, the Social Democratic Party (SPD). The SPD simply picked up after World War II where it had ended in 1933, when the Nazis installed their 12-year reign of terror. The CDU, by contrast, was the first conservative party in German history that was pro-Western, pro-American, and dedicated to free enterprise tempered by welfarism.

Konrad Adenauer, West Germany's first chancellor, was already 73 years old when he stepped into his new office. An aging man, a conservative Catholic, he was yet in many ways more modern than any of his predecessors. Though not an uncritical admirer of the US, he liked American dynamism and enterprise; he also got on well with Americans. (The second Frau Adenauer was a cousin to Mrs John McCloy, wife of the US High Commissioner in Bonn, 1949–52.) Under Adenauer's auspices, the CDU adopted "American" electoral techniques. However much Adenauer was resolved to cooperate with France, he would always give priority to West Germany's links to the US. And it was West Germany which turned out to be the US's most powerful European ally, the keystone of NATO's defense in Central Europe and of Europe's economic revival. Disillusioned by the Nazi Party's grim record and by the experience of total defeat, West Germans looked for a new role model. Many of them found it in US constitutional democracy and US civic culture. US films, US business methods and modes of merchandising, US or US-influenced science and technology, even styles of architecture, acquired great popularity; new American-style freeways and suburbs went into construction, and new high-rise buildings, new fast food chains, and American-style skylines spread throughout West Germany.

Bonn was quite unlike Weimar in that there was no serious opposition to the new republic. The Federal Republic of Germany, like the US, prized its constitution, the *Grundgesetz*, and its bill of rights. The old right had discredited itself by the grim record of the Third Reich. The old left had lost its reputation by the record of the German Democratic Republic (GDR), distinguished by that peculiar blend of self-righteousness, brutality, and incompetence which distinguished the "first German Workers' and Peasants' State." Neither anti-Semitism nor anti-clericalism had disappeared in West Germany, but they were politically taboo; neither the constitutional right nor the constitutional left would touch them. Both West Germany and the US believed in fundamental rights. Both were federal systems (unlike their main NATO allies in Europe). Both lacked a capital in the sense in which London, Paris, Rome and Madrid were national capitals. As regards the nitty-gritty of politics, the German federal chancellor in some respects functioned like a US president (with the difference that the chancellor wielded much greater power within his own party). The very choice of its capital, Bonn, a provincial city on the left bank of the Rhine, symbolized West Germany's political orientation. Adenauer's personal ethos, moreover, was civilian and constitutional. He disliked not merely communists but also the bureaucratic, militaristic dominance of Prussia in the old German state. Before Adenauer died, he warned his friends that Germans were untrustworthy, and that he feared unification because East Germans would dominate a reunited Germany. As an ex-mayor of Cologne, he was heir to a long tradition of Cologne's municipal liberty as well as of the ancient Cologne Episcopal Principality's pro-French orientation. Above all, *der Alte*, "the old man," was the first German chancellor who regarded generals as on the same level as chiefs of fire departments, totally unimpressed by the glitter of medals and dress uniforms.

Immediately after World War II, West Germany, even more than the US, became a country of immigrants *par excellence*. By the early 1950s, one-fifth of the Federal Republic's population consisted of refugees, Germans who had fled to West Germany from the East German regions annexed by Poland, from the Sudetenland in Czechoslovakia, and from the GDR. These men and women had come to West Germany as new settlers, penniless for the most part, determined to rebuild their lives in what was to them a different country. Moreover, in West Germany, as in Japan, the old class differences had eroded. The aristocracy and the traditional urban elite lost their former influence; but the Catholic minority increased its influence and status in West Germany. The Jewish *haute bourgeoisie* had been destroyed, just like all other Jewish groups. To be a junker, or a general, or a senior civil servant no longer carried the same social cachet as in prewar days. Henceforth West Germany's leading politicians overwhelmingly came from modest circumstances – *kleiner Leute Kinder*, the children of little people. Even Adenauer derived from a relatively modest background. The days were past when, during the Weimar Republic, President Friedrich Ebert had been widely jeered at by the well-born because his father was an impecunious tailor.

Nevertheless, there were also striking differences between the US and West Germany. The US was a young nation with an old state. Germany was an old nation inhabiting two new states (set up in 1949 – 173 years after the US Declaration of Independence). The Vietnam War apart, the US had known only victories; the Germans in the twentieth century had experienced only disgrace and defeat. The US was united; Germany, forcibly divided into two rival republics. East Germany enjoyed no legitimacy in the eyes of its people. West Germany did – but even West Germany, until 1990, had to put up with a variety of limitations on its sovereignty. The US was confident in its national identity – West Germany was not. Hence "it was the broken continuity of German history and the ensuing uncertainty of German national identity which lent the United States willy-nilly a role in Germany's post 1945 existence that in this form exists nowhere in Europe."[10]

Just because the Federal Republic of Germany was so deeply entangled with the US, any critiques of the West German state and society easily translated into anti-Americanism. The critiques derived from the right as much as from the left of the German political spectrum. They took for granted the assumption that America was a bastion of materialism and crass selfishness, taking no account of American religiosity, charitable endeavors, or the prominent place of the hard luck story in American literature and folklore. But anti-Americanism in Germany was directed even more against "Americanized" Germans than "real" Americans: those *Bundesdeutschen* (federal citizens) who supposedly worshipped only one Trinity – the dollar, yen, and D-Mark. Ambivalence toward the US remained deeply embedded in Germany, and colored even debates on highly technical subjects such as currency fluctuations. For instance, when the value of the dollar sharply declined during the early 1980s, the Americans were blamed for "exporting inflation" and endangering German exports. But when the dollar thereafter greatly appreciated, the US still incurred criticism – this time for diverting German investments into the lucrative American market.

Anti-American sentiments were muted during the Adenauer era. There was massive US investment in Germany (followed later by reciprocal German investments in the US). Businessmen, tourists, professors, and students crossed the Atlantic in both directions. Moreover, West Germany, during the Adenauer era, took a hard line against the German Democratic Republic. This was not surprising, given the GDR's entire dependence on the Soviet Union, and given also recurrent Soviet provocations, especially with regard to West Berlin; hence the US alliance remained popular among West Germans (and, surreptitiously so, among most East Germans). President John F. Kennedy especially aroused profound personal admiration by his winning personality, chic, expertise on the television screen, his glamorous wife, and especially his ringing declaration at the Berlin Wall: "*ich bin ein Berliner*" (I am a Berliner). In the long run, however, the construction of the Berlin Wall (1961) led to West German disappointment with the US, which supposedly had possessed neither the power nor the will to prevent the Wall from being built. West German politicians (including such former hard-liners as Willy Brandt, formerly mayor of West Berlin, later federal chancellor) henceforth looked to conciliation. By a new *Ostpolitik*, Brandt hoped to achieve in East Germany *Wandel durch Annäherung* (change through rapprochement). At the same time the West Germans sought to improve relations (détente) with the Soviet Union and its Warsaw Pact satellites; a soft line would help to expand German trade to the East, whilst preventing West Germany from being outflanked diplomatically by the US which pursued its own policy of rapprochement (expressed in such arrangements as the Quadripartite Agreement on Berlin signed in 1972 by the US, the Soviet Union, Britain and France.)

US-German relations were troubled also in other ways. There were disputes over NATO burden-sharing. There was disagreement when German farmers complained about destruction from NATO tanks, and the annoyance for men and beasts created by low-flying NATO aircraft. No country in the world, after all, contained as many armed men, armored vehicles, and missiles on so small a space as Germany East and West. There was controversy when Bonn refused to support Washington in "out of area" disputes affecting countries such as Iran, Israel, and Nicaragua. There was friction over a wide range of economic matters, including trade and currency. Disagreements of a technical kind were apt to be heightened by differences in historical experience, and by different lessons drawn from the disasters of the post-World War I period. For Americans, and also for Britons, the first priority was to avoid unemployment – better fiscal extravagance and inflation, provided there were jobs for all. The Germans, by contrast, dreaded hyper-inflation, to which they attributed the political collapse of the Weimar Republic and the rise of Nazism; hence German political culture insisted on fiscal orthodoxy and a deflationary macroeconomic policy aiming at price stability.[11]

During the Vietnam War, the US lost prestige even among its most loyal German supporters. In Germany, as elsewhere in Western Europe, there was a new and affluent youth culture. The German youngsters who reached the age of majority during the 1960s were not necessarily against the US; but they had no personal memories of postwar miseries, the Marshall Plan, the intense desire of defeated Germans to be occupied by the Americans rather than the Russians. On the other hand, the "New Politics," oddly enough, created new transatlantic linkages. German "Greens" learned from US ecologists. The "New Left" in Germany greatly profited from the experience of the "New Left" in America. Rock music, drugs, youth fashions, youth jargon, confrontational politics, spanned the Atlantic. The American-tinted youth culture also penetrated into East Germany – much to the disgust of the communists' traditional youth movement *Freie Deutsche Jugend*, with its love for camp fires, shorts, hiking songs, bannerets, and recorder music, inherited from the German *Jugendbewegung* (youth movement) predating World War I. The massive peace rallies directed against NATO nuclear armaments might be encouraged, to some extent even supported financially and organizationally, from East Germany. But the West German peace demonstrations – unstructured, seemingly spontaneous – differed fundamentally from those uniformed, disciplined marching formations which had pitted right against left in the days of the Weimar Republic. A minority of German militants might bitterly hate *Amerika*. (The German spelling was exported to the US for the use of American radicals). Nevertheless, German activists, like activists all over Western Europe, adopted American jeans and an Americanized jargon. Even anti-Americanism was now to some extent made in America.

Political difficulties between the US and West Germany were magnified by tensions between the US and the EEC. The Americans had numerous, and justified, complaints with regard to EEC subsidies and discrimination against US exports. There was further controversy as the EEC currencies achieved convertibility and the dollar-exchange standard crumbled, and with it an important source of US power. The creation of the European

Monetary system (EMS) in 1978, in a sense, represented a German-led declaration of monetary independence from the dollar.

Fundamental issues apart, there were clashes between personalities from the late 1960s on. For instance, Social Democratic chancellor Helmut Schmidt, French president Giscard d'Estaing, and President Ford managed to achieve a remarkable period of cooperation in Atlantic affairs. This collaboration quickly ended with President Carter's election, as Schmidt could not abide Carter, and bitterly distrusted both Carter's assertive trade policies and what he regarded as Carter's sanctimonious moralism in the pursuit of human rights. Trouble continued in the Reagan era. Whereas Reagan was popular among British conservatives, he held no such appeal in Germany. There was no Thatcherism in the CDU. It was during the Reagan era that the US budget deficit rose sharply as a percentage of the GDP; so did the respective real interest rate differentials, the real discount interest rates, and the trade balance. The government of Chancellor Helmut Kohl, "the other Helmut," resisted US entreaties on a variety of contentious issues, whether to abandon fiscal prudence, or to impose an oil pipeline embargo on the Soviet Union (1982).

Nevertheless, the US and West Germany remained close. German public opinion polls continued to favor overwhelmingly West Germany's link to the Atlantic alliance, despite continued disagreement over such issues as the deployment of US intermediate-range missiles on German soil. West Germany and the US stayed linked by ties of NATO, commerce, investment, tourism, personal friendships, academic cooperation, and suchlike. Left-wing students at the Free University of Berlin might demonstrate against what they described as US hegemony; but the mass of Berliners, indeed the mass of Germans, were grateful for the US presence. Whether they liked or disliked the US, Germans understood perfectly well that of all West Germany's allies, the US was least opposed to Germany's ultimate reunification; hence a majority of Germans approved of the presence of US troops on German soil. There was indeed substantial evidence that "the Germans constitute very loyal allies of NATO and the United States in general."[12]

FRANCE

France, by contrast, found itself in a much more ambiguous position in postwar Europe. After the end of World War II, France, on paper, was a victor; a French army was stationed in occupied Germany; General de Gaulle, head of the provisional government, claimed to speak for a great power; glory had been restored. But France had also suffered the greatest defeat in its history, further tarnished by fratricidal strife between the French, collaboration with Germany, and betrayal. Americans might respect France as a great cultural power, homeland of General Lafayette, homeland of great thinkers and artists; but few Americans at the end of World War II were willing to concede to France the role claimed for it by de Gaulle. There was, moreover, no French ethnic lobby in the US, few French people having emigrated during the preceding century to the US (or even to French-speaking Quebec in Canada).

During World War II, Franco–American relations moreover worsened by dint of personal factors. President Roosevelt disliked de Gaulle as an upstart soldier, hungry for glory, but unrepresentative of the French nation at large. Had Roosevelt had his way, France would have initially been placed under Allied military occupation. Roosevelt's distrust of de Gaulle was widely shared by American liberals of many stripes who had a visceral hostility to de Gaulle, a right-winger, Catholic, and reputed royalist. It was only at Britain's behest that France secured admission to the Yalta Conference, and was allocated its own zone of occupation in vanquished Germany. No wonder de Gaulle looked upon the US with a mixture of wariness and disdain. By contrast, critics of de Gaulle, men such as Representative L. Mendel Rivers, a US Democrat, called de Gaulle "the most ungrateful man since Judas Iscariot betrayed Jesus Christ,"[13] a description no doubt regarded as a courteous understatement by de Gaulle's domestic opponents in France itself.

However, de Gaulle resigned from the presidency of the provisional government in 1946, and the Fourth Republic, established after World War II, generally worked in an understanding way with the US. Despite its ill-merited reputation for incompetence, it was the Fourth Republic which rebuilt France. (Thanks to the Marshall Plan, the overall rate of French economic expansion was actually even greater during the Fourth Republic than during de Gaulle's stewardship.) It was during the era of the Fourth Republic that France joined NATO and the EEC. The Fourth Republic, however, foundered on the colonial issue. The French lost the war in Indochina (1946–54). They failed to win the struggle in Algeria (1954–62), a bloody confrontation which diverted French military manpower and resources into what both NATO planners and de Gaulle regarded as an African sideshow. Moreover, the colonial issues worsened Franco–American relations in an oddly contradictory manner. The US incurred censure from French colonial lobbies for the US failure to support France – indeed, for taking an anti-colonial position (as over the war in Algeria). At the same time, the US earned blame for its so-called neocolonial designs, and for its assumed alliance with the most reactionary segments of society both in metropolitan France and the French empire.

In the end, it was de Gaulle who cut the Gordian knot. After he returned to power in 1958, he finally granted independence to Algeria (1962). He expanded France's nuclear arsenal (inherited in fact from the Fourth Republic), determined that France should have a modern, mechanized army, as well as a commanding voice within both the EEC and the Western Alliance as a whole. The general's prejudices with regard to the US were in no wise comparable to the visceral dislike of the US evinced by the bulk of the French intellectual establishment, including André Malraux on the right and Jean-Paul Sartre on the left. De Gaulle simply wanted a greater say for France within Western councils. In 1958, he unsuccessfully asked for a reorganization of NATO under a tripartite directorship, with France, the US, and Britain as members. During the Cuban crisis he was further disillusioned at the US's failure fully to consult its allies. De Gaulle (and even many critics of de Gaulle) resented the Americans' perceived sanctimoniousness and unreliability. His distrust of the US found expression when in 1966 he caused France to withdraw from NATO's military structure; he harshly censured in public US policy in Vietnam, convinced that the US forces could not succeed where the French professional army had failed. De Gaulle likewise denounced the dollar's dominant position in international trade, and vaguely spoke of a Europe stretching from the Atlantic to the Urals.

Nevertheless, de Gaulle's policies must be seen in perspective. He understood perfectly well that Western Europe needed the US. Moreover, by cooperating with West Germany, and by rebuilding France as a military power, he indirectly strengthened Western defense. At the end of the 1960s, moreover, when the US seemed much less powerful and menacing than 20 years before, de Gaulle once more drew closer to Washington. So did his successor Georges Pompidou (elected to the presidency in 1969); so in turn did Valéry Giscard d'Estaing, who became president in 1974. The French economy increasingly opened to US investment; the French and US governments engaged in amicable discussions in an effort to control the effects of a major world economic crisis after 1973. In 1976 France agreed with the US, Britain, and West Germany that financial assistance to countries such as Italy should be conditional on there being no communists in the government.[14] Cooperation in politics was paralleled by economic collaboration. (For instance, the French government gave its blessing to the takeover of the French computer firm CH by the American Honeywell-Bull Company, an arrangement that surely would have aroused de Gaulle's well-phrased condemnation.)

Franco-American collaboration continued under President François Mitterand, installed in office in 1981. Mitterand was the rising hope of French socialism: he had reorganized and strengthened the formerly moribund

French Socialist Party; he had started off as a man of the left; his government at first contained several communists, and completed the nationalization of the French banking industry. But in the long run, Mitterand's elections marked a decisive shift to the right. The French Communist Party henceforth ceased to be the most important left-wing party in France; pride of place in this respect was taken by the socialists. The alliance with the communists soon broke down (1984). Even more important, perhaps, Marxism ceased to be chic among leading French intellectuals even before the erosion of communism in the Soviet Union was fully understood abroad. The French Communist Party thereafter went into irretrievable decline, while the French Socialist Party turned into a champion of welfare capitalism – French style. Mitterand himself lacked the emotional anti-Americanism that had distinguished so much of the French left; his regime was rather "Europeanist" (indeed, many leading functionaries within France's new Euro-establishment, men such as Jean Monnet and Jacques Delors, were socialists). Mitterand's regime also rejected any return to France's traditional protectionism, and instead opted for a liberalized international economy. On a personal level, Mitterand got on well with German federal chancellor Helmut Kohl, himself pro-American. Mitterand thus backed Kohl in his resolve to deploy those new American missiles that Helmut Schmidt had originally requested to balance growing Soviet strength.

Not that Franco-American relations were unclouded. There was wide disagreement, for instance, on the Middle Eastern question, as French policy under Giscard d'Estaing openly sided with the Arabs, while America's slanted toward Israel. The French were willing enough to see US missiles on German, but not on French, soil. As far as the US was concerned, the French were overly friendly toward Castro in Cuba and the Sandinistas in Nicaragua. There were also Franco-American clashes of a more intangible kind. Frenchmen of all political orientations resented the decline of French as an international language and its replacement by American English. Frenchmen of all political orientations were apt to make fun of President Reagan and his occasional *gaffes*, attributed to American *naïveté* and lack of general sophistication. (Though a matter of fact, no American could compete in this respect with Giscard d'Estaing's foreign minister Jean Sauvagnargues, who welcomed visiting pianist Arthur Rubinstein as "Monsieur Toscanini", and apostrophized President Sadat from Egypt as "president of Israel.")

Nevertheless the US and France continued to cooperate. The cordial nature of Franco-American relations under a socialist government in Paris would have surprised experts such as Crane Brinton who, little more than a decade before, had predicted a turn for the worse, if de Gaulle were to be succeeded by a government of the left.[15] Moreover, it would have been difficult to imagine two statesmen more different than Presidents Mitterand and Reagan. Nevertheless, the two got on surprisingly well – at this time traditional socialist verities were becoming *démodé* among the French vanguard, and even Californian wine had come to be chic in France. Indeed, Mitterand went out of his way to praise both Reagan as an individual, and the Americans as a people. As Mitterand put it, the American nation was "vibrant, powerful, full of energy and character"; American democracy guaranteed that "the greatest number will enjoy a liberty that is genuine, lived, practical."[16]

Not that there was all-round agreement. Within the NATO alliance, US influence became less influential than in the past. The Americans' relative economic position within NATO somewhat weakened (1969 was the last year in which the US could boast of a balanced budget.) The US was much less able than in the past to enforce its views with regard to contentious matters such as trade in strategic items within the Soviet Union, or the Arab-Israeli dispute. Mitterand criticized the US for supporting right-wing dictatorships in Latin America, while emphasizing France's own obligations toward the Third World. Mitterand later reacted to the 1992 race riots in Los Angeles and elsewhere in the US by blaming the disparity between rich and poor allegedly widened by President George Bush's policies in particular and by the capitalist, conservative nature of US society in general. But Mitterand regarded the US as an essential counterweight both against Germany within the EC, and against the former Soviet Union within the global context. Mitterand thus strongly supported the 1979 NATO decision to install Pershing II missiles in Europe. In 1982 French and US troops cooperated in an ill-starred intervention in Lebanon for the purpose of backing a national Lebanese government, and getting both Israelis and Syrians to withdraw. (It ended in disaster.) A year later, the US went out of its way to support French intervention in Chad for the purpose of safeguarding Chad against Libyan aggression. As far as Washington was concerned, it was all to the good that France should not succumb to the "European disease" but maintain a Western stake in Africa and the world at large. For all their many quarrels, no fundamental issue would divide Paris from Washington.


## THE SMALLER DEMOCRACIES OF NORTHERN EUROPE

The US faced somewhat different problems in dealing with the smaller European democracies within NATO – Holland, Belgium, Norway, and Denmark. All four of these countries had highly developed agricultural systems; all the them had built substantial industries, with Belgium as one of the world's pioneers in the industrial revolutions; all four had set up massive welfare states, above all the Dutch; all four combined a constitutional monarchy with a well-tried parliamentary system; all were committed to the rule of law. All four, however, had sought an inglorious neutrality before the start of World War II. Unlike Switzerland, none of the four had properly prepared its defense; hence they were all rapidly overthrown by Nazi Germany, and subjected to occupation. All four owed their liberation to Anglo-American forces, and all four emerged from World War II in a chastened mood, ready to seek security through wider alliances.

The most constructive approach came from Holland and Belgium. Both suffered considerable trauma through decolonization: Holland's loss of the former Dutch East Indies, later known as Indonesia (1949); Belgium's abdication from rule over the Belgian Congo (1960), later styled Zaire. Both had to deal internally with the problems of *verzuiling* ("pillarization") whereby entire social groups operated in quasi-isolation from one another. (In Holland, Catholics and Socialist rarely mixed though both spoke the same language; in Belgium, French-speaking Walloons and Flemings likewise lived apart.) Nevertheless, both Holland and Belgium took a most constructive part in making the new Europe. "Benelux," an economic association between Belgium, the Netherlands, and Luxembourg (begun in 1948), was an early model for a wider European union. Both Belgium and Holland were leaders in the movement toward European integration; both provided a disproportionately large number of "Europeanist" statesmen and administrators (including the Belgian Paul-Henri Spaak, one of the architects of the EEC). Both Belgium and the Netherlands were founder members of the ECSC and the EEC. During the troubled 1960s, the Dutch in particular strongly favored including Britain into the EEC, as against de Gaulle's opposition.

Holland and Belgium were also founder members of NATO. Both generally followed the US lead, especially Holland, the first continental country to accept US nuclear weapons on its soil.[17] When de Gaulle moved to eject the NATO forces from France in 1966 and 1967, the Dutch and Belgians played a major part in seeking a new solution; NATO military commands were transferred to the Benelux countries and Brussels became the new NATO headquarters. Contrary to the stereotype of the long-haired Dutch soldier eternally on strike, the Netherlands forces – like the Belgian – turned out to be "small, modern, and excellently equipped."[18] The same generalization also applied to Belgium. During the 1970s relations between the US and the Low Countries declined, in part as a result of the Vietnam War, in part as a result of quarrels over the modernization of

NATO's nuclear forces. But overall, the Low Countries remained an essential component of the NATO structure.

Denmark and Norway, by contrast, had strong pacifist traditions. Both were initially loath to join the EEC. (Denmark became a member in 1973, together with Britain and Ireland. Norway, by contrast, refused to do so after a highly emotional referendum campaign in 1972.) Both Norway and Denmark were influenced by neutralism, Swedish-style. Sweden, governed by a series of Social Democratic governments, believed that Swedish neutrality evidenced superior virtue; in its dealings with the former Soviet Union, Stockholm adopted an almost universally conciliatory stance. During the Vietnam War it was the US which seemed to Swedes the world's chief disturber of peace: Washington's preachiness had met its match. Norway, unlike Sweden not having enjoyed the luxury of neutrality in World War II, joined NATO, but subject to certain reservations. (In particular, Norway insisted that no allied troops and no nuclear weapons might be stationed on Norwegian soil in peacetime, this despite a massive Soviet military buildup in the Kola Peninsula adjoining her remote northern province.) From a military standpoint, it was, however, Denmark which constituted NATO's weakest link, even more vulnerable than Norway.[19] On the other hand, the Danes and Norwegians maintained close civilian links with the US. Both were, in a sense, transatlantic states. Numerous Scandinavians had emigrated to the US; English was almost universally understood in the Scandinavian countries; and while the Scandinavians – with their own moralistic tradition – were ready enough to criticize the US, none of these countries ever remotely considered a break.


## ITALY


When the Italian Republic came into being after World War II, it seemed destined to be an Ugly Duckling. The war had left Italy physically wrecked, ideologically divided, and economically ruined. The peace treaty imposed by the Allies on Italy was harsh because Churchill insisted; even a distinguished anti-Fascist such as the philosopher Benedetto Croce denounced the treaty. The new Republic was far from popular; in 1946 only 54 percent of the electorate had voted for the Republic as against the monarchy. Unlike Germany, Italy had seen bitter civil strife; unlike Germany, Italy possessed a strong communist party with massive backing among workers, farm laborers, and intellectuals; it was the most powerful and most flexible communist party in Western Europe. The major parties all turned into patronage machines, whose political self-interest seemed to transcend all considerations of national unity. The Italian Communist Party (PCI) at first bitterly opposed Italy's membership in NATO ("Italy out of NATO – NATO out of Italy!"). Moreover, Italy was divided by striking regional disparities, especially between the backward South and the industrial North; for many years there was heavy unemployment, and Italy supplied a source of migrant labor for its more prosperous neighbors beyond the Alps.

Yet the Italians, like the West Germans, staged a political and economic miracle of a kind that no political forecaster had foreseen. The Christian Democratic Party provided permanent leadership. (Between 1945 and 1981, every prime minister was a Christian Democrat, even though individual cabinets rapidly changed in composition.) Italian politics have been compared to the Italians' *commedia dell'arte*; masks change, but the casts remains much the same. It was only with the breakup of communism in the Soviet Union that the Italian Communist Party fatally weakened, while the Christian Democrats likewise declined in numbers and cohesion. Thereafter new groups emerged, including the *Lega Nord* (Northern League) parties which thrived on anti-Rome and anti-South feelings.

In the initial phase of the Italian Republic the US performed a vital role; it supplied massive aid – direct subventions, loans, and other advantages. (These included not merely Marshall Aid, but also subsequent grants such as a credit of more than $1 billion provided in 1964.) There was indeed a "special relationship" of a peculiar kind between the US and Italy. This derived in part from the links that existed between the US Catholic community and Italy, and in part from the power exerted by the Italian-American lobby. (By 1970, the Italians in the US formed one of the largest bodies of the "foreign stock" Americans born in Europe, as distinct from Americans of remoter foreign ancestry.)[20] Italian-Americans gave private assistance to relatives in Italy; they gave generous aid to pro-Western parties (especially the Christian Democrats) and to Christian trade unions. Italo-American links were further tightened through private US investments in Italy, military cooperation within NATO, expanding trade, ecclesiastical connections, and US technical advice, and also popular imports to the US from Italy. (Movies, perfumes, and high-fashion clothes and accessories created an image of Italy as the land of feminine beauty *par excellence*; Italian-manufactured cars and mopeds stood for tasteful styling and high-grade engineering; Italian espresso and cappuchino served in outdoor cafés represented sophistication.)

Debate continues regarding the full extent of the American impact and its benefits. The Americans' direct (as opposed to their indirect) influence was impermanent; already by 1948 the US had largely "forfeited its already feeble control over the internal economy and politics of Italy."[21] Whilst the US largely shouldered the financial burden of the peace settlement imposed on Italy, US advisers could not impose their own version of Keynesianism on Italian policy-makers. US trade unionists were more indirect in their methods. American labor advisers supported schisms within the communist-led CGIL (Italian Confederation of Labor); US Ambassador Clare Boothe Luce announced in 1955 that the US Defense Department would award no further US contracts to Italian firms in which CGIL candidates won more than 50 percent of the votes in its elections to its internal commissions. More importantly, successive US administrations tried to influence Italian general elections by threatening to withhold aid to Italy, if communists were included in any Italian cabinet. Even the Carter administration, in 1978, issued a warning against including the PCI in any new government, and expressed the hope that communist strength would decline in the next elections.[22] No one can say for sure how effective these pressure tactics in fact turned out to be. In all probability, they made little difference. The Italian trade union movement had always been badly split. The greater part of the Italian electorate remained hostile to communism (not surprisingly so, given the communists' record in the Warsaw Pact countries, and even in Yugoslavia, Italy's next door neighbor).

The Western connection thus remained overwhelmingly popular in Italy. Italy took a leading part in the creation of the EEC; of all of its members, Italy may well have benefited the most from the freeing of restrictions on trade, labor, and investment. In the end, even the EEC's critics came to accept Italy's membership, including the Italian Communist Party. The Italians unhesitatingly accepted the stationing of US missiles in their country; the US fleet in the Mediterranean could rely on Italian naval bases – an important consideration, especially at times when Turkey and Greece, two other NATO allies in the Mediterranean, were at daggers drawn. For Italy, membership of NATO also had other uses. South Tyrol contained a German-speaking minority which objected to Italian overlordship. Austria brought the matter to the UN (1960 to 1961). In 1969, Austria and Italy signed an agreement which essentially favored Italy, a member of NATO and EEC, as against Austria, a neutral country. The German-speaking Tyroleans, for their part, never managed to gain acceptance by the international community as an oppressed nationality on a par with Basques or Palestinians. German-speaking revisionists at the time were out of favor with the other European nationalities on both sides of the Iron Curtain.

The Italians thus remained deaf, not only to communist but also to Gaullist entreaties. (For instance, Italy opposed de Gaulle's project for a "Big Three" directorate within NATO, and a plan for a Mediterranean Pact under French leadership.) Even the Italian Communist Party finally agreed to Italy's membership in NATO (1974). At the same time, Italy carried out its own form of *Ostpolitik* by strengthening its relations with the successor states of the Austro-Hungarian Empire, irrespective of their social systems. In 1978 Italy thus joined the "Alpe-Adria" group, together with Austria, Hungary, and Yugoslavia. In 1990 this was expanded into the Pentagonal Group which included Czechoslovakia, also a former Hapsburg possession.

Again, agreement in principle did not prevent harsh disputes on particulars. For instance, Ambassador Luce bitterly fought efforts by the large and aggressive government-owned oil corporation ENI (National Hydrocarbons Trust) to gain exclusive exploration rights in the Po Valley, a design opposed by foreign corporations as well as Italian business interests. But as Norman Kogan, a leading American scholar, points out, its attempt probably backfired by stimulating Italy's nationalist feelings. There were further disagreements over Italy's self-styled "Mediterranean Mission." Italy had a particular stake in the Arab world through its oil interests, its concern with industrial exports, and the role of Italian firms as construction contractors engaged in building dams, bridge, roads, and factories. The "Mediterranean Mission" involved a pro-Arab slant in questions such as international terrorism, or the future of Israel (an issue further complicated by the Vatican's unwillingness to give diplomatic recognition to the government in Jerusalem). The Italians were at first weak and inefficient in controlling Arab terrorists. Nevertheless, Italy remained a firm supporter of the transatlantic connection.

Italy also successfully dealt with internal terrorism, a subject that merits a brief digression. Terrorism became widespread after World War II when it was employed as a weapon against colonial overlords by national groups as varied as Algerians, Cypriots, Malayan Chinese, and others. During the 1960s and 1970s, there were also small groups of domestic terrorists in industrialized countries, especially Germany, Italy, and Japan – the three powers defeated in World War II. These terrorist groups shared certain common features. Their members were generally young, well educated, and in revolt against their own middle-class origins. They claimed to be *purs et durs*, pure and hard. They looked toward Messianic forms of socialism. Unlike national independence movements, they lacked any kind of popular support. Indeed, the terrorists were totally out of touch with those "toiling masses" that they claimed to represent.

According to a widespread orthodoxy popular in Western campuses at the time, terrorism was somehow a new phenomenon, dependent on technical innovations such as the automobile, plastic explosives, the walkie-talkie radio, and, above all, the publicity engendered by television. In fact, terrorism is as old as the hills. By contrast with terrorist groups such as the Thugs in nineteenth-century India or the Zealots in ancient Judaea, bodies such as the Red Brigades in Italy or the Red Army Fraction in West Germany were of scanty importance. It is true that modern terrorists enjoyed the advantages offered to them by television, which turned murder into a spectacle. But publicity itself proved a double-edged sword. It interfered with operational secrecy. Publicity, moreover, was likely, in the long run, to turn the viewers against the terrorists rather than to gain them public sympathy.

In Italy, as elsewhere, the terrorist movement was rooted in the student activism which swept through US and Western European universities during the 1960s. In Italy, as in the US, the militants worshipped men such as Mao Zedong, Fidel Castro, Che Guevara, and Ho Chi Minh. The activists idealized revolutionary murder campaigns such as the Cultural Revolution in China. They looked to destabilizing the Italian Republic, and to discrediting the "Old Left" (including the Italian Communist Party). Above all, the militants hated the US, the modern activists equivalent of the Scarlet Woman, the Great Whore of Babylon, while copying cultural styles from Berkeley, California.

During the first part of the 1970s, the Italian terrorists primarily attacked property. From the mid-1970s, they increasingly turned against people – judges, journalists, businessmen, police officials. The most distinguished victim was Aldo Moro, head of the Christian Democratic Party, and five times prime minister. Moro was kidnapped, and later murdered (1978). Moro's murder, however, did not profit the terrorists. The Italian public decisively turned against the Red Brigades; the Republic successfully rallied in its own defense without, however, abrogating the civil rights of ordinary citizens. If anything, terrorism proved that the Italian Republic was more stable than its detractors had assumed. Neither did terrorism have an appreciable effect on Italo-American relations. On the contrary, the terrorists' super-heated anti-Americanism may have worked in the Americans' favor, as popular hatred against the terrorists increased, and anything associated with terrorism fell into discredit.


## SPAIN AND PORTUGAL


If Italy was one of Washington's best-liked allies, Spain, for long, was the most detested. The Spanish Civil War of 1936–9 had been a catastrophe for Spain. It had also engaged the world's attention to a greater extent than any previous civil conflict in history. For supporters of the Republic, the conflict seemed destined to decide the future of democracy as against Fascism; for Franco-backers, the war would play a crucial part in the defense of Christianity against revolutionary atheism. In fact, the Spanish war remained a European sideshow; Europe's fate was not decided on the Ebro. General Francisco Franco, once in power, cheated on his supporters as well as his enemies; instead of establishing either a monarchy or a Falangist state, he created one of the most long-lasting personal dictatorships in European history: his rule over Spain as a whole endured from 1939 until his death in 1975.

As long as Franco ruled, his name was anathema to American and European progressives and leftists. While remaining neutral in World War II, Spain had initially slanted toward the Axis powers. Franco had outlawed independent trade unions and opposition parties. Later on, the Franco regime sided with the Arabs against Israel, a US ally. Franco offended Britain, a major NATO partner of the US, by calling for the restoration of Gibraltar. Worse still, Franco represented everything that progressives hated in politics: clericalism, feudalism, militarism, authoritarianism. President Truman disliked Franco even more than President Roosevelt had done.[23] There was, moreover, no Spanish ethnic lobby in the US to plead Madrid's case, for emigrating Spaniards had generally preferred Spanish-speaking to anglophone America.

On the other hand, however, Franco received political support from high-ranking US army and navy commanders, as well as from ultra-conservative politicians who were anxious to have bases in the Iberian Peninsula and to integrate it into the Western defense system. Moreover, Franco played his cards with skill: he had never persecuted the Jews; his reprisals, though bloody, were infinitely less harsh than Stalin's; his regime gradually softened; Spain altered through growing links with the rest of Europe, through tourism, mass entertainment, commerce, and through the exodus of Spanish workers to Northern Europe. In 1953, the US and Spain concluded a defense treaty which established a significant American presence in Spain; Spain had also received economic aid from the US – appreciably less than the other West European countries, but nevertheless considerable.

From the 1960s onward, the Spanish economy began to alter beyond recognition, and Spain replicated the Italian miracle. The proportion of Spaniards employed in agriculture declined; cities grew apace; industrial production expanded; television sets, cars, refrigerators, became commonplace possessions. Economic growth went with political transformation. By the early 1970s, the men who had risked their lives in the trenches during civil war had become old, and the intense loyalties and hatreds of the war came to seem incomprehensible to men and women born after World War II; for most of them the Beatles' music seemed more appealing that the strains of military bands. Moreover, Franco himself had established a formal procedure for initiating change. In choosing Juan Carlos I as the future king, Franco had unwittingly selected a monarch who would peacefully liquidate the Franco regime in 1976. Contrary to all predictions, Spain thereafter developed a stable party system and a workable democracy. Spain governed by a socialist administration, headed from 1982 by Felipe Gonzalez Marquez, turned out a model of private enterprise. Spain's rate of economic growth consistently stood above the EC's as a whole. Spain's former insularity disappeared, and Spain created new industries, new transport links, new educational facilities, new financial institutions. Spain, once berated for its backwardness, itself became an exporter of capital, especially for Latin America, and an importer of labor. Spaniards as a whole became increasingly prosperous: according to Spanish critics, the new Spaniard was interested only in the "three 'c's" – *coche* (car), *casa* (house), and *compañera* (girlfriend).

Not that relations between the US and democratic Spain were unclouded. Former opponents of Franco resented military cooperation between the US and Franco Spain; there was widespread hostility to the existence of US bases on Spanish soil. There were Spanish memories of the US-Spanish War of 1898 – for Spanish intellectuals the most traumatic event in modern Spanish history after the Civil War. Spain, moreover, began to renew its cultural and economic links with Latin America (including Cuba). Nevertheless, Spanish antipathies toward the transatlantic connection diminished over time. By 1979 even the Spanish Communist Party (now a reformist body) argued that a continued American presence in Spain was essential for the preservation of the balance of power in Europe. In 1982 Spain joined NATO, and in 1986 Spain (like Portugal) became a fully fledged member of the EC. Despite inflation, labor unrest, and political violence on the part of militant Basque separatists, democracy survived in Spain while Hispano-American relations gradually improved. (According to a 1982 survey, seven times as many Spaniards preferred "friendship with the US" to "friendship with the Soviet Union" – 28 to 4 percent).[24]

Neighboring Portugal underwent a similar transformation, albeit with greater violence and greater risks. From 1928 to 1968 Portugal had been subject to the personal rule of António de Oliveira Salazar, an economics professor turned politician. Although he deeply feared an American imperialism in Africa after World War II, Salazar's relations with the US had been fairly amicable. During World War II Portugal had observed a neutrality that hesitantly slanted toward the Western Powers. In 1959 Portugal became a founder member of NATO, an arrangement that involved Luso-American cooperation in military and naval matters. Alone among Western European countries, Portugal backed the Nixon administration in giving massive aid to Israel during the crisis of the Yom Kippur War in 1973. Faced with widespread anti-colonial risings in her African possessions, Portugal moreover increasingly opened its doors to foreign, including US, capital.

At long last, however, the Portuguese dictatorship foundered, regretted in the US only by ultra-conservatives. Like the Fourth Republic in France, it broke on a colonial issue – with the difference that the French army had wished to go on fighting in Algeria, whereas the Portuguese army was tired of the wars in Angola, Guinea, and Mozambique. In 1974 a military government took over in Lisbon, and negotiated the independence of the Portuguese colonies, a solution welcomed by American liberals. (Under President Kennedy the US had indeed briefly given covert support to one of the Angola independence movements.)

The new military government in Lisbon thereafter soon lurched sharply to the left. For a time it seemed that Portugal might turn into a Western European Cuba, controlled wholly or in part by the most Stalinist and hard-line of communist parties in Western Europe. The Portuguese Communist Party received aid from its "fraternal" associates in the Eastern Bloc; this was the USSR's last attempt to extend the communist sphere of influence in Europe. The Portuguese left, however, was too weak and divided to succeed, whilst its opponents drew on massive assistance from Western European socialists (especially the West German Social Democratic Party), the Western European Christian Democrats, and also from Portuguese emigrants in the US. In 1975, parliamentary government was restored in Portugal; the Iberian Peninsula increasingly became integrated into Western Europe as a whole. After a lengthy time lag, the Portuguese economy recovered; prosperity spread; despite its socialist constitution, Portugal increasingly encouraged private enterprise. The last communist takeover bid in Western Europe ended in failure, and Europe thereafter stood secure.

# 4

# Germany: Key to a Continent

The 1989 revolutions in Eastern and Central Europe caused a seismic shift throughout Europe, and within two years thereafter the Soviet Union disintegrated. By contrast, the economic power of the European Community became even more overwhelming. By 1990 the "Europe of Twelve" consisted of some 320 million people and accounted for about one-third of the world's currency reserves. The EC, in other words, was the world's largest trading partner; its stake in global commerce exceeded the combined shares of the United States and the Soviet Union. (In 1984 the Organization for Economic Cooperation and Development countries accounted for 44 percent of global commerce compared with 13 percent for the United States.) The ratio of trade to the gross domestic product rose steadily, and intra-European integration became ever more effective. Europewide companies expanded their business in manufacturing, retailing, finance, and transport. Whatever fears pessimists might harbor regarding a future "Fortress Europe," the EC as a whole had become dependent on the world economy and the EC's component national economies had become integrated with one another.[1] Within the EC and within the North Atlantic Treaty Organization, Germany occupies a key position. Germany is the most powerful European partner in terms of conventional arms, the most populous state in Europe and the best armed after the Soviet Union, and the only country that forms a part both of Western Europe and of Central and Eastern Europe – *das Land der Mitte*, the land between. It has not always been thus.

## WEST GERMAN SUCCESS STORY

At the end of World War II, Germany lay prostrate and Britain still occupied the leading position within Western Europe. But from 1961 onward, West Germany's economic production began rapidly to outpace Britain's (followed by France's in 1966). By 1990, Germany's lead had become even more impressive – strengthened as it was by a widespread political consensus. Germans might disagree bitterly, but ever since the Social Democrats abandoned Marxism in 1959, German politics had clustered round the center; only a few militants – left and right – refused to accept the reigning social market economy. Even the main think tanks, run in association with the leading political parties, tried to be "scientific" and "value free."

There were good reasons for this underlying concern: above all, Germany's overwhelming economic success. Germany, reunited in 1990, had now by far the largest population (nearly 80 million) of any European state outside the former Soviet Union.[2] Even without the adhesion of East Germany, West Germany accounted for about 26 percent of the EC's Gross Domestic Product. West Germany was the major partner of virtually every EC member state and consistently ran a trade surplus with its European partners, with the exception of the Netherlands, Norway, and Ireland. Germany was the most important supplier for the Italian, Spanish, Portuguese, and Turkish markets. Even the French economy, the second largest in Europe, was fully integrated into that of Germany. Germany also had a great stake in Eastern and Central Europe, where German continued to be widely understood, where Germans had worked for centuries, and where the new governments in Poland, Czechoslovakia, and Hungary all looked toward the West, particularly Germany. The Germans possessed additional advantages. The defunct German Democratic Republic had been a major partner in East European trade, and East Germans had acquired special expertise in certain of these markets. Even before German reunification, West Germany had been Eastern Europe's second-largest foreign supplier after the Soviet Union.

West Germany's commercial strength reflected German industrial efficiency. The Germans, with one of the world's best industrial training systems, excelled at turning out highly qualified workers, supervisors, and managers. The Germans were good at applying technology to commercial ends and skilled at marketing abroad, in part because of their highly developed language skills. Having experienced disastrous hyperinflation after World War I, the Germans insisted on fiscal conservatism and took special care to develop small, high-value-added niche markets for one-of-a-kind products (for instance, highly specialized machine tools). German capitalism as a whole emphasized diversity more than size. Whereas the world's 1,000 largest firms included 353 US and 345 Japanese companies, West Germany accounted for only 30. By contrast, the Germans had a huge number of middle-sized businesses – flexible, adaptable, and just as export-oriented as the giants. As a result, the West German economy did not depend for its prosperity on a relatively small number of huge companies. Germany's export base was broader than Japan's and not dependent on a single main customer, unlike Japan's reliance on the United States. Germany exported 2.5 times as much per capita as Japan, and its positive trade balance exceeded that of Japan.[3]

By the late 1980s the Deutschmark had become Europe's principal currency, the core of the European Monetary System (EMS), and the primary link between the EMS currencies, the dollar, and the yen. The Bundesbank (the German federal bank in Frankfurt) played a major role in managing currencies worldwide. Germany had a massive current account surplus. As William Wallace, a leading British expert, points out, Germany also played a crucial role in technical advances.[4] In 1985 about 40 percent of all European patents derived from Germany, with France second, and Britain third. German influence spilled across its borders in many other ways, for instance, in the exchange of students. Up to the early 1980s the United States was the most important foreign destination for students from Western Europe; thereafter Germany assumed the leading place. Germany also became the leading foreign host country for Americans studying abroad. West Germany likewise supplied more tourists to other European states than any other country. Germans bought more second homes abroad than other Europeans; indeed, the Germans' proclivity for buying houses and real estate became a political issue in countries such as Denmark, Spain, and Austria.

Notwithstanding numerous pessimistic forecasts to the contrary, German economic vigor showed no signs of abating. The Germans, fearful of inflation since their disastrous experience after World War I, managed to maintain the value of their currency more effectively than their main competitors. In 1990 the change in consumer prices over the previous year stood at 2.7 percent for Germany, 3.4 percent for France, 9.5 percent for Britain, and 5.3 percent for the United States. The Germans also maintained a favorable trade balance. In 1990 the trade balance, in US billion dollars, free on board, amounted to $70 for Germany, minus $8.5 for France, minus $32 for Britain, and minus $110 for the United States.[5]

Germany was also tied to the United States, West Germany's most important trade partner outside the EC. (The bilateral trade between the United States and West Germany in 1987 amounted to $39.7 billion.) Until the early 1980s, US-German commerce was balanced. From 1982 on, however, the US deficit continued to grow (amounting to $16.3 billion in 1987, about 10 percent of the US total trade deficit). In contrast, there was a rough equilibrium as regards foreign investment. By the end of the

1980s, Germany had invested about $37.8 billion in the United States, compared with $35.5 billion by Americans in the Federal German Republic. German funds played a particularly important part in US chemical industries, followed by commerce, electric machinery, cars and trucks. Americans for their part put their money in a variety of joint German partnerships, real estate, office machines, other specialized machinery such as computers, and chemicals. Alongside Canada and Japan, Germany currently constitutes the United States' largest economic partner and strongest political ally.

For all the Germans' economic successes, however, their country also faced serious challenges. Germany was superbly good at manufacturing goods and selling them abroad. Indeed, West Germany's share of exports as a percentage of the gross national product – 32 percent – exceeded that of any other country; of this, manufactures made up the lion's share: 77 percent. But by the late 1980s expertise in manufacturing was no longer as important a guarantee of economic success as it had been in the past. The Germans lagged behind Japan and the United States in a variety of new industries such as computers. Germany also suffered from a relatively high rate of unemployment. By 1990, West German business was investing a smaller percentage of the national product than its main competitors. (Japan stood at the top of the list with more than 20 percent, followed by France, Britain, and the United States.)[6]

Germany, moreover, had to confront numerous problems derived from its social market economy (*soziale Marktwirtschaft*, or welfare capitalism), in which most Germans take great pride. The public sector grew apace. The heavily regulated German economy gave massive public subsidies to agriculture and selected industries (especially those connected with aerospace, energy saving, and environmental protection). Labor costs were surely the highest in Europe. Contrary to their reputation, German workers had the lowest number of annual working hours in the industrialized world. There was massive protection for workers against what the courts regarded as unfair dismissals. A declining birth rate caused the indigenous labor force to shrink; productivity increased more slowly than in the past. (The rate of growth fell from 4 percent a year in the decade 1967–77, to only 1.5 percent over the next ten years.) There was a high rate of taxation and an extremely complex system of regulating business practices and wages.[7] Germany's labor costs continued to rise, as Germany's powerful trade unions (united in the Deutsche Gewerkschaftsbund) increased their demands. German business reacted by shifting manufacturing jobs abroad. As Daimler-Benz chairman Edzard Reuter put it in 1992, the revered label "made in Germany" might one day have to be replaced by the label "made by Mercedes-Benz."

In the early 1990s unemployment was high, especially in East Germany. Admittedly, joblessness no longer threatened the political system, as it had during the waning years of the Weimar Republic. The scale of benefits was generous. (The German unemployment system pays benefits for two years at a substantial percentage of previous earnings, more than two-thirds for the average worker. A worker expecting to be laid off soon would therefore do well to ask for a higher wage, and hence the resultant entitlement, before the axe falls.) A high level of unemployment pay also discouraged some workers from seeking employment, a complaint frequently heard among East Germany's emergent entrepreneurs, who spoke of labor shortages at a time of high unemployment. Whatever the explanation, unemployment was serious, striking particularly at young Germans whom employers were reluctant to hire during an upswing for fear they could not get rid of them during a period of slackening demand. German plants were typically under-utilized. Moreover, fiscal generosity reduced labor mobility and also caused a further rise of public expenditure. Demands on the state increased in other ways, too. As the German population continued to age, it required growing public expenditures on pensions and health services. Not surprisingly, the public sector ran into debt. (By 1992 the total German public sector debt, including debts accumulated by the federal government, the states, and the local communes had attained 46.1 percent of the gross national product; it was estimated that by 1995 the debt would reach 51.4 percent.)

## TRIALS OF UNIFICATION

All these problems faded into insignificance when compared with the difficulties entailed in absorbing East Germany. When the Berlin Wall opened in 1989, hardly any German, East or West, understood the enormity of the disaster that 45 years of communist rule had inflicted on East Germany. Even the most strident anti-communists underestimated the extent of the environmental, economic, and political crises that beset Eastern Europe. By and large, Western intelligence agents, journalists, television commentators, and scholars had failed to uncover East Germany's shortcomings. East Germany seemed more prosperous than its eastern neighbors, and whatever reservations might be held with regard to Romanian or Polish socialism, few doubted that the countrymen of Marx and Engels would succeed in making a socialist economy work with accustomed Teutonic efficiency. From the late 1960s on, a whole school of "GDR-ologists" in the United States set out to show that the German Democratic Republic could not fairly be described as a totalitarian state based on terror. On the contrary, the GDR supposedly rested on "consultative authoritarianism" that could rightly boast of considerable social and economic achievements. As Norman M. Naimark, a leading scholar in the field, put it many years ago, "contemporary scholarship distorts reality [in the GDR] as egregiously as did that of the Cold War era. Fear and resentment among the East German population is not mentioned. The Berlin Wall is defended by even more involved arguments than those proffered by East German ideologues."[8]

The favorable impression of the GDR in fact rested on propaganda and fabricated statistics put out by such party worthies as Günter Mittag, former economic secretary of the Socialist Unity Party's (SED's) Central Committee and head of the East German economy. Falsified data found credence among Western college professors, statisticians, and intelligence agents. The height of absurdity was attained by the Statistical Abstract of the United States, a most reputable publication that credited East Germany with a per capital income (in US 1984 dollars) higher than West Germany's.[9] Any East German truck driver or housekeeper would have known better. Like the rest of communist-dominated Europe, East Germany was in fact a disaster area, disfigured by poverty, pollution, urban decay, and industrial obsolescence.

Making use of the anti-Fascist appeal, East German propaganda portrayed the regime as the first German "Workers' and Peasant' State," which supposedly stood for the toiling masses and the young, the future. But East Germany's rulers, in fact, created neither a new socialist consciousness nor a new pride in the East German state. East Germany represented the past – traditional industries such as coal mining and shipbuilding as against the new computer-based and biochemical industries developed in the West, especially the United States. The GDR had a touch of militarism absent from West Germany: elderly West Germans would travel to East Berlin and nostalgically watch the changing of the guards, carried out in proper Prussian style. In its appeal to the young, the SED embodied the pre-World War I youth movement, with its camp-fire romanticism and banners, as against the post-World War II youth culture that seeped in from the West complete with rock music, jeans and jargon. The SED prided itself on communicating to the young a traditional morality opposed to the hedonism of the West. But the East German family labored under even heavier strains than did its counterpart in the West, and the SED was unable to enforce its notions of socialist virtue. (Thirty-five percent of all children in East Germany were born outside wedlock, as opposed to about 8 percent in West Germany.)[10]

The SED faced innumerable other contradictions. It professed to speak for the common people, but the SED's cultural functionaries, in their hostility to regionalism, looked down on dialects and dialect literature. Instead, the SED was associated with an elitist party jargon (*Parteichine-sisch*) often spoken with a Saxon intonation, giving rise to popular jokes about the "Greater Saxon Reich." The SED had promised a great cultural revival, but there were no successors to Marx and Engels. All the giants of Marxism were products of the Victorian era. Although the SED preached an egalitarian ethos, everyone knew that the *nomenklatura* were living in luxury, with their dachas, their special shops, and special privileges. (The segregated housing compound at Wandlitz was surrounded by high walls; because of the Volvos parked outside the functionaries' houses, the settlement was known as "Volvograd."). The SED exalted the downtrodden in German history, but also rehabilitated such royal rulers as Frederick the Great, greatest of Prussian militarists, and King August the Strong of Saxony (whose sobriquet referred to his sexual prowess as much as to his physical strength). For all but its direct beneficiaries – a not insignificant group – the SED state lacked legitimacy. It was therefore unrealistic for West German politicians to call for a transitional period before completing the amalgamation of the two German states. However desirable such a solution might have been in theory, the mass of East Germans would not wait, and the organs of the East German state lost all authority when the Wall was opened on 9 November 1989. The East German state rapidly disintegrated, and unification had to be accomplished helter-skelter (*Hals über Kopf*).

The picture was not entirely bleak, however. East Germans had done well in certain traditional industries – the manufacture of toys, musical instruments, optics, and garden tools – and maintained quality in certain specialized branches of metal production, nonmetallic minerals, ceramics, glass precision engineering, weapons, and steel fabrication. In these areas the technological gap between the two Germanys remained small.[11] But East Germany failed to keep abreast of world standards in mass consumer goods, as witnessed by the inferior quality of East German Trabant cars. The East Germans had also failed to pioneer new industries or new informational services, in part because the leadership wanted to keep control and not let computers speed the exchange of information. (Robotron in Dresden was one of the biggest microelectronic firms in the communist world, but their computers lagged behind Western products.) Even more seriously, the East Germans had permitted their housing stock, roads, bridges, railways, and telecommunications to decay. By 1989 East Germany was bankrupt economically as well as politically. The GDR was no longer able to repay its foreign debts – a matter still treated as a state secret, but well known to the Soviet authorities. As regards more intangible factors, the GDR was deficient in managerial initiative, as private enterprise had been endlessly defamed by the *nomenklatura* and derided by the intellectuals. Not surprisingly, East German job seekers were reluctant to apply for positions that entailed risks, preferring positions where they could check in every morning, work their stint, and go home at night.[12] Much of the labor force needed to be retrained so that, say, mechanics used to repairing a simple Trabant could work on a complex Mercedes. Above all, many East German workers – demoralized by long years of communist mismanagement – had to learn a new work ethic.

The task of renovation was to prove much harder than Chancellor Helmut Kohl anticipated. Academicians the world over had produced innumerable works on how to transform a capitalist into a socialist economy. Not a single major study, however, was available on how to reverse the process. Moreover, the euphoria in East Germany occasioned by unification soon turned into disillusionment. Too many East Germans, skeptical of their own country's propaganda, overestimated West Germany's riches and Bonn's financial ability to help the stricken East. The "soft left," which remained influential among intellectuals and in the Lutheran church, continued to criticize the free market economy, deride successful entrepreneurs, and abuse anti-communist politicians such as Ronald Reagan. (Visiting Berlin in 1987, Reagan called on Gorbachev to tear down the Berlin Wall; he was thereafter dismissed as a *schiesswütiger Cowboy*, a gun-happy cowboy.)[13] Most Western experts, by contrast, had underestimated the East German communists' incompetence. The vast majority of the East German industries (possibly more than 90 percent) proved noncompetitive on the world market.

The most doleful part of the communist legacy, however, was massive unemployment in East Germany. Workers lost their jobs as overstaffing in industry diminished and uncompetitive factories closed down. Although workers were shielded from misery by high rates of unemployment compensation – equal to those prevailing in West Germany – there was much dislocation and suffering. By 1992 more than three million East Germans were registered as unemployed, a sharp rise from the preceding year. All too many East German companies remained overstaffed and uncompetitive. Fearful of social unrest and political opposition, the Bonn government had, moreover, concealed the extent of hidden unemployment by "make-work" programs of dubious worth, by putting workers in uncompetitive companies at half-day shifts while allowing them nevertheless to draw almost full pay. The government also sought to counter unemployment by offering early retirement and retraining programs – yet a good many smaller employers complained that they could not get qualified applicants.

West Germany, of course, had its own unemployment problem; by December 1990, West Germany had a jobless rate of 6.8 percent.[14] But whereas the West German economy's output went up, production in East Germany slumped disastrously. In 1990 alone, the gross national product in East Germany fell by 15 percent. Not surprisingly, the initial euphoria concerning reunification turned to bitter discontent; there were riots and demonstrations in East Germany. Disillusioned West German citizens resented the imposition of massive new taxes to support East Germany and the other former communist states. (In 1992 Bonn was scheduled to pay an estimated 180 billion DM into East Germany, just 13 billion DM short of the region's gross national product for 1991. Seventy-five percent of this cash was intended for unemployment payments and civil service salaries – in other words, to finance East German consumer spending.) The burden on West German taxpayers was increased by massive subsidies paid to East German industries. Not surprisingly, Kohl's reputation declined. In the 1991 Land elections in Rhineland-Palatinate, Kohl's own state, the Christian Democratic Union (CDU) lost to the Social Democrats – surprising in that conservatively-minded, relatively rural Land, traditionally a Christian Democratic bastion.

East Germany should at least have done better than Poland, which faced similar problems, for East Germany was part of a huge free trade area, the EC, and had – collectively speaking – a rich uncle, the West German taxpayer, whose purse was imagined to be enormously large. But whereas Poland had been free to devalue its currency, and thereby gain a temporary advantage for its exports, East Germany now shared a single currency – the Deutschmark – with its neighbor; and for political reasons, monetary union had taken place at an unrealistically high exchange rate. Unlike Poland, East Germany could in theory draw on a great reservoir of skilled labor in West Germany to supply scarce industrial and administrative skills; but few West Germans wanted to work in decaying cities where housing was cramped and the drains smelled. Above all, there was irresistible pressure for East German wages to rise to West German levels. Indeed, in many industries pay quickly went up to between 50 and 80 percent of the West German level. This would not have mattered, had pay rises been matched by corresponding improvements in productivity; for a variety of reasons, this did not happen, however, and East Germany lost its only remaining economic advantage: low wages to attract industry. German policy-makers were impaled on the horns of a dilemma: If they were too slow in closing the wage gap between East and West Germany, the most skilled and enterprising workers would leave for the West. But if the wage gap closed too fast, investors would fail to come and East German products would become too expensive to compete.[15]

There were other problems as well. The communist regime in the GDR had ambivalent feelings toward the West. It needed West German money but hated West German political and cultural influence. The East Germans had denounced the United States as the bastion of monopoly capitalism, yet East German head of state Erich Honecker's greatest ambition was to be received in the White House. Even after the United States officially recognized the GDR in 1974, the quality of East German scholarship concerning North America remained poor even by the modest standards of *Amerikakunde* in West Germany. (Gus Hall, general secretary of the Communist Party of the United States, continued to be cited as a leading "scientific" observer of the American scene.) In East Germany, as in the other communist countries, travel to the West was reserved as a privilege for "approved" academics who never criticized the GDR when abroad. On the US side, only a handful of scholars – fortunately including such distinguished experts as George Iggers, Norman M. Naimark, David Pike, Arthur Hanhardt, James McAdams, and Tony Judt – paid any attention to the GDR. Trade between East Germany and the United States was negligible; in 1987, the United States occupied only the 26th place among the GDR's commercial partners.[16]

The first step toward reunification was dismantling the East German state. Contrary to widespread misconceptions, the state machinery had been extremely inefficient; only the SED and the Stasi (State Security Service) had been run well. The local authorities were ineffective; the law courts were distrusted; the financial system was in disarray; and no free enterprise system could be established without completely restructuring the state and the laws that governed its operation. The process began on October 3, 1990 when Lieutenant General Jörg Schönbohm of the Bundeswehr took command of Territorial Force East, the remnants of the demoralized East German army. Some National People's Army (NVA) personnel were absorbed into the Bundeswehr, and many West German civil servants took up key positions in the former East German bureaucracy. By 1991, 12,000 West German officials were employed on a temporary basis, but even this number was inadequate. In contrast, the swollen and hugely inefficient East German state apparatus meant that, according to 1990 estimates, between 650,000 and 1,000,000 East German officials would lose their jobs. That number included some 1,700 East German judges who would be replaced, at least for the time being, by West Germans. The creation of a new court system would be a tremendous task. The judges appointed under the communist system were loyal party members who had avowedly enforced party justice according to the party's precepts. These judges would now have to be scrutinized for their ideological biases by an evaluation committee. This by itself was a horrendous assignment. Saxony's Minister of Justice estimated in 1991 that more than one-third of the *Land*'s current judges and district attorneys would fail their evaluation. Given the tremendous increase in case load, Saxony needed more than 1,500 jurists; there were currently no more than 60, of whom about 20 would have to be let go.

East Germany also had to eliminate at least part of its huge academic establishment, which was replete with lecturers trained in Marxism-Leninism and fit only to teach "Diamat" (dialectical materialism), *Polök* (political economy), and other pseudo-sciences. Even scientists faced a harsh future; only half would retain their jobs. The bulk of East Germany's military officers and foreign service officers would have to go because only loyal communists had been appointed to such posts. The future, however, appeared brighter for technical employees such as post office and railway officials. Whatever happened, there would be many hardships and many hitches. Concluded a senior West German official, "A lot of lawyers are going to make a lot of money before it is all sorted out."[17]

An equal challenge was restoring the free market. Between 1990 and 1991 some 500,000 new businesses opened their doors in East Germany; mostly small and medium-sized, the new entrepreneurs were tailors, butchers, builders, cobblers, restaurant keepers, building contractors, shopkeepers, mechanics, and electricians, who provided a huge range of services that had been neglected under the *ancien régime*. These petty entrepreneurs had plenty of problems – lack of capital, red tape, legal uncertainties – but at least they would no longer have to fear confiscation of their property for the supposed good of the proletariat.

Far more complicated was privatizing the *Kombinate*, the huge, vertically integrated state corporations that had dominated East German industry. The *de facto* unification of Germany occurred when the Berlin Wall fell in 1989; on March 1, 1990, the GDR's reform-minded prime minister, Hans Modrow, set up a public trust agency (*Treuhandanstalt*) to oversee the privatization of East Germany's state-owned enterprises. In June 1990 the economic union between the two Germanys was concluded, and the *Treuhandanstalt* announced that it would speed up privatization. The privatizers faced numerous obstacles. There were few meaningful financial records. Under the old regime the book value of these undertakings had been grossly inflated, and there was no way of knowing how any given firm would have fared in a free market economy. Even statistics concerning exports to the West provided no reliable evidence, for such sales had been highly subsidized. The *Kombinate* had been heavily in debt, and existing firms were pressured to continue their operations, however unprofitable, to provide jobs for workers who would otherwise be unemployed. For instance, the factory making Wartburg cars was temporarily saved from closure after thousands of workers at Eisenach took to the streets, demonstrated, and blocked the main motorway through town.[18]

The *Treuhandanstalt*'s policy was to sell entire firms, not individual assets, while restructuring the businesses under its control. Its operations were facilitated by new guidelines that gave priority to the claims of new investors over those of former owners. Privatization accelerated; ongoing privatization produced new funds that the "Treuhand" could use to write off East German company debts. Moreover, by the beginning of 1991, the Treuhand seemed on the verge of persuading Bonn to forgive a much larger portion of these debts or at least to assist in refinancing them.

In the eyes of its critics, however, the Treuhand could do nothing right. On the one hand, the agency encountered condemnation from Western economists and investors for not proceeding fast enough with privatization and for subsidizing companies that should have gone out of business. On the other hand, the Treuhand was accused of a lack of social sensitivity in its rush to privatization; censors from the left included trade unionists, SPD politicians, and CDU politicians concerned with the political consequences of widespread unemployment. These critics insisted that the Treuhand should do more to preserve East German jobs. In addition, the Treuhand was expected by many officials to help pay the costs of German unification. Instead, the Treuhand added enormously to these costs. Although the agency had liquidated, by the middle of 1991, some 330 East German companies incapable of surviving, it paid out billions to keep 7,000 additional enterprises from going under and from discharging some 4 million employees. Liquidity loans of 30 billion DM preserved entire sectors, from shipbuilding to steel. The Treuhand became the world's largest industrial holding company.[19]

The Treuhand also encountered bitter opposition from those who viewed the agency as an instrument of West German "colonization." A case in point was the planned merger between Carl Zeiss East (the original optical firm in Jena) and Carl Zeiss West (a spin-off set up in the US zone of occupation after World War II). The two firms quarreled for years over who had the right to use the famous Carl Zeiss name; later there was a bitter dispute on how the two firms should be merged. Zeiss West, by far the stronger and more up to date of the two firms, submitted a plan to the Treuhand whereby Zeiss East would be left with fewer than 5,000 workers (having already cut its work force from 70,000 to 23,000). The Treuhand would have been glad to approve the deal, even agreeing to write off 1 billion DM of its debts before the transfer to Zeiss West, but protests by Zeiss East managers induced the local *Land* government of Thuringia to demand a new deal of the Treuhand, leaving Zeiss East to operate with participation from the *Land* government. The Treuhand agreed. Under the new arrangement, Zeiss East would remain an independent corporation with at least 10,000 workers; the Treuhand hoped that Zeiss West would continue to be a major investor in its restructured eastern counterpart.[20] Far more commonly, however, East German corporations were simply allowed to go under (for instance, Interflug, the East German airline) or taken over by West German firms. This was hardly surprising, as the West Germans owned the bulk of the available private capital; more important, West Germany commanded most of the available entrepreneurial skills, especially now that so many enterprising East German men and women had come West.

Even more difficult were the intangible psychopolitical problems. For the second time in recent history, a great number of Germans had to come to terms with their past. For the second time, an army of men and women claimed to know nothing of atrocities or argued that they had only obeyed the orders of a lawfully constituted state enjoying international recognition. Who in fact had been responsible for the failures of the past? What should happen to those who had participated in political murders, executions, or the gunning down of refugees trying to escape from the GDR? Had the citizens of East Germany all been helpless dupes ("seventeen million perpetrators searching for seventeen million victims")? Should all former communist officials and Stasi informants be banned from positions of authority? Should allowances be made for those who had changed their political affiliation or for those with indispensable skills? What of genuine idealists who had truly believed in Marxism-Leninism? Or did avowed Marxist-Leninists have any claim to sympathy when they had given allegiance to doctrines that sanctioned, indeed glorified, revolutionary terror? Unfortunately, the problems of "decommunization" were confronted less effectively in East Germany than in the other former Warsaw Pact states. There was no relation between the enormity of the crimes committed and the penalties exacted. In future, the unmastered communist past would form as heavy a burden as the unmastered Nazi past.

Moreover, the old anti-communist solidarity soon disappeared. In East Germany, as in the other states formerly under communist rule, hostility against "them," the *nomenklatura*, originally united most people against their self-appointed rulers. When the dictatorship broke asunder, so did popular unity. This even happened in Poland, where the militant trade union Solidarity had pioneered resistance to the communists and served as an inspiration to all Poland's neighbors. Political fragmentation was also, however, a symptom of national recuperation; after a lengthy Ice Age, normal dissensions returned.

Moreover, East Germany, like all the former communist countries, had to cope with radical changes in its class structure. All communist countries contained three separate, though interconnected, strata – the *nomenklatura*, the intellectuals, and the workers (Poland had a fourth group, the agricultural smallholders). The *nomenklatura* disappeared; many went down on the social scale, as former officials turned into truckers or dishwashers. Others managed to use their technical knowledge and connections to make it into the new bourgeoisie.

The intellectuals faced special problems. All those who had radically disagreed with the regime had been imprisoned or expelled, finding refuge in West Germany. The vast majority of East German intellectuals were therefore Marxists, including numerous Marxists who wished to reform the system. There were no intellectuals left in East Germany who opposed socialism as a matter of principle; in this respect East Germany strikingly differed from post-communist Czechoslovakia or Poland. The Marxist heritage was, however, extremely troublesome. Marxists of every kind had in the past looked to a cultural renaissance that would follow the creation of a workers' and peasants' state. In practice, East German achievement in the arts, the sciences, in literature, history, or the social sciences remained modest, especially when compared with those attained in Germany's "bourgeois" past. It was only East German Olympic athletes who made their country famous, and this by dubious methods.

Under the communist regime, intellectuals had been given certain privileges in return for singing the right tunes. Some had gone into opposition. Even those dissidents, however, in an odd and indirect manner, depended on the regime for their subject matter and for their sense of self-importance. They might be penalized by the government, but at least the government took their work seriously. What would they do, what would they write about, once the tyranny had disappeared? Who would read their books now that the public wanted to forget about socialism? The dissident intellectuals moreover shared the *nomenklatura*'s contempt for the bourgeoisie and petty bourgeoisie. Not for them the frankness of Lech Walesa, who, on a visit to London, explained to a British audience, "Great Britain has built her prosperity on a strong middle class. Forty-five years of communism in Poland has virtually destroyed this social class. Poland needs it badly."[21] Given the extent of anti-bourgeois prejudice within the intelligentsia, we may expect, after a decent interval, the emergence of a new school – *schön war's doch*, all the same, life had been good in the olden days.

The industrial workers likewise had to make major readjustments. The communists, who regarded the workers in the heavy industries as the equivalent of Napoleon's Imperial Guard, saw the economy centered on huge industrial combines specializing in the production of coal and steel and the manufacture of ships and railway engines. These enterprises would be staffed by large and well-disciplined armies of labor. But the communists' version of the industrial future was in fact the image of the past;

East German workers – like their colleagues in the rest of Europe – had to adjust to an age of high-tech and service industries, an age that none of the Marxist theoreticians had been able to predict. This was a hard assignment. With the GDR's collapse, guaranteed employment ended and hundreds of thousands of East Germans were made jobless. Bonn responded with massive job creation programs (*Arbeitsbeschaffungs-Massnahmen* [ABM] in lengthy German bureaucratese). By the end of 1991, more than 400,000 jobs had indeed been created (30 percent in construction, 27 percent in farming and environmental programs, 15 percent in social services).[22] Nevertheless, unemployment remained a serious problem, made worse by generous unemployment benefits which discouraged jobless people from taking low-paid jobs.

Prospects were equally gloomy for East German agriculture. Like the rest of the East German industries, farming in the GDR suffered from inefficiency and over-manning. Few of East Germany's 4,000 agricultural collectives were likely to compete successfully with EC farmers; few would be able to survive as Western-style cooperatives or private farms. The change-over thus accelerated East Germany's flight from the land. East German agriculture was dying, complained the East German Agricultural Labor Union. Particularly hard hit was the *Land* Mecklenburg-Vorpommern, as whole villages came to stand empty. The East German farmers' economic problems worsened through a legacy of distrust, hate, and envy which made life intolerable for many villagers. "Whoever is able to do so, leaves for the West. Especially young, intelligent, and socially mobile workers do not want to live anymore in a countryside which grows ever more desolate."[23]

Even the Protestant Church in East Germany came under severe and justified criticism. East German churchmen had taken pride in the way in which the churches had formed centers of moral resistance against communism. But once the Stasi files were open to public scrutiny, the reality turned out much grimmer. The churches had been coopted by the communist state and thoroughly infiltrated by the Stasi. Infiltration began in the "classic" manner through communist front organizations such as the German Peace Union. In addition, thousands of pastors agreed to serve as Stasi informers, including some bishops.[24] The East German churches were heavily subsidized by their Western coreligionists. This did not, however, prevent East German churchmen from taking a high and mighty moral line against West Germany, whose social system was endlessly denounced for its assumed selfishness, greed, materialism, and other sins supposedly not practiced with the same assiduity east of the Elbe. The East German churches, of course, stood for *Kirche im Sozialismus* (church within socialism); they wished to mend not end the communist system;

the bulk of East German churchmen were probably as disappointed at the results of the East German elections of 1990 as the left-intellectuals in secular occupations. Following on the Protestants churches' dubious record in Nazi Germany, their tale of moral dereliction in East Germany is a sorry one – not improved by the manner in which so many parsons after the *Wende* managed to correct their resumés.

Given the extent of these problems, there was by 1993 a widespread air of despondency in East Germany. Friction occurred between "Ossies" (East Germans) and "Wessies" (West Germans), especially those who had come to East Germany on temporary appointments as administrators, managers, or technical experts. Ossies were supposed to be lazy, demanding, and backward; Wessies were lampooned as arrogant know-it-alls. There were fears of a neo-Nazi revival as skinheads, German street-corner thugs, and right-wing groups such as *Republikaner* (National Party) assaulted foreigners from Eastern Europe and the Third World.

East Germans and West Germans also had a different perspective concerning Germany's past. Many East Germans considered that they had borne a much greater share of Germany's wartime and postwar misfortunes than West Germans; distributive justice required that West Germans should now assume their proper burden.[25] By contrast, many West Germans felt that, after more than half a century of totalitarian rule, first under the Nazis, then under the communists, East Germans would distort the democratic values of West Germany and reintroduce into the Federal Republic that unblinking intolerance and authoritarianism that had helped ruin the Weimar Republic. Moreover, forecasts concerning East Germany's recovery likewise tended to be pessimistic. According to some estimates, it would take ten years to raise East Germany to the level West Germany had reached in 1989, and there would still be striking differences between the two countries' economic performance. Ambitious East Germans would still migrate to the "Golden West."

Pessimists also have other apprehensions about East Germany and its vulnerability to propaganda from the extreme right as well as from the extreme left. Despite the anti-Fascist line taken by the defunct East German regime, East Germans have never come to terms with the Nazi past in the same way West Germans have. Although the legacy for Nazi crimes has been laid on West German shoulders, in 1933, when Hitler gained power in Germany, the pro-Nazi vote had actually been higher, on average, in central and East Germany than in West Germany. Today, East Germans remain more critical of the West in general, and of the NATO alliance and the US connection in particular, than West Germans. East Germans also go to church much less often than West Germans, nearly half of whom are Catholics. More friction derives from the continued, though diminishing, presence of Soviet soldiers in East Germany. At the time of writing, about one-third had been withdrawn; their morale and discipline had suffered, however, and hostile incidents were on the increase. There was, moreover, widespread discontent in East Germany. Not that East Germans wished to rebuild the discredited German Democratic Republic, or restore to the German tricolor the former communist emblem with hammer and compass. But there was widespread discontent with the West German-dominated parties. (In the local elections held in Berlin in 1992, the East Berlin voters showed political preferences very different from those of their West Berlin compatriots. In East Berlin, the PDS (Partei des Demokratischen Sozialismus), successor to the discredited SED, East Germany's former ruling party, gained 29.7 percent of the votes, as compared to 11.3 percent in West Berlin. The left-leaning "Coalition 90" and the Greens obtained 12.6 percent and 13.3 percent respectively. In other words, the left-wing dissidents in East Berlin won 42.3 percent of the total in East Berlin – not a healthy sign for the republic.)

Nevertheless, the present authors feel confident about Germany's political future. After the shock of World War II and the innumerable atrocities committed by the Nazis, many scholars assumed that Germany's terrible history under Hitler had somehow been predestined, that all German roads had been bound for the Third Reich. But Germany also had a host of indigenous traditions totally different in kind. There was the Hanseatic spirit of independence in cities such as Hamburg; the legacy of social christianity and responsible citizenship developed in Catholic Germany; the tough defense of working-class brotherhood and international understanding cultivated in the industrial regions. There was the inheritance of what might be called Grand Ducal Germany – Saxe-Weimar Hesse and Baden – with their restrained constitutionalism. There was the Lutheran legacy of reformers such as von Stein and Hardenberg, with olden-days' Prussia's austere commitment to honest government and a *Rechsstaat* (rule of law).

The constitution adopted by the Federal Republic of Germany in 1949 recognized the existence of fundamental human rights and the binding force of an unwritten moral law superior to the laws made by the state. These fundamental assumptions, consonant with Catholic doctrine, strikingly departed from the positivist tradition of German jurisprudence in Wilhelminian days. Under the new dispensation, created under the FRG, the citizens' rights were also protected by a powerful court. The German constitution and the Republican flag met with almost universal approval – unlike in the Weimar Republic, where the bourgeoisie and even many working-class people had despised both the state and its banner. In a profounder sense, defeat in World War II, with its terrible aftermath, had shattered much of the Germans' traditional respect for the state – an authority satirically personified by Thomas Mann (in our translation) as Field Marshal Doctor von State ("General Doktor von Staat"). Comrade Commissar State was equally unpopular in East Germany. For all their boasting, both the Nazis and the communists had turned out to be history's losers. Neither the Nazis nor the communists could rebuild a powerful political party; the main parties in Germany are firmly committed to democracy – Bonn is not Weimar. The skinheads were not the first to introduce violence into postwar German politics; working-class skinheads merely follow the example of leftist intellectuals once committed to terrorist groups such as the RAF (*Rote Armee Fraktion*, Red Army Fraction). The skinheads fear foreigners who compete with Germans, including unemployed Germans, for jobs, housing, and social services. The skinheads do not want to live in a multicultural society. They look to what they mistakenly imagine was a better past. They have to be treated with a strong hand – but they will not endanger the German state as Nazis and communists between them once wrecked the Weimar Republic.

The FRG's Basic Law grants asylum to those who have been politically persecuted (Article 16) and to people of German descent (*Volkszugehörigkeit*) who return to Germany and obtain German citizenship (Article 116). In the past, the number of applications for asylum was relatively small, but during the 1970s the figure rapidly rose and continued to go up. In 1990 an estimated 193,000 persons applied for asylum; by November of 1991 more than 205,000 had applied. The asylum seekers competed with ethnic Germans as well as with migrants who have moved from East Germany to West Germany. The immigrants included a great variety of nationals: Turks, Arabs, Gypsies, and Angolans (of whom an estimated 170,000 arrived in the first half of 1991).

Between January 1989 and the end of 1991, some 2.5 million or more people were relocated in Germany. By 1992 something like 6 million foreigners were living in Germany. Once a country which used to send emigrants abroad, Germany had become a magnet for immigrants. In statistical terms, the number of newcomers was small, compared with the 12 million Germans, refugees, and expellees absorbed in West Germany after World War II, when Germany's economic prospects seemed infinitely worse than they do now. But the recent arrivals were foreigners, not Germans, and have therefore angered many and frightened more. Although Germany's population is aging and more immigrant workers will be needed in the future, popular resistance to immigration has grown apace.

In Germany, as in so many other countries, foreigners are accused of living on welfare, but at the same time for taking away the native-born people's jobs. Foreigners are denounced for keeping aloof from Germans, but also for seducing women. Foreigners talk funny! How happy we would all be if they would only go back to where they came from! In 1992 an expert in the good city of Düsseldorf actually made a study of what would happen to the town if the skinheads got their wish, and all aliens were to depart. Düsseldorf has 576,000 people, 79,700 of them foreigners. The latter comprise 33,000 persons in employment. Each month they earn 102 million marks gross. Of this income, they pay 20 million marks in income tax, and 18 million marks in pension contributions. If they were all to decamp, Düsseldorf shopkeepers would lose a great deal of business; pensioners would see a decline in pension funds, and there would be less money to spend; hence industrialists would have to lay off more workers. The foreigners would be missed not only as consumers but also as producers. Many of them are employed in manufacturing (especially metal work), construction, road building, and service industries. Others work in the health care industry, as drivers and ticket collectors on buses, in catering. (For instance, more than a third of the waiters are foreigners.) Foreigners, on the average, are younger than Germans; they contribute a disproportionately large share to pension funds. Hence Düsseldorf would be ill served if all foreigners were to leave.[26]

Federal president Richard von Weizäcker, known for his humanitarian sentiments, has called for a new European immigration policy: in effect, quotas. There is a limit to the number of immigrants Germany can absorb while rebuilding East Germany. United Germany, with a population of nearly 79,000,000 people and an area considerably smaller than California, is densely populated. (Were the US's population density to equal Germany's, the US would have a population exceeding two billion people.) Hence it is not only skinheads who believe that there are ecological and demographic limits to Germany's ability to absorb massive new foreign immigration. French, English, or Spanish skinheads are no nicer than their German friends. Neither the French nor the other EC states are keen to open their gates to huge numbers of asylum seekers from Eastern Europe or the Third World, and Germany cannot solve the problem on its own. (Social assistance to asylum seekers runs at more than 5 billion DM a year, and many more newcomers, including Poles, Russians, Gypsies, Croats and others, arrived in 1992.) The immigration problem in the long run can be solved only by an all-European quota system and by active economic development in East-Central Europe.[27]

It is worth stressing that the new xenophobia is not merely a German, but a European, indeed, a transatlantic problem. Although the new Europe attracts immigrants from all over the southern and eastern periphery, unlike the United States (and to a lesser extent Canada and Australia), Europe does not regard itself as a continent created by and for immigrants.

Legally, a naturalized citizen in Germany, Britain, France, or Sweden stands on a par with the native-born. But few native-born regard the new citizen as a German, English, French or Swedish person. There is, moreover, universal contempt for the unskilled or allegedly unskilled foreigner. The French widely look down on Arabs, Italians on Albanians, Britons on Indians and Pakistanis. (Indeed, English "Paki-bashers" on vacation have at times joined their German comrades in beating up blacks.) Right-wing parties have increased their vote. But there are crumbs of comfort. Despite countless forecasts to the contrary, there was no effective Nazi revival after World War II, no Fourth Reich. We believe that there will be none in the future. Neither will communism have a chance to recover its reputation. The PDS will continue to attract a handful of idealists and a much larger number of former *nomenklatura* members; for them the PDS will serve as a kind of veterans' organization. But self-appointed political vanguards of whatever political complexion are at a disadvantage in East Germany. *Nie wieder Sozialismus* ("socialism never again"), runs a widely repeated slogan (socialism being identified with the "real existing socialism" created by the SED).

In general, experts widely feared that East Germany's political culture would turn out to be more authoritarian, more averse to compromise, than West Germany's. After more than half a century of totalitarian government, such an outcome would hardly be surprising. In East Germany there were grievances aplenty which cut across traditional party lines, and occasioned projects for the formation of an East German Party, an *Ostpartei*, to give expression to the blend of depression, defiance, and nostalgic pride widely found east of the Elbe. Nevertheless, the dissenters' influence should not be exaggerated. By the end of 1992 reconstruction in East Germany had made great progress; construction workers were busy at building sites throughout the new *Länder*. There was also political progress. For instance, Saxony, East Germany's most important and relatively most successful *Land*, at the time of writing was governed by the CDU, enjoying an absolute majority in the *Landtag* (state legislature). Nevertheless, there was a good deal of give and take between the governing party and the opposition. Whereas party allegiance had hardened in West Germany, political parties in Saxony cooperated more successfully; there was more parliamentary cross-voting, more civility than in West Germany, and less party discipline. (Party discipline was unfavorably associated in the public mind with "democratic centralism", formerly practiced by the SED.) Moreover, East German parliamentarians take their newly found freedom seriously: they attend parliamentary sessions with great conscientiousness and practice a camaraderie that derives from the solidarity of anti-Communist resistance days.

As regards the economy, pessimists should take heart by remembering Germany's condition in 1945, when all the experts displayed the most extreme pessimism with regard to the future. Germany experienced enormous losses in World War II: millions dead and wounded, millions of refugees, bridges blown, factories burnt, telephones out of action, houses gutted, hunger and despair. Yet within a few years Germany experienced an astonishing revival and greater prosperity than the most cheerful optimist ever imagined. The reasons for this astonishing achievement were not hard to find. In 1948, West Germany underwent a thoroughgoing currency reform resulting in a new Deutschmark worth working for. The complex system of economic controls dating from the Third Reich was largely dismantled. West Germany was integrated into Western Europe through the Marshall Plan, the European Coal and Steel Community and the European Economic Community, and the NATO alliance.

East Germany, by contrast, faced special problems when the communist regime collapsed, which in some ways equalled those of Germany at the breakup of the Third Reich. The communist regime had lied to its people and the world. Worse, the regime had left a legacy of hatred and distrust. The Stasi was discovered to have relied on an army of informers even larger than the Gestapo's; lifelong associations broke up when neighbors, colleagues, friends, and relatives were revealed as Stasi spies. The East Germany economy was in a parluous condition, worse in certain respects than the German economy had been after World War II. During the war, Allied bombers had heavily damaged German cities, but the bulk of the Third Reich's productive capacity had remained intact. Even the Nazis had properly maintained the country's housing stock and infrastructure in peacetime. German factories were at least as modern as those of its neighbors. Not so in East Germany after the breakdown of communism. In East Germany, as in the formerly communist world at large, the industrial investments made by the communists were largely sub-standard; few of the new factories could compete on the world market. Most of the new capital investments were devalued from the start. Communist planning, moreover, had made inadequate provision for maintenance. Hence roofs leaked; drains smelled; houses decayed – as did rolling stock, roads, and the rest of the infrastructure. Pollution was much more widespread than in West Germany. The human capital was in even worse shape. For 45 years, commercial and entrepreneurial skills had been defamed by socialist propaganda. Farmers and industrialists had been robbed of their property, and in many cases had left the country. The formerly communist countries had endured an economic catastrophe unequalled in the twentieth century, the bulk of their capital uncompetitive, their labor force demoralized. Nevertheless, there were bright spots. Entrepreneurial skill had not disappeared from East Germany. Contrary to many pessimistic forecasts, there was indeed indigenous capital formation, which provided the wherewithal for artisans and traders to open shops. Above all, East Germany, unlike the other East European countries, will gain massive assistance from West Germany and the EC. Perhaps the West German *Wirtschaftswunder* will be replicated east of the Elbe River.

## THE FUTURE OF A UNITED GERMANY

What of the wider effects of German unification: will a united Germany once more threaten its neighbors? Will Germany seek to establish its own "new order" in Europe as a whole? Will the ghosts of two defunct totalitarian regimes return to haunt Germany? Will US-German relations deteriorate as Germany keeps getting stronger? As we see it, the answer

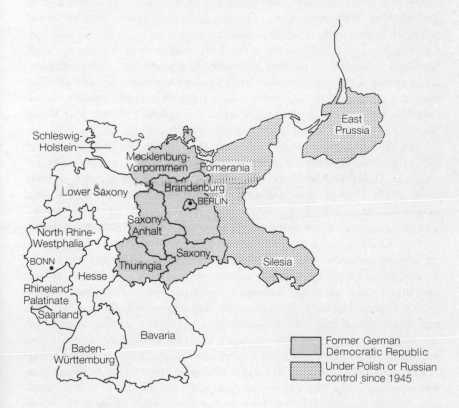

*Figure 4.1* United Germany.

to all these questions is no. Let us set forth the reasons for our relative optimism.

On the face of it, united Germany should once more long to acquire its lost eastern territories. After World War II, Poland acquired a substantial share of what had been the former Reich: East Prussia, Pomerania, Silesia. But contrary to expectations, irredentism never developed into a powerful political force in East or West Germany. (In 1990, while the GDR still existed, both the East German and West German parliaments formally recognized the existing Polish frontier.) The refugees driven from the former East Germany had been absorbed into West German society; their children knew no other home but West Germany and spoke German with a Rhenish or a Bavarian accent, not with Silesian or Pomeranian inflections. United Germany will certainly take a major role in the economic development of its eastern neighbors. German will continue to be the language of trade in the new Central Europe – more than 160 million people can speak German. But German will not revive as a language of command, as in the days of the "Greater Germanic Reich." Neither would many Germans wish to settle again in what was once East Prussia or German Silesia. On the contrary, the drift of migration is now westward. Although a handful of fanatics remained who wished to reclaim the lost lands in the East, and although the Kohl government initially irritated both the United States and France by its apparent ambivalence over the Oder-Neisse border, in the end German recognition of the post-World War II frontier was unequivocal.

German-Czech relations likewise bear the burden of a bloody past. In 1939 the Nazis dismembered the Czechoslovak state and occupied the country. At the end of World War II the Czechs expelled the German minority. In 1968 the East German army joined the Soviet army in once more invading Czechoslovakia and putting an end to the "Prague Spring." The struggle against communism, however, gave to German and Czech a common enemy. Thereafter German economic influence became predominant in Czechoslovakia. (By 1992, pledged German capital amounted to about 80 percent of all pledged foreign capital.) Despite the Czechs' enthusiasm for America and all things American, German remained the most widely known foreign language. Czechs might feel ambivalent about what some regarded as the threatened "Germanization" of their country; nevertheless, the bulk of Czechs approved when in 1992 Chancellor Kohl and Czech president Vaclav Havel prepared to sign a German-Czech friendship treaty.

There are other grounds for optimism. The specters of totalitarianism have gone. At the time of writing, at the end of 1991, a handful of ultra-leftists still labored in terrorist organizations such as the RAF, which has been responsible for some spectacular assassinations. But the mass of the population looked on these murder squads with a mixture of disgust and incomprehension; there is no future in Germany for the armed dictatorship of the left-wing intellectuals. Not that all was well with Germany. Germany, especially East Germany, was plagued after unification by violence against foreigners. Germany had the world's most liberal asylum laws; asylum seekers were maintained at public expense while their respective cases were under judical consideration. Their numbers were large and kept growing, at a time when Germany was experiencing rising unemployment, a growing tax burden, and widespread disillusionment with conventional party politics. (By May 1992, about 100,000 regular party members had resigned from the major parties.) There was widespread rioting, arson, and murder – especially in East Germany, where Nazi memories were stronger than in West Germany. These outrages committed against foreigners seemed even more objectionable as German policemen and German courts applied more lenient standards to right-wing than to left-wing extremists. These disorders must, however, be seen in perspective. German violence against foreign asylum seekers and work seekers was paralleled in other European countries, in Spain, France, even Switzerland. Rampaging thugs and their political supporters must be taught a stern lesson. (Saxony, one of the new German *Länder*, serves as an example to the rest.) But Bonn is not Weimar. The rioters who yell "foreigners out" will not put a new *Führer* into power. For that purpose they lack cohesion, leadership, a common doctrine, and mass support. Neither will there be a revival of Prussian militarism. In the Wilhelminian Reich (and also under the Weimar Republic) Prussia had been by far the most powerful of German Länder; Wilhelminian and Weimar Germany alike had been built on Prussian foundations. But Prussia has long since disappeared from the map. The new Germany rests on West German foundations linked to the EC and NATO; it is, in effect, a new Western state based on a democratic political culture, not an authoritarian, militaristic Prussian one.

What of Germany's position within the EC? On paper, united Germany looks enormous. But in terms of population, the adhesion of East Germany to the Federal German Republic does not mean as much as might be imagined. East Germany's population is no larger than that of Rhineland-Westfalia, a single West German *Land*. In terms of national production, East Germany, as we have shown, will for many years be a debit rather than a credit to united Germany. Although united Germany's gross national product greatly exceeds that of France, Britain, or Italy, any of these two countries combined outweigh united Germany in terms of national production. Moreover, the EC as a whole is experiencing an economic shift that lessens the previous imbalance between North and

South, both within the EC as a whole and within its individual components. Both Italy and Spain have made substantial economic progress. Within individual member countries of the EC, *Länder* such as Bavaria and Baden-Württemberg have gained in new industries, but so has southern France as against northern "rust belt" towns.

Germany will continue to play a leading role within the EC, but Germany's integration into the EC also has the distinct advantage of weakening economic nationalism. Germany, moreover, also faces grave economic problems. Unemployment is heavy; so are Germany's budgetary commitments for social services. Contrary to the stereotype of the German workaholic, German workers take longer vacations and work shorter hours than their American colleagues. Only 52 percent of working-age Germans have jobs, as compared to 63 percent of Americans. German labor costs continue to soar in a manner dangerous for a country that depends on exports to a much larger extent than the US. The high costs of doing business in Germany (*Standort Deutschland*) is forcing some German business to leave Germany.

Germany is also obliged to rebuild East Germany – at the expense of a reluctant West German taxpayer. ("We are one people," enthusiastically exclaims an East German to a West German. "We too" goes the West German's answer!) According to labor expert Wolfgang Scheremet of the German Institute for Economic Research, Berlin, another 20 years will elapse before East Germany's living standards reach those of West Germany. East Germany's need for capital seems almost limitless, despite massive West German investments. (According to the German Institute for Business, Cologne, private business in 1992 expected to invest 113 bn DM in East Germany by the end of 1995.) Germany has also taken over major financial obligations in assisting the former Soviet Union, in return for assuring the withdrawal of Soviet troops from East Germany. Germany will also pay a share of the Gulf War of 1991. The total cost of these commitments has proved immense. In 1991 alone Germany planned to invest $58 billion in East Germany and committed $33.7 billion to the Soviet Union. The $17 billion to Eastern Europe constituted about 3 percent of the German Gross National Product;[28] and a *Wall Street Journal* article in 1991 estimated that East Germany was costing about 5.5 percent of West Germany's GNP. Germany also holds the highest percentage of any country of the former Soviet Union's hard currency debt, a debt that may or may not be paid, but certainly not when due. Powerful as it is, the German horse has been made to pull too heavy a load.

Still, Germany remains the key to the European continent. Despite unfavorable publicity regarding the German economy, the German worker remains one of the world's most productive. Germany manufacturing productivity has continued to rise (by an annual average of 3 percent between 1991 and 1992.) Within the EC, the Deutschmark by 1992 enjoyed a special position, serving as the anchor of the European Exchange Rate Mechanism (ERM). The Bundesbank, the world's strongest and most independent central bank, steered its monetary policy in the direction of keeping inflation down and interest rates up. For the other European countries, pegging the local currency to the Deutschmark insured against monetary instability. The cost of unification and additional massive state expenditure, however, greatly raised Germany's budget deficit (to 6 percent of GNP). In 1991 the current account of Germany's balance of payments swung from the world's biggest surplus in 1990 to a deficit. The German inflation rate rose (exceeding that of France, which also had the smallest budget deficit in the ERM).[29] According to the above figures from the International Monetary Fund's growth estimate for 1991, Germany remained Europe's key country.

Nevertheless, the means at Germany's disposal remained limited. By 1992 there was indeed in Germany a mood of pessimism about the country's future; this sentiment went alongside considerable apprehensions concerning the Maastricht agreement on an economic and monetary union by 1999. There was *Angst* even in such bastions of the German establishment as the Bundesbank, fearful of Maastricht's financial implications. *Angst* was even more widespread within the German electorate. Traumatized by massive inflation following both World War I and World War II, the Germans looked for financial stability to the well-tried Deutschmark; it seemed unlikely, therefore, that the Ecu, the proposed new Euro-currency unit, would ever be acceptable. There was equal reluctance among German taxpayers to take on increasing monetary obligations whereby the "rich" countries of the EC, foremost among them Germany, would pay ever-increasing subsidies for the development of "poor" countries such as Ireland, Portugal, Greece, and Spain. Whether formally accepted or not, the Maastricht treaty was unlikely to work in the way intended by its makers.

Whatever Maastricht's future, there would, however, be no German-dominated "new order" in Europe, but a multinational partnership in association with the EC of 1992. For all united Germany's strength, its international options are strictly circumscribed by reason of its membership in bodies such as NATO, the EC, the Western European Union (WEU), and the Conference on Security Cooperation in Europe (CSCE), although from 1991 on, Germany took a much more independent line in foreign policy than in the past. (In 1991, Germany recognized Croatia's and Slovenia's independence from Yugoslavia and forced the EC to go along. Germany argued that the Croats and the Slovenes had as much right to self-determination as East Germans. The British, French, and especially the Spaniards, by contrast, feared separatists in their own countries, be they Northern Irish Catholics, Bretons, or Basques.)

Nevertheless, the Germans could not be accused of throwing their weight about. In the European Parliament, Germany had to be content with 81 members, with many more allocated for France, Britain, and Italy. The Germans were even outnumbered by members from the Iberian Peninsula, although Germany's combined population (79,000,000) was much larger than the combined numbers for Spain (40,000,000) and Portugal (10,000,000). Likewise, no other member of NATO had gone as far to integrate its military forces and command structure into NATO's multinational organization. The EC members – Germany included – negotiate as an international unit. For example, when Europeans take part in negotiations ("rounds") within the General Agreement on Tariffs and Trade (GATT) to cut tariff rates, the EC is represented by a single delegation. Although united Germany will have great influence in policy-making, Germany does not dominate the EC or the other Euro-organizations. On the contrary, German critics point out that the Germans provide the "foot soldiers" – well-trained experts and administrators in medium- and upper-medium-level positions – to the organizations. By contrast, the French, especially gifted French *énarques* (graduates of the elite Ecole Nationale d'Administration), and, to a lesser extent, the British, make up a disproportionate number of the decision-makers at the EC headquarters at Berlaymont in Brussels.

What of Germany's relations with the United States? Journalists too often stress the bad news. Although the dreadful legacy of the Third Reich continues to cling to Germany, more than two-thirds of all Germans now alive were born after the end of World War II, few of whom dream of a Fourth Reich. Indeed, the greatest miracle experienced by Germany after the collapse of the Third Reich was not just the *Wirtschaftswunder* but also the revival of German democracy. West German democracy has gained full legitimacy. Germany has also experienced a politico-military miracle. Germans of great insight and integrity – professors, clergy, unionists – foresaw that German rearmament would inevitably lead to a revival of militarism. Germany did rearm, but the Bundeswehr never proved a danger to German democracy. No West German general ever even considered a *coup d'etát*. The Bundeswehr is a democratic army that serves to defend a democratic people. The Bundeswehr is, moreover, the strongest force within the NATO alliance in Europe and forms an essential component of Western defense.

What of the *Angst*-ridden German, perpetually taking out his private discontent on his neighbor? He exists, but apparently more often in novels and psychological tracts than in reality. According to a recent issue of *Eurobaromètre*, a standard series of public opinion studies, 87 percent of West German respondents declare themselves to be satisfied, or fairly satisfied, with life. The bulk of West Germans want to be good Europeans. Seventy percent of respondents favor unification; 64 percent believe that West Germany has benefited from membership in the European community. Anti-Semitism, Germany's ancient curse, has ceased to play a significant part in West German politics. Although West German historians in the late 1980s conducted a bitter controversy (*Historikerstreit*) concerning the nature of the Holocaust, no professor, serious journalist, or politician seeks to justify past crimes. German-Jewish leaders now argue over the wisdom of officially exempting descendants of Holocaust victims from being drafted into the Bundeswehr, but they don't complain of anti-Semitism in the West German army – a remarkable advance. It is more often in the Muslim world that Nazi Jew-baiters are still remembered with nostalgia. (Manfred Koch-Hillebrecht, a German public opinion expert, was horrified when he visited Aden in the Arab peninsula and constantly heard praise of one Akmán, a great German patriot, who turned out to be Adolf Eichmann.)

What of informal US-German contacts? On the whole, the Germans are popular in the United States, ranging just behind the British and the French. Germany is accounted the land of the Mercedes-Benz and the BMW, of quality engineering and reliability. In the United States, as in France, it is the well-educated who tend to be most pro-German. The United States is heavily involved in the German economy, with an estimated 20,000 US businesses in Germany. American veterans of World War II are not, as a group, more unfriendly toward Germans than their compatriots who did not wear uniforms.[30] Germany makes a favorable impression on visiting US tourists, businesspeople, and academics; US soldiers prefer being stationed in Germany to Korea or the Middle East. Even the never-ending series of World War II movies has not harmed the German image. In these tales, Germans invariably take the place of American Indians in Wild West films; the Germans fight well and are invariably beaten.

There are complications. Americans' friendly feelings toward Germany (and other foreign countries) are not reflected in the teaching of foreign languages or the history of foreign countries. In fact, language teaching has declined; by 1991, one-fifth of all US high schools provided no foreign language instruction and one-half of US state colleges required no foreign language study whatever. The teaching of German in particular has diminished. German literature is little known in the United States, and German movies are rarely shown (with a few exceptions such as *Das*

*Boot*, the story of a German U-boat in World War II). By contrast, US films and US rock music continue to make a profound impact in Germany, while English remains by far the most widely spoken foreign tongue and the lingua franca for many groups such as athletes, airline pilots, soldiers, merchant seamen, businesspeople, scientists, and academics. From the standpoint of both multicultural enrichment and commercial advantage, the United States can make no better investment than to improve the teaching of foreign tongues at its high schools and colleges.

There are also problems from the German perspective. After World War II the US example influenced the new West German constitution, German education, German business methods, German popular arts, and German academia, science, and technology. The new generation of Germans, however, was more apt to be influenced by anti-American stereotypes derived from the Cold War, the Vietnam War, Watergate, the Iran-Contra affair, and real or supposed US sponsorship of reactionary regimes in the Third World. Left-wing militants took up a new form of neutralism that curiously blended residual German nationalism with concern for ecology, sympathy for the Third World, and a visceral dislike for the United States and Israel. (By contrast, German critics of the United States never regarded real or alleged offenses committed by France – its massive reliance on nuclear power, its substantial share in polluting the Rhine river, and its support for such former African tyrants as the emperor Bokassa – with the same censorious distrust.)

There was more to the partial German-American estrangement than generational change or sentimental hostilities. There are, for example, misunderstandings derived from differences in political culture. Americans of whatever persuasion tend to be suspicious of state authority and state-supported religion; many of their ancestors had, after all, left home because they disliked the existing public authorities in the old country. Germans of whatever political complexion are more likely to be respectful of the state, particularly in its capacity as a welfare agency. This generalization applies to the CDU as much as to the SPD. American conservatives are therefore mistaken to look at the CDU as yet another conservative party, for the CDU is as much committed to welfarism as its opponents. Despite its fervent call for solidarity with Washington, the CDU only tepidly supported US sanctions against the Soviet Union during the early 1980s. The CDU was also much more willing to support Gorbachev's Soviet Union than US conservatives. From the CDU's standpoint, hard cash was a small price to pay for the withdrawal of Soviet troops from East Germany.

For all its pro-American stance, the CDU was always uneasy about US actions outside Europe, as were many British and French conservatives.

Like the other European powers, Germany was more likely than the
United States to tilt toward the Arab side in the ongoing Arab-Israeli
dispute. In 1986, Kohl refused to support the United States in its air raid
against Libya (only Britain supported it). West Germany proved lax in
preventing the sale of military technology (including manufacturing facilities for the production of poison gas) to Libya and Iraq, outlaw states.
Germany did not participate militarily in the Gulf War, insisting that the
German constitution forbade any such venture and that the Middle East
was outside NATO's sphere of action. Only the British gave unstinting
military support to the United States in the Gulf War, supplying 37,000
regular soldiers, one-quarter of their army's effective strength. Germany
did provide massive financial aid ($6.6 billion) for a war that greatly
enhanced US military prestige all over Europe; but although Kohl thereafter proposed a constitutional change making possible future German
intervention outside NATO's traditional context, it seemed unlikely that
German troops would ever be massively employed overseas.

The German left was even more ambivalent toward the United States
than the CDU. Old-style Social Democrats such as Helmut Schmidt were,
and continued to be, like Mitterrand in France, firm Atlanticists. But,
unlike that of the French Socialists, the German Social Democrats'
conversion to Atlanticism came late (starting in 1959). Schmidt encountered heavy opposition within his party over issues such as the
deployment in Germany of intermediate-range missiles. President Reagan
met bitter hostility from the SPD, and leftists within the party, such as
Oskar Lafontaine, toyed with a partial German withdrawal from NATO.
Lafontaine also expressed much skepticism with regard to German unification. The Greens, influential among the young and well-educated, took
an even harder line. Anti-Americanism, moreover, finds a parallel in the
dislike of a minority of East German intellectuals for West Germany,
supposedly a land of capitalism, soulless materialism, and insensitivity, a
country that has brought to East Germany crime, drugs, unemployment,
and, above all, greed.

Yet when all is said and done, Germany and the United States remain
close allies. The Vietnam war with its traumas is almost forgotten. For
all the German pacifists' concern about the US military, the US army
remains popular; (according to a Pentagon estimate the net contribution
to the German economy made by the US armed forces in 1991 amounted
to $4.7 billion.) A British journalist investigating conditions in the US
garrison at Schwabach found that the crime rate was no different from
any other town with German soldiers based in it. Indeed, there was a
feeling of gratitude, and regret for the day when Johnny would go
marching home.[31] Even the SPD is not truly anti-American, though it is

divided on numerous issues affecting German-American relations (such as the future participation of German soldiers in UN peacekeeping forces). No matter who rules in Bonn or Berlin, the United States and Germany will remain closely linked economically and politically. The United States cannot afford to lose the German market any more than Germany can do without the United States. Germans rightly emphasize the value of Germany's links with France, but France can never be a military substitute for the United States. French and British nuclear guarantees cannot replace nuclear guarantees provided by the American superpower. Of all Germany's allies, only the United States had no deep-seated fears with regard to a united Germany; of all the allied statesmen, it was President Bush who gave most support to Kohl over the unification issue. The French were less enthusiastic; popular support for German unification, expressed in public opinion polls, rapidly declined in France. France could never replace the United States as Germany's chief associate. It was the American connection that counted for Germany, and on essentials German and US policies went in tandem. In 1991, US secretary of state James Baker and German foreign minister Hans-Dietrich Genscher met in Washington, DC. Calling for expanding contacts between NATO, Central and Eastern Europe, and the Soviet Union, they likewise looked to enhancing NATO's political component. Genscher (a Liberal Democrat and the recipient of, among other honors, the Distinguished Statesman Award from the Anti-Defamation League of B'nai B'rith) would not be accused of anti-Americanism from any part of the US political spectrum – and it was politicians like Genscher who, for 20 years before his resignation in 1992, shaped German foreign policy.

Anti-Americanism in Germany, moreover, must be seen in its wider context. No German chancellor after World War II, neither Adenauer, Brandt, Schmidt, nor Kohl, has ever desired to undo the US alliance. According to public opinion polls, anti-American feeling actually declined from the late 1950s to the early 1980s (when political tensions between the United States and West Germany were at their height). The conventional anti-Americanism of the left is itself a form of Americanism. German critics of America object to particular US policies: they appeal to "the America of civil rights workers, reformers, of peacelovers"; they attack US acts in Central America. The general public in Germany likes the United States; as Kurt Sontheimer, a German, puts it: "anti-Americanism, whether cultural or political, does not play a significant role in today's political system in West Germany."[32] Looking at Germany's past, it is an immense change for the better.

What of policy recommendations for the future? The United States and Germany are not deeply divided on any major issues. There are, however, disagreements, especially on economic matters, that transcend German-American relations. One hinges on inflation. Whereas in 1991 the United States requested Germany to lower its interest rates, Chancellor Kohl, on a visit to Washington, insisted on future stability. The United States would be ill-advised to push Germany over this issue, for fear of inflation is deep-seated in German political culture. After World War I, Germany suffered from superinflation that ruined those hard-working German savers who had trustingly put their money into state securities; the Weimar Republic never got over the shock. It is not surprising that the Bonn Republic should regard inflation as a supreme evil. We warmly agree with the British *Economist* that the best industrial policy is "to keep inflation low, real interest rates gently positive and exchange rates stable."[33] Then ordinary citizens will save and businesspeople will invest money.

The United States cannot directly influence the EC. American indirect influence should, however, be legitimately employed in the service of free trade. Washington calls on the EC to diminish discrimination against US exports (especially in agriculture). The United States should set an example and champion the cause of lowering subsidies and maintaining low tariffs, when the clamor for protecting specific industries is getting louder in both Europe and the United States. Washington should likewise support those Europeans who oppose industrial policies designed to introduce state guidance and state support for key manufacturing enterprises. The state has done poorly as an industrial guide and planner in Eastern Europe; the state is not likely to do better in Western Europe, despite the faith displayed by champions of state enterprise such as Edith Cresson, the strident former French prime minister. European Community subsidies, be they to agriculture or Airbus, should be opposed by the United States.

Similar considerations apply to foreign investment. Kohl has rightly called for increased foreign (including American) investment in East Germany. In both Europe and the United States there is, however, a strong movement that favors curbing foreign investments. We should oppose such a movement. Foreign investment entails an influx of new capital and, in many cases, new entrepreneurial, managerial, and technological skills. American prosperity in the nineteenth century depended heavily on imported (especially British) capital. Prosperity in the twenty-first century will be certain to owe a great deal to the willingness of foreigners to place their capital where it can be used to its best advantage.

So far as Eastern Europe and the former Soviet Union are concerned, US and German policies have diverged in certain respects. In the Yugoslav imbroglio, Germany, and Austria leaned toward Croatia and Slovenia (former parts of the Austro-Hungarian monarchy). The US State Department, by contrast, tended to support the cause of Yugoslav "integralism," desiring to preserve the status quo. The Germans gave massive aid to the Soviet Union and their Eastern and Central European neighbors and felt aggrieved that the United States and other West European countries did not show similar generosity. But Americans are reluctant to be generous to foreigners at the US taxpayers' expense.

As regards US–German military cooperation, we shall limit ourselves here to a few general remarks. In days gone by, the French joked that they wanted a German army larger than the Soviet army and a French army larger than the German army. If Central Europe is considered on its own, these French pundits may get their wish. Existing arrangements between the Germans and the Soviets provide for a gradual withdrawal of all Soviet troops from East Germany; the Bundeswehr will be reduced to 370,000 men (less than the French armed forces, which numbered 466,000 in 1990). Germany will continue to occupy a major place in European defense, however. In 1991, the United States substantially reduced its existing commitments, but we should not heed the advice of those neutralists who call for a complete US withdrawal from Europe. Neither should Washington place any confidence in those Europeans who wish to rely for their defense on a Western European Union or the Conference on Security and Cooperation in Europe to the exclusion of the United States. Despite the collapse of the Warsaw Pact, the United States still has essential roles to play as owner of the world's main nuclear deterrent and as a mediator in intra-European issues. Neither the British, the French, the Poles, the Russians, nor the bulk of Germans want the US military totally to depart from Europe; their motto is "Yankees, stay put! but in smaller numbers."

There are certain demands that Washington should legitimately make of Bonn. The United States must insist that Germany enforce strict limits on private-sector exports of atomic, bacteriological, and nuclear weapons to the Third World. Washington should, however, go easy on Germany regarding the deployment of German troops outside NATO's defined sphere of action. The extent to which Germany should take on new military commitments is being debated in an inter-German dispute in which the United States should not interfere. The participation of Bundeswehr soldiers would certainly have been welcome in the Gulf War; nevertheless their presence was not essential. In fact, by continuing to shoulder the main burden of defending NATO's central front in Europe, the Germans facilitated the deployment of US troops in the Middle East. Germany was also assiduous in contributing financial help.

We should not therefore exaggerate the extent of US–German disagreements. Chancellor Kohl, on his Washington visit in 1991, rightly commented on the good relations that existed between the two countries and stressed their common commitment to the reconstruction of Central and Eastern Europe. Germany has an essential part to play in this reconstruction, as well as in rebuilding its own eastern *Länder*. Germany, however, has enormous financial commitments and, though productive and prosperous, also faces serious economic problems. These problems do not derive only from difficulties with East Germany. Given the size and ubiquity of the German welfare state, industry in Germany has now become expensive. (According to the prestigious Institut für Deutsche Wirtschaft, it now costs more to employ a German than a US or Japanese worker.) Germany has now overtaken both Switzerland and Sweden as the world's most expensive industrial location. German workers in industry work fewer hours a year than their US or Japanese competitors; the German trend is for less work and more pay. (Within the EC, only Denmark has higher labor costs than Germany.)[34] Although healthy and well fed, the German cow cannot be milked *ad infinitum*. The United States should therefore not encourage Germany into excessive expenditure at the German taxpayers' expense.

## GERMAN UNITY: THE INTERNATIONAL RESPONSE

German unification brought divergent reactions from Europe and the United States. The Soviets counted on German help to rebuild their economy and to pay for getting Soviet troops out of Germany and back home. The French were ambivalent: Politically, they welcomed unification as benefiting Europe and helping France grow economically. Privately, they feared a bigger, more powerful, and economically successful Germany that would look eastward. The British strongly supported German unity, but the Italians feared that a greater Germany might overwhelm Europe economically. The Poles, mindful of historic threats from Germany, had misgivings, but border guarantees allayed their fears. The Russians, even though twice invaded by Germany in this century, had to be pragmatic. They knew they could not stop German unification and therefore sought to gain financial concessions from West Germany. The former Soviet Union counted on German help to rebuild its economy and to promote Russian links to the EC. The smaller neighbors of Germany (Austria, Czechoslovakia, Belgium, Holland) were uneasy. The Dutch, Belgians, and French wanted to tie Germany more closely to the EC and NATO to counter Germany's strength and eastward-looking policies.[35]

The United States throughout the postwar period supported German unification (but did not think it likely), and wanted a greater role for a new Germany in Europe and in developing Central and Eastern Europe. A united Germany was perceived to be the dominant state in the EC and thus a force for keeping the EC a free trade area. In keeping with the "special relationship" the United States has enjoyed with West Germany since 1948, President Bush offered the Germans a "partnership in leadership." The United States did not anticipate the sudden collapse of East Germany and thus did not immediately accept Chancellor Helmut Kohl's ten-point unification plan. Instead, the United States tried to control the process by claiming, as a conqueror, the right to decide the future of the two Germanys. Washington initially pushed for economic integration, not political unification. Fortunately, the United States did not hold to this policy but sought unification through talks between the two Germanies and the four main allies of World War II. Events, however, moved too fast; West Germany had the initiative, and Kohl wanted speedy, full unification, no matter what the United States and the other Allies desired. Therefore he seized the only possible moment in the summer of 1990. The uniting of Germany and the ending of the Cold War then posed problems for the US and its defensive shield NATO.

NATO cannot survive in its present form because the Cold War has ended; the Soviet Union has been replaced by a loose economic union, with the Russian Federated Republic as its leading member. In 1991, President Bush announced far-reaching changes in military policy, including withdrawing all ground-launched short-range nuclear artillery and weapons to the United States. This decision will eliminate numerous points of friction between the United States and its NATO allies. As the danger of a Soviet invasion recedes, all the West European countries have diminished the size of their defense forces. With the unification of Germany, a new order began in Europe, and German-American ties are certain to undergo further far-reaching changes in the 1990s.[36] With the end of the Cold War, which reduced German and Western Europe's military dependency on the United States, a new European-wide security system has to be found for Europe.

Meanwhile the United States and the EC need to ensure Germany's adherence to the Community, to NATO, and to the Atlantic alliance. American policy should strengthen the EC so that it can contain a reunited Germany. The special relationship with Britain and Germany must continue. Washington should remain a major partner in the new Europe, but not the chairman of the board. The "European house" still needs US power and economic strength to ensure peace, prosperity, and economic growth.

Franco-German relations will likewise play a crucial part in the new Europe. During the 1980s, Paris and Bonn worked out a close relationship built on several pillars: the Atlantic alliance, the EC, and hope for ultimate self-determination in Eastern and Central Europe. France learned to accept Germany's concern for *Mitteleuropa* but remained distrustful of Soviet intentions and of Bonn's perceived inability to understand the extent of the Soviet threat. Whereas France wanted to play a global role, West Germany did not; the Gulf War debacle showed that the majority of Germans were pro peace and against interventionism. Whereas Germany was primarily concerned with a policy of peace, France was determined to "fulfill her international obligations." France and West Germany had worked together to strengthen the EC and develop an EC foreign policy instrumentality (European Political Cooperation); but the disappearance of the Berlin Wall on 9 November 1989 undermined French-German assumptions and policies on Eastern Europe. President Mitterrand, who was not consulted by Kohl on the ten-point plan, hence went to the GDR and Moscow and talked about controlling German power in Europe.

The Kohl-Gorbachev meeting leading to the agreement to withdraw Soviet troops and to Germany's staying in NATO came as a shock to France. With the "two plus four" negotiations, Germany had established its independence and primacy in Europe. After German unification, Paris and Bonn were reconciled and called for monetary and political union in the EC. A France determined to play a global role and a Germany unwilling to act outside Europe, however, will continue to trouble the EC and Franco-German relations. Ironically, France, which since 1945 has feared Germany once again becoming a military power, is now concerned over German reluctance to act as a world power.[37] Unfortunately, the EC seems incapable of quickly forming a new security system; the Western European Union is too narrow and the CSCE too large to act quickly and coherently, as events since 1991 in Yugoslavia have shown.

For French diplomacy, the collapse of the Soviet Union was hard to take. In the olden days, Paris could always threaten to outflank Bonn diplomatically by dealing directly with Moscow. Thereafter the Soviet counter-weight disappeared, and Germany once again became the predominant power in *Mitteleuropa*. Relations between Kohl and Mitterand had never been as close as those which had existed between Charles de Gaulle and Konrad Adenauer or Giscard d'Estaing and Helmut Schmidt. Mitterand was displeased by Kohl's failure to consult his ally over his plan for German unification, by lack of German participation in the Gulf War, and over a variety of other issues. Nevertheless, Germany was France's most important economic partner, accounting for the largest share of French foreign trade. Germany and France cooperated militarily by expanding mixed units; and France and Germany had to collaborate in matters of ecology (for instance in cleaning up the Rhine). The ties were too close to snap.

Unification proved immensely more costly both in financial and political terms than Germans had ever imagined. *Post victoriam omnes cives tristes sunt*, said the Romans, after victory all citizens grieve. United Germany had to contend with a revival of chauvinism, and with remaining divisions between East and West Germans. Far from being celebrated as a new Bismarck or a new Cavour for unifying his country, Kohl met with bitter criticism. Even within the ruling CDU itself, the East-West division now became more important than older differences, between the party's Christian social and its free enterprise wing. All the same, the consequences of German unity strike us as overwhelmingly positive. Over time, West German values, institutions, law, and economy will dominate East Germany and integrate it into the constitutional democracy and economic prosperity of West Germany.[38] The disappearance of the East German state should be good news to all Europeans; after all, East Germany was one of the most Stalinist members of the Warsaw Pact and played an unsavory part in exporting arms and experts in guerilla warfare and Stasi police methods to Marxist-Leninist governments in the Third World. A unified Germany will, in fact, have more stability and pose less of a threat than a divided Germany. The GDR possessed a large army that was trained to fight the Bundeswehr; the GDR, moreover, had on its soil some 400,000 Soviet troops and a massive array of conventional and nuclear weapons, all poised to strike at the West using the element of surprise. This menace has gone. Soviet troops are being withdrawn; the East German army has been disbanded; the Warsaw Pact has dissolved. The new Germany is a democratic and constitutional state. The old Prussia extended its power through war, and the old Austro-Hungarian Empire through marriage alliances (*bella gerant alii, tu, felix Austria, nube*: let others wage war, you, happy Austria, marry!). The new Germany, by contrast, seeks global influence not by war or marriage but by extending its trade.

Many Europeans of course remain uneasy about the Germans now that Germany has once more become united, bigger, and even more powerful. There are fears that Germany will be an economic superpower dominating both the EC and the former communist countries in East-Central Europe. There is concern about the revival of an older Germany – diligent, efficient, order-loving, but also power-hungry and autocratic, if not worse. We do not share these apprehensions. We believe there will never be a Fourth Reich; Germany is too firmly linked to the EC, too closely tied to the transatlantic economy, too Western in its political culture to revert to a Nazi or Stalinist past.

"Deutschmark nationalism" has certainly played a leading role within the EC, but it aimed at improved markets, wages, consumer goods, not at militarism or *Lebensraum*. "Deutschmark nationalism" should not be feared either by the United States or by Germany's neighbors.[39] By the middle of 1992 Germany was certainly in no condition to dominate its neighbors – Germany's deficit was proportionally higher than the US's. Moreover, from its very start, the Federal Republic of Germany was committed to democracy and the rule of law; this democratic culture is now being extended to the former GDR. The problems of unification are difficult but not insoluble. The task of rebuilding East Germany will keep the Germans busy for at least a decade. In the meantime, they will become even further committed to transnational bodies such as the EC, the WEU, and the CSCE. Europe and the world have indeed been fortunate.

# 5

# East-Central Europe: The Great Transformation 1985–1992

Socialism is the wave of the future: thus ran the communist slogan proclaimed throughout the "socialist third" of the world, and widely outside. This form of socialism had nothing to do with the system desired, say, by the French Socialist Party or the German Social Democratic Party – socialism, in Soviet parlance, entailed the dictatorship by a communist *nomenklatura*. Doctrinal differences regarding socialism, thus understood, differed, of course, widely. Soviet, Chinese, Vietnamese, North Koreans, Cubans all vied with one another in asserting the special validity of their own brand. But at least there was general agreement that socialism was immensely superior to capitalism economically, morally, politically, even aesthetically. Marx and Lenin were universally honored as the Founding Fathers of an all-conquering ideology which ultimately would create a new society, a new world, and a "New Man." The battle would be won under the command of a self-appointed vanguard which would lead the backward masses to eventual triumph. The end of history would be a new Messianic age within a classless society.[1] A sign outside of Moscow once proclaimed: "We are living in an age in which all roads lead to Communism." No longer.

## BACKGROUND TO REVOLUTION, 1945–1985

Until the arrival of this New Dawn, how would communist-ruled states conduct their affairs? How would they deal with the capitalist countries beyond the pale? Opinion was divided. But the Soviet line at any rate was clear. The Soviet Union was the workers' fatherland, the fount of socialist wisdom ("to learn from the Soviet Union means to win," as the East

German slogan put it). The Soviet Union was the "big brother" of its Warsaw Pact allies in Central and Eastern Europe. By contrast, monopoly capitalism in the West was set toward irreversible breakdown. Soviet policy must aim toward the "peaceful coexistence" of state systems. Such was the doctrine enunciated at the 20th Party Congress of the CPSU (Communist Party of the Soviet Union) in 1956, later incorporated into the Party Program of 1961, and thereafter reiterated in official directives and party documents throughout the Soviet Union and the Warsaw Pact countries until the changes brought about by Mikhail Gorbachev from 1985. However, "peaceful coexistence" applied only to the foreign relations between sovereign states. There could be no "peaceful coexistence" between competing social systems, between socialism and capitalism. On the contrary, "peaceful coexistence" implied the intensification of the international class struggle by all means – economic, propagandistic, cultural, diplomatic, even military. Military intervention in Third World states was therefore justified by a new doctrine of "proletarian internationalism," according to which the embattled working class of one country might be rightfully supported by armed force in the liberation struggle in another. The Soviet Union continued to consider itself as the center of a great revolutionary movement, with an intricate and far-flung network of intelligence and propaganda organizations in the West. More importantly, the Soviet Union continued to expand its military forces and its long-range missile strength. Determined not to suffer another diplomatic defeat such as the Soviet Union had sustained over Cuba in 1962, the Soviets, during the 1960s and 1970s, built a powerful navy. In addition Moscow supported so-called liberation wars in various parts of the world, sustained in Africa particularly by Cuban proxy forces and by East German specialists in military matters and police procedures.

Throughout the 1960s and 1970s the Soviet official mood remained optimistic. The international correlation of forces would continue to shift in Moscow's favor. The Soviet Union and its Warsaw Pact allies continued to gain massive loans from the West, complete with a variety of indirect trade advantages. In a more intangible sense, Marxist-Leninist propaganda had apparently created within the socialist countries a new counter-reality, even a new language; the *nomenklatura* forced its subjects, so to speak, to become bilingual, with one idiom for public and another for private use. The official Marxist-Leninist vocabulary even penetrated to the West, as leftist intellectuals widely adopted pseudo-scientific terms such as "monopoly capitalism" (free enterprise) and "kulak" (an agricultural smallholder).

It was an astonishing propaganda success – the greatest in human history – even though Marxism-Leninism had failed everywhere. Already by the 1970s the economies of the Soviet Union and its Warsaw Pact allies were in disarray, their systems of government corrupt, their party dignitaries hated by the common people. In demographic terms, Soviet communism had turned out to be the most homicidal system in European history. The number of its victims was variously estimated at between 40 and 60 million – many times more even than the total number of people starved, gassed, hanged, or shot by the Nazis. In economic terms, Marxism-Leninism, far from outproducing capitalism, had done poorly by comparison with the capitalist states at a similar stage of economic development. (South Korea performed infinitely better than North Korea, Taiwan and Hong Kong better than the People's Republic of China, Austria better than Czechoslovakia or Hungary, and, most important of all – West Germany greatly outproduced East Germany.)

World communism, moreover, became increasingly divided. In 1948 Yugoslavia, under Marshal Tito, broke with Moscow, and he thereafter gained substantial Western support in maintaining his dictatorship. More seriously, the People's Republic of China and the Soviet Union fell out. The split was made public in 1963; the People's Republic built its own nuclear armory, and instead of remaining a support for the Soviet Union turned into a threat and a competitor for leadership of the world communist movement. Militant leftists in the West thereafter increasingly admired the People's Republic of China rather than the Soviet Union. Despite the blood-curdling horrors committed before, during and after the Cultural Revolution of 1966–8, it became chic among campus militants to cite Mao Zedong's Little Red Book, and to repeat the most extraordinary fairy stories about China's progress. (The very mosquitoes and snails supposedly had departed from China under Mao's beneficent rule.)

The deficiencies of socialism should have been amply studied in Western academies. As Sir Ralf Dahrendorf put it many years later: "What we did not know (though we might have known had we listened to some of the independent voices 'from underneath') was the extent of the physical, social, and moral degradation of the countries of Communist Europe."[2] This was not merely Dahrendorf's personal omission. It was a failure on the part of a substantial part of the Western academic intelligentsia (and by no means only the leftist intelligentsia). There was no lack of evidence regarding the incompetence, greed, and corruption of the *nomenklatura* in all communist countries. Millions of refugees had come to the West, especially to the US, from countries as far afield as Poland, Romania, Ukraine, Cuba, China, and Vietnam. But their accounts were all too frequently dismissed as propaganda. Scholars such as Adam Ulam, Richard Pipes, Walter Laqueur, Paul Hollander, David E. Powell, Walter D. Connor, Marshall Goldman, Warren Nutter (who cast doubts on the assumed magnificence of the Soviets' economic achievements), and Robert

Conquest (whose classics on Stalin's terrors were secretly translated in the Russian underground press) met with considerable hostility from the left. To be known in elite universities as a "Cold Warrior" was widely regarded as a badge of fanaticism or folly.

Hence there was not much of an academic effort in the US to enquire into the durability of the Soviet system, or to investigate the problems that would derive from transforming a communist into a free market economy. In 1970 Andrei Amalrik, a Soviet dissident living abroad, published *Will the Soviet Union Survive Until 1984?*, which predicted that communism would disintegrate quickly, not slowly. But on the whole, such enquiries were commonly held in academia to be fit only for East Bloc expatriates with an ax to grind, or for aging ladies wont to predict the future from the Book of Revelations. The US intelligence organizations did no better; indeed, the CIA consistently overestimated Soviet economic production and underestimated Soviet spending on the military. Only a minority of scholars took a different line – for example, Harry Rowen – and this at a price. A group of academicians who met in a conference to investigate the possible consequences of a communist breakdown earned widespread derision for their endeavor. The resultant four-volume work, edited by Alexander Shtromas and Morton A. Kaplan, was widely reviled or ignored.[3] In Europe enquiries were made into alternative solutions for communism by bodies such as the Institut für Wirtschaftspolitik at Cologne University, the Institut für Wirtschaftssystemvergleich, Zürich, and the Institute for Policy Studies in England. Nevertheless, the breakdown of communism came almost everywhere as a shattering surprise.

Norman Stone, a British scholar writing in the *Sunday Times* (London, September 1, 1991), pointed out that all too many Western experts had a persistent theme: supposedly, the Soviet Union was like the West, with similar problems. All too many were reluctant to hear the truth: that Soviets overspent on defense, that communist regimes oppressed their subjects, and that the Communist Party was a privileged elite. Why should so many intellectuals have deceived themselves and others about the ills of Marxism-Leninist governments or ignored their fragility? (This particular failure was by no means confined to the liberal-left; there were also self-styled conservatives who misjudged communism, while many of its most trenchant critics derived from the left.) Anti-communism was sometimes identified with Nazism. Dr Goebbels and his minions had denounced the Soviet Union; hence the Soviet Union could not be as black a devil as its enemies would assert. There also still clung to Marxist-Leninists an aura of moral worth – their methods might be despicable, but at least their aim was noble. Their world view, in principle, claimed to be scientific. They were optimistic, committed to the assumption that humankind was infinitely perfectible (a view that no Christian can adopt). Marxist-Leninists also shared with many leftists (and also many conservatives) a widespread intellectual and clerical prejudice against "trade," against businesspeople, a prejudice originally taken over from the traditional European aristocracy.

During the 1960s, leftist militancy seeped into seminaries and theological training colleges. The Protestant mainline churches turned to the left; the World Council of Churches identified itself with the Third World as against the West. The Catholic Church also modified its former anti-communist militance, partially in response to the new course set by Pope John XXIII and the Second Vatican Council (1962–3). The Vatican, several times in the postwar world, claimed communism was closer to Christianity than was capitalism! Many clerical people – Catholic, Protestant, and Jewish alike – henceforth would use "cut-throat capitalism" as an abusive cliché; "cut-throat socialism," by contrast, went unmentioned and uncensored. Another stereotype, identified the stockholders of large corporations with "fat cats," without understanding that stockholders were not necessarily rich, or without realizing that poor working people's pension funds might be invested in those very corporations that leftist divines were wont to denounce.

The "soft left" also included a new breed of historians, such as Gabriel Kolko and William Appleman Williams, the so-called revisionists, who laid the blame for the Cold War wholly or almost exclusively on the US. Stalin, the reader is left to conclude, should have been trusted by his erstwhile allies. Never mind that Stalin had betrayed the most prominent of his domestic associates – nearly all the Old Bolsheviks, the cream of the pre-World War II officer corps, the cream of the intelligentsia. Never mind that Stalin had murdered even more people than Hitler. Never mind that the doctrine of global class warfare was inherent, not merely in Stalinist but also in Leninist doctrine!

Overall, the "soft left" might criticize the Marxist-Leninists; but at least the Marxist-Leninists received credit for having regard for the well-being of the common people. Given a choice, these backward masses would rather have a full belly than civil rights – or such was the mistaken assumption widely spread among professors at the time. As a popular college text book put it during the 1960s with regard to Italy:

Impoverished Italians and those who smart under other forms of social oppression because of their humble station and non-conformism to middle class standards would gladly exchange the freedom of elections and democratic constitutionalism for the tangible rewards of socialism: permanent employment; three meals a day; meat, sugar, and milk in the diet; decent housing; educational opportunity; entertainment; vacations and excursions; etc. To the growing millions who want higher living standards, security, and social equality, communism is attractive.[4]

How far did the so-called opinion-makers actually shape public opinion? The evidence conflicts. But there is no doubt that Marxist-Leninists themselves believed that the Cold War was going in their favor during the 1970s. The Western economies suffered from successive oil shocks. Unemployment became widespread in the West; inflationary pressures increased. The "Thirty Golden Years" that had started with the postwar recovery drew to a close. The West seemed anxious to make economic concessions to the Soviet Union and its Warsaw Pact allies, as massive loans were extended to the communist governments (most of them yet to be repaid).

Marxist-Leninists also made major political gains. The peace treaty negotiated for the purpose of ending the Vietnam War soon foundered, and in 1975 South Vietnam fell to the communists; Cambodia and Laos soon followed. The breakdown of the Portuguese empire (1974) led to the creation of two self-proclaimed Marxist-Leninist republics, Angola and Mazambique, both led by "vanguard parties" in close touch with the CPSU (Communist Party of the Soviet Union). Cuban soldiers were deployed in Angola, and also in Ethiopia, where the monarchy had fallen in 1973, to be replaced later by another Marxist-Leninist dictatorship. Marxist-Leninist revolutionaries also seemed to be making good progress in the New World. In 1979 the Sandinistas seized power in Nicaragua, committed to the international class struggle, dedicated to helping other revolutionaries in Central America, sustained by aid from Cuba and the Soviet Union. Above all, Soviet forces in 1979 invaded neighboring Afghanistan. For the first time since World War II, the Soviet Union intervened directly with its own military forces in a foreign country, without even bothering to use proxies, whether soldiers from Cuba, or police and security experts from East Germany.

Soviet confidence seemed to be matched by self-questioning and self-disparagement in much of the West. For instance, Britain during the 1960s experienced both social and parliamentary instability, culminating in the "winter of discontent" of 1979. In the US there was the trauma of race riots, the trauma of Vietnam, the trauma of Watergate, followed by the Iranian hostage crisis. There was, in the mainline churches, in academia, and in the prestige media a period of intense American self-criticism. As far as the leftist intelligentsia was concerned, it was the US that stood on trial, not the Soviet Union, not Cuba, not the People's Republic of China, not the German Democratic Republic. By this time, moreover, memories of World War II victories and the astonishing revival thereafter had faded.

Whereas the first postwar generations of US academics had mostly served in the military during World War II, this generalization no longer applied to their successors. Having already been widely evaded by graduate students, the US draft ended in 1973. Thereafter a majority of college professors consisted of men and women who not only had never worn uniforms, but who lacked friends and acquaintances who had done so. By the time that the great Allied wartime generals were carried to their graves – Eisenhower in 1969, de Gaulle in 1970, Montgomery in 1976 – it appeared as if they had derived from another age.

Nevertheless, the tide was turning. The new Marxist-Leninist states all ran into desperate economic difficulties. Angolan forces and their Cuban allies failed to subdue the armed opposition organized by Unita (National Union for the Total Independence of Angola), rebels who were in turn supported by South Africa. In Mozambique, the government could not control widespread revolts nominally coordinated by Renamo (National Resistance of Mozambique), again sustained with South African help. The Sandinista experiment in Nicaragua oppressed its people, depressed the economy and could not defeat its opposition. Marxist-Leninism likewise ran aground in Ethiopia. Above all, the Soviet empire – as the British Indian empire before – proved unable to subdue the mountaineers of Afghanistan, a defeat fraught with much graver consequences for the Soviets in the twentieth century than it had been for the British in the nineteenth.

There were problems also with regard to military technology. During World War II the Soviet-produced T-34 tank had astounded German and Allied experts alike by its excellence. Forty years later the Soviet lead seemed to have disappeared. Western-built planes scored a decisive victory in Israeli-Syrian air battles against Soviet-built planes and anti-aircraft missiles in 1973. In 1986 the Chernobyl nuclear disaster invited shattering comments concerning Soviet nuclear engineering. By the time of the breakup of the Eastern Bloc, Eastern Europe's and the Soviet Union's ecological problems had reached catastrophic proportions. Wherever Marxism -Leninism had been tried – in the Soviet Union, Poland, East Germany, Czechoslovakia, Vietnam, Cambodia, North Korea, Cuba, Angola, Mozambique – the result had been disaster. Not a single success story brightened the Marxist-Leninist tale of woe. The unsophisticated anti-communists of old had been proven right beyond their wildest dreams. In much of Eastern Europe, the very term "socialism" itself became a term of abuse, and political debate reverted to issues and to the terminology of the nineteenth century.

There was a corresponding loss of confidence within the leading cadres of the various communist parties. Internal opposition grew apace in the

Soviet satellite states, as Churchill's "V" for victory sign replaced the clenched fist as the symbol of liberation. "We will bury you," Nikita Khrushchev had boasted to Richard Nixon in 1959. Khrushchev did not mean that the Soviet Union planned to inflict a nuclear Pearl Harbor on the US, but that Marxism-Leninism would outproduce capitalism. Thirty years later, no communist wanted to be reminded of Khrushchev's prediction. By this time the mass of Eastern and Central Europeans as well as of Soviet people had become totally disenchanted with a system that had promised so much and delivered so little. The "true believers" willing to die for socialism had dwindled in numbers to a small minority. The very successes gained by the socialist regimes in speeding urbanization and industrialization had stimulated new consumer demands and demands for personal freedom that the existing socialist regimes could not satisfy. At a time when leftist intellectuals in the West denounced Reagan's America with ever-growing distaste for the assumed greed and insensitivity of "casino captialism," Central and East Europeans increasingly looked on America as the promised land.

There was also widespread change within the Western states. There was growing disenchantment among Western European intellectuals with Marxist models. This change was particularly notable in France, once a great bastion of intellectual Marxism. Sometime between 1973 and 1978 the stranglehold of Marxism on the French mind was broken.[5] In France, as elsewhere in Western Europe and the US, the intellectual initiative overwhelmingly passed to critics of Marxism, including such brilliant expatriates as Aleksandr Solzhenitsyn and Leszek Kolakowski. Free enterprise economics once more became intellectually respectable. (In 1977 Milton Friedman received the Nobel Prize; in 1982 P. T. Bauer, the British Milton Friedman, advanced to the House of Lords.) Western Europe as a whole regained its self-confidence.

There was also an end to "Eurosclerosis" and "Eurogloom." The Atlantic economies (especially the US economy) began to recover. During the 1980s, the global shortage of oil turned into a global oil glut. Newspaper accounts and learned tomes full of gloomy forecasts proclaiming ever-increasing shortages of vital raw materials began to gather dust on library shelves. In the US, the Reagan era (1981–8) saw a striking decline in inflation, a striking expansion in jobs, while the ratio of debt to the US gross national product remained much lower than in West Germany and Japan, the two countries against which Reagan's critics would most often measure the US's supposed failure.[6] Numerous misconceptions notwithstanding, unemployment in the US declined, inflation diminished, and the US gross national product substantially increased during the 1980s, including the value of US manufacturing output.[7] Above all, the Reagan administration accelerated the rearmament program begun during the last years of the Carter presidency. Reagan's expressed hostility to the Soviet's "evil empire" aroused substantial criticism within the ranks of US opinion-makers who considered Reagan's approach to be naive, if not worse. But the bulk of US public opinion was much more strongly in favor of "containing communism" than the opinion-makers.[8] Poles, Czechs, Lithuanians, Latvians found even less to complain about in Reagan's description of the "evil empire" which held them in thrall. Clearly, the West was getting stronger and even Soviet experts ceased to predict the inevitable breakdown of capitalism. Reagan did not confine himself to the verbal castigation of communism. Armed opposition to Marxist-Leninist governments received US support in countries as far afield as Nicaragua, Angola, Ethiopia, and Afghanistan. The president's Strategic Defense Initiative (SDI) and massive US rearmament set limits to past Soviet attempts to gain strategic predominance and overstretched the Soviet economy. As far as the US was concerned, communist advances would no longer be regarded as irresistible and irreversible. The "international correlation of forces" clearly began to shift toward the West.

At the same time, the EC continued to make substantial progress while the Comecon countries were in disarray. The admission of Greece to the EC in 1981, and of Spain and Portugal in 1986, had shown the EC's ability to accommodate new members with relatively backward economies. Spain, Portugal, and Greece all did relatively well within the EC's framework; their economies expanded – rapidly so in the case of Spain – and their parliamentary institutions became increasingly secure. The EC itself improved its performance in a variety of ways. For instance, in 1968 the EEC's last internal customs barriers came down. Inter-Community commerce expanded. Workers who settled in another EC country received equality of treatment in terms of employment, and general working conditions. Professional qualifications acquired in one EC country increasingly became accepted in others. The inter-Community movement of capital was liberalized. The EC developed a comprehensive policy regarding research and development. At the same time the movement for Western European political unification gathered strength. Jacques Delors, president of the EC Commission, was a "Europeanist" as well as a socialist; he resolved both to improve the EC and extend its scope – much to the disgust of latter-day Gaullists such as Margaret Thatcher, who wished to preserve the undivided sovereignty of member states, and were determined to prevent meddling in the member states' social policies by an overweening bureaucracy in Brussels.

After lengthy delay, the movement for Western European political association began to pick up speed. In 1985, the European Commission issued a major White Paper on the elimination of those numerous restrictions that still remained in the EC. (These comprised, among many other things, vexatious border inspections of goods in transit; restrictions on the movements of peoples; differences in national product norms; problems connected with differential taxation; patents; standardization in service industries, computers, communications, and such like.) In 1986 the EC promulgated the Single European Act (entering into force on 1 July 1987). The new program was designed to create an economic and monetary union and to sweep away the remaining obstacles to free movement of people, goods, capital, and services within the Community.[9]

The movement for European association also widened its social support. The Treaty of Rome in 1957 had drawn its main support from a small minority – bureaucrats, intellectuals, some prominent politicians, and magnates of heavy industry. The program for "1992," the new target date for the "Single Market," by contrast, could rely on broader backing. Advocates of a united Europe now included corporate capitalists engaged in a broad range of enterprises which had already extended the scale of their operations through massive trans-frontier mergers.[10] EC "1992" was backed likewise by professionals with transnational outlets for their respective skills, and by those who wanted a united Europe for its own sake – generally a confident lot.

By contrast, critics of a united Europe tended to be pessimists, people who felt themselves on the defensive – small farmers, many small-scale employers, unskilled workers, and the indigent, who looked for relief to their own national governments, not to some remote Euro-bureaucrat in Brussels. Along with hostility to closer association went hostility to immigration. By the late 1980s, immigration had become a major issue, as France, Britain, and Germany had all acquired substantial alien minorities, including Islamic minorities which presented Europe with cultural and political problems of a kind never faced before. There were Algerians in France, Turks and Serbs in Germany, Pakistanis in England. These Muslim newcomers had little in common; yet they all aroused popular hostility, especially among the poor. The newcomers met with strong prejudice regarding their color, customs, and religion. At worst, this hostility might find expression in skinhead thuggery. Enmity, however, was also accompanied by many other apprehensions – fears of an overweening Euro-bureaucracy, a remote Euro-judicature bent on expanding its power, and more general fears concerning a super-Europe transcending traditional cultures in a Babel of *franglais*, computer-speak, *Gastarbeiter* jargon, and Euro officialese. However, as a trade association the EC worked perfectly well. Hence the former Comecon states and the EFTA countries (Norway, Sweden, Finland, Austria, Switzerland, and Iceland) became increasingly willing to join the EC. Above all, the EC now also seemed a desirable model for Eastern and Central Europe.

By contrast, the Soviet Union had slithered into a profound crisis by the early 1980s, as had all its Warsaw Pact allies. The Soviet economy faced one emergency after another, as the Soviet Union increasingly confronted over-centralization, corruption, inflexibility, managerial ineffi- ciency, waste, misguided investments, over-manning, industrial obsoles- cence, consumer shortages, and consumer demoralization. Far from fusing into one Soviet people, the various ethnic groups (more than 200 in all, including ethnic Russians) regained their confidence; far from declining as a spiritual force, religion revived – Christianity, Judaism, and Islam. Marxism-Leninism had largely been reduced to a collection of empty litanies; no creative impulse derived from a dying ideology. The Soviet economy was in deep trouble, the environment despoiled, the heroes forgotten, but not their exploitation of Soviet citizens. By now even the more intelligent members of the *nomenklatura* began to understand that things could not continue in the accustomed fashion, that their own living standards would fall unless the economy improved. By the 1980s entire state enterprises were surreptitiously passing into private hands, with the secret connivance of high officials who profited personally from such deals. The highest stage of socialism turned out to be thievery, and those who ruled it a "kleptocracy." More seriously still, the Soviet Union faced desperate new demographic challenges, as the general mortality (especially infant mortality) increased; at the same time fertility declined in the European (though not in the Muslim) parts of the Soviet Union. (This diminution came in part as a result of numerous abortions made necessary by the absence of reliable contraceptives. These abortions, often crudely performed, left all too many women unable to bear children.)

Neither could the Soviet Union quiet discontent at home by victories abroad. The empire in Eastern Europe proved costly to sustain, as did "fraternal" help to Cuba and other pro-Soviet states. A time traveller from the late Czarist era visiting Russia in the early 1980s would have found much of the oppositional literature quite familiar – there were Western liberals and slavophiles, ethnic nationalists, dissident socialists, religious conservatives, free traders, and many more. At long last, the ice broke. The first major crack may have opened when Konstantin Chernenko took over power in 1984 – indeed Amalrik's question "Will the Soviet Union Last until 1984?" (published 1970) was more perceptive than the author could have known. Chernenko tried to improve relations with the US. In the same year, almost unnoticed by the world at large, Mozambique, a Soviet ally in the Third World, concluded at Nkomati an accord with South Africa whereby the two signatories agreed not to foment subversion beyond their respective borders. Even a few years earlier such an arrangement would have seemed inconceivable, given the Marxist-Leninist assumption that South Africa was a Western financial colony, run by a reactionary, racist clique doomed to speedy extinction. In 1985 Chernenko died, to be replaced by Mikhail Gorbachev – and relations with the West thereafter underwent a fundamental change.[11]

Gorbachev was a product of the communist system; he began his career as a convinced Marxist-Leninist who looked to the world revolution. Neither did he intend to dismantle the Soviet empire. (As late as December 1989, he told the CPSU's Central Committee that the existence of two sovereign German states had to be accepted.)[12] At home Gorbachev wished to mend communism, not end it, to render the state more efficient, more humane, and more acceptable to the citizenry. Reform was to be administered in homeopathic doses; some critics even drew comparisons between Gorbachev's "New Thinking" and the approach of those Czarist police officers who organized official trade unions for the purpose of channeling and controlling the workers' wrath. But, faced with a troubled economy and widespread discontent among workers, intellectuals, and ethnic minorities, Gorbachev soon went much further than he had meant to go. In 1986 Andrei Sakharov, noted Soviet physicist and civil rights activist, was permitted to return to Moscow from exile. Gorbachev himself consolidated his personal power. (For example, in 1989 he also took over Andrei Gromyko's position as head of state.) He revised Soviet doctrine, insisting that ideological differences should not be translated into international relations. He called for advice from reformers, and sacked a few hard-liners.

Gorbachev created for himself the image of a flexible politician, maneuvering between the hard-liners on the one side and reformers on the other; he used force when convenient (for instance, against Kazakhstan in 1986), and conciliation where inevitable. Gorbachev authorized such previously prohibited institutions as private and cooperative enterprises and joint ventures with foreigners; then he backpedalled, while failing to sanction essential reforms such as the privatization of land. The federal republics gained a degree of autonomy that would have given apoplexy to Stalin; but Gorbachev during the late 1980s had no intention of ending communism or permitting any republic to secede – not even the three Baltic states, whose incorporation by the USSR in 1940 had never been recognized by the US.

Gorbachev's reputation has declined since the 1991 coup. Critics within and without the Soviet Union stress his vacillations, his inability or unwillingness to take his initial reforms to their predestined conclusion. These objections are well taken. Yet, when all is said and done, it was under Gorbachev that the Soviet citizens secured for themselves what they had ardently desired – freedom of speech, freedom of assembly, freedom of religion – those "bourgeois" freedoms that the workers allegedly do not prize as much as a fat wage packet. There were constitutional reforms under Gorbachev; these culminated in 1990 when the Central Committee of the Communist Party of the Soviet Union gave up the party's constitutionally guaranteed monopoly of power. Practice might differ from theory – but even minor changes would have appeared utterly scandalous to yesteryear's true believers.

Above all, there were major changes in foreign policy, forced on the Soviet leadership by domestic weakness. It was the supreme merit of hardened *apparatchiks* such as Gorbachev and his foreign minister Eduard Shevardnadze to understand the new realities, and reset sails accordingly. Having waged a long, bloody, unpopular, and inconclusive counter-insurgency war, the Soviet armed forces withdrew from Afghanistan in 1988. In the same year, the Soviet Union. South Africa, and Cuba negotiated a treaty providing for the Cuban army's withdrawal from Angola. The class struggle was virtually repudiated as the basis of Soviet foreign policy. In military terms, the Warsaw Pact armies were, by this time, dubious assets, given their uncertain loyalty. In economic terms, the Eastern European satellites (and also Cuba) had become a heavy burden to the over-taxed Soviet consumers – and were perceived as such by the Soviet public. Except for Yugoslavia and Cuba, the communist regimes had all been established by Soviet bayonets or surrogates; none enjoyed popular legitimacy. Addressing the Council of Europe at Strasbourg in July 1989, Gorbachev announced that the Red Army would no longer intervene in domestic disorders in the Soviet Union's satellite countries in Central and Eastern Europe. Henceforth "real existing socialism" was doomed, for the various Quisling regimes could not rely on the loyalty of their own armies.

By contrast, there was in all Eastern and Central European countries a universal longing to be accepted by the West as Europeans; there was a universal wish for "normality," a universal disgust with the pretension and privileges of the *nomenklatura* – their special shops, special apartments, special dachas, special travel permits. Instead opposition was expressed in a thousand different ways: through sermons; through classical plays and poems reinterpreted to fit present-day circumstances; through radio broadcasts from the West; and through political jokes, a potent form of popular oral tradition.

Opposition also came from the churches. Admittedly, these operated in an ambiguous fashion. All officially sanctioned churches had cooperated with Caesar in some fashion or other. But they also criticized Caesar, or at least provided some facilities of silent opposition on the part of individual believers. By and large, the Orthodox clergy were least likely to play the rebel. The reasons for this state of affairs were complex, linked to the Orthodox churches' long tradition of cooperation with the state, and to the ability of communists in Romania, Bulgaria, and Serbia to purge the churches immediately after their takeovers following World War II. Some Protestants, particularly in East Germany, played a somewhat more active role. Committed as they were to maintaining a "church within socialism," they nevertheless opposed the government on matters concerning ecology and armaments. The most active opposition, overall, derived from the Catholics, especially Polish Catholics. (According to a 1990 poll, 84 percent of Poles called themselves believers, as opposed to only one person in three in Czechoslovakia, and one person in four in East Germany.) The Poles drew special inspiration from the election in 1978 of a compatriot, the Cardinal of Krakow, to the Papacy. The new Pope, John Paul II, was a brilliant statesman, determined to bring change to Eastern Europe. His visit to Poland in 1979 proved, in Soviet foreign minister Andrei Gromyko's words, "a psychological earthquake."[13]

Communist power weakened in other ways. The communist societies might remain backward technologically; nevertheless, computers and fax facilities began to make their influence felt by opening a broad range of new communication channels.[14] There was universal contempt for the *nomenklatura*'s disembodied party-speak with (in the East German version) its *Diamat* (dialectical materialism), *Polök* (political economy), *Gewi* (political philosophy), *Wiso* (scientific socialism), and other ugly acronyms. Only a handful of old true believers – including a diminishing contingent of Western visitors – still accepted that old-fashioned poster world in which young men and maidens forever carried banners, marched uphill, and fixedly stared into the sun. There was universal revulsion against those indispensable servants of totalitarian rule, the KGB and the informer – perhaps a jealous colleague at work, perhaps the kindly-looking concierge next door, who would act as a stool pigeon for the police. There was widespread awareness of socialist backwardness compared to the capitalist West.

Gorbachev did not create these conditions. He never meant to lead a revolution. He did not initially desire to end the role of the Communist Party or of the KGB. He did not desire to create a free market economy; he took a tough line against opposition. He did not truly appreciate the force of ethnic nationalism (including Russian ethnic nationalism) or of religion, a subject to which we shall return in relation to the 1991 coup. Gorbachev lacked a popular mandate in the sense of never having been elected to office, and he failed to dismantle the military-industrial complex or the top-heavy machinery of economic control. *Time* magazine in its January 1, 1992, issue, selected Gorbachev as the "Man of the Decade."

According to *Time*, he was a master politician who generated a sense of purpose, and who led the regime and the opposition alike. According to scholars such as Dimitri Simes, a Russian emigré, Gorbachev was a man with a mission only waiting for a chance to downgrade the Communist Party. Gorbachev was in fact none of these things: he was a communist determined to save communism from its own excesses. Nevertheless – within the Soviet context – Gorbachev was the most outstanding reformer that his country had produced. He understood that the Soviet Union could not continue as before; he determined therefore "to eliminate the operative role of the party in the economy," – but this only after a lengthy period of economic decline. Gorbachev operated against bitter opposition within the Politburo and the Central Committee; he became increasingly radicalized as traditional methods (campaigns against alcoholism and corruption, personnel changes) proved wholly ineffective.[15] Gorbachev did not overthrow the communist system: this was the achievement of leaders such as Boris Yeltsin. But Gorbachev was the chief agent in the liberation of Eastern and Central Europe, for it was he who refused henceforth to sustain the bankrupt Soviet satellites by Soviet armed force. Thereafter Soviet foreign policy underwent a decisive change.[16]

What was the role of Western Europe and of the US in these developments? The Western European impact was indirect. *Samizdat* authors gained a great deal from being able to publish with private firms in the West. Western Europe and the US were role models in countries where locally made merchandise was automatically regarded as shoddy, and Western goods as of superior quality. Western Europe was free; Western Europe did well economically; Western Europe did well politically, as the movement for Western European unification gathered speed. (In January 1989 Delors launched a plan for linking the six countries of the EFTA (European Free Trade Association), comprising Switzerland, Austria, Norway, Sweden, Finland, Iceland, to the EC by creating a European Economic Space, EES. In April, an EC committee headed by Delors proposed a three-stage plan toward European Monetary Union, EMU.) By this time, every Central European country looked toward Western Europe for salvation.

As regards the US, it clearly posed no direct military danger to the Soviet Union in a conventional war. Whatever Soviet propagandists might say in public, they must have realized in private that a superpower which had accepted defeat in Vietnam, and which tolerated Fidel Castro's dictatorship 90 miles off Miami, was not likely to plunge into military adventures in Eastern Europe. Neither would its Western European allies – certainly not West Germany, where Federal Chancellor Helmut Kohl, the Christian Democratic leader, had in 1987 rolled out a red carpet for

Erich Honecker, the East German head of state, when "Red Erich" for the first time paid a state visit to West Germany. Neither the State Department nor any of the US intelligence organizations apparently had the slightest inkling that Soviet rule in Eastern Europe was about to collapse. While libraries were filled with works on socialism, there were few books explaining such vital topics as the economic weakness of the system, the loss of legitimacy of the party, the role of the extended family within the communist ruling cadres, or the place of the "Second Economy" within a communist country – despite the vital role played by underground enterprise in helping the socialist countries to survive at all. Likewise, on taking over, the Eastern European revolutionaries initially found no academic guidance on the fundamental problems of the late twentieth century: how to restore private enterprise in a socialist economy, or how to get a socialist country out of the red.

Nevertheless, the US did exert a tremendous indirect influence. Millions of Eastern Europeans had earlier settled in the US; their letters home, their visits, provided relatives, friends, and former neighbors with much more accurate information than did official propaganda. Radio Free Europe and the Voice of America had a wide audience in Eastern Europe; so did Western scholars such as Milton Friedman and Robert Conquest. While President Reagan widely encountered contempt among intellectuals and the media at home when he spoke of the Soviet Union as an "evil empire," millions of Poles, Czechs, Balts, and Georgians knew Reagan spoke the truth. The US remained influential – not so much for its diplomacy, but for the international demonstration effect of a free enterprise society and its superpower status. The very stridency of communist propaganda worked in America's favor. The mass of the people east of the Elbe had ceased to take the communist media seriously; anything they said was distrusted; far from being despised, the US was more apt to be romanticized.

## THE COLLAPSE OF COMMUNISM: THE NORTHERN TIER STATES

In 1989 revolutions broke out all over Eastern and Central Europe – nothing comparable had happened since 1848. Except in Romania, these revolutions were all peaceful. They had other features in common. They all had mass support. None of the revolutions hinged on those categories dear to self-styled progressive scholars in the West: race, class, or gender. All revolutions centered on traditional demands for national independence, freedom of religion, personal liberties, the rights to individual property, and parliamentary institutions. There was to be an end to self-appointed vanguards, to the "New Man," and the "radiant future." Everywhere, the communist establishments were divided and demoralized, once they had grasped their inability to rely on Soviet power. Moreover, the communist *nomenklaturas* could not possibly be romanticized in retrospect. Scores of novels and successful TV plays – *Upstairs, Downstairs, A Passage to India* – have cast glamor on the former British imperial ruling class. Whatever their failings, they were at least colorful; they were also gentlemen, or at any rate claimed to be such. By contrast, no viewer would conceivably want to watch East German or Soviet party bosses at play. To be boorish as well as tyrannical proved a fatal handicap.

A special role in this upheaval fell to Poland. Poland had been the first Central European country to be occupied by the Red Army during World War II, the first to endure communist rule, the first to be liberated from its thrall. Poland, like Slovakia, Croatia, and Lithuania, was overwhelmingly a Catholic country. Poles looked toward Rome as a countervailing power to their own state. Poles took pride in the election of a Polish Pope, John Paul II, whose visit to his native country in 1979 marked the beginning of a new epoch. As Timothy Garton Ash, an insightful British observer, put it, "the Pope's first great pilgrimage to Poland was the turning point. Here, for the first time, we saw that massive, sustained, yet supremely peaceful and self-disciplined manifestation of social unity, the gentle crowd against the Party-state which was both the hallmark and the essential catalyst of change."[17] Poland was unusual in other ways. Poles had settled extensively in the West, above all in the US, also in Canada, Britain, and France: Poles, therefore, had innumerable private contacts and pressure groups abroad. Poles had long experience in resisting foreign rulers with an alien religion. Poles had a long history of anti-Russian revolts; and they had not forgotten the World War II Katyn massacre (involving the mass execution by the Soviets of captured Polish military officers) and similar atrocities; Poland's national anthem itself proclaimed that Poland was not yet lost.

Poland also had some peculiar features. Alone in Eastern and Central Europe, communist-ruled Poland had managed to retain an independent peasantry, restricted though it was by innumerable economic and political disabilities. Poland, in a sense, was also a pioneering land. After World War II, Poland had been compelled to shift its geographical center. Eastern Poland had been lost to the Soviet Union; the Polish population of the former eastern provinces was forced to move. In partial compensation, Poland was given part of eastern Germany, whose population was likewise forcibly expelled. (Possibly between 1 and 1.5 million German-descended people remain in Poland today.) Poles resettled their own new West, but the colonists remained bitterly anti-Russian.

In Poland there had also been long-standing opposition to communism among all other strata of the population – intellectuals, church people, smallholders, and workers. "Solidarity," a trade union founded in 1980 against bitter government opposition, developed into the first independent political movement in the Soviet bloc, in effect a national front more than a mere labor organization. It was led by Lech Walesa, a union leader as patriotic and tough as Marshal Józef Pilsudski, modern Poland's founding father, whom Walesa curiously resembled in appearance. Solidarity's moment of triumph came in August 1989, when Poles installed as the new prime minister Tadeusz Mazowiecki, a practicing Catholic and a leading member of Solidarity. (It was Mazowiecki who, at enormous risk to his personal popularity, initiated during his brief period of office from 1989–90 a major reform program.) His installation was a crucial event – almost precisely 50 years after the signing of the Nazi-Soviet Non-Aggression Pact in 1939, and two centuries after the French National Assembly had proclaimed the Rights of Man during the French Revolution. Gorbachev recognized the new government; even the KGB sent a congratualatory cable; Poland had regained its effective independence as a country, lost in 1939, and Poles would now recover their civic rights.

Thereafter Poland took the lead among former communist countries in the restoration of private enterprise. The country began to privatize numerous state-owned industries (with workers of a privatized company entitled to buy up to 20 percent of the shares at half price). The Polish currency was made convertible, a key feature in the reform program, and one imitated by Russia in 1992. Inflation declined; price controls and subsidies were largely eliminated. Shops opened throughout the country, giving a more cheerful air to the cityscape and much-needed services to the people. Unemployment in 1990 was at least kept down to acceptable levels.[18] (Given the size of the "Second Economy," the real extent of unemployment was much lower than official statistics suggested, a generalization true of all formerly communist countries.) In 1992 the government extended its privatization plans in an attempt to restructure and salvage crumbling state-owned enterprises. Poland, an overwhelmingly Catholic country, enjoyed a degree of cultural cohesion equalled in no former Comecon country; this invisible asset (symbolized through massive church building after liberation) also helped to facilitate Poland's material rehabilitation.

Not that Poland was in good shape. Parliamentary power was fragmented: by 1992 there were 29 political parties in operation. Key workers (including teachers, scientists, civil servants) mostly found themselves worse off than they had been in the bad old days. The country was heavily indebted to Western countries, which had improvidently lent to Poland something like 38.9 billion in dollars; much of Poland's industry was antiquated, (including, for instance, the great shipyards at Gdańsk, a stronghold of Solidarity). The state had abandoned attempts to control food prices, ration meat, or fix wages. The result was a massive increase in food prices, long queues fo panic buyers outside shops, and a wave of strikes as workers sought to compensate for rising prices by bigger wage packets. In Poland, as in the rest of Central Europe, there was also an ecological crisis. (A report submitted to the Polish Academy of Sciences indicated that the envirommental balance had totally collapsed in 27 provinces,in which one-third of the population lived, with undrinkable water, unusable beaches, endemic disease, and the danger of genetic human damage.)

Equally troublesome were the effects of those intangible factors which operated in Poland perhaps to an even greater extent than in the remainder of Central Europe. Poland had been the first to modify the communist system; Poles did so by a series of compromises which at first left the communists with greater residual power than they would enjoy in East Germany and Czechoslovakia. The Polish communists, moreover, had an early start in the creation of *nomenklatura* capitalism. The process began in the late 1980s when Poland took steps for the limited privatization of state enterprises and the creation of joint state-private companies. The head of the state enterprise, a communist, would often thereafter become president of the private company, enriching his own enterprise at state expense. The communist successor parties moreover inherited much of the former Communist Party's property; hence, communists retained a considerable stake in the new economy. "Clean" capital, locally engendered, was hard to find – a problem that beset every country formerly under communit rule.

Poland also faced difficult relations with its new neighbors. As long as Poland had formed part of the Soviet empire, Poland was at least shielded from disputes with adjoining states. Once the Soviet empire collapsed, there was a striking change in Poland's geopolitical situation. Instead of a weak and discredited German Democratic Republic, Poland in the West now faced a strong and united Germany. True enough, Germany had renounced all claims to those territories taken from Germany by Poland at the end of World War II. But what would happen if a future Germany were to move to the right? Not surprisingly, the Poles were to the fore among those Eastern Europeans who looked alike to the EC and to the US to maintain a new balance of power.

In the east, there was a revival of long-standing friction between Poland and Lithuania. Vilnius (Polish Wilno), the Lithuanian capital, had formed part of prewar Poland; a substantial Polish minority remained in Lithuania;

ill will continued on both sides of the border: among all of Poland's foreign relations, those between Poland and Lithuania were the worst. By contrast, Poland's relations with Russia and Belarus were correct, though not cordial. (Except for the Russian enclave at Kaliningrad, Poland now lacked a common border with Russia.) There were also complications with Ukraine, a country twice as large at Poland, with a larger population and an expanding army. Ukrainians and Poles had fought for centuries. The Western Ukraine became part of Poland after World War I, but was then seized by Stalin as part of the territorial changes brought about by the Hitler-Stalin Pact of 1939. During and after World War I, Ukrainian guerrillas fought against both Germans and Poles; Ukrainians also attacked Poles living in Ukraine. But Poland was also the first country to recognize Ukraine's independence; despite friction in Western Ukraine concerning church property and other complex matters, no major Polish party now makes territorial claims on its neighbor. Moreover, a substantial number of Ukrainians work in Poland. Poland will also take satisfaction in an agreement concluded in 1992 between the US and Ukraine requiring Ukraine (as well as Kazakhstan and Belarus) to relinquish all nuclear weapons, leaving Russia the only member of the CIS with nuclear arms. (The Ukraine's status remained doubtful, however.)

More seriously, Poles of whatever political complexion had endured during the twentieth century a series of unparalleled bloodlettings. The Nazis had murdered most of the Polish Jews (three million), and an equal number of Polish Christians, especially those whom the Nazis considered to be potential leaders). Then came the Red Army and its Polish communist allies; the latter continued the persecution of middle-class people and of independent-minded dissidents of every kind. Countless Poles had fled abroad; no country suffered from the brain drain more than Poland. How would Poland deal with these problems? Post-communist Poland, like pre-communist Poland, again developed a multiplicity of parties. Henceforth, according to a Hungarian sociologist's pun, there would be three poles in Poland: "Social Democracy, Christian Democracy, and Free Market economics. They form a triangular field of force which now determines what is happening in Poland."[19]

Given the troubles that beset their country, Poles acted with remarkable speed and efficiency. By 1993 more than 80 percent of the country's industry had been turned over to private ownership through investment funds distributed to workers, or through corporate shares nominally owned by the treasury but available for purchase. By the end of 1992, private firms in Poland accounted for over 40 percent of the GDP and nearly 60 percent of the labor force. In Poland alone among the former Soviet satellites estimated industrial production for 1993 would exceed production in 1990. The Warsaw Stock Exchange (set up in 1991) had become a power in the economy; many new jobs had been created in private enterprises. Foreign capital investment was on the rise, albeit slowly (from an estimated $250,000,000 in 1990 to $1 billion in 1992). The expansion of small business had altered the physical appearance of cities and the shape of politics alike. Poland's problems remained enormous, but Poland was ethnically homogeneous. The Catholic Church provided common cultural standards as well as a common religion and a host of voluntary social services. The Polish example was keenly watched by the Russians, and in turn greatly influenced the policies subsequently followed by Boris Yeltsin.

The next domino to fall was Hungary. Hungary had emerged from both World Wars as a two-time loser. Defeat in World War I had reduced Hungary to a rump of its former self. In World War II, Hungary, with Nazi help, had regained from Romania a part of the disputed province of Transylvania (mainly populated by Hungarians); but in the postwar settlement Transylvania was once again lost. But the Hungarians had gained distinction in 1956 by staging the only armed rising that had ever been launched against Central Europe's Soviet overlords. The revolt was brutally crushed, and its leaders executed, but Hungary thereafter developed its own form of "goulash communism," a more benign version of the tyranny exercised by the communists in the neighboring countries.

On the face of it, the Hungarian communists should thus have done better than the rest. By the 1980s, the Hungarian churches, unlike the Polish churches, stood compromised by extensive cooperation with the government. The first Hungarian opposition party (the Hungarian Democratic Forum) was only formed in 1988, followed thereafter by more than 50 other organizations. Nevertheless, the Hungarian communists had by then incurred too much hostility from those "toiling masses" whom the party ideologues would always invoke. Even within its own ranks, the party suffered from divisiveness and disillusionment. By the late 1970s already, as the party's standard history observed, "within the party itself, the revolutionary zeal of earlier times has been largely swept under by the tide of secular values intrinsic to modernization."[20] The ruling party (then known as the Hungarian Socialist Workers' Party, HSWP) sought to weather the storm by changing its program and its name (October 1989). By that time, Hungary now stood committed to a multi-party system, a new constitution, a new electoral law, a reformed criminal code, and a mixed economy. On October 23, 1989, the anniversary of the 1956 uprising, Hungary once more proclaimed itself a Republic instead of a People's Republic. Freedom of emigration became a fundamental right; the "Iron Curtain" disappeared, as Hungarians and foreigners alike might freely cross the Hungarian border.

Not that all was well with Hungary. The country's economy was in a desperate state; inflation was rampant; compared with communist misrule, even the reactionary regime of Admiral Miklos Horthy had been a model of efficiency. Hungary lacked a national organization such as Solidarity. As Elie Abel put it, "the Hungarian opposition seems to resemble a cluster of competing political boutiques whose merchandise, while stylish, interests no more than a fraction of dispirited working-class voters."[21] In Hungary, as elsewhere, there was moreover a revival of traditional nationalism, complete with traditional chauvinism and anti-Semitism. Alone in Nazi-occupied Central Europe, a fairly substantial Jewish minority in Hungary had managed to survive the Nazi persecution. Jews were well represented in journalism and academia. Jews overwhelmingly lived in Budapest, the capital; they were traditionally associated with "liberalism" and "cosmopolitanism." The infighting between organizations such as the Hungarian Democratic Forum and the Free Democrats sometimes had an ethnic edge, when Free Democrats were accused of lacking the true Hungarian spirit – and everyone knew exactly what *that* meant. But Hungarians were confident. Hungary had already made substantial progress before the 1989 revolution; Budapest already looked more like a Western city than any other behind the Iron Curtain. Hungary opted for a moderate right-center government (headed by József Antall, president of the Hungarian Democratic Forum). There were good grounds for hope.

The Hungarian revolution had equally beneficial effects internationally. Even before Hungary's *ancien régime* ended, the Hungarians opened their borders, and thereby allowed numerous East Germans to emigrate legally to West Germany. *Republikflucht* ("flight from the republic," a punishable offense in East Germany) could no longer be prevented. The Hungarian revolution thereby intensified a long-standing crisis in the German Democratic Republic, whose very existence as a state depended on its ability to keep its unwilling citizens at home.

East Germany was, of course, unique in Europe in that it was a communist state in competition with West Germany, a prosperous capitalist state that shared East Germany's nationality. If the two Germanies were to be reunited, East German reconstruction would be facilitated by West German aid – an option not available to any other communist country in Central and Eastern Europe. Not that this seemed a likely prospect in the mid-1980s; no one anticipated the speed with which the two German states would once again fuse. The partition of Germany after World War II had, after all, appeared most convenient to all of Germany's neighbors who uniformly feared the re-emergence of a German world power. (The US was the only Western country which had no dread of a reunited Reich.)

Communists worldwide had a special stake in East Germany's success; East Germany was advertised as the most advanced part of the communist world; the East German *Kombinate* (industrial aggregates) were supposedly doing wonders. Germans were said to be hard-working, disciplined, and efficient. Germans were also the compatriots of Marx and Engels, socialism's founding fathers. If the Germans could not make a success of socialism, no one else would. The East German state, moreover, had supposedly attained permanence. East Germans – so went the story – had acquired a new pride in their own state, a new socialist consciousness. Hence the division of Germany would remain permanent until such times as West Germany also turned socialist. Academic forecasts concerning this subject make embarrassing reading in retrospect. To give just two examples: according to Philip Windsor, an Englishman contributing to a standard work on Western Europe, published in 1986, there would be no German reunification in the foreseeable future;[22] and F. Stephen Larrabee, an American writing in 1989, the year in which the GDR collapsed, argued that reunification had ceased to be a real issue. Even more absurdly, US official statistics claimed that the per capita GNP in West Germany was lower than East Germany's.[23]

How did highly intelligent people arrive at such conclusions? On the surface, observers apparently had good reasons for their confidence in the GDR. East Germany, like the Federal Republic of Germany, celebrated its fortieth birthday in 1989. Both states had endured longer than the Weimar Republic and the Third Reich between them. On both sides of the border there was now a new generation – men and women in their forties – who had never known a united Germany in their lifetimes. East Germans had experienced 40 years of communist indoctrination at school, in the youth movement, in the army, at the workplace; their very language had been modified by communist terminology. West Germany, by contrast, had been integrated into the West – militarily, economically, culturally, politically. Particularly strong was the US influence. Even the most militantly anti-American student demonstrators took their rock music, their jeans, and their jargon from America as well as their science and technology. East Germany and West Germany seemed worlds apart; surely they would stay apart. From the 1960s onward, the bulk of West German scholars, diplomats, and businessmen dealt with the GDR on the basis that it would last. So did the great majority of West German politicians. The West German Social Democrats, the SPD (whose sister party was banned in East Germany), actually joined with the East German ruling party, the SED, in a "Joint Commission on Fundamental Values" in 1982. The SPD's object was *Wandel durch Annäherung* (transformation by rapprochement). SPD leader Willy Brandt certainly did not anticipate that the GDR would soon disappear. The governing party, the CDU, was not quite that effusive. All the same it was Helmut Kohl, CDU leader and federal chancellor since 1982, whose government indeed improved on his predecessor's policy by multiplying political and economic contacts with the GDR.

Nevertheless, the "objective correlation of forces," in communist terminology, changed more rapidly than the experts had foreseen. The permanent existence of the GDR as a separate state depended on certain assumptions. The Soviet Union would always be willing to defend its satellites within the Warsaw Pact against internal subversion. The Warsaw Pact states would maintain "socialist solidarity." The organs of the East German state, including the National People's Army, would always prove reliable. The East German economy would perform with reasonable efficiency, and so would the East German welfare services. The East German population could somehow be shielded from Western influence – this despite the availability and popularity of West German TV programs, the growth of tourism, and, above all, those ties of culture and kinship that continued to link Germans on both sides of the border.

By 1989, however, all these conditions had ceased to apply. The "fraternal" socialist states were crumbling. Poland, East Germany's next-door neighbor, had already made great strides in freeing itself from communist tyranny. Gorbachev was clearly unwilling to deploy the Red Army in support of the satellite regimes. Ever since its foundation in 1946, the governing SED (Socialist Unity Party) had effusively praised the Soviet Union as Germany's great example. Now this propaganda turned against its makers, as Gorbachev became the hero of the crowds. In East Germany there was widespread agitation and huge demonstrations, led at first by dissident leftists who desired "socialism with a human face." Intellectuals (including leftist Lutheran clergymen) united in such bodies as the "New Forum." But these reformers were soon left far behind by popular opinion. By now the *nomenklatura* and its allies were totally discredited by East Germany's economic failure, by the privileges enjoyed by the self-styled vanguard of the proletariat and by the evident mendacity of official propaganda. The *nomenklatura* itself lost heart, many of its own members bitterly disillusioned. Indeed, some highly placed former dignitaries, such as Günter Schabowski, an ex-member of the East German Politburo, went further in their denunciation of communism than many old-style anti-communists. According to Schabowski, the entire system had been irredeemably perverted from the start, since Marxism-Leninism itself rested on mistaken premises.[24]

In the end, only the *Staatssicherheitsdienst* ("Stasi" or State Security Service, an armed state within the state) would have been willing to fight.

But no reliance could have been placed on the East German army. The Soviet divisions stayed in their barracks. The East German police lost confidence, and proved both unable and unwilling to cope with mass demonstrations that involved hundreds of thousands. By now the communist leadership had obviously become dispirited and divided; none would take personal responsibility for occasioning massive bloodshed. The hardliners were totally isolated, and the bulk of communists were fearful for their own personal future. On October 18, 1989, Erich Honecker, "Red Erich," a surviving hardliner, fell from power. At this point, communists of any stripe could no longer master the situation. On November 9, 1989 – on the very day when the Kaiser's government had signed an armistice in 1918 – the East German communist government capitulated to its people by opening the Berlin Wall. Nine days later East German authorities announced that five million of their citizens – almost one-third of the GDR's entire population – had applied for travel papers to West Germany. On December 1, the East German parliament abolished constitutional provision guaranteeing the SED's leading role. The East German state disintegrated with a speed that surprised West German politicians and bureaucrats, who would have preferred a slowly-paced handover.

In March 1990, East Germany held free elections – the first there since Hitler's takeover in 1933. They were amongst the most important held in modern German history; they would deliver the people's verdict on "real existing socialism"; they would also play a decisive part in shaping the future of a united Germany. Left-wing intellectuals such as Christa Wolf, the well-known East German writer, hoped that East Germany would wish to preserve its socialist achievements. The workers surely would now put their trust in a democratic form of socialism, free from the "deformations" of the old system. These hopes came to nought. After 40 years of socialism in East Germany, 48.1 percent of the East German voters opted for the conservative Alliance for Germany, led by the Christian Democrats. The Social Democrats received 21.8 percent of the votes on an ultra-moderate program that accepted a free market economy. The Party of Democratic Socialism, the PDS (the refurbished SED under new management) obtained only 16.3 percent of the votes, despite the party's newly-found commitment to democracy and a mixed economy. Worse still from the left's standpoint, the East German workers deserted socialism, even in areas such as Saxony, once a center of proletarian militance. The most loyal supporters of socialism were now the intellectuals. The "new politics," represented by feminists and "Greens," failed to make an impact.

According to the left-wing intelligentsia, the East German workers had permitted themselves to be lured by Western television sets and D-Marks – by crude consumerism. This was only a half-truth. East Germany and

Czechoslovakia were the most prosperous of the Central European countries. By a calculus of economic self-interest they should have been the most contented. But they voted against tyranny, and also against those privileged intellectuals impudent enough to censure ordinary folk for wanting to spend their own money in their own way and for complaining about the lack of goods and services and of freedom and trust. Further, the GDR turned out to have been an informer society *par excellence*.

The election over, the two Germanies were bound for unification. Re-union would be negotiated on conservative terms, led by two conservatives, with Helmut Kohl, the West German chancellor, very much the senior partner, and Lothar de Maizière, the East German premier, also a CDU man, very much the junior partner. The CDU also scored major successes in the now reconstituted five eastern *Länder* which replaced the unitary regime set up under communist auspices in East Germany. The military side of reunification was handled by direct arrangement with the Soviets. The combined forces of the reunited German state would not exceed 370,000 men, less than the existing Bundeswehr the West German army. The East German army would disappear. United Germany would remain a member of NATO, but no NATO troops would be stationed in the East. In theory, this was a partial disarmament treaty. In practice, Germany remained militarily the strongest country in Central Europe, as there was no way in which treaty limitations on the size of Germany's forces could be effectively enforced, as the Warsaw Pact disintegrated and as the Soviet forces prepared to withdraw from their former empire by the end of 1994.

As regards "inner-German" relations, East and West Germany concluded a treaty (in force as of July 1, 1990) which created a monetary, economic, and social union. West Germany's "social market economy" became the norm for a united Germany. The Bundesbank (the federal bank of West Germany) became the central bank for all Germany, the D-Mark became the currency for all Germany, with elaborate provisions for the exchange of East Marks into West Marks. The reunification treaty – 900 pages long – guaranteed security for foreign investors, unified the tax laws and the legal system, and went a long way toward solving the difficult question of property rights, and unifying working conditions, as well as social services. On October 3, 1990, "Unification Day," Germany's new national holiday, East Germany joined to West Germany.

Not all Germans were satisfied. (There was no compensation for those Germans who had lost their property between 1945 and 1949, while East Germany had been governed by the Soviet Union.) Moreover, a fog of forgetfulness descended on East Germany; no one had ever served as an informer – well, hardly anyone – and no one had ever known of, much

less practiced Leninist theories of revolutionary terror against the enemies
of the working class, except a few frightened old men awaiting or fearing
trial. The very initials of the former German Democratic Republic passed
into popular oblivion. They were replaced by newly-coined acronyms such
as BGD, *"beigetretene Gebiete Deutschlands"* (newly joined German provinces) or according to the Berliners' cynical humor, FOB (meaning not
"free on board," but *Fass ohne Boden*, "bottomless barrel"). Chancellor Kohl
and his coajudators had enormously underestimated the extent of East
Germany's economic predicament, the cost of rehabilitating the country,
the psychological destruction effected by communism in eroding the work
ethic, depressing the entrepreneurial spirit, and disrupting confidence
between individual citizens, and the resentment as well as the admiration
felt by so many East Germans for the "Golden West." The burden on the
West German tax payers kept growing as inefficient East German industries
were increasingly rehabilitated at public expense. But at least the nightmare
of East Germany's "real existing socialism" was over.

The revolutions in Poland, Hungary and East Germany left Czechoslovakia's regime geographically isolated. Czechoslovakia had been the only
Eastern or Central European country where the communist takeover in
1948 had enjoyed popular support—albeit support from a minority only.
Czechoslovakia was then a relatively highly industrialized country with a
class-conscious proletariat. Irrespective of class affiliation, the Czechs had
felt themselves betrayed by the Western powers through the Munich
Agreement of 1938 with Hitler; and the Czechs had traditionally looked
on Russians as fellow Slavs who would back them against the Germans. After World War II, the Czechs expelled their German minority,
three million people in all, and thereby simplified, though did not
eliminate, the country's ethnic problems. (Under the Nazis, the Slovaks
had enjoyed an illusory independence; they continued to resent Prague's
predominance and regarded themselves as a separate people. Within the
Czech-speaking lands, Moravia put forward regional autonomy claims as
against Bohemia.) Bohemia and Moravia had been the most industrialized
part of the Austro-Hungarian Empire. Czech engineering skill thereafter retained its international reputation – for example, the standard
British machine-gun in World War II, the Bren gun, was of prewar Czech
design. Czechoslovakia, moreover, had suffered little material damage in
World War II.

When the communists took over, Czechoslovakia thus started from a
higher material level than any other Soviet satellite country except for
East Germany. By Eastern European standards, there was plenty for the
communists to squander, and plenty to loot (including, as in western
Poland, the property of the expelled Germans). But because of communist

mismanagement, the country's relative standing within the industrial world declined; there was widespread corruption and decay – so much so that intellectuals referred to their country as "Absurdistan," Kafka's nightmares transformed into a system of government. The Czechs bravely attempted to reform the system during the Prague Spring of 1968; but Soviet tanks put an end to the experiment. Henceforth, socialism itself stood widely discredited – even "socialism with a human face."

In Czechoslovakia, as in the rest of Eastern and Central Europe, socialism – a term once charged with hope – acquired negative connotations. There was widespread repression; there were extensive purges which had the unintended effect of further weakening the regime by removing most of the remaining able people from positions of authority, and by terminating all serious discussion on how to improve the economy. It was rule by the incompetent over the time-servers. The communists attempted to deal with their predicament by a dual strategy – selective terror on the one hand, limited economic reform on the other, concessions to the workers, and limited autonomy for professional people.

By the late 1980s, however, the regime was at the end of its tether. Existing fissures widened within the ranks of the ruling party. There was an increased turnover of incumbents in leading positions; the "stability of cadres" ended; the leadership became more divided, less experienced, and less confident than before. There was constant vacillation in the way in which the rulers dealt with dissidents – this at a time when the leading cadres tended to be younger than before, and less sure of the future than the Old Guard. There was a rapid increase in the number of oppositional bodies concerned with politics, religion, poetry, ecology, peace, areas highly charged with politics. Discontent increased among the workers, the intellectuals, and the Slovak nationalists.[25]

The people as a whole no longer looked to the "radiant future" but to the golden past, to the democratic institutions, the personal freedom, and the relative prosperity of Czechoslovakia as it had existed in the prewar period. Tomás Masaryk, Czechoslovakia's Founding Father, now seemed infinitely preferable to Marx, Lenin, and the entire socialist pantheon. There was total disillusion with the compromises of yesteryear; there was a new generation gap; there was indeed a feeling of guilt among those who had made the successive compromises. The opposition movement also had the good fortune to secure numerous men and women willing to make great personal sacrifices – foremost among them Václav Havel, a playwright turned resistance leader, a man of peace, and yet of steely resolution.

In Czechoslovakia, as in East Germany, the communist regime thereafter collapsed without bloodshed, threatened by mass strikes, mass demonstrations, universal hostility, and massive defections, – and faced also with events in East Germany where the Berlin Wall had opened. On December 10 President Gustav Husak resigned. Thereafter a parliamentary regime was installed; the Czechoslovak People's Republic became the Czech and Slovak Federal Republic. (The Slovaks would not even tolerate a hyphen to link Czech and Slovak into one word.) Absurdistan ended with Havel, and "absurdist" writer, installed in the presidency.

The post-communist government's task, on the face of it, seemed unmanageable. Apart from the usual problems of industrial obsolescence, a decaying infrastructure, and catastrophic pollution, there were intractable ethnic problems. Slovaks and Czechs could not see eye to eye. Slovakia, the republic's most backward part, had been saddled by the communists with a huge military-industrial complex whose future outlook was grim. Slovakia was a Catholic country whose citizens widely distrusted what they regarded as the Czechs' secularism, and also the Czechs' assumed indifference to Slovakia's special needs. In 1993 the Czecho-Slovak state thus broke into its two constituent components. But at least the Czech-Slovak divorce – like the Czecho-Slovak "velvet revolution" – was peaceful. Within the Czech republic, the reformists, led by Václav Klaus, determined to proceed at full speed in joining the West. The Czechs managed to maintain a relatively stable currency, reduce unemployment, and privatize state enterprises through a complex voucher system – leaving the Slovaks far behind. The Czech republic seemed destined therefore to become in future what it had been in the past: the most democratic and economically the most advanced country in East-Central Europe.

## THE COLLAPSE OF COMMUNISM: THE SOUTHERN TIER STATES

The Northern Tier states – Poland, Hungary, East Germany, and Czechoslovakia – had traditionally formed the most developed part of East-Central Europe. They were also ethnically more homogeneous than their neighbors, Poland and Czechoslovakia having carried out their version of "ethnic cleansing" after World War II (mainly at the cost of the Germans). The Southern Tier states, by contrast, were poorer, and also more divided in an ethnic sense. Recovery from the communist nightmare would prove even harder for them than for their northern neighbors; within a new political context, moreover, former communists managed to hold on to power far more effectively than they did in the Northern Tier states. However, Romania was the only former Warsaw Pact country where the overthrow of communism led to internal warfare.[26] On the face of it, Romania should have had an easier path to freedom than its neighbors. The country's dictator, Nicolae Ceauşescu had begun his rule as a reputed reformer; Romania had attained greater independence from the Moscow connection than its neighbors. Accordingly, Romania had received plentiful help from the West, including extensive credits (Romania enjoyed trade agreements with the US, the EEC, and was the first state in Eastern and Central Europe to adhere to the major international financial agreements.) Romania prided itself on being a credit-worthy state; when Western loans ceased to be easily available, Romania set out to repay its foreign loans at enormous sacrifice. Ceauşescu was showered with foreign honors, titles, decorations, doctorates whose profusion would have delighted a Roman Caesar. Ceauşescu was pragmatic in permitting Romanian Jews to emigrate to Israel, ethnic Germans to leave for West Germany – all in return for hard cash. At the same time, Ceauşescu built a huge security apparatus, while reducing the army to little more than an ill-paid labor service. Ceauşescu skillfully played the various interest groups against one another – regular military services, the Patriotic Guard (an armed organization under the party's control), the Securitate (secret police), the navy, the air force, the party. Above all, the president's own family members controlled the key positions in the state. In Romania, as in North Korea, the highest stage of socialism turned out to be the political family business.

Ceauşescu's Romania, however, labored under grim disability, not all of communist making. Romania prided itself on its Latin legacy, a Roman enclave surrounded by Slavs and Magyars. But Romania – unlike Poland – was not a Latin Roman Catholic, but an Orthodox country. Romania shared with Russia, Ukraine, Serbia, and Bulgaria the legacy of the Byzantine Empire in which supreme religious and secular power had been fused. Not that Orthodox states lack freedom-loving traditions of their own. But in all of them, the break from communism was slower than in Catholic states (Poland, Lithuania) or predominantly Lutheran countries (East Germany, Estonia). Moreover, Romanians, having themselves been oppressed in the past by Ottoman Turks and Magyars, had developed an intense nationalism of their own, intolerant all too often of their own ethnic minorities – Hungarians, Jews, Gypsies. Romania, after World War I, had taken Transylvania from the defunct Austro-Hungarian Empire. The "Old Kingdom" was thereby much enlarged. However, Romania's original core had been the most backward part of Greater Romania – as if Italy had been unified by the Bourbon Kingdom of the South rather than by Savoy. Not surprisingly, Romania faced a host of troubles at the best of times.

During the 1980s, Romania's condition enormously worsened, in part owing to the megalomania of Ceauşescu and his wife.[27] Their lust for glory was insatiable. Ceauşescu was exalted as the supreme leader, the supreme military commander, the supreme hero of the working class. He was also the supreme builder (responsible for countless construction projects, gigantic, yet shoddy); he was the supreme theoretician (having published 30 volumes concerning Romania on the "Way of Building Up the Multi-laterally Developed Socialist Society" – thus his entry in the *International Who's Who*. Ceauşescu's spouse Elena matched her husband's delusion of grandeur; she considered herself as Romania's liberator, Mother and leading woman scientist – an amalgam of Joan of Arc, Mother Teresa, and Marie Curie. (Elena had in fact never finished grade school.) Between them, the Ceauşescus and their host of hangers-on wrecked the economy; worse still, Ceauşescu formulated plans for wiping out Romania's tradi-tional villages and transferring their people to agro-towns – Cambodia's man-made catastrophe in reverse.

In the end the Romanian regime collapsed. Gorbachev's reforms in the Soviet Union and the revolutions in Eastern Europe left Ceauşescu isolated; he could no longer claim to be defending Romania's independence against Soviet ambition at a time when Soviet intervention no longer seemed credible. The mass of the population was totally alienated from the regime; there was widespread discontent even within the ruling party and the armed forces. The spark of revolt was supplied by rioting in the town of Timişoara, where Hungarians joined with Romanians. Fighting spread; on December 22 1989, the Ceauşescus fled the capital. They were shortly thereafter caught, summarily tried, and shot on Christmas Day.

The role of the Soviet Union remains obscure in these events, especially that of the KGB. So does the part played by rivalries within the ruling party for whose leadership Ceauşescu had clearly become a liability. What is clear is that the National Salvation Front seized power after bitter fighting against the Securitate. Thereafter Petre Roman, the provisional prime minister, and son of a veteran communist, announced a new program designed to assure "an historic transition of unprecedented scope, namely the transition from a super-centralized economy to a market economy."[28] The Front's leaders comprised many former communists who had held high office under Ceauşescu but who now professed to be model demo-crats. In 1990, at general elections held in May, the National Salvation Front gained a decisive victory, although there was widespread talk of electoral fraud, with corruption, brutality, new strikes and further unrest thereafter. In theory Romania henceforth also stood committed to reform; in practice former communist chieftains continued to play a a leading role. The new Romania therefore found it hard to shed the evils of the old – authoritarianism, obscurantism, and ethnic intolerance tempered by cor-ruption. But at least the horrors of the Ceauşescu regime were over.

Neighboring Bulgaria, by contrast to Romania, had always been loyal to the Warsaw Pact; Bulgarians had traditionally felt gratitude for Russia's historic role in liberating their country from the Turkish yoke. The

Bulgarian communists had ruled with great harshness; the methods of Bulgaria's secret police differed in no wise from those of the Securitate. But the Bulgarian communists had shown greater ability. (For instance, more resources had been devoted to agriculture in Bulgaria than in Romania; the Bulgarian communists, moreover, showed greater caution in the face of the approaching storm than Ceauşescu.) In October 1990 the Bulgarian communists agreed to far-reaching reforms; on November 10, hard-line president Todor Zhivkov resigned; the communists then began talks with the Union of Democratic Forces, and thereafter the communist party endorsed a multi-party democracy, and changed its name to the Bulgarian Socialist Party. In Bulgaria, as in Romania, former communists retained considerable power; but the communists' monopoly of power had been broken. Their position further declined as Zhelyu Zhelev, an advocate of private enterprise, leader of the Union of Democratic Forces, was appointed head of state in 1990.

Yugoslavia, by contrast, had not formed part of the Warsaw Pact; Yugoslav communism had not been imposed by Soviet bayonets. Marshal

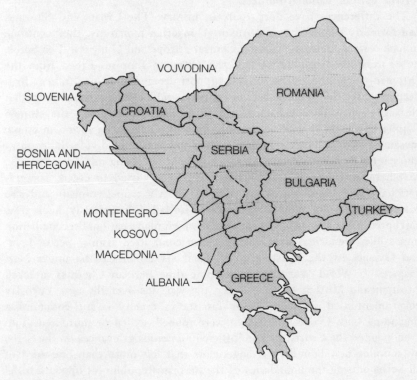

*Figure 5.1* The Balkan area.

Josip Broz Tito had broken from the Soviet connection and ruled mainly by force over a multinational state – "the last of the Hapsburgs," as British historian A. J. P. Taylor called him in a half-joking fashion. Unfortunately Taylor was mistaken. Yugoslavia was indeed a multinational state, like Austro-Hungary; but none of its rulers managed to create an all-embracing Yugoslav identity that would transcend the national divisions, especially between Serbs and Croats. The communist party and the Yugoslav army attempted to serve as transnational institutions; neither of them succeeded. This was a tragedy, for, despite their mutual hatred, Serbs and Croats have much in common. Their ethnic origins are similar; they speak what is essentially the same language, a tongue divided into several dialects and different alphabets. There are religious divisions – the Serbs are mainly, though not wholly, Greek Orthodox; the Croats are primarily Roman Catholics; and Yugoslavia also contains a substantial Muslim minority, part Albanian, part Slavic in origin. But again, the Serbo-Croat dispute does not mainly hinge on religion. In Yugoslavia, as in Northern Ireland, it is not the most devoted church-goers who provide the bulk of volunteers for the various national militias.

The differences have deep roots in history. The Croats and Slovenes had formerly belonged to the Austro-Hungarian monarchy; they continue to look toward German-speaking Central Europe and Hungary. The Serbs, by contrast, had formed part of the Ottoman Empire. Freed from the Ottoman yoke, the Serbs sought support from Russia or France. In a deeper sense, the division between Croats and Serbs corresponds to that cleavage which once separated the Byzantine Greek from the Roman Empire. To make matters even more difficult, Yugoslavia forms an ethnic mosaic of extraordinary complexity. It is impossible to divide the country into nationally homogeneous provinces without uprooting millions of people. Marshal Tito (himself half Slovene, half Croat) tried to create a supranational state based on the principles of Marxism-Leninism and the partisan tradition of World War II. But Tito failed disastrously; his regime corrupted Yugoslav society to an extent which made national reconciliation impossible. Genocidal atrocities had been committed against Serbs, Jews, and Gypsies by the Quisling government set up in Croatia under Nazi auspices in World War II. At the same time Serbian Chetniks attacked Croatian and Muslim villages. When the war was over the new Yugoslav government vied with the Croat fascists in cruelty – anti-communists (including both Croats and Serbs) were robbed, exiled or murdered. Tito even angered the Croats; he also inflicted numerous grievances on the Serbs by complex new boundary arrangements that left more than one-third of all Serbs outside the boundaries of the Serbian Republic (as opposed to 22 percent of Croats dwelling beyond the confines of Croatia.)[29] Neither did the federal army survive as a transnational body in a way in which the "Imperial-Royal Army" had done in the former Austro-Hungarian Empire. Yugoslavia was an artificially constructed country, like Czechoslovakia: both were Wilsonian creations derived from the post-World War I settlement, and both collapsed as soon as they were put under stress.

With the coming of the 1990s, the various republics increasingly began to act as sovereign states and enforced trade restrictions against one another. In 1991 Slovenia formally seceded. Croatia followed suit. There was no adequate provision for minority rights or boundary revisions, even though under the terms of the treaty of St Germain-en-Laye of 1919, the founding document of the Yugoslav state, major disputes should have been submitted to international adjudication. The Serbs, bitterly conscious of the massive atrocities against them in Croatia during World War II, insisted that if Croatia were to go its own way, it must modify its existing boundaries and cede to Serbia those districts mainly inhabited by Serbs. Croatia insisted on retaining the existing boundaries; the Serbs replied that these had been arbitrarily drawn by the former Tito regime, that they deliberately put Serbs at a disadvantage, and should therefore be revised. Neither Croats nor Bosnian Muslims would accept this contention. In 1991 bitter fighting broke out; the conflict arrayed the Yugoslav federal army, now in truth a Serbian force, as well as Serbian guerrillas, against the Croats.

The Serbo-Croat war in turn worsened all other ethnic quarrels in every republic. Thus in 1991 Macedonia, another republic, declared its independence, thereby reawakening new hostilities. (Bulgaria had long-standing claims to the region; Greece had concerns that a sovereign Macedonia would regard Greek Macedonia as a *terra irredenta*.) Toward the end of 1991, Bosnia-Hercegovina declared its independence, thereby adding further fuel to the fire. (The country was divided into Muslim, Croat, and Serb groups, territorially intermingled, sometimes intermarried.) Bosnia was an artificial state; its citizens lacked a common loyalty; neither Croats nor Serbians wished to live under Muslim-dominated governance. Serbia again backed local Serbian insurrectionaries, insisting that Serbian minority groups should be allowed to join a Greater Serbia. Serbia and Montenegro in 1992 formed a Yugoslav rump state; Serbian president Slobodan Milosevic, a former communist turned ardent nationalist, switched from war to negotiations. The UN agreed to send 14,000 "peacekeeping" troops to the troubled region (stationed mainly in Yugoslavia, but with their headquarters in Sarajevo, capital of Bosnia). By 1992 the outlook as yet remained grim. By the end of the year Croats and Serbs apparently agreed to divide Bosnia at the Muslims' expense; but "ethnic cleansing" continued, as Serbs (and to a lesser extent Croats) murderously expelled minorities from disputed territories occupied by their respective armed forces. Civil strife had done great physical damage, worsened all problems connected with ridding the stricken lands of their communist heritage, and further embittered relations between ethnic communities that were hostile and yet akin. Only one thing was certain – the old Yugoslavia would never be put together again. Yugoslav integralism (aimed at uniting all Southern Slavs under one flag) had become a lost cause, no matter whether represented by kings or commissars.

In theory, the various republics should be able to cooperate, for they have much in common culturally, and have a common stake in a wider market. In practice, they were split by bitter historical memories that seemingly live forever. For a time Europe itself was divided over the Yugoslav imbroglio in a manner that faintly recalled the battle lines of World War I. Germany, Austria, Hungary (the former "Central Powers") sympathized with the Croats. (Indeed, Germany's unilateral recognition of Croatia, without any provision for possible boundary revision, helped to fuel conflict.) By contrast, Russia sympathized with the Serbs. (Twenty-five million Russians lived outside Russia's borders, reduced to minority status in former Soviet republics adjacent to Russia; hence Moscow naturally supported Belgrade.) France, Britain, and Spain (hostile respectively to Breton, Northern Irish Catholic, and Basque separatists) initially sympathized with the Yugoslav federal government. Worse still, conflict might as yet spread if Serbia were to invade Macedonia. In 1993 the EC and US attempted to put an end to the fighting by threatening massive intervention in Bosnia, and by attempting to impose a compromise by which Bosnia would be divided into 10 autonomous regions – a patchwork plan certain not to work in practice. However, there was one small consolation. Albania, under one of the most oppressive communist regimes, was also affected by the breakdown of communism in Yugoslavia.[30] The communist party weakened; mosques re-opened; beards – offensive to the militant secularists – were legalized. And in 1991 Fatos Nano, the new prime minister, announced a program for transforming the country's socialist system into a free market system. The last of the dominos had fallen.

To summarize, scholars such as J. F. Brown, Charles Gati, William E. Griffith, and Richard F. Staar have explained the revolution in Eastern Europe as the result of several factors: the loss of political legitimacy of communist ruling parties, and the economic deterioration of the Soviet Union and its allies. Western academic opinion had widely held that "fat" communists were easier to handle than "lean" communists, that the West should therefore seek to improve the communists' economic position so as to make them more amenable to compromise. In practice, however, the economic decline of the Soviet Union benefited the West by weakening the Soviets politically. Equally important was Gorbachev's withdrawal of support for the other Warsaw Pact governments, a resolve likewise linked to the Soviet Union's ongoing economic troubles. Moreover, the accelerating domestic crises in the Soviet Union made it difficult for it to compete with the US arms buildup, or to continue to dominate Eastern Europe. Armed intervention might have destroyed the Soviet Union itself. Once Gorbachev decided he would not intervene, the local communist rulers weakened, and their political legitimacy was undermined.[31]

The triumph over communism in East-Central Europe was quickly followed by disillusionment. The collapse of communism was followed by severe economic crises, political instability, and unanticipated pangs of readjustment. Forty-five years of socialism had produced a situation unparalleled in history. The investments made in industry and agriculture over this period were already obsolescent, in most cases, at the time they were made. The infrastructure was in decay; labor demoralized. There were great differences between the various communist countries, and also within the borders of the same country: hence there was no single road to recovery. Much depended on the historical conditions and cultural heritage specific to each of the formerly subject nations, assets which no statistician can quantify. But overall there was a decline in material well-being before the benefits of democracy could be realized. Hence, ethnic nationalists provoked war in the former Yugoslavia, and occasioned the peaceful dismemberment of Czechoslovakia.

The new states all face almost insurmountable problems. Communism has disappeared, but communists have stayed on, many of them in leading positions in the state and the economy. The Third Reich was destroyed by outside force, followed by a clean sweep; in the formerly communist countries, by contrast, numerous communists cooperated in the transformation of the former regimes, or at any rate pretended to do so. The "velvet revolutions" left all too many former bosses well provided – to the disgust of innumerable dissidents who had languished in jail. No planner, no statesman moreover, found a method of painless replacing "real existing socialism" by a market economy. The member states of the former Warsaw Pact had possessed centrally owned and planned economies; they were also linked to the Council for Mutual Economic Assistance (CMEA). CMEA aimed to ensure Soviet domination of the region, separate the members of CMEA from the West's economy, and supply goods and raw materials to the Soviet Union. No balanced, diversified economies were allowed to develop; rather, each state was assigned a particular economic role to benefit the Soviet Union. CMEA failed and left the members poor and without significant bilateral trade links with the West.

The need for reform is evident but the strategy to follow from socialism to free enterprise is problematic. The requirements for a market economy are many: political authority to force reforms, support of citizens for these reforms, structural changes in the economy. These include an end of price controls and subsidies; a policy designed to let the market allocate prices, a return on capital, and wages; privatization, and a vigorous program for rebuilding the infrastructure. New systems of law, accounting, communications and regulation will have to be developed, as well as an effective welfare system, a valid tax structure and honest auditing. There is much disagreement on how to make all these changes – by shock therapy or by slow evolution. There are arguments over the pace of price reform and privatization. There is no consensus on what role the West should pay in restructuring the former communist bloc. The IMF and the World Bank are important players, but both institutions have met with severe criticism on the ground that their respective policy-makers do not fully comprehend the differences between the ex-communist states. Only one thing is certain: large-scale Western aid is not likely to be forthcoming in future; the ex-communist countries need to earn dollars, yen, and D-Marks by selling to the West; the Western countries can best aid the former communist states by lowering trade barriers. Other troubles bedevilling the former Warsaw Pact members concern military and security affairs. The Warsaw Pact broke up on February 25, 1991, but no one is quite sure what to put into its place. Refugees from East-Central Europe are a problem for the EC, especially for Germany. Reforms in most East-Central European countries have proceeded at varying speeds – but at least change is under way. The way to the future is no longer the way to nowhere.

## AFTER THE REVOLUTION

By the first half of 1990, the first phase of the great revolution had largely run its course. The revolution entailed the breakdown of the Soviet empire in East-Central Europe – a generation after the demise of the Western European empires overseas. Like the British rulers of empire, the Soviets had lost faith in their own mission, and also in the belief that empire was essential for security abroad and prosperity at home. An army of empire-builders – policemen, military advisers, propagandists, political and economic advisers – now had to look for alternative employment. The certainties of Marxism-Leninism, with its faith in "irreversible progress," ceased to be acceptable.

The Soviet hegemony was over. But the millennium expected earlier by so many militant opponents of communism did not materialize. Eastern and Central Europe continued to suffer from, bitter national hostilities, and from dislike of immigrants seen as competitors for jobs, housing, and social services. Everywhere there were long-standing hatreds against members of the former *nomenklatura*, the secret police, and the army of informers that had made life a misery in the past. There were new antipathies between jobless workers and demobilized soldiers, jobless party functionaries and intellectuals on the one hand, and workers in employment on the other, as well as the new class of independent businessmen and self-employed artisans.[32] There was widespread distrust of politicians – no matter which party they supported. There was a great deal of political fragmentation, particularly in Poland where democratic reform was impeded by a multiplicity of weak parties. As Adam Michnik, a hero of the Polish liberation struggle, put it, the real danger henceforth derived not so much from communism but from "a combination of chauvinism, xenophobia, populism, and authoritarianism, all of them connected with a sense of frustration typical of great social upheavals."[33]

Nevertheless, few Europeans wanted the Old Order to return – not even the communists who henceforth changed their propaganda, programs, and prognoses. All over Eastern and Central Europe, small entrepreneurs once more set up shop: – butchers, tailors, mechanics, builders, electricians went into private business. Indeed, Marx's predictions might be reversed – it was the petty bourgeoisie that turned out to be the rising class. Henceforth all Eastern and Central European countries emphasized their links to the West. The German word *Mitteleuropa* regained its popularity, as the proponents of *Mitteleuropa* forgot its past unsavory connection with German imperialism during the Wilhelminian era. Freedom from Soviet domination was henceforth equated with a market economy. Thus at a meeting of the Conference on Security and Cooperation in Europe (CSCE), representing the US and Canada, the Soviet Union, and all European countries except Albania, the participants approved of a document which recognized the links between a pluralistic democracy and free enterprise.

The Eastern European revolutions moreover profoundly affected the USSR. When the communist dictatorships began to crumble in Eastern Europe, conventional wisdom still asserted that the USSR could stay aloof. After all, the revolution itself had not been imposed from outside; it had lasted longer and supposedly had deeper roots. Nevertheless, the USSR was shaken. As Stephen Sestanovitch, a leading expert, put it, in the brief period from the winter of 1989 to the following spring, the Soviet communists traveled almost the entire route that Poland had traveled from 1981, when General Wojciech Jaruzelski had imposed martial law, to 1989, when he had begun talks with Solidarity.[34] Indeed, the Soviet Union was in even greater trouble than Poland, for communist tyranny had lasted much longer there and had been even more destructive. (There were few Russians who had not lost at least one member of their extended family during the Stalin terror and its aftermath.) The breakdown of Marxism-Leninism also raised anew the "national question," as Soviet troops intervened in Azerbaijan. The Baltic states formally declared independence, and ethnic Russians once more proclaimed their allegiance to a separate Russian nation. In a military sense, the Soviet Union for the time being remained a superpower; in a political sense, the USSR's long-term survival seemed even more questionable than it had been 20 years ago.[35]

Most important of all had been the religious or pseudo-religious dimension of communism. The true believers of olden times had regarded the party as a new mortal god, for all practical purposes all-wise, all-good, and all-powerful. By 1990, there were few such faithful left outside old-age homes and lunatic asylums. The builders of communism had seen their venture as a heroic task; the party would be like Prometheus, who stole fire from the gods. Half a century ago, communism had still produced heroes; the volunteers who had fought in the International Brigades in Spain had genuinely risked their lives for socialism. By the end of the 1980s, this faith had largely evaporated. Everywhere, the end of communism was supremely unheroic. Leading cadres denounced their party's past; communist hangers-on changed their respective resumés. The heirs of Prometheus now sued for their pension rights; communism had ceased to be a living faith. Contrary to all Marxist forecasts, it was the traditional religions that survived.[36]

There was also an end to Marxism-Leninism as a self-professed science. As Marx put it, bourgeois historians had already elucidated the role of economics and of class struggles in history. Marx's own originality, he believed, consisted in his scientific demonstration that capitalism must inevitably lead to socialism, and that socialism would bring communist prosperity. Obviously, this had not happened in any socialist country. Why? Marxist-Leninists henceforth put the blame on "Stalinist deformation." It was not a satisfactory argument from the Marxist-Leninists' own perspective. If one wicked man or a clique of wicked men can change a social system and thereby throw history off its course, what becomes of Marx's materialist interpretation of history? And why were Marxist-Leninists unable to predict their own system's impending demise?

Marxism-Leninism survived in Europe – but only as a minority creed. All over Central and Eastern Europe, and thereafter all over the Soviet Union, red stars came down from public buildings; statues of Lenin disappeared from public squares; street names were changed; the vocabulary of politics changed with almost incomprehensible speed. But the economic consequences of Marxism-Leninism could not be eliminated so easily. In every instance, socialist countries at a comparable level of social development at the time of the communists" takeover had fared much,

much worse than adjacent countries under capitalism. Czechoslovakia by 1989 was much less prosperous or economically developed than Austria, North Korea than South Korea. East Germany in particular had been turned into Germany's equivalent of the Italian *Mezzogiorno* ("backward south"). To be fair, not all problems of industrial decay were of communist making. The 1970s and 1980s had seen "rust belt" decline in cities as far afield as Belfast, Glasgow, Essen, Lille, and Namur in Western Europe, where traditional industries could no longer compete on the world market. But the communist regimes turned out to have been particularly mendacious in their promises, unresponsive in adjusting to change, uncreative in the development of new industries and novel services. Everywhere the defunct communist governments left behind antiquated factories, ill-managed farms, buildings in disrepair, railway tracks and rolling stock poorly maintained. There were horrendous ecological problems; many of the nuclear power installations, for example, were disasters waiting to happen. There was no parallel in economic history for the predicament which faced the former communist countries. The bulk of the huge capital investment made in industrial and agricultural enterprises turned out to be out-dated; the labor force suffered from poor morale and, frequently, from lack of adequate training. Military hardware apart, the great majority of the merchandise produced in the formerly socialist countries could not compete on the world markets. *Wiso* (*wissenschaftlicher Sozialismus, Scientific Socialism*) – turned out to be history's greatest consumer fraud, and the world's biggest environmental disaster.

More daunting still were the problems of a psychological kind. Who had truly been responsible for the failures of the past? What should happen to those who had participated in political murders, torture, executions? The communist cadres got off lightly – much more so than the Nazi cadres after World War II. There was no clean sweep, as there had been in Germany and Italy after World War II; perhaps the "velvet revolutions" were too velvety. In countries as far afield as Serbia, Poland, Ukraine, Romania, former communist bosses entered politics as reborn democrats. At the same time former cadres used their political connections and organizational skills to become successful capitalists or to halt reforms. The communists certainly had little to complain about any retribution they might receive when a reckoning is made of the total number of people robbed, exiled, jailed, or killed under their auspices. But then ordinary people too found themselves under a cloud of suspicion. Had the ordinary citizens really all been innocent victims? After all, all communist regimes had depended on a great army of informers, average citizens who had been willing to profit themselves or to avenge private wrongs by denouncing their real or assumed enemies to the secret police. As an East German taxi driver bitterly put it, the DDR (*Deutsche Demokratische Republik*, "German Democratic Republic") should really have been known as *Deutsche Denunziantenrepublik* ("German Stool Pigeons' Republic"). How would former supporters of the regime explain their past political conduct to their own children? What of the sense of betrayal experienced by genuine idealists?

Then there were the political problems of establishing parliamentary regimes in countries such as Romania and Hungary which had suffered from repressive governments even before the communists had taken power. The communists turned out to be even more brutal than their predecessors. Having gained power, the communist elites treated their subjects as minors. (The German phrase is *unmündig*: "incompetent to speak.") The new ruling parties endeavored to organize every aspect of life – not just politics, but also culture, recreation – nothing was to escape the party's guidance. For more than 50 years, the rulers and subjects alike had become accustomed to "double speak" – a public truth and a private truth. As Václav Havel put it in his 1990 New Year's address as president, "we are all morally sick, because we all got used to saying one thing and thinking another." Havel was fortunately not quite right – there were a few courageous men and women like himself who never bent the knee to Baal – but how many other Czechs, Poles, East Germans, Romanians could claim as much?

A market economy would be equally hard to reconstruct. The old order had worked – after a fashion. The Soviet Union and its Warsaw Pact allies had formed a protected enclave whose members traded with one another, without having to meet world standards. As least on paper, workers had a right to guaranteed jobs and social services; good might often be unavailable in stores, but at least on paper their prices were controlled. Reconstruction entails profound institutional changes. Under socialism, the ordinary citizen had been like an enlisted man or a non-commissioned officer in a great army of labor; in a free economy, some of this army of labor would be demobilized because they were unproductive. The means of production – farms, factories, and their like – would have to become efficient and privatized; the state would cease to own and finance major enterprises; banks would have to expand their functions. The liberated countries would need, above all, a stable currency. They would have to reconstruct a private banking system and a free financial market, with new institutions such as a stock exchange. Claims for compensation from former owners would have to be settled.

The pangs of transition were great. Appearances notwithstanding, the state machinery in the formerly socialist countries had been weak: only the military, the ruling party and security services had been well organized. The creation of a market economy required, not a weak, but a strong state – an efficient tax system, an efficient legal system, efficient social services capable of providing a "safety net" for the poor. In addition, the formerly socialist states needed that huge network of employers' organizations, labor unions, trade associations, and other lobbies that permit a democratic state to function. The problems seemed countless. For instance, the closing down of uneconomic enterprises would entail both an immediate decline in national production and heavy unemployment. There would be a great "overhang" of savings accumulated by ordinary citizens at a time when there was little to buy in the shops. The termination of state subsidies would cause a rapid rise in the price of food, housing, transport, and other services. (For example, in Czechoslovakia, during the first quarter of 1991 alone, industrial output declined by 12 percent, while consumer prices rose by 40 percent.)[37] Complex property claims would have to be settled. New legal codes would have to be put into operation. The tax system would have to be reformed. National currencies would have to be made internationally convertible. Government financing of specific economic enterprises would have to end. Central planning would have to be abandoned, state ownership reduced, and economic decisions left to the operation of the market place. The state would have to create a host of new social services to cope with unemployment, and to retrain workers with obsolescent skills. Monopolies would have to end – no matter whether public or private. Central and Eastern Europe would once more have to link fully to the economies of Western Europe, indeed the world economy at large.[38]

On the face of it, such efforts would daunt a Hercules. For more than half a century, the population had been asked to make sacrifices for a golden future somewhere beyond the horizon. Now the sacrifices would begin again. Except in Czechoslovakia, the state had played a major part in the economies of all East-Central European states even before the communist seizure of power. Afterwards, the new ruling parties went one better and controlled all "commanding heights of the economy." Private entrepreneurs had been wiped out or driven underground. In so far as the official economy functioned at all, it did so because it was sustained by a huge "Second Economy" in which buyers and sellers, suppliers and clients alike, operated in a chiaroscuro of sanctioned illegality. There were entrepreneurs aplenty; but they too depended of necessity on protection; there was to their enterprise the element of gambling on the football pools – hardly a prescription for turning out a vigorous, self-respecting bourgeoisie.

There were also complex administrative issues. Despite their self-proclaimed efficiency, the communist-ruled states had been sketchily organized; even in East Germany only the ruling SED (Socialist Unity Party) and the State Security Service had been efficiently run. But in the end, even these bodies had lost their cohesion; the party cadres' morale had begun to falter, as leading communists tried to steer away their own children from party careers, with their boredom and their dangers, and encouraged them rather to go into the academic progessions, the arts, or careers in science. Now the entire administration would have to be recast, the laws revised, including the inadequate and distorted administrative codes. The ruling parties had created for themselves huge and interlocking financial empires. Was it now not just for the expropriators in turn to be expropriated?

Even these were minor questions compared to property relations in general. Most of the farms, mines, factories – even most small-scale enterprises – had been forcibly transferred to state ownership. There was no precedent in history for dismantling a socialist state or for compensating former owners. Few academicians or investigative journalists had even considered such matters, for socialism was supposedly irreversible. Not surprisingly, the post-revolutionary investment climate was full of uncertainties, with claims, counter-claims, and mutual recriminations. Bonn took over the public trust agency, the *Treuhandanstalt* or "Treuhand," set up by the GRR's reforming prime minister Hans Modrow in 1990 to deal with the situation in East Germany. But its task proved awesome. So did the job of reorganizing the East German bureaucracy, huge, costly and inefficient. (Whereas the various ministries in Bonn in 1990 only employed about 25,000 civil servants and other salaried personnel, the various ministries and agencies in East Berlin alone had 220,000 men and women on their respective payrolls.)

How far could indigenous capitalism be reconstructed? Leftist theoreticians had for long asserted that the process of socializing the means of production was irreversible. This contention proved wrong. Every communist-ruled country had possessed a large underground economy; there were concealed private holdings of gold, hard currency, and other assets. There was some entrepreneurial skill: there were plenty of people willing to save, to start afresh, and to go on accumulating capital. In a city such as Dresden in eastern Germany, private shops and sales booths reappeared as if by magic. They were run by small merchants willing to sell anything from ladies' underwear to second-hand trucks; or by technicians able to repair shoes, bikes, refrigerators, whatever. Advertising posters came back; color once more returned to Dresden's formerly grey and depressing townscape. The return of capitalism, however, also created unfortunate political problems. The communists mostly lost political power, but the former *nomenklatura* still ran industries and state businesses, still had political connections; some had technical expertise and knowhow. There remained communist networks (*Seilschaften*, in East German parlance – groups of people willing to pull the same rope); a good many communists thus made money in private enterprise and created what might be called a new form of *nomenklatura* capitalism. Not surprisingly, success aroused immense popular hostility.

As of late 1992, the economies of all former East Bloc states remained inefficient, with too many workers producing shoddy goods with obsolete technology. These economies had only been able to produce goods for CMEA; they could not compete in the world market. Most communist-run plants and collectives needed to be closed down; others needed to be modernized and run by fewer workers. At issue was the speed with which this transformation should be brought about. According to reformers such as Thomas Moore, senior fellow at the Hoover Institution, the answer was "privatize now or fail later."[39] This analysis was criticized by scholars such as Hans Peter Widmaier, a German economist, who pleaded for a slower and more circumspect approach. Privatization, argued Widmaier, may be desirable, but privatization in and of itself does not necessarily produce new capital in a poverty-stricken land. Privatization does not necessarily improve management methods in a country where inefficiency is rife. To integrate the formerly socialist economies into the world economy at one fell swoop is enormously difficult, since none of these economies can compete on a global market. Transitional arrangements may therefore be necessary, depending on the local situation.

No matter what approach they adopted, the successor governments all found the going hard. All too many entrenched lobbies resisted reform. These included high-ranking communist bureaucrats who had managed to adjust to the new situation and henceforth passed for militant nationalists. Many worker councils resisted reform. Government ownership had usually led to overstaffing and low incentives; and worker-managed firms are seldom efficient – they favor immediate benefits for the worker over investment or sales, and therefore inflate wages. In communist-ruled societies, the state and the party owned from 80 to 100 percent of the modes of production and business assets. To transform these systems would be difficult, and the West could do little to help until structural reforms were in place, and privatization had been substantial. Technical advice can help; loans to the private sector can stimulate the economy somewhat. But the best medicine for the East is trade, not aid. If the EC and the US would lower or eliminate trade barriers to Eastern Europe's products (computers, steel, textiles, agriculture), progress would be possible.

The ex-communist members of the Warsaw Pact faced similar problems in this period of transition to capitalism. Property rights were not well defined. Workers, managers and communist party members acted as if they, not the state, owned the property.[40] Poland and Hungary began to give management functions to worker councils; but these councils were neither efficient nor productive. Previous ownership claims were another problem for the states that fell to the Soviets after World War II. Reprivatization would not be easy and would slow up investment. Who wants to invest in a contested piece of property? (Only in eastern Germany was the problem partially solved as the all-German government assumed responsibility for future claims over ownership.) Everywhere (except in eastern Germany) privatization affected at first only small firms. Without a proper capital market, who could buy large firms? The public had few assets, and selling to foreigners created political difficulties. How to evaluate assets was yet another nightmare. Voucher schemes were developed to let citizens buy shares in enterprises, but this too raised problems, especially from employees of the firms that opposed privatization and sales except to themselves. In Poland and Hungary, many workers resisted privatization and claimed that they should run the firms themselves.[41] Fortunately, there were some differences in this pattern among former East Bloc countries. The rate of privatization varied greatly. As a rough and ready generalization, the states once belonging to the Austro-Hungarian monarchy did comparatively well – the Czech Republic, Hungary, Slovenia, also Poland – whereas Romania and Serbia fared ill. Hungary, for instance, looked to privatize 2,500 firms a year, but the State Property Agency faced internal opposition. Nevertheless, there was progress, and by 1993 Hungary had become the largest recipient of direct foreign investment in East-Central Europe (followed by the Czech republic). Poland went farthest toward a market economy; it abolished most price controls, freed the private sector, and cut government subsidies. High inflation and unemployment widely slowed reforms; but, the Polish budget was in surplus, and there was a large currency trade balance for 1992. The Polish state still owned a substantial portion of the economy, but private enterprise made substantial advances in retailing and service industries. Big firms were as yet heavily overstaffed, and the agricultural sector needed to lose a large percentage of its workers, leading to higher unemployment rates as privatization expanded. The government, however, paid too much in unemployment benefits; the need to print money to pay for them threatened even higher inflation. In Czechoslovakia the task was equally hard. Within the newly separated Czech Republic the market reformist notions of finance minister Václav Klaus prevailed over those favoring a slow pace of transformation. Klaus's task was particularly hard. Prices had been rigidly controlled until the beginning of 1991; a large variety of consumer products had been subsidized; two-fifths of Czechoslovakia's exports had gone to the former Soviet Union; hence new markets would have to be found at a time of economic disruption. But Klaus pushed ahead. A voucher system was devised to sell off companies to private citizens (an arrangement poorly understood by the ill-educated, who did not grasp the system and felt left out). Small shops and businesses multiplied. By the end of 1992 the Czech republic seemed on the road to slow recovery, whereas that of Slovakia limped behind, as in pre-communist days.

The role of the foreign investor was also controversial. In prewar Central and Eastern Europe it had not only been the communists who had distrusted foreign lenders. In fact, nationalists of every stripe had looked with disdain or fear at those who supposedly promoted the "alienation" of national wealth. By the 1990s, when capital was scarce even in the developed world, such attitudes in particular had to change. Interestingly enough, it was Romania, politically still the most authoritarian country, which went farthest in favoring foreigners. In 1991 a new investment law permitted foreign investors to hold 100 percent equity in Romanian enterprises, to acquire a stake in existing companies, to acquire new ones, and to repatriate profits in hard currencies.[42] In addition, tax on profits was waived for five years – a concession regarded as unwise by those economists who considered that no privileges should be made available to foreign entrepreneurs which were not equally available to local entrepreneurs.

Finally, there was the role of the intellectuals. Winston Churchill, himself a writer of distinction, later described his own part during the desperate year 1940 with uncharacteristic modesty: it had been the British people who had been the lion; he himself had merely supplied the roar. This was not the way in which the bulk of intellectuals envisaged their part in the revolution of 1989. "The politics of the revolution were not made by workers or peasants. They were made by intellectuals."[43] On the face of it, Timothy Garton Ash had plenty of justification for this generalization. The list of revolutionary leaders reads like an extract from an authors' and artists' *Who's Who*: the playwright Václav Havel in Czechoslovakia, the editor Tadeusz Mazowiecki in Poland, the conductor Kurt Masur in East Germany, the philosopher János Kis in Hungary, the communist engineer Petre Roman in Romania. But for all their distinction, these intellectuals would have counted for nothing had the communist regimes not been hated by the great mass of the people. It was the people who had disbelieved their own government's propaganda and tuned in to Western radio and TV stations. They had resisted communist indoctrination; they had sabotaged official plans by working to rule, by going absent without leave, by turning a blind eye to infractions at work, by fiddling on the black market. Unlike the intellectuals, these anonymous citizens had lacked access to the international media; but it was the man and the woman in the factory, the office, the home, who had caused communism to die the death of a thousand cuts.

The intellectuals' role of course had been ambivalent, perhaps even more so than the role of non-intellectuals. Some writers, novelists, poets, journalists and churchmen had resisted heroically; but many more had made their peace with the regime, and profited from those petty privileges that were available to trimmers. The left-wing intellectuals faced additional problems. They said they would avoid alike the ills of unreconstructed Marxism-Leninism and of "Wild West capitalism *à l'américaine*;" instead they would take as their model humanitarian countries such as Finland, Austria, or especially Sweden. But the problems stemming from the Swedish model were overlooked. Sweden had developed a great welfare state on the foundations of private enterprise. The farms and the factories were privately owned; only about 5 percent of the means of production were in state ownership. Sweden was a monarchy; Sweden had an old established patriciate with great families such as the Wallenbergs. Sweden drew on a dual tradition of enlightened monarchy and Lutheran respect for the power and legitimacy of the state. Sweden's welfare state also entailed a huge tax burden and an overweening bureaucracy. The Swedish model would prove hard to export; in any case, the Swedes themselves were resolved to modify their own system.

Despite these and many other difficulties, the formerly captive nations managed to attain a number of striking successes, within a relatively short time. The Old Guard changed, and younger men and women stepped into positions of responsibility. Opinion differed widely on the best way of privatizing the economy, on methods of change, and their pace. But at least there was some consensus; very few East Europeans wanted to return to "scientific socialism." Poland was a particularly striking example. By January 1, 1990, most prices were already freed. A host of new shops and stores opened for business; there was a striking improvement in the quality of services rendered and of merchandise sold. Polish cities began to alter in appearance as private enterprise gained in vigor. Government mono- polies largely disappeared. (By 1991 only the railway and the post office remained monopolies.) Poland, like Czechoslovakia, attained a budget surplus, as subsidies designed to shore up prices for designated merchan- dise rapidly declined in value. Taxation was reduced, from a maximum of 85 percent in the private sector to 40 percent, somewhat less than in Sweden. Budgetary expenditure rapidly declined as a proportion of the gross domestic product.

Not that success came easily. Poles suffered bitterly from electoral apathy, unemployment, and inflation. In Poland, as in the rest of Eastern and Central Europe, the communists renamed, reformed, and reorganized their movement. Operating as moderate parties, these successor organiza- tions would once again draw on popular resentments and disappointments.

During the 1991 elections in Poland, for example, the so-called "Left Alternative" did surprisingly well. Whereas the representatives of the Solidarity movement obtained an absolute majority, they were badly splintered. (In part, the splintered vote derived from an electoral law so permissive that even the "Friends of Beer Party" attained a few representatives in parliament.)[44]

The 1989 revolution raised once more those complex questions concerning nationalism which communism had been unable to resolve. How would the freed nations deal with one another in future? On the face of it, there were grounds for pessimism. In Romania, Hungarians and Romanians had cooperated in the original rising against Ceauşescu in 1989. But only a year later, violent conflict erupted in Transylvania between the two nationalities. The Bulgarian ex-communists promised all manner of reforms; but the Turkish minority in Bulgaria bitterly complained of discrimination. Anti-Semitism persisted, even in countries such as Poland where they were hardly any Jews left. Things were even worse in Yugoslavia (independent from the Soviet connection since Marshal Tito's days, and not part of the former Warsaw Pact), where the various nationalities moved even further apart, and by 1991 Serbs and Croats were involved in a particularly ferocious and apparently insoluble conflict.

Far from diminishing, national hostilities may actually have grown under socialism. For once the state controls all the means of production, control of the state machinery becomes for each ethnic group not merely a matter of pride, but of prosperity. The very ferocity of communist persecution heightened nationalism – for instance in Ukraine, whose people will never forget the famines and mass slaughter engineered by Stalin. Certainly, existing national antagonisms persisted under communism, and became more audible than before. (According to a recent example of black humor from Ukraine, a newly elected member of parliament wants to be recognized by the assembly's president. "I won't call on that man" says the president to himself. "He is a furious nationalist, and will probably say that all Russians should be hanged." A second deputy wishes to be heard. "I won't call on him either," thinks the president. "That man is a fierce anti-Semite and will demand that all Jews should be drowned." Finally a member of the Green Party is allowed to address the House. "Fellow citizens," he begins, "our forests are dying; our lakes are running dry. Disaster looms – and where then shall we hang the Russians, and where shall we drown the Jews?")

All too widely, nationalism in Eastern and Central Europe continued to serve as a salve for injured collective vanity, or as an alibi for national failure. One's own national group may have failed to succeed in business or politics – but look at its deep spiritual qualities, its splendid cultural legacy! This form of collective self-deception both misrepresented the present and falsified the past. Great cultural centers such as Vienna, Prague, Budapest, Vilnius had always drawn their vigor from the ethnic diversity that had distinguished them in the past. Prague had once been a German and Jewish as well as a Czech city. *Don Giovanni*, Mozart's masterpiece, had first been performed in Prague, not in Vienna. It was a dangerous piece of self-deception for Czechs to commemorate the occasion, when the real Mozart and his wife would have been expelled from the city as Germans, had they chanced to live in Prague in 1945.

Eastern Europe henceforth looked at new forms of transnational cooperation (including a long-forgotten World War II project for linking Poland to Czechoslovakia). Adhesion to a united Western Europe promised a more popular alternative. Hungary joined the Council of Europe in 1990; Czechoslovakia followed suit in 1991; all the former Warsaw Pact states looked to ultimately joining the EC. The "Alpe-Adria" group, founded in 1978 as an association of Italy, Hungary, Austria, and the former Yugoslavia, with shared regional concerns, expanded into the "Pentagonal" group with the inclusion of Czechoslovakia in 1990.

But Europe was itself a vague concept. How far did Europe stretch? Who had the right to call himself a European? What was characteristically European? Humanitarian-minded politicians such as János Kis in Hungary, Václav Havel in Czechoslovakia, looked to a European union which would transcend the bigotry of national conflict. They were opposed inside their own country by ethnic traditionalists who remained suspicious of alien influence and who identified the West with rootless cosmopolitanism. There was a division between those who looked to a free market, based on mass consumption, and traditionalists who idealized their own nations and dreaded the assumed greed, vulgarity and materialism of free enterprise.

The various nations of Eastern and Central Europe, and also those of the former Soviet Union, remained intensely suspicious of one another – Germans (especially East Germans) of Poles and Czechs, Hungarians of Romanians. The constituent parts of Yugoslavia broke asunder; but Yugoslavia's fragmentation only resulted in bloody fighting and bloody persecution, as there was no way of slicing up the country without leaving substantial minorities on the "wrong" side of the various borders. Western progressives had widely accepted that traditional politics were about to be superseded by the new politics of class, color, and gender. These forecasts proved quite mistaken. Gender played no part in the revolutions of Central and Eastern Europe; race prejudice proper was of small account, as Croats and Serbs did not argue about their respective genetic inheritance. It was the traditional divisions that remained, defined by language, religion, and nationality or historic rivalries. As the Soviet threat began to wane, internal ethnic tensions increased. Czechs and Slovaks reverted to their past disagreements, and Czechoslovakia broke up. (According to a pre-World War II joke, a citizen of the republic was either a Czech or a Slovak; if he called himself a Czechoslovak he was a Jew.) But Czechoslovakia's ethnic problems were of small importance compared to Yugoslavia's, or even Romania's, or Bulgaria's or those of Azerbaijan. There were deep internal fault lines, not only in Yugoslavia, but also in Romania and Bulgaria, where the leading ethnic group of each respective state made up only 80 percent or so of the population, with much debate concerning the size of Turkish, Hungarian, and Gypsy minorities.[45]

Above all, there were serious ethnic splits transcending neighboring countries. Hungary claimed with some justification that something between 1.5 million and 2.3 million Hungarians in Transylvania in Romania were denied civic rights. Serbia, aggrieved at the size of the Serbian minorities living outside Serbia's borders, challenged the boundaries drawn between the various provinces under Tito's regime. The Serbs, as already mentioned, took to arms and seized territory both from Croatia and Bosnia-Hercegovina for the sake of uniting as many Serbs as possible in a great Serbian homeland.[46] Serbia thereby increased the territory under its control – but at great cost. Conquest commonly entailed "ethnic cleansing," "purification," the expulsion of non-Serbs, in a misguided and cruel effort to unscramble the ethnic omelette. (Croats of course had also resorted to similar practices, as had other Balkan peoples at the height of national struggles.) Serbia, moreover, found herself diplomatically isolated. By 1992, Germany and her allies within the EC opposed Serbia. Both Russia and the US had distanced themselves from the cause of a united Yugoslavia which they had once sponsored. Serbia's allies consisted of an ill-assorted collection – the People's Republic of China, India, Indonesia, and Zimbabwe, all of them hostile to ethnic dissident movements within their own borders, but none of them able to help. Serbia's currency reserves were exhausted, inflation rampant, shop windows empty, fuel almost unobtainable. (Proclaimed Serbian ultra Vojislav Seselj, "if we Serbs can't get gas, we'll go on horseback.") When Macedonia proclaimed its independence, the Balkan puzzle became even more perilous. Serbia and Greece looked askance at the new state, whereas Bulgaria hastened to recognize Macedonia. If Serbia were to intervene in Macedonia, Bulgaria would surely resist, whilst Albanians in the Serbian province of Kossovo would be encouraged to seek union with Albania. Romania laid claim to the former Soviet republic of Moldova; Bulgaria had quarrels with Turkey and Romania – a witch's cauldron from which the US should stand strictly aloof.

However, Western Europeans could not afford to regard such problems with indifference. First of all, they had their own minorities to consider:

German-speaking Tyroleans in Italy, Basques and Catalonians in Spain, Bretons in France. More explosive still was the problem of immigrant minorities – Arabs in France; Turks in Germany; North Africans in Italy; Indians, Pakistanis, and West Indians in Britain. Their total number remains a matter of dispute, as they include permanent residents, illegal immigrants, labor migrants on contract, asylum seekers, many of whom desire to stay permanently in the land of their choice. As José Camarena Delgado, a senior staff member with the European Parliament's United Left group, put it, "with eight million legal immigrants and perhaps half again as many illegals, immigrants constitute already what some people call the Community's 13th state."[47] In the EC, as in the US, the newcomers filled many jobs that natives were reluctant to take. The migrants also benefited their respective homelands by massive remittances sent to relatives back home. But everywhere the immigrants aroused hostility, especially those from Eastern and Central Europe and the Islamic world. There was fear of *Überfremdung* (being swamped by foreigners), as the tide was expected by some to gain enormous strength in the future. (Mgr Stimpfle, the Catholic bishop of Augsburg, Germany, estimated in 1989 that 120 million newcomers might enter the EC during the next 20 or 30 years.)[48] The newcomers aroused intense fears and intense detestation, not merely among German skinheads and English "Paki-bashers," but also among respectable politicians such as Jacques Chirac, a French conservative leader. As he put it,

"The French worker sees on the landing of his crowded HLM [subsidized apartment block] a father, with four wives and a score of children, all on welfare – without working, of course," Chirac told supporters in Orleans. "Add to that the noise and the smell, and the French worker on the landing goes crazy."[49]

What would happen if economic conditions worsened and millions of Poles, Ukrainians, Russians, Romanians, Belorussians, Croats and Slovenes joined Turks, Algerians, and Pakistanis? Europe would surely be ungovernable, and existing national identities would dissolve in cosmopolitan chaos! The demise of communism, thus created a new specter that none had considered while the Iron Curtain had still been in existence.

Nevertheless, there was also hope. Freed at last from the Soviet threat, Czechs, Hungarians, and Poles all cut their respective military forces.[50] On the face of it, there was more money left for civilian expenditure. Eastern and Central Europe, even the Soviet Union, experienced much less violence than they had half a century ago. (Even Croatia and Serbia have not experienced in their new war anything like the human losses they had suffered respectively during and after World War II.) In Poland, Czechoslovakia, East Germany, and Hungary, the revolution had come with little violence. In Romania there had been fighting – but nothing as ferocious as the terror experienced in World War II. The Soviet Union witnessed bloody disturbances in republics as far afield as Georgia, Lithuania, and Armenia. But this was child's play compared with the revolution of 1917 and its aftermath. Poland, Hungary, and Czechoslovakia had become ethnically more homogeneous than they had been before World War II. But this was not the whole story. In the traditional societies of East Central Europe, social class, occupations, nationality, and religion had often coincided: Germans filled the trades in cities; Jews were village traders; Ukrainians labored on the land, and so on. Industrialization, urbanization, a common experience of communist tyranny, however, all helped to weaken these distinctions. There were also political changes. The new Germany integrated into the EC, the new Russia striving for democracy were much better neighbors than Imperial Russia and Imperial Germany had been, not to speak of the Third Reich and the Soviet empire. Within the newly liberated countries, rule by the mailed fist was at a discount. The Mazowiecki government in Poland adopted a much more humane approach toward both Jews and Germans than any previous Polish administration; similarly, the Kohl government in united Germany went out of its way to reassure the Poles. (Václav Havel's humanitarian attitude toward national minority questions was miles apart from that of Eduard Beneš, president of Czechoslovakia from 1945 to 1948. The newly liberated countries now looked West – toward the European Community.

The formerly communist-ruled countries also had other assets. The Messianic hopes of yesteryear had gone. The liberated nations were ready for a change. Overall, the formerly communist countries emerged from their servitude more urbanized and better educated in a technical sense than they had been before World War II. They no longer idealized their respective armies. The tasks before them were immense. They would have to grant civic rights to all citizens of whatever ethnic ancestry; they would – at the very least – have to create stable currencies; they would have to end all legislation against private traders, manufacturers, and farmers; they would have to rid themselves of those vulgar prejudices against middlemen, the so-called "speculators." The assignment was immense – but at least there was hope.

# 6

# Embattled Empire: From Soviet Union to CIS

Russia stood on the edge of an abyss. It seemed as if the country was boiling over from anger, envy, and resentment of every imaginable kind which until then had been kept under a lid of awe and fear. Now that the population had lost respect for the government, there was nothing to hold society together: neither civic sense nor patriotism. For it was the state that had made Russia a country, not vice versa.

(Describing Russia at the time of revolutionary outbreaks in 1904, quote from Richard Pipes, *The Russian Revolution*, New York, Vintage Books, 1991.)

The first half of the twentieth century witnessed the breakdown of three great empires. The Austro-Hungarian and Ottoman empires collapsed at the end of World War I, and the European colonial empires broke asunder after World War II. However diverse, they had ruled over a multiplicity of peoples and had relied on supranational armies not formally identified with any one ethnic community. But in the end, they all proved unable to cope with the discordant forces of nationalism. Only one great empire seemed destined to survive – the Soviet Union. Formed of 15 republics nominally equal in status, the Soviet Union made up a huge multi-ethnic conglomerate, composed of an estimated 287,015,000 people, extending over 8,849,496 square miles, two and a half times the size of the US, by far the world's largest country, with immense natural resources. Its people contained all manner of European and Asian stock. The Soviet Union's "core" state was the Russian Federated Socialist Republic, which accounted for about three-quarters of the Soviet Union's territory, two-thirds of its

GNP, and over half of its population. Table 6.1 shows the composition of the former Soviet Union.

Table 6.1 The Soviet Union, 1989

| Republic | Population (in millions) | Net output (as a percentage of each republic's contribution to the Soviet Union's net output) in 1988 |
|---|---|---|
| Russia | 148.0 | 61.1 |
| Ukraine (Ukraina) | 51.8 | 18.2 |
| Byelorussia (Belarus) | 10.3 | 4.2 |
| Lithuania | 3.7 | 1.4 |
| Latvia | 2.7 | 1.1 |
| Estonia | 1.6 | 0.64 |
| Moldavia (Moldova) | 4.4 | 1.2 |
| Georgia | 5.5 | 1.6 |
| Armenia | 3.3 | 0.9 |
| Azerbaijan | 7.1 | 1.7 |
| Kazakhstan | 16.7 | 4.3 |
| Uzbekistan | 20.3 | 3.3 |
| Tajikistan | 5.2 | 0.8 |
| Kirghizstan | 4.4 | 0.8 |
| Turkmenistan | 3.6 | 0.8 |

Source: Financial Times, August 27, 1991, p. 7

Two years later, this huge empire disintegrated. Following an unsuccessful coup by Soviet hard-liners in August 1991, central control ceased to operate effectively. In the Soviet Union, as in the remaining Warsaw Pact countries, the ruling communist party, the secret police, the military, and the military-industrial-scientific complex had worked effectively. It was they who assured the empire's cohesion. The rest of the central state machinery had been surprisingly weak, and could not therefore assure imperial cohesion, once the ruling party fractured. The same weakness beset the opposition. Of oppositional groups there had been plenty; but most of them were local in their impact; few were organized on an all-Union basis; none therefore could take over the Soviet Union as a whole, when the communist party failed.

By the end of 1991, map makers had to redraw the frontiers on existing globes and atlases. The three Baltic republics (Latvia, Lithuania, Estonia) had, in 1991, achieved independence de jure. All other republics, except Russia and Kazakhstan, declared independence de facto. (A key event in this regard was Ukraine's declaration issued on December 1, 1991, backed by an overwhelming majority of the electorate, including the ethnic Russian minority in the country.)[1] Thereafter, in December 1991, Russia,

*Figure 6.1* The Commonwealth of Independent States (CIS); at the end of 1992 Georgia was not yet a member.

Ukraine, and Belarus joined in a loosely structured Commonwealth of Independent States (CIS), with its administrative seat in Minsk. Its members would supposedly enjoy the same independence as did the members of the British Commonwealth. Unfortunately the history of the British Commonwealth gave no guidance to the new post-Soviet association, a body not likely to survive for many years. In case of war, would the members join in a common military effort, as the British dominions had done in two World Wars? Or would each of the various republics remain neutral, as India, Ghana, and other new states insisted in the new British Commonwealth?

At the time of writing (1992), the Russian Federation had taken command over its own armed forces, subject to its own defense ministry, and the CIS was a mere paper organization. The Russian Federation still maintained troops outside its own borders (including East Germany, from which the troops were gradually being withdrawn, the Baltic republics, and Moldova). General Pavel Sergeevich Grachëv, the new minister of defense, was engaged in what he called the creation of a new Russian army from nothing. When finally reorganized, the new force would number between 1.2 to 1.3 million men, much smaller than the old Soviet Army, but with a much larger professional contingent, supported, as before, by a massive industrial complex. The new force will benefit from physical consolidation within a much smaller land mass than the old Soviet Union, and from ethnic homogeneity, as the non-Russian ethnic component will largely disappear. R & D expenditure, as a percentage of military expenditure as a whole, has increased. According to General Grachëv, Russia's sphere of interest includes all former Soviet republics on Russia's land borders; hence the military claim the right to intervene if any of these states – the three Baltic republics, Ukraine, Belarus, Azerbaijan, Georgia, and Kazakhstan – are threatened.[2] The Russian military establishment has a number of allies among the former Soviet republics: Kazakhstan, Turkmenistan, Kirghizstan, Uzbekistan, Tajikistan, and Armenia all signed treaties of cooperation with Russia in 1992. Georgia, however, was not aligned with Russia, while the three Baltic states, Moldova, Azerbaijan, and above all, Ukraine, had assumed an anti-Moscow stance and built their own armed forces.

At the time of writing, Russian controlled the bulk of the former Soviet Union's strategic weapons. But the position was far from clear. (At the end of 1992 Ukrainian Prime Minister Leonid Kuchma insisted that his country was unwilling to destroy its missile silos or hand over all long-range weapons to Russia. Belarus and Kazakhstan had agreed to give up their nuclear weapons altogether, but none of their respective parliaments had as yet ratified the relevant agreements signed in 1991.) The nuclear threat apart, there was ongoing proliferation of military technology, since Russia remained a major exporter of non-nuclear arms. To make matters worse, the Russian armed forces faced serious morale problems, as numerous officers and men had volunteered for the non-Russian (especially the Ukrainian) national armies, thereby leaving the rest with a sense of uncertainty. The naval forces had been gravely weakened, as Ukraine claimed the bulk of the Black Sea fleet. The military-industrial-scientific complex suffered from a brain drain, as some highly qualified people left for abroad. There was widespread anxiety with regarding Russia's future, and also such mundane problems as accommodation, pay, and career prospects.

Throughout its history the Russian army has shown astonishing powers of recuperation; it will surely remain one of the world's leading military establishments. The army's political loyalty, however, remains in dispute. True enough, the army has never run Russia in the past. But the army has increasingly come to distrust the politicians – all the more so since the army is now controlled by generals who made their reputation in Afghanistan; as these veterans see it, the war was started by civilians, mismanaged by civilians, and ingloriously terminated by civilians. Hence no civilian government in future can take for granted the army's unstinting obedience.

Whatever the future of Russian politics, Russia will play the decisive role within the huge land mass formerly comprised within the Soviet Union. None of Russia's neighbours can afford to quarrel with Russia, especially since about 25,000,000 Russians live outside Russia's boundaries. (Only a million French-speakers lived in Algeria; yet France was willing to fight a long and costly war, in part to defend the settlers' interests.) It is in Russia that the greater part of the former Soviet military-industrial complex is located; it is Russia which has by far the largest population. Some form of cooperation must continue between Russia and its neighbors, lest a Yugoslav-type disaster ensue.

The breakup of the Soviet Union was not what the US had wanted, any more than the US had desired the disintegration of Yugoslavia. President Bush had supported President Gorbachev to the hilt – to the extent of warning Ukrainians against the risks of independence. There was concern, above all, with the question of who would control the 30,000 or so nuclear weapons accumulated by the former Soviet Union, how disarmament would proceed, how the spread of weapons and technology could be avoided. And would the missile forces maintain their discipline at a time when the future looked so insecure?

By mid-1992, it was far from clear how these problems would be resolved. Clearly, not even the military would be able to put the former Soviet Humpty Dumpty together again. To make matters worse, the individual republics faced numerous and intractable problems of their own. The reins of power were held mostly by ex-communists such as President Leonid Kravchuk in Ukraine; Kravchuk himself had graduated from an impassioned opponent of "bourgeois nationalism" to its staunchest defender. Political opportunism, however, was but a minor complaint when compared with the divisive force of ethnic nationalism. Most of the new republics were themselves complex ethnic mosaics.[3] (In the Soviet Union, as formerly constituted, there were some 200 ethnic groups.) The most homogeneous republics were Armenia (where some 85 percent of the population belonged to the dominant ethnic group), and Russia (with just over 80 percent). By contrast, in Kazakhstan less than half the population comprise Kazakhs. Hence all republics faced in miniature those problems which had confronted the former Soviet Union as a whole.

The Russian Federation was no exception. By the end of 1991, President Boris Yeltsin expressed fears that Russia might break up into warring fiefdoms. Yeltsin had some reason for his apprehension. The Muslim region of Chechen-Ingushetia demanded independence from Russia, and was led by a former Soviet air force general, Dzhokhar Dudaev, who threatened terrorism if his demands went unmet. There was secessionist sentiment in Tatarstan (historically a Turkic speaking territory, now with a large Russian minority, with its capital in Kazan). There was agitation for a Far Eastern Republic in cities such as Vladivostok, which looked to the Pacific. By contrast, many ethnic Russians in other republics demanded that they should rejoin Russia. These included the mainly Russian population of the Crimea (part of Ukraine), Russians in the Dnester area of Moldova, and Russians in North Kazakhstan.

Ethnic rivalry within the former Soviet Union was aggravated by all the other social ills inflicted on the people by 70 years of communism. Poverty was all-pervasive – far more so than in any Western country.[4] The demographic effects of communist tyranny had been shattering. Indeed, the Soviet Union had formed the most effective killing machine of modern times. (According to some estimates, the Soviet regime between 1917 and 1987 murdered nearly 62 million people – nearly 55 million of whom were the Soviet Union's own citizens.)[5] Even much lower estimates agreed that the Soviet Union's homicidal record had been much worse even than Nazi Germany's. The economy was in desperate straits. As an investigation of Magnitogorsk, "Steeltown USSR," explained, the problem was not merely that the citizens were exploited; they also had to wait for an average of 15 years for a separate apartment, while breathing air containing a level of pollutants 33 times higher than that regarded as perilous in the US, and – if they were men – die on average only three years after retirement. Central planning, moreover, created its own form of obsolescence; under conditions of free competition, within an international market economy, the Magnitogorsk steel industry simply could not compete.[6]

Speaking in more general terms, civil society had been gravely injured under communist rule. The aristocracy, the bourgeoisie and the peasantry had disappeared. Minorities had been decimated in a "cold war" waged by Moscow against its own subjects. (Supposedly one-half of Kazakhstan's population died under Stalin.) Government by force and fraud had shaken public confidence. Soviet citizens had become habituated to being lied to by official propaganda and official statistics. They took for granted that the concierge downstairs, or the next-door neighbor, or the supervisor at work might be a police informer. Soviet theoreticians believed that Soviet socialism was irreversible. Yet central planning never worked. The planners' ineffective efforts to create an efficient, centrally controlled economy came to nought. Instead, these policies created perverse incentives that misallocated resources on a vast scale; the mass of Soviet citizens thus became truly alienated from their own system.[7]

Soviet patriotism was replaced by national or ethnic sentiments centering on individual republics. According to Marxist-Leninist theory, such a development could not take place; on the contrary, the various nationalities were destined to fuse by reason of improved communications, ongoing urbanization, rapid industrialization, advancing education, and the consolidation of an industrial working class. (A similar analysis was applied with equal futility to other multi-ethnic countries such as South Africa.) Soviet practice, however, proved very different. Improved communications, especially television, introduced ordinary people to cultures and life-styles other than their own; but they also diffused national cultures, and strengthened the viewers' interest in their own traditions.[8]

The Soviet successor states differed enormously in their makeup and political orientation. By far the most Western parts of the former USSR were the three Baltic republics which had looked in the past and would look in the future toward Scandinavia and Western Europe. They are also distinct from the remainder of the former Soviet Union in a religious sense. Lithuania is, like Poland, a mainly Catholic country; Latvia and Estonia are mainly Lutheran. All three states have Russian minorities; their ports provide bases in the Baltic for the Red Fleet, and maritime outlets for Russian trade. But all three Baltic republics had always looked back with nostalgia to their status before World War II, before Stalin annexed them to the Soviet Union and installed governance by terror. Baltic politics are moderate and democratic – at least by comparison with those of the Caucasus and in Muslim Asia. It should not be beyond the bounds of statesmanship to arrive at a compromise that secures to Russia adequate commercial and naval access to the Baltic, and gives protection to ethnic minorities (including Russians, Belorussians, Jews) who choose to stay.[9]

What of the Balts' relations with the US? Overall, they have not been skilled at making their case. There are not many Estonians and Latvians in the US. The Lithuanians, by contrast, are relatively numerous. (Something like five million people of Lithuanian origin live in the US, more than twice as many as in Lithuania.) But the Lithuanians – unlike the Irish or the Jews, or, to a lesser extent, the Croats and Ukrainians – do not constitute an effective ethnic lobby in the US. The Balts, however, enjoyed a great political advantage in that the US never legally recognized the Soviet occupation of the Baltic republics. All three states will manage to survive as independent entities.

By contrast, Georgia and Armenia are Christian outposts in the Muslim world. Both have their own national churches and a culture that dates back to antiquity. Their secession did not injure the Soviet Union either strategically or economically. Having achieved their independence, both states must confront a precarious economic situation, widespread unrest, weak governance, and lack of confidence in the future. Both states, moreover, find themselves in a difficult strategic position. Armenia at least may be able to rely on aid from a large and influential diaspora whose members look on Armenia as their homeland. Armenia, however, has had repeated clashes with Azerbaijan. The armed struggle began in 1988 when the Armenians asked Moscow to reverse the 1921 accord which attached the enclave of Nagorno-Karabakh, populated by Armenians, to Azerbaijan instead of to Armenia. Blockades led to violence as both sides obtained tanks and heavy weapons. Both sides must accept the Moscow agreement, but although in February 1992 the two sought a truce over the enclave, it is unlikely the Azerbaijanis will give up Nagorno-Karabakh.

Georgia, by contrast, contains a substantial Muslim minority. Bordering on a Muslim sea, both Georgia and Armenia will have a hard road to independence, and would surely profit from an economic association with Russia, as would the Baltic states. Some factions within the Republic of Moldova wish to join Romania, to which Moldova formerly belonged. But Moldova too has substantial ethnic minorities, primarily Russian. Romania's own record is poor in treating its minorities (especially Hungarians and Gypsies). Hence Moldova's future remains uncertain. The same applies to the Soviet Union's Muslim republics in Asia. They are poverty-stricken even by Russian standards; they are by culture and religion even more distinct from Russia than the non-Russian territories in Europe. But given their economic difficulties in subsisting on their own, they will probably remain linked to Russia in some form or other. Such a forecast seems all the more reasonable since backward and strife-torn Muslim countries such as Afghanistan and Iran do not make persuasive counter-models. Turkey, on the other hand, seeks to promote its influence with perhaps more success.

From the former all-Union standpoint, the departure of these smaller republics made only a minor difference. More critical was the decision taken by Ukraine in December 1991 to seek complete independence. Ukrainian industry and mineral wealth had been important to the Soviet economy; Ukraine had also been one of the Soviet Union's great bread baskets. (In 1987 it accounted for 18.2 percent of Soviet consumer goods and 22.3 percent of its agricultural output.) Ukraine's population was larger than that of Poland and Czechoslovakia combined, and nearly as large as that of France (51,740,000 as against 56,400,000), but with a considerably larger land area at the Ukrainian people's disposal.

Like Russia, Ukraine is culturally varied. About 90 percent of its people worship in Ukrainian Orthodox churches, others are Uniates (Catholics with a Slavic rite). Ukraine's frontiers, like those of the other republics, were drawn by imperial overlords. After World War II, Ukraine greatly enlarged its territory as a result of the Soviet victory. Ukraine acquired Eastern Galicia and Volhynia from Poland (the so-called Western Ukraine).

Czechoslovakia ceded Sub-Carpathian Ruthenia. Romania yielded Northern Bukovina and part of Bessarabia (Moldova). But most important of
all, Ukraine in 1954 gained the Crimea from Russia as a "gift" from Nikita
S. Krushchev.

But unrest remained. There were a variety of nationality problems.
(About two-thirds of the Crimea's population consists of ethnic Russians;
Ukrainians make up one-quarter; other minorities comprise Poles, Jews,
Belarussians, Moldovans, and others.) More seriously, Ukraine had a long
history of brutal exploitation. The Nazi invaders plundered the country
in World War II, widely treated Ukrainians as *Untermenschen* (sub-humans),
and murdered every Jew and Gypsy they could find as part of a continental
murder campaign. Even after being widely greeted as liberators on their
arrival, the Nazis through their destructive acts sacrificed the opportunity
to mobilize Ukrainians, Russians, Jews, and others against their Soviet
oppressors; not surprisingly, Germany lost the war. But Nazi tyranny,
however bloodstained, lasted for only a few years, whereas except for the
Western Ukraine, Soviet domination endured ever since 1917 – despite
bitter and prolonged resistance in Ukraine as well as in other parts of the
Soviet Union. The results of communist and Nazi cruelty combined were
shattering. "When the casualties of civil war, collectivization, the purges
and the Second World War are combined, more than half the male and
a quarter of the female population perished."[10]

In part as a reaction against totalitarian oppression, Ukrainian nationalism became a powerful force which animated not only a variety of opposition groups, but which also penetrated into the Communist Party. Under
the leadership of Leonid Kravchuk, the former communist Republic's first
secretary, Ukraine asserted its right to a national destiny, separated both
from the Soviet Union and from neighboring Russia. Kravchuk's regime
rested on a compromise between the old *apparatchiks* and the nationalists;
reforms remained largely on paper; the old bosses largely kept their jobs;
but at least Ukraine achieved independence from Moscow. Fortunately,
however, relations between ethnic Russians and ethnic Ukrainians within
Ukraine are nothing like as troubled as those between Croats and Serbs
in Yugoslavia. Ukrainian nationalism and distinctive Ukrainian ways are
strongest in Western Ukraine; but in general ethnic Ukrainians and ethnic
Russians have much in common in a cultural sense – as do Danes, Swedes,
and Norwegians who are nevertheless politically separate. At the time of
writing, the old *nomenklatura* still controlled industry and trade and stifled
privatization efforts. As a result, little had been done to make Ukraine a
viable economic democracy.

Once Ukrainian independence had been consolidated, Russia resembled
territorially the former Russia as constituted under the terms of the

Brest-Litovsk treaty, forced on the Bolsheviks by Germany in 1917. In territorial terms, it was a disaster of a kind no empire had ever sustained without a long preceding period of catastrophic war. Russia and the other republics faced enormous difficulties. Many of their boundaries were quite artificial, having been drawn with the same unconcern for the indigenous population as those of the Western colonial empires in Africa. There were other problems. To mention just one: the former British and French colonies in Africa had attained independence at a time of global prosperity; the Soviet successor states, by contrast, had gained their sovereignty during a worldwide recession. Nevertheless, their future potential remains great. Russia is likely to continue as a great power, given its resources, the abilities of its peoples, and the extraordinary capacity for recuperation which Russia has displayed after every disaster in its history.

## A FADING VISION

How did this huge and relatively bloodless revolution occur? For 45 years after World War II, Moscow's word was law from the Elbe to the Pacific.[11] No fundamental change seemed possible – so much so that even only a few years ago as respected a critic of Soviet rule in Eastern Europe as Charles Gati still warned Westerners to seek for the Soviet dependencies no more than "evolutionary or within-system changes' rather than "noble, desirable, but unrealistic objectives."[12] Commentators Jerry Hough and Stephen Cohen likewise argued that *perestroika* would work and there would be a slow evolution from communism. But in the end, Moscow's hegemony collapsed with unimagined speed. Thereafter, trouble spread from the Soviet Union's "outer empire" to its "inner empire" – a process that raised fundamental questions concerning the essential character of Soviet imperial rule before the Gorbachevian revolution.

According to what might be called the Russo-centric school, the Soviet empire was merely a Russian empire writ large. Despite the power once wielded by potentates such as Stalin (a Georgian), it was essentially Russians who ruled; it was the Russians who had imposed their own peculiar stamp on the Soviet empire. The Russians, the argument continues, had been successively ruled by Mongols, then by indigenous autocrats. The Russians had experienced neither the liberation force of the Renaissance nor of the Reformation; the Russians were the last Europeans to abolish serfdom. Greek Orthodox in their religious backgrounds, the Russians were traditionally subjected to a Caesaro-Papism that merged the power of Church and State. Not surprisingly, the Russian people were habituated to the might of tyrannical cliques, be they Czarist or communist. Worse still, this industrious, obedient people had always faithfully served its rulers in constantly expanding Moscow's power. This interpretation appeals to many – including Polish, Georgian and Lithuanian and many other nationalists. Moreover, it has long antecedents. Already in the mid-nineteenth century scholars as different as Karl Marx, the German revolutionary, and Constantin Frantz, a German reactionary, agreed on one issue; Russia was a threat to Europe. Unless the European powers cooperated, Russia would expand to the West until her influence stretched all the way from Gdańsk to Trieste – not a bad guess as regards the expansion of Soviet influence by 1945.

There are, however, problems with this Russo-centric interpretation. It ignores those anti-authoritarian and democratic legacies that Russia inherited from its past. Moreover, the Russians, unlike other empire builders, do not particularly idealize martial splendor. (The Red Army was always inferior in prestige to the Imperial German or the Imperial Japanese Army, despite the victories of World War II.) Wars of expansion – for instance, the recent war in Afghanistan – were thoroughly unpopular in Russia. Few demobilized Russian conscripts looked back to army life with pride or pleasure. And, fortunately for Russia, the country had no previous experience of a military dictatorship.

The true beneficiaries of the Soviet empire were the members of the Soviet *nomenklatura*, all senior functionaries within the communist party. The members of the *nomenklatura* gained advancement not so much through their technical ability, but through their real or assumed loyalty to the party, and lack of scruple in furthering their respective careers and the party's interests. The *nomenklatura* dominated the key institutions of the Soviet state, and in every Soviet agency there was a natural conflict between the technicians, appointed for their specialized skills, and the "partocrats" who ruled the roost.

The *nomenklatura* was essentially a supranational pool of people. It is true that many key positions within the *nomenklatura* were held by ethnic Russians; but these men and women – like their opposite numbers in the non-Russian republics of the Soviet Union and in "fraternal" parties abroad – were molded more by their party than by their national identity. They formed part of an international ruling class that displayed remarkable homogeneity. Whether trained in Moscow, Warsaw, or East Berlin, a leading communist would feel at home in party offices anywhere, read similar directives, and spoke the same party jargon with the same stilted terminology. The senior cadres in the various pro-Moscow parties saw themselves as part of an international brotherhood, in part an all-encompassing old boys' network, in part a party, a club, a Mafia, and a counter-church. In more concrete terms, the party provided the senior cadres with a considerable income, and numerous special privileges, including special housing and special shopping facilities. The cadres were sustained by a great network of research organizations and academies whose publications, cast in the same transnational party idiom, read today as if they had been written on another star.

Not that national loyalties ceased to count within the socialist world. (Many East Germans, for instance, were wont to compare themselves more to West Germany and to speak of their eastern neighbors with contempt as *Polaken*, polaks.) But overall, the leading cadres of the ruling communist parties, and even of major non-ruling communist parties, had more in common with each other than they had with their respective fellow citizens. The leading communist cadres saw themselves engaged in an international class war in which, ultimately, capitalism would vanish from the globe, the bourgeoisie would be destroyed worldwide, and the pro-letariat would prevail – led, of course, by an enlightened vanguard, the communist party. Compromises would have to be made on the way, temporary alliances would have to be concluded. But the long-term aim never varied: world revolution, except for a period of coexistence between nation-states but not between competing social systems. It is a mistake, therefore, to assume that the Cold War started or ended at any particular date, or that the Cold War derived from Stalinist deforma-tions or from diplomatic misunderstandings. The Cold War was implied by the very nature of the Soviet regime; the Cold War began when the Bolsheviks forcibly seized power in Russia in 1917; the Cold War ended when the Communist Party of the Soviet Union was banned in 1991. The Cold War, and the domestic terror practiced to a greater or lesser extent by all communist regimes the world over, was linked to the conviction that service to the party justified anything and everything. Indeed, the party ruled the senior cadres' public and private lives to the extent of making or breaking marriages. Any kind of moral turpitude was accept-able for the party's good – better to denounce a friend than let an enemy go free.

The international counter-church depended not merely on military power, but also on a moral appeal. Communism, in the eyes of the faithful, was irresistible, its progress irreversible. During the 1970s Marxism-Leninism, the Soviet empire's pseudo-religion, still seemed on the upswing worldwide. The US had been humiliated in Vietnam; Marxist-Leninist governments had gained power as far afield as Angola, Mozambique, Af-ghanistan, Laos, Vietnam, Cambodia, and Nicaragua, with Grenada thrown in as a sop. Even during the 1980s, the majority of Western academics, the bulk of officials in the CIA and the US State Department believed the communist system would stay in place for a long time.

During the 1980s, however, the tide turned. President Reagan's denunciation of the Soviets' "Evil Empire" resounded all over the world, even inside the Soviet Union. The Soviet invasion of Afghanistan met with bitter resistance, soon to be supported by the US. The Soviet-backed regimes in Angola, Mozambique, and Ethiopia – all professedly Marxist-Leninist dictatorships – faltered; all incurred bitter civil strife and economic disaster. Marxism-Leninism no longer seemed the wave of the future; on the contrary, Margaret Thatcher's government in Great Britain both publicized and practiced the new concept of "privatization," a major departure. By the late 1980s, the Soviet empire in East-Central Europe and in the USSR itself was in disarray. Mikhail S. Gorbachev's accession to power signified a sea change – a fact understood with remarkable political instinct by President Reagan, who backed the Soviet Union's last leader. Subject to constant pressure from within, Gorbachev, from 1985 onward, embarked on reluctant reforms symbolized by the terms *glasnost* and *perestroika*. Discouraged and dispirited, the Soviet leadership was forced to make a virtue of necessity. In June 1989 President Gorbachev, addressing the Council of Europe in Strasbourg, specifically renounced the use of force against former or present members of the communist bloc.[13] Moscow policy-makers apparently believed that the Soviet Union could maintain its predominance in East-Central Europe by those methods of "Indirect Rule" once used by British empire-builders. But the Soviet leaders had apparently failed to understand just how unpopular the communist satellite regimes were with their own people and how dependent these governments had been on Soviet support. The empire therefore collapsed with startling rapidity. Judging by the public discourse, new style, nobody – well, hardly anybody – had ever been a communist, and those who had been were either exiled, dead, or in a state of repentance.

Imperial breakup abroad helped to delegitimize Soviet power at home. If Poland could be free, why not Ukraine? Why not Georgia? Why not Russia? Thereafter, a great many misconceptions popular also among a great many Western academics and media people suddenly had to be discarded. Such bankrupt notions included the convergence theory (according to which communism and democracy were becoming alike due to increasing technical requirements of modern complex states). Equally discredited was the moral equivalence concept (which denied any essential difference between Western, especially US, democracy and Soviet communism). Discredited were also those who sought a "Third Way" between communism and capitalism. (As the Czech minister for finance, Václav Klaus, put it, "the 'Third Way' leads to the Third World!") Rehabilitated was the concept of totalitarianism which regarded communism and Nazism as hostile

twins – an interpretation widely contested in academia during the 1960s
and 1970s. Not surprisingly, world-famous historian Robert Conquest
cheerfully insisted that now indeed the time had come for the righteous
to gloat – it being "in the public interest that victory over the forces of
falsification, ignorance and stupidity be rubbed in as hard as possible."[14]

Within the Soviet Union itself, the cult of Lenin came to be seen for
what it was – a blend of idolatry and kitsch. Soviet history increasingly
appeared in its true colors, not a noble enterprise temporarily "deformed"
by deviations, but an endless tale of lies, betrayals, murder, incompetence,
militarism, collectivization, and thievery. By contrast, the West seemed
ever more attractive, especially the US. For some opponents of the Soviet
regime, Ronald Reagan became a hero. As Arkadii Murashev, a liberal
close to Boris Yeltsin, put it in a question to David Remnick: "he called
us the "Evil Empire." So why did you in the West laugh at him?"[15]

Dissent spread into the highest ranks of the *nomenklatura*; men and
women were losing faith in the very system that had catapulted them to
power. They included hard-boiled *apparatchiks* such as Eduard Shevardnadze, who at one time had ruled Georgia with a rod of iron, but later
claimed to have become completely disillusioned, convinced that the
regime had become rotten and required fundamental change.[16] By contrast,
the West, especially the US, now served as a popular counter-model. In
purely commercial terms, the US impact was small. (US exports to Eastern
Europe as a whole formed an insignificant part of US foreign trade.
Between 1979 and 1987, moreover, the value of US exports to Eastern
Europe went down by more than one-half.)[17] But in moral terms the US
influence was considerable, through visits to the West, by Radio Liberty,
films, rock music, literature legally or illegally imported into the Soviet
Union, through links with emigrants (including millions of Ukrainians
settled in the US and Canada, as well as Balts, ethnic Russian sectarians,
Russian Jews, and many others).

Reagan's successor as president, George Bush, moreover had competent
advice. He was one of the first major statesman in the West to catch the
changing mood when, in a speech at Mainz, in May 1989, he called for
a Europe whole and free. Further, there was within the US and other
Western countries a minority of committed scholars such as Conquest,
Leszek Kolakowski, Richard Pipes, and Adam Ulam who reshaped public
opinion in the face of much academic hostility. (The history department
at Stanford, Conquest's own university, for years has denied teaching
privileges to Conquest, a "Cold Warrior" by reputation and conviction.)

Within Russia there was widespread intellectual opposition.[18] This included intellectual giants such as Andrei Sakharov, one of the world's
leading nuclear physicists (father of the Soviet hydrogen bomb), and by

conviction a liberal who looked to the West. Even more important perhaps was Aleksandr Solzhenitsyn, the greatest writer produced by the former communist world. Solzhenitsyn, a slavophile in the traditional mold, was a man of unbending courage, neither bribed nor broken. Above all, he stood for a humane form of Russian nationalism, averse to dreams of conquest, averse to holding down other nations by force, averse to those anti-Jewish, anti-Asian, and other ethnic phobias widespread among ultra-militant nationalists in Russia and East-Central Europe alike.

Anti-communism became a popular creed in every republic in the Soviet Union, mingled with contempt for the Soviet Union's revolutionary allies abroad. At its most unsophisticated, this derived from hostility to supposedly ungrateful Third World peoples who were thought to be living high on the hog by means of astronomical foreign aid remittances supplied at the Soviet citizens' expense. (In this respect, the Soviet's own propaganda with regard to the generosity of their foreign assistance programs backfired.) On a higher intellectual plane there was a new comprehension for the murderous frivolity with which, for example, Nicolae Ceauşescu, a self-confessed Marxist-Leninist, destroyed villages to build socialist agro-towns in Romania, whereas the Khmer Rouge, also self-confessed Marxist-Leninists, emptied towns of their people to build a socialist countryside in Cambodia. By the late 1980s, it was thus a common sight to see great lines of workers on parade in Moscow with banners proclaiming "Marxism-Leninism on the garbage heap of history" or "seventy-five years on the road to nowhere."

The mass of the Soviet peoples were by now well aware that the regime was bankrupt morally as well as financially. (By 1991 the Soviet Union's foreign debt had risen to more than $70 billion; the country suffered from hyperinflation; the national budget deficit had jumped by 230 percent over the previous year; the gross national product had plunged; 24.8 million persons were said to be unemployed.) The Soviet Union had many other problems. Traditional socialist societies extracted revenue directly from state-owned enterprises. Prices did not operate as an instrument for allocating scarce resources, but were arbitrarily fixed. Households built up large savings, but these could not be effectively used because there were few goods available at the shops. Liberalization, once begun, was uniformly accompanied by loss of government revenue, as the state gave up control over state enterprises. (Between 1985 and 1989, government revenue supposedly fell by 6 percent of the gross domestic product, from 47.3 percent to 41.00 percent. Thereafter the decline rapidly accelerated, and thereby played a major part in cracking the "center's" control over the Soviet Union at large.) Liberalization, moreover, went with inflation. This derived in part from governmental deficits incurred to finance inefficient enterprises: enterprises then built up excessive inventories as a substitute for money, which was losing its value. By doing so, they further contributed to the loss of public trust in the currency. Effective reform would prove impossible, unless accompanied by the creation of an effective tax system and an Internal Revenue Service.[19]

To make matters even worse, the preceding 75 years of communism had turned the Soviet Union into a warfare state. (The US, by contrast, was a welfare state which spent in 1989, as part of its national budget, nearly three times as much on social welfare as it did on defense.) Even on its own terms the warfare state encountered serious difficulties. The massive rearmament under way in the US during the last years of the Carter administration, and thereafter under the Reagan presidency, increasingly threatened the Soviet position. So did the development of "high tech" warfare, in which the West had an evident advantage, as demonstrated first by the Gulf War, later by other technical innovations which made even the Gulf War technology seem out of date. In the military as in the civilian sphere, communist rule consistently failed to outproduce capitalism.

Above all, communist rule failed to win over those toiling masses whom the communist rulers never failed to eulogize. Given the size of the Soviet underground economy, there was indeed a widespread belief that poverty would lessen if socialism were to end. As one expert study put it:

> These expectations stem from a conviction common to many Soviet economists that there are enormous reserves of talent and energy in the country not being properly or otherwise utilized by the state enterprise system. These hidden resources are believed to exist in the population at large, as well as in the so-called "shadow economy" and are capable of being brought into the economy through cooperatives. One Soviet economist, for example, estimated that this "shadow economy" has a turnover of 70–90 billion rubles per year, then commented that by opening the way to coops and individual labor activity "many shady phenomena have come to light, been legalized and begun to work for the state, if only because tax is being paid now."[20]

Revisionist scholarship in the US has tried to reinterpret history in terms of race, class, and gender. But these had no relevance to the great revolution that shook East-Central Europe and the Soviet Union from 1989 onward. In the Soviet Union, as elsewhere, these revolutions hinged on nationalism, free market initiatives, and religion. In a profounder sense, the disintegration of communism entailed the breakdown of a secular faith. In the past, communist believers – like the Nazi faithful of old – had seen themselves as embattled soldiers whose struggle would end the world's woes. "So comrades come rally the last fight to face" proclaimed the *Internationale*, the communist party anthem. *"Zum letzten Mal wird zum*

*Apell geblasen*" (for the last time the trumpet sounds the roll call) ran the Nazi party's battle song: thereafter victory – splendid, refulgent. It was this millenarian vision which vanished. The communists' very symbolism sickened the people at large. Thus in 1991, a city-wide referendum in Leningrad, the city of Lenin, demanded that the city's name revert to St Petersburg. Boris Yeltsin, on being inaugurated in July 1991 as the first popularly elected president of the Russian Federation, took good care to restore the imagery of the past. The Kremlin Hall of Congresses was stripped of its Soviet trappings. The traditional Russian flag took the place of Lenin's statue. Priests, pastors, rabbis, and mullahs sat in the first row. Alexei II, the patriarch of the Russian Orthodox Church, blessed the new president and asked him to remember the law of Christ. It was as if 70 years of Marxist-Leninist indoctrination had been wiped off the slate.

## THE NEW POLITICS

Lenin had envisaged the communist parties of the future as chosen vanguards. They would differ from other political parties as did trained Guards regiments from hastily raised militia units. Hence "democratic centralism," that is to say rigid party discipline, would always prevail over a disunited opposition, however numerous. Lenin's party never quite worked as its maker had intended; but following Gorbachev's takeover, internal disagreement within the CPSU became ever more severe. By 1991 disunity had become so apparent that Gorbachev himself spoke of three or even four different factions within the CPSU. With 16 million members, the CPSU did remain by far the most numerous and best financed organization within the Soviet Union. Nevertheless, its numbers declined, and so did morale. (As of January 1990, the party had 19.2 million members; a year later membership dropped by 3 million.) Moreover, communists, incredibly, complained of being insulted or ignored. Thus nearly one-third of all party members questioned in a public opinion survey complained of psychological discomforts inflicted on them by colleagues ill-disposed towards communism.[21]

The party had other problems. The economic situation kept deteriorating. (By July 1991, the gross national product for 1991 was estimated to have declined between 15 and 20 percent from 1990.) Confidence lessened in the party's future. This was a particularly serious matter, for all totalitarian regimes depend on a huge anonymous army of informers willing to denounce acquaintances, colleagues, and neighbors. By doing so, the informer gets in the good books of the authorities; he or she enjoys the illusion of sharing in the party's power, and punishes personal enemies at public expense. This game is, however, only profitable as long as authority is firm. Once trust in the ruler's future breaks, informers cease to ply their trade, and the ruler's authority further diminishes. This is precisely what befell the CPSU; hence there was a shortage of able and dedicated leaders at all levels, while the party's loss of absolute power left the old-time functionaries with a sense of bewilderment. Whatever their personal preferences, Soviet rulers could no longer attempt to make up for failure at home by glorious victories abroad.

The Soviet Union also faced an ecological crisis of stunning proportions. Communist rule had produced a great network of unsafe nuclear installations; the Chernobyl disaster might as yet be repeated many times. There was shocking industrial pollution, matched only by the ill usage of soil and water resources. Lakes and rivers were widely polluted. Required to meet even more unreasonable production targets, collective and state farms had carelessly used mountains of chemical fertilizers and pesticides which polluted drinking water. Official attempts to cut down on the expense of irrigation works often cause proper drainage to be omitted; hence there was extensive soil salinization which destroyed soil fertility. The same problems also affected the capitalist world – but overall no capitalist country could quite equal the ravages of socialism.

The Soviet armed forces likewise faced severe internal dissensions. There were disciplinary problems as conscripts complained of harsh treatment inflicted on them by long-service men; there was disagreement between the various branches of the service, especially between the army and the navy (the latter a particularly capital-intensive and expensive service); there was a natural rivalry between the Communist Party political officers and the military professionals, a rivalry that mirrored the wider divisions of Soviet society. There was discontent with regard to the war in Afghanistan, waged unsuccessfully by the Soviet Union, and the Gulf War, fought successfully by the US against a Soviet ally. There was hostile competition between the army's military intelligence and the KGB. There was discontent among junior officers, non-commissioned officers, and enlisted men alike with regard to poor pay, poor housing, and poor food. There was indiscipline and drunkenness. There were ethnic tensions, especially between Slavs and Muslim Asians. Many conscripts refused to report for duty, not only in the dissident Baltic and Caucasian republics, but also in Moscow. Within the defense forces there were horizontal divisions between the high command and junior and middle-grade officers. The continuing withdrawal of Soviet forces from Central Europe had affected morale, and also multiplied more mundane problems of finding domestic accommodation for officers and men, and training facilities for large units. To make matters worse, there was the sorry record of the Soviet forces with regard to environmental damage. The Red Army had left behind environmental devastation in East Germany, Czechoslovakia, Poland, and Hungary; now the Soviet Union itself would have to take the additional strain.

Faced with a deteriorating diplomatic situation and an ongoing domestic crisis, the CPSU fractured. There was, for instance, bitter disagreement between what might be called the centralizers who wanted to concentrate all power in Moscow, and devolutionists who were willing to grant local self-government, or even dominion status, to associated republics. There was dissension between economic reformers and traditionalists; there was the clash between Westernizers and slavophiles. This sketch is of course somewhat schematic. Not all democrats favored decentralization; not all practicing Christians were slavophile. Some thorough-going communists (such as Ukrainian communists) wanted more power for the republics as against the center. But overall there was a cleavage between communist hard-liners who favored central planning in the economy and a tough line toward dissident republics, and those who advocated political devolution and private enterprise alike.

By the middle of 1991, the hard-liners were in retreat, but their power was far from broken. Though divided, the CPSU was still powerful, with countless financial tentacles at home and abroad, its total wealth hard to estimate. Equally important was the KGB, a huge and diverse organization with its own private armies. The KGB constituted a state within the state – a hybrid between an intelligence organization, police department, customs service, economic surveillance agency, public opinion research group, and crime syndicate.[22] The hard-liners likewise were well represented within the military-industrial complex, a major part within an economy where most quality goods of any kind were produced, in the first place, for the Communist Party members and the military and their dependents. (In 1991 a group of hard-liners thus issued a general condemnation of reformers who looked to foreigners for inspiration. The signatories included Deputy Defense Minister Valentin Varennikov, as well as Deputy Interior Minister and Afghan War hero Boris Gromov.) In addition, there were hard-liners within the Russian Orthodox Church. (An appeal made to Gorbachev in 1990, asking him to declare a state of emergency so as to prevent a takeover on the part of "separatists" and anti-communist elements, was signed, among others, by the Russian Patriarch Alexei II.[23]) The hard-liners had support within the ranks of the major all-Soviet ministries (whose members feared for their jobs, in case the Soviet Union were to disintegrate). The hard-liners were equally powerful within the KGB, with its great army of informers; the hard-liners also controlled about a quarter of the seats within the Soviet parliament, as constituted before the abortive coup of 1991.

Above all, the hard-liners put their trust in the armed forces and the KGB. In retrospect, theirs seems a poor choice. But at the time, the hard-liners apparently still had good reason for their confidence. The armed forces had remained the regime's favorite in receiving hardware, indeed armaments continued to accumulate. A few examples must suffice. According to reports issued in 1990, a new submarine was added to the Soviet navy every six weeks; two aircraft, six tanks, and one missile were produced every day. Reductions were largely confined to absolete or aging weapons and vessels. The US Under Secretary of Defense reported small decreases in the production of fighters, fighter-bombers, and bombers; but these were balanced by increases in the production of light armored vehicles, mortars, short-range ballistic missiles and tanker aircraft. Overall, modernization of the armed forces proceeded at a rapid pace. (Indeed, Soviet TV mentioned for the first time hitherto secret "space troops" reported to create a Soviet analogue to SDI.)[24] In terms of costs, the military outlay likewise stayed impressive. The Soviet defense budget was more than double the official figure of 77 billion rubles.)[25] According to published Soviet figures, ascertained by Ambassador Richard F. Staar, military expenditure had actually gone up, from 26 percent of the national budget in 1990 to 36 percent in 1991. Much to the reformers' disgust, there had been, through 1991, no effective switch from military production to peacetime investment. (According to Soviet press reports, only five or six of some 400 defense enterprises planned for conversion had fully switched to manufacturing consumer products by the beginning of 1991.)[26]

Neither had the Soviet armed forces apparently followed the spirit or the letter of the conventional forces treaty in Europe (CFE) signed by the NATO and former Warsaw Pact powers in 1990. The treaty provided for reductions in five weapons categories (tanks, armored combat vehicles, artillery systems, combat aircraft, and attack helicopters.) But, asserted the critics, between 1988 and 1990 the Soviets had moved more than half of their equipment in the first three categories from Central Europe to east of the Urals, that is to say outside the area specified by the treaty for reductions. Three armored divisions had been transferred to coastal defense – thus not subject to CFE reductions. The Soviet forces embarked on a massive buildup on the Kola Peninsula and in the Pechenga Valley, within striking distance of Norway's borders. Finally, as Ambassador Staar, himself a former arms negotiator, points out, armed forces had moved from East-Central Europe to the Russian Federation, ostensibly for the purpose of protecting rocket installations and nuclear warheads against ethnic disorders. However, such tensions were evident only in areas such as the Caucasus, far from such missile sites.[27]

Nevertheless, the hard-liners now faced ever-increasing popular opposition. In the dissident republics of the Baltic and the Caucasus, communist power largely disintegrated. In the Slavic republics there were also national communists, such as Kravchuk, concerned only with their own separate republics. There were various reform groups whose influence continued to grow to such an extent that some hard-liners threatened to leave the communist party rather than to remain with an increasingly "social democratic" organization. The democratic factions enjoyed massive support among intellectuals, technicians, and the workers, supposedly communism's chief beneficiaries. (Contrary to the Soviet intellectuals' widespread disdain for the great unwashed masses and their supposed submissiveness to tyranny, it was the workers who disliked communism even more than the well-educated. According to a poll taken early in 1991 by the All-Union Center for Public Opinion in the Soviet Union, only one in three still supported communism among the college graduates; only one in five among those without any higher education at all.)[28]

Caught between hard-liners (mistakenly referred to in the Western press as "conservatives") and the reformers, Gorbachev found himself between two fires. Gorbachev himself was the product of an unregenerate communist system, a loyal Marxist-Leninist who originally had looked to the world revolution. But as the system foundered, he turned to reform after 1985: *perestroika* and *glasnost*. By 1988 Gorbachev had apparently resolved – as de Gaulle had decided two decades earlier with regard to Algeria – that the Soviet Union's "outer empire" should no longer be sustained by Soviet troops. But without this armed support, the "outer empire" collapsed, and Gorbachev – seemingly frightened by the indirect consequences of this upheaval – once more switched to the right. Thereafter, Gorbachev – in Marxist terminology – faced an irresolvable contradiction. He wished to reform a bankrupt system; but he could do so only with the aid of a Soviet establishment with a vital stake in the system's continuance. Reform, however tentative, would delegitimize the ruling Communist Party, while nationalism within the individual republic grew by leaps and bounds.

In March 1991 Soviet voters held a union-wide referendum. Voters were ambiguously asked whether they wished to preserve the Union of Soviet Socialist Republics as "a renewed federation of equal sovereign republics, in which human rights and the freedoms of all nationalities will be fully guaranteed." Armenia, Georgia, Estonia, Latvia, Lithuania, and Moldova would not participate. By contrast the Muslim republics voted for union with surprisingly high majorities. (Vote tampering may have contributed to the high totals.) In the Russian Federation there was a substantial "no" vote (26.4 percent, with 52.8 percent of the eligible voters going to the polls). In Ukraine 28 percent voted in the negative, with 58.2 percent of eligible voters taking part. In Belarus, the no vote was only 5.8 percent, with 69.7 percent of the voters participating.

As the central power continued to decline, a new Union Treaty, drafted in 1991, was designed to transform the Soviet Union into a loose federation, leaving much more power to the republics than those enjoyed by the states forming the United States.[29] The CPSU was no longer referred to in the draft treaty, and not surprisingly communist morale thereafter slumped. The hard-liners were even more upset when, in July 1991, Gorbachev put to the CPSU's leadership a new program which would have earned its authors a death sentence in the olden days. Henceforth, the program asserted, no political organization should ever again aim at the compulsory transformation of society. The CPSU should become a party of democratic reform, political and economic freedom, social justice and all-human values. The Soviet Union should aim at the creation of a multi-party system, a mixed economy, should create a convertible ruble, and free prices. The party itself must become democratized – individual members should enjoy the freedom to dissent from the party, the freedom to be a believer. Finally, in a lapidary sentence that alone deserves to enshrine the party's last secretary-general in his country's memory, it declared: "the party forever excludes from its arsenal the principle – the end justifies the means."[30]

By this time, however, power was rapidly slipping from Gorbachev's hands. The various republics were each going their own way – above all the Russian Federation itself. In July 1991, for example, Soviet law-makers approved legislation that permitted the establishment of stock exchanges. To a believing Marxist-Leninist this was worse than sanctioning official brothels. The law-makers put an end to the monopolies previously enjoyed by state companies. Taxes on business profits diminished. Together with earlier legislation to sell two-thirds of state-owned enterprises during the next two years, and to allow foreign investors additional access, the state-owned economy was further modified – at least on paper.

Attempting to regain domestic support by garnering foreign aid, Gorbachev travelled to London for a conference of the world's seven most highly industrialized nations (G7) and linked foreign aid to internal reform. Without Western aid, he threatened, the Soviet Union would face social uprising. As part of the new course, the Soviets expected Western investment and membership in the International Monetary Fund (IMF); in return the Soviets would make the ruble convertible, liberalize prices, and privatize state-run industries. However, these proposed reforms were still based on profound ignorance of the way in which free enterprise systems should work. In the Soviet's opinion, investment should not depend on whether an individual Western company thought it could make a profit. Rather the Soviets negotiated in the belief that Western governments could tell companies what they should do. As Gorbachev put it, "if the Japanese government does not favor cooperation with a country, Japanese capital will never invest in that country. It is the same for other countries. If the IMF invests $1 million, at once $10 million will be invested by private capital. The policies of the IMF are determined by the Group of Seven."[31] It was a fatal misconception – particularly dangerous at a time when the Soviet Union's staple exports were in trouble. (Gold prices in 1991 had fallen. The oil-producing countries of the Middle East and Latin America were courting Western companies for additional investment – this at a time when Soviet industries and the Soviet infrastructure were decaying.)

How would the Soviet economy be restructured? In 1991 a group of leading reformers issued a seven-page plan designed to turn the Soviet Union into a pluralist democracy. The signatories spoke for a new Democratic Reform Movement (DDR) that might turn itself into an independent political party – a course of action to be decided in September 1991. They included a group of prominent politicians, among them Gorbachev's former foreign minister Eduard Shevardnadze, a communist Saul now turned free enterprise Paul. Other influential members were Leningrad's reformist mayor Anatoli Sobchak, Moscow mayor Gavriil Popov, Russian prime minister Ivan Silaev, Russian vice-president Col. Aleksandr Rutskoi, and Russian president Boris Yeltsin. For the time being the reformers dominated both the parliament and government of the Russian Federation.

Whereas Gorbachev looked for foreign aid to sustain his reforms (and was largely thwarted at the London Conference), the reformers in the Russian Federation looked to do without assistance from abroad, and overwhelmingly backed private enterprise. (Thus in 1991 the Supreme Economic Council made an arrangement with Stanford's free-enterprise-directed Hoover Institution for advice on the restoration of capitalism in Russia.) By now the Russian legislature had become at least partially committed to a market economy, and acted accordingly. (For instance, the coalmining industry was transferred from all-Union control to the Russian Federation so as to facilitate the industry's privatization.)

The reformers had a stony road to tread. Their difficulties were even greater than those of their colleagues in Hungary, Poland, and Czechoslovakia. In these countries opposition to communism had drawn on a strong sense of nationalism and hostility to the Soviet occupiers, memories of prewar parties and the prewar state survived. Above all, Czechs, Slovaks, Hungarians, and Poles all desired that their respective countries should "return to Europe." In Russia, by contrast, there was no common agreement regarding the meaning of Russian nationalism. In the past Russian and Soviet nationalism had been confused; moreover, the age-old debate between slavophiles (that is to say cultural isolationists) and Westerners remained unresolved, having been suppressed during the long years of communist tyranny.

Of parties there were many – all too many. But they were small, with a fluctuating membership, puny financial resources, and weak organization. They lacked mass appeal. Their programs were apt to be ill-defined, if not visionary – not surprising at a time when the state agencies were widely in a chaotic state, and the best of party programs could not translate from theory to practice. Russia, moreover, shared another weakness with the remaining successor states of the Soviet empire. All had adopted systems of proportional representation, instead of the Anglo-American system of plurality voting. Whatever its theoretical merits, proportional representation tends to fragment parliamentary parties, and gives undue influence to extremist groups, a generalization applicable to countries as varied as Russia, Poland, and Israel.

The Russian parliament (elected in 1990, before the Communist Party had been discredited, and before opposition parties had consolidated) moreover contained a substantial number of hard-liners both on the left and on the right who opposed Yeltsin. There was a bewildering number of political parties (between 30 and 40 by 1992). They comprised former communists, socialists, anarcho-syndicalists, right-wingers, Christian Democrats, Liberal Democrats, Social Democrats, as well as a new Entrepreneurs' Party. (The Christian Democrats took the German CDU for a model.)[32] By 1992 there were three loose coalitions. "Democratic Russia" suffered from numerous internal divisions, but on the whole backed Yeltsin and his acting prime minister Yegor Gaidar in their attempt to create a Western-style market economy. Democratic Russia was supported by the new class of independent entrepreneurs and by reform-minded intellectuals.

The center was occupied by the Civic Union, which comprised disillusioned democrats, directors of state-owned factories and farms, members of minor centrist groups. While endorsing a market economy, the Union insisted on a much slower pace of reform than Gaidar's. Aleksandr Rutskoi, a much-decorated hero from the Afghan war, Yeltsin's vice-president, and also one of his bitter critics, looked to the creation of a strong state. According to Rutskoi, Russian statesmen should learn from the example of Peter Stolypin, the last of the great reforming ministers of the Czarist era. Stolypin had tried to link reform to a strong state; no other formula would do. Only a strong state could create the rule of the law; only the rule of the law could assure the creation of a market economy. Russia could not be cured by shock therapy, but only by treatment of a more cautious kind.[33] The Union also took a strong line toward ethnic minorities within Russia's borders while supporting the grievances of ethnic Russians living in the other republics. The Union occupied a strategic position in the Russian parliament. Yeltsin's survival would depend on his ability to maneuver between the Union and Democratic Russia – a difficult feat.

The right was represented by the National Salvation Front, an incongruous coalition of hard-line nationalists, monarchists, and communists – "red and brown," meaning National Socialist (Nazi) according to the Front's critics. The Front rejected reform, called for the restoration of Russia's armed might and Russian leadership within the former Soviet Union, while blaming Jews, foreigners, and home-grown evil-doers for Russia's ills. The Front associated the West with spreading crime, drug addiction, prostitution, a raucous youth culture, and contempt for authority in general. The Front commanded support particularly within the military, among party officials without employment, workers without jobs, and a host of other citizens. Ordinary Russians were irked not merely by high unemployment and rising prices, but also by a sense of moral decay – the prestige accorded to whores available for hard currency, the sight of grim-faced men who drove in unmarked luxury cars, parked their vehicles illegally whenever the drivers pleased, and were assiduously saluted by police officers. Fearing a right-wing coup, Yeltsin banned the Front. At the same time he attempted to create his own machinery, based on a security council under his own control, and a nation-wide network of factory managers and heads of workers' collectives to advise the council. But there was no clear distinction between the powers of the president and parliament; provincial bosses openly flouted the central authority. Neither bans nor administrative changes could dispose of those grievances which had led to the formation of the National Salvation Front in the first place. As the knowledgeable observer Richard F. Staar put it, the future might well belong to a right-wing coalition representing the High Command of the armed forces and the military-industrial complex – not a reassuring prospect to contemplate.[34]

Nevertheless, Russian democracy, young, ill-experienced, and ill-financed, did a great deal better than the prophets had expected. Between 1991 and 1992 Russia had managed to reduce its budget deficit from 20 percent to 5 percent of the gross national product; prices had been freed without riots, and the economy had partially opened to international trade.[35] There was freedom of speech, freedom of religion, freedom of the press, freedom to form political parties. The Soviet empire had been dismantled much more peacefully than the British empire in India, the French empire in Algeria, or the Portuguese empire in Angola and Mozambique. It is true that many problems remained. Foremost among them was inflation which, ironically enough, struck with particular severity at democracy's most loyal supporters – teachers, professors, scientists. Patriotic Russians complained that declining living standards went with a decline of Russia's prestige abroad, as even the small Baltic states now dared to defy Moscow over the grant of full civic rights to the resident Russian minorities. Communist and ultra-nationalist hard-liners remained powerful. But over the long years of communist tyranny the Russian people had become increasingly urbanized, increasingly educated in a formal sense, increasingly reluctant to accept the claims of political Messiahs. In all probability, therefore, the New Right will not muster enough strength to take over Russia, much less the former Soviet Union as a whole – given the strength of anti-communism amongst the bulk of the population.

Outside Russia proper there was an immense array of local national parties which varied from ultra-nationalist to fully democratic organizations. The ultra-nationalists included Zviad Gamsakhurdia, a gifted linguist and an environmentalist of note, who became president of Georgia's first freely elected government since 1918. Gamsakhurdia (later displaced from power) soon earned for himself the sobriquet of "Georgian Mussolini" as he cracked down on dissidents and threatened to drive them out of the country. On the other hand, Vytautas Landsbergis, Lithuanian president from 1990 to 1992, was a convinced democrat, a man of personal integrity. A prominent musicologist, he thereafter turned to dissident politics, and became leader of Sajudis, the Lithuanian national movement. The future may well depend on whether the leaders of the Soviet successor states will take Gamsakhurdia or Landsbergis as role models.

## THE SOVIET UNION FRAGMENTS

In July 1991 the Communist Party of the Soviet Union issued an unheard of complaint. The Party's Deputy General Secretary Vladimir Ivashko lamented that party organizers were being thrown out of industrial and agricultural enterprises, and that the human rights of loyal party members were being violated.[36] Quite so, agreed Gamsakhurdia: communists should be "chopped up" and "burned out of the Georgian nation with a red-hot iron."[37] Compared to such rhetoric, the language of old-fashioned anti-communists in the US had begun to sound tame. What was at stake for them personally was their own past. Could former *apparatchiks* truly admit that they had served all their lifetime an evil, or at least a futile cause? What was at stake for the world was the future of the greatest surviving empire. The hard-liners now comprised a strange alliance between old-fashioned imperialists such as lieutenant-colonel Victor Alksnis, a professional officer who would have felt thoroughly at home among French airborne officers during the Algerian war, and hard-line communists. This alliance now drew its most persuasive arguments from the armory of traditional imperialism which, in its Western form, the Soviet had always denounced – unwisely so, for the Russian neo-imperialists' self-interest. The demise of great empires in the past had always come at a great price. Suppose the Soviet Union were to disintegrate? What would happen to those numerous national minorities located on the "wrong" side of the new borders? What would be the fate of those 25 million ethnic Russians who live outside the Russian Federation? Would they be treated any better than the million Europeans who had been expelled from Algeria when that country had attained independence, or the 600,000 to 800,000 Portuguese and Euro-Africans who had been thrown out of newly independent Angola and Mozambique? Already Russia has begun to brace herself for an invasion of refugees from dissident republics. (For instance, as many as 60 percent of Tajikistan's Russians supposedly want to leave.) Not all migrants were ethnic Russians; fighting between Azerbaijan and Armenia in 1990 occasioned massive emigration of refugees derived from both nationalities who sought the relative safety of the Russian Federated Republic).

Only a strong empire, the centralizers' claimed, could rebuild the Soviet Union as a great free-trading area. Only a strong empire could afford to tax rich provinces to help poor regions. (This particular argument lost some of its force when in 1991 the Russian Federation agreed to subsidize poverty-stricken Kirghizstan.) Only a strong empire could contain the bitter strife that divides ethnic communities such as Armenians and Azerbaijanis. The centralizers foresaw that the a breakup of the Soviet Union, in promoting ethnic anarchy, would play a disastrous game of beggar-my-neighbor, holding on to scarce resources and thereby contributing to economic fragmentation and general chaos. The Soviet successor states might conceivably become involved in a civil war in which even nuclear weapons might be employed. Such wars would inevitably engulf foreign countries, producing a global catastrophe.[38] The Soviet Union might fragment – with Yugoslavia as a paradigm. As Gorbachev put it:

> The events [in Yugoslavia] are a lesson for all the peoples in the Soviet Union, and also a warning. . . . What is happening now should make everybody understand that it is necessary to pursue the road to renewal and not disintegration.[39]

If the Soviet center failed to hold, the hard-liners' argument went on, a domino effect would start and the process of dissolution would continue. The US would then be left as the world's only remaining superpower. This was a prospect that should daunt not only Soviets but also all foreign patriots. In addition, the hard-liners employed cultural arguments. Why break up the Soviet Union and thereby make its peoples more vulnerable than ever before to Western evils? Better stay with traditional values tried and true. Such were the views of "Archie Bunkers," Russian style, who disliked outsiders – Jewish or Gentile – with equal ferocity.[40]

The hard-liners therefore felt that only a putsch could avert disaster. (It was an attempted palace revolution, since the plotters included the most senior members of the Soviet government, including the prime minister, the minister of defense, and the head of the KGB.) The most immediate cause was the new union treaty, due to be signed on August 27, 1991. The full story remains to be told, but the outlines are clear. The coup leaders, men whom Gorbachev had fully trusted, arrested Gorbachev and tried to seize power through military force. They were not, however, an impressive lot. Gennedy Yanaev, the Soviet vice-president, Gorbachev's personal choice; Vladimir Kryuchkov, chairman of the KGB; Marshal Dimitry Yazov, defense minister; Boris Pugo, minister of the interior, and their friends would all have incurred from Lenin the harshest censure possible for their lack of resolve and deficient organizational skills. Indeed, they made every mistake in the book – as noted by Marshall I. Goldman, a respected American Sovietologist who happened to be in Moscow at the time. The plotters overlooked Yeltsin's personal popularity[41] and failed to understand the changes in the Soviet political climate brought about by Gorbachev's *perestroika*. The Soviet public was neither that docile mass of communist imagination, nor that ferocious, unwashed mob that Russian intellectuals had so often dreaded in the past. On the contrary, the public was firm, yet committed to legality; Soviet citizens were in fact truly upset that the conspirators had violated legal procedure, a point reiterated by speakers in the Russian parliament.

Above all, the conspirators could no longer rely on the army, their chosen instrument. Many years earlier, Alexander Shtromas, an émigré scholar in England of Lithuanian descent, had made a striking prediction. If once the Communist Party's power were to weaken, there would come into existence a "second pivot." This might be almost any existing institution within the Soviet state, but suddenly popular power would come to hinge on this "second pivot," until Soviet power would be displaced. In August 1991, it was the parliament of the Russian Federated Republic which turned out to be the "second pivot." The deputies met in internationally televised sessions. From Moscow to London to New York audiences could listen to debates which once more extolled those constitutional liberties that communists and their friends had defamed for several generations: constitutional government and the rule of law. Outside parliament, Muscovites rose, linked arms, and dared the "State Committee for the State of Emergency" to send in tanks. The plotters seemed helpless; tank crews refused to obey orders; Yeltsin proved an inspirational leader of boundless courage, and the coup collapsed.[42] The leaders were arrested on August 22. Just over a week later, on August 30, 1991, the Supreme Soviet of the Soviet Union, by a huge majority, suspended the activities of the Communist Party of the Soviet Union. Thereafter the central power continued to weaken. Nothing was left for the hard-liners but *sauve qui peut*, save your skins!

## A TIME OF TROUBLES

By the end of 1991, the Soviet Union had ceased to exist as a state; effective power had swung to the republics, above all to Russia, the giant among them. Russia is twice the size of the US. Its population stands at 147,386,000, with an annual growth in 1989 of 1.5 percent. Russia's resources are enormous. They include an estimated 50 percent of the world's coal reserves, 20 percent of the world's estimated gold deposits, with oil, natural gas, iron ore, diamonds, copper, silver, timber – a veritable treasure house. Overall, the breakdown of the huge Soviet edifice had come much more swiftly and much more peacefully than the most optimistic forecasters could have imagined. By the end of 1991, Yeltsin thus had assumed control of the former Soviet Union's economic ministries, and its key foreign ministry. Gosbank, the Soviet state bank, was running out of cash to pay official salaries and other outstanding debts. It was the republics, Russia chief among them, which took over all outstanding obligations. Those who paid the piper would henceforth call the tune.

It was not only the central civilian administration which was in disarray. There were laws – but no constitution. There was open talk about an army coup on the part of disaffected, politicized soldiers backed by hungry crowds in the streets, by former party bosses without jobs, and by that great host of informers who had formerly served the KGB, and now stood in fear that their past activities would come to light. The armed forces suffered from a serious malaise. They remained immensely powerful in terms of numbers and weaponry. But they were beset by poor morale, divided loyalties, and uncertainty concerning their mission, career prospects, and pay. There was ethnic rivalry, and problems of alcoholism and illiteracy.[43] Discontented officers organized an "Officers' League," led by Colonel Terechov, who openly gave subversive interviews to the foreign press, including *Der Spiegel* in Germany.[44] Terechov claimed that the League was particularly influential among field grade officers – majors and colonels (the very group which had set off the Portuguese military coup in 1974 and the Spanish Civil War in 1936). The League complained that the army was in desperate shape – ill-housed, ill-paid, ill-respected, and ill-led. Arms were being stolen *en masse*; supplies were sold by corrupt soldiers and civilians. Two-thirds of the conscripted failed to report for duty. Not surprisingly, morale had slumped; discipline was gravely impaired. Only the National Salvation Front, said the colonel, could restore Russia's past greatness.

These problems became even more pressing as the other republics began to form their own security forces. Pessimists therefore feared that dispirited troops might mutiny – as the *Force Publique* had done with disastrous effects in the former Belgian Congo 30 years earlier and again in 1991. But this time, a military breakup would affect a military force of immense power, armed with nuclear weaponry. This included an estimated 30,000 ICBM and tactical nuclear weapons – missiles, bombs, mines, artillery shells – many of them small enough to be easily transported. What would happen if corrupt military officers or civilian officials were to sell them on the international black market to Third World dictators, terrorists, or plain criminals?

There was also a great deal of crime. For all the former propaganda, crime was omnipresent throughout the lands that had once composed the Soviet Union. The former ruling party and its intelligence agencies and police had been linked to illegal arrests of citizens, and crime, as had its economic agencies. The ordinary Soviet citizen always had to walk along a narrow line, as the distinction between legal and illegal activities could never be clearly drawn. Crime had pervaded society. As a Soviet journalist, forced to leave his country because of his investigation into organized crime, put it: "until people totally untarnished by the system (read Mafia) come into power in the Soviet Union, there are no hopes for a brighter future."[45]

The economy was equally in trouble. (According to official estimates, the GNP of the Soviet Union as a whole had declined by 10 percent in the first half of 1991 and was estimated to fall by another 8 to 10 percent by the year's end. Foreign trade was down by 37 percent.) The major failing was the government's inability or unwillingness to create a new currency. The ruble kept losing its value. (By the end of 1992 inflation was running at 1,300 percent a year.) German recovery after World War I and World War II respectively had been made possible by the creation of a sound mark; Russia would not be able to repeat this feat without a sound ruble.[46] By the end of 1992 much of the country was reduced to a barter economy. The separate republics issued their own rubles, thereby worsening their problem, since the bank notes issued by other republics were no longer interchangeable. Neither were bank deposits freely convertible into currency. The banks remained state-owned, linked to state-run enterprises.

Bank loans therefore went to state firms rather than to small business in need of credit. The country in fact used a dual currency – rubles and dollars (or other hard foreign currencies). There was no properly constituted Internal Revenue Service; the Russian state drew the bulk of its revenue from state enterprises; hence there was an inbuilt opposition to reform. Government in many areas could not enforce its own laws; there were extortion rackets; the country was plagued with conflicting jurisdiction, legal uncertainties; foreign investors could hardly be blamed for looking at Russia with extreme suspicion at a time when risk capital was scarce world-wide – a fact inadequately understood by Russian bureaucrats. To reform Russia meant working with international agencies such as the IMF and the World Bank, ignorant of Russia's special problems. It was a task that would have tested alike the wisdom of Solon and of Solomon.

This was not the end of Russia's problems. In 1992 the former ruble zone broke up, as coordination of basic fiscal, monetary, and credit policies proved difficult between the various republics. Inter-republic trade faltered in the face of numerous artificial restrictions. The collective security agreement, signed at Tashkent between Russia, five Central Asian states, and Armenia, was in trouble. Parcelling out the assets of the former Soviet Union remained a divisive subject. Equally difficult was the task of cutting down Russia's (and also Ukraine's) bloated arms sector (important also as a source of foreign currency through international arms sales). On a conservative estimate it accounts for over a third, and perhaps as much as half of the Soviet Union's total industrial output.[47] The switch to a peacetime economy, with a Russian army of between 1.2 million to 1.3 million men, will be tremendously difficult.

Yeltsin tried to meet the problem head on by privatization through a complex voucher scheme whereby 150 million Russians received cream-colored "privatization checks" with a picture of the Russian parliament. Each voucher could be sold for cash, placed in some new investment fund, or used to buy shares in state enterprises being shed by the state.[48] But success remained far from certain as confusion prevailed, for ordinary Russians widely distrusted the project as yet another government ruse. There were lengthening bread lines, energy shortfalls, traffic breakdowns, widespread popular anxiety about the future. Precise statistics are of course unavailable, given the huge size of Russia's "Second Economy" concealed from census takers and tax collectors. But Russia's natural resources remained enormous. Russia remained the world's largest oil producer. Russia's true gold reserves were much larger than indicated by official statistics, as a good deal of gold coins remained hidden in stockings and jam jars. There was probably more food available through underground channels than official spokesmen would admit. (Caroll Boger, a visiting

US journalist, found in 1991 plenty of shortages, much hoarding, a decline in food consumption, but no evidence of starvation.)[49] By the middle of 1992 a shopper in Moscow or St Petersburg could buy anything he or she desired – the choicest foods, the finest cars. But only the rich could afford such luxuries. Purchasers who went to state stores found food at more reasonable prices and lesser quality. In the villages the food situation was generally better than in the cities. The main sufferers were people on small, fixed incomes – teachers, clerks, manual workers, and pensioners. But few were actually starving. Moreover, the former Soviet Union had accumulated a huge Strategic Grain Reserve, designed to tide the country over an extended war. (According to some estimates, the Strategic Grain Reserve was large enough to feed the country for three, perhaps even four years.) If these supplies were properly distributed, hunger could surely be avoided.[50] Moreover, published statistics in Russia underplayed the extent of total economic production. They did so because a large portion derived from clandestine enterprise, both official and private, largely escaped the attention of statisticians and tax gatherers.

Nevertheless, conditions were bad enough. An overgrown arms industry kept turning out military hardware, thereby adding to existing stocks which themselves had to be maintained and guarded from would-be thieves. A metropolis such as Sverdlovsk, Yeltsin's native city, largely depended on the manufacture of arms. What was Yeltsin to do in his native city? Would he close down all factories at once and thereby ruin his hometown? Or would he do so by degrees? A solution would have to be found; otherwise Sverdlovsk (now known again as Yekaterinburg), just like other cities, would not supply enough consumer goods to pay the farmers; thereafter bread lines would further lengthen, and once more threaten the very existence of the new regimes.

In the bad old days of the Soviet Union, the rulers had relied heavily on coercion to extract food from the villages. Farmers were forced to deliver their assigned quotas, or pay the consequences. The cities had been subsidized by the countryside, with disastrous effects for the country's supplies of meat, milk, grain, and vegetables. Private farmers had been robbed of their land, jailed, and murdered – the so-called kulak (small-holder) of communist demonology, in fact Russia's most hard-working and efficient cultivators of the land. Independent rural traders (many of them Jewish) fared no better; their demise gravely weakened the distribution network in the countryside, and deprived villagers of local credit facilities otherwise unavailable. Not surprisingly, Soviet agriculture suffered from all the ills that also beset urban industries – inefficient planning, an uneco-nomic pricing system, inadequate maintenance of equipment; managerial inadequacies; deficient storage facilities; insufficient transport – the list goes on. Discipline weakened; morale declined. As a Lithuanian farmer's wife put it to a visiting American scholar, "since independence nobody at the kholkoz [collective farm] wants to work. Everyone is waiting. Production is falling." Drunkenness, she continued, was on the upswing; laborers would not turn up for work. The only thing to do was to turn the kholkoz into a cooperative run by the most efficient of small farmers – "but then all the drunks and the freeloaders would have to go."[51] Reconstruction involved even more: a private farming industry, a network of private trade, a system of private credit would have to be rebuilt – and all from scratch.

There were yet other problems connected with Soviet science. The scientific enterprise was essential for reconstructing the economy – but science was in disarray. Scientists had for many years been intimidated by party bosses and ideologues. It was a miracle how much they did achieve, even after Stalin's purges had decimated the academic professions. But as the Soviet economy continued to deteriorate, even these achievements were threatened. Soviet scientists experienced increasing difficulties in securing scientific equipment, specialist publications, even the most essential raw materials. These troubles were multiplied by ethnic discrimination, particularly against Jews. Science cannot flourish under conditions where a Jewish petrochemical engineer (now living in the US) was told, on wanting to hire another Jewish expert, "don't make a synagogue in your laboratory."[52] Not surprisingly, Soviet science was threatened by a massive exodus of scientists and other specialists, many of them Jewish; one of the Soviet Union's most crucial enterprises thus stood in danger of collapse.

For 70 years, Soviet opinion-makers had tried to poison the mind of ordinary citizens against allegedly greedy foreigners supposedly who rejoiced in sucking the lifeblood from exploited workers. Reformers such as Yeltsin realized that such fairy tales would no longer serve in future. Even so, a foreign investor, for example, would have to seek answers to innumerable questions. Which of many conflicting agencies would deal with his application? What would happen to existing Soviet debt to Western countries?[53] Would the republics take over the former Soviet Union's foreign debt? At the time of writing, Western creditors were insisting that the republics should deal with the debt collectively, and indicated that they would grant no new credits if the republics acted separately. How would the former Soviet Union's existing reserves of gold and foreign currency be apportioned between the republics? It was infinitely easier to frame queries than supply answers.

The resolution of all these questions hinges on politics. Russia may not remain committed to a market economy. The military might take over, either directly or indirectly. But even if the reformers retain power, their difficulties remain. No market economy can function without a powerful state with a well-organized legal system, incorruptible judiciary and an efficient and honest police to enforce the rule of law. A market economy likewise requires a sound currency, banking system, effective social service agencies, a competent internal revenue service, census bureau, archives department, and many other official agencies whose performance Western businessmen and economists take for granted. The republics will also have to frame new citizenship laws, itself a highly charged political question which involves minority rights as a whole. (For example, on occupying the three Baltic republics before World War II, the Soviets deported and murdered the bulk of the indigenous elites; numerous Russians thereafter settled in the Baltic lands, where they came to make up more than 30 percent of the population in Estonia, and more than 40 percent in Latvia. The new republics fear for their cultural as well as national survival; they will have to settle the difficult problem of which Russians will be accepted as citizens, and who will have to depart.) All these tasks will have to be accomplished with slender financial means, insufficient trained personnel, impoverished political institutions – and this during an ongoing economic crisis, and at a time of great political uncertainty. It is an assignment that would have daunted Hercules.

The formation of the CIS (Commonwealth of Independent States) did not halt the threatened slide into chaos in some parts of the former Soviet Union. Some experts indeed talked of "disintegrative reorganization"! They forgot Aristotle's warning: Better tyranny than anarchy. The old Soviet Union had gone, but no coherent cooperative structure had as yet taken its place.[54] At the time of writing there was violence in Georgia, Azerbaijan, Moldova, and Armenia. The distribution system, always poor, had become even more inefficient as the various republics put up new trade barriers, while withholding food for their own use. Policy-makers bitterly disagreed on how to reform the country. As the London *Economist* put it, "Russia displays the curious phenomenon of a government full of monetarists and a central bank full of Keynesians."[55] But there were also some hopeful signs. A start had been made on privatization, and also on improving Russia's primitive system of taxation. Price subsidies were largely ended; budgetary controls became stricter than before.

## WHAT'S TO BE DONE?

How then should Washington act toward the Soviet Union's successor states? On a political plane, Russia is the key to the new post-communist world. Russia is by far the largest and most powerful of the successor states; whatever turmoil the country may undergo for the time being,

Russia will surely re-emerge as a great power, as it has always done. Great diplomatic skill will be required to maintain good Russo-American relations in future: the army remains powerful; former communists run the big industries, nuclear weapons abound. But there are no natural disputes between the two countries. Even a military dictatorship in Russia would be vastly preferable to the defunct communist regime, for a military government would merely look out for Russia's interests as a great power without being ideologically committed to the international class struggle and the world revolution. Neither the US nor Russia want territory from the other; both have raw materials and "living space" aplenty. Oddly enough, Russia and the US also share certain more general features. Both are huge in size; both countries had the experience of endless moving frontiers. Both are varied in their ethnic character. Both have a strong streak of religiosity that foreigners have consistently failed to appreciate to its full extent. Both countries have an ambivalent attitude to Europe – half out, half in.

Foreign relations are influenced by intangible considerations as well as *realpolitik*. All too many Europeans, including many Russians, mistakenly believe, for example, that the US is both a libertine and a materialistic country, run by men with cold hearts and bulging wallets. US information agencies need to point out that these views are quite mistaken, that the US is indeed, by any standards, a remarkably religious country. The overwhelming majority of Americans of any color reject drugs, sexual immorality, or criminal behavior of any kind. The television screen does not provide a true mirror of US society.

US diplomacy also needs to emphasize that America has no quarrel with Russia as such, as distinct from the discredited communist system. A strong Russia may indeed be necessary in future as a counter-weight against the People's Republic of China, or perhaps against new Muslim Fundamentalist challenges. This consideration should be kept in mind with regard to US diplomacy concerning ethnic minority rights. Russia now seeks to protect the 25 million ethnic Russians outside Russia's borders. Before foreigners criticize Russia for doing so, they should remember than France fought a bloody and extended war in part to safeguard just 1 million *pieds noirs* in Algeria. In so far as the US is able to exert diplomatic influence, it should be used to protect minority rights in the Soviet successor states, including minority rights for expatriate Russians. Neighboring states may have a case in restricting the influence of Russian settlers within their respective countries. Nevertheless, they should desist, for it is imprudent on the part of Russia's smaller neighbors to poke the eyes of the Russian bear when it is sick. They should be left in no doubt that no US soldier (or, for that matter, no EC soldier) will ever fire a shot to defend Russia's neighbors in a quarrel occasioned over minority rights or frontier rectifications. By the same token, US diplomacy may have to stress in future that Russia's own national interests are best served by a policy of compromise. France did not become weaker, but stronger, by retreating from Algeria; Britain emerged stronger, not weaker, by conceding independence to Eire. These are valid examples for militant Russian nationalists to follow.

Among economic issues, one of the chief concerns is the role of foreign aid. Should the US provide foreign assistance? And if so, how much? Should aid be extended to the failing Soviet state, or to the individual republics? Should the US concentrate on food aid? (At the end of 1991, the former Bush administration resolved to provide $1.5 billion of food aid, to be channeled through the republics rather than the center in Moscow.) What was to be done about the crushing burden of debts assumed by successive Soviet governments? (By 1991, the Soviets owed an estimated $74 billion to Western creditors alone; of these $28 billion were due to Germany, by far the Soviet Union's largest creditor, with additional debts to Middle Eastern countries, South Korea, Taiwan, and elsewhere.) In November 1991, the Group of Seven (G7, comprising the US, Japan, Germany, France, Britain, Italy, and Canada) offered a $1 billion "bridge loan" to tide the Soviets over their short-term obligations. This was not the end of Western generosity. In 1992 the Western countries drafted a $24 billion aid plan for Russia, with strong support from the Bush administration in Washington. Russia and most of the other republics won full admittance to the IMF (International Monetary Fund) and the World Bank, thereby gaining additional access to funds provided for the most part by Western taxpayer. In addition, the US and ten other Western countries tentatively agreed to provide financial assistance to prop up the failing ruble. Nevertheless, expert opinion remained convinced that even these outlays would not suffice to put Russia and the remaining republics back on their feet.

The advocates of massive aid therefore asked for much greater commitments. The US should furnish food in the short run, and industrial and infrastructural assistance in the long run, linked to extensive technical advice. As aid advocates see it, the former Soviet Union faces catastrophe. Hunger may sweep through the new republics. The social order may collapse; hence communism might be replaced by new forms of home-grown fascism. Washington therefore allegedly has a vital stake in the Soviet Union's future prosperity.[56] Even at its most selfish, the US must strive to preserve some kind of a central Soviet coordinating machinery to assure control of an estimated 30,000 nuclear weapons in the combined arsenal. It is not in the US's interest that Russia, Belarus, Ukraine, and Kazakhstan (where nuclear weapons are stationed at present) should all become nuclear powers in their own right, or that they should seek to make money by selling nuclear weapons to Third World powers. Hence the US should give aid to the individual republics, and, at the same time, strive for the preservation of a central coordinating body.

There are other arguments for giving aid. The US cannot afford to leave East-Central Europe and the former Soviet Union to the West Europeans alone, particularly the Germans, as a field of economic interest. Some advocates of aid indeed paint even scarier pictures. If the economies of the various republics collapse, there will be a huge exodus of Ukrainians, Russians, Balts, and others. These poverty-stricken and embittered emigrants will seek homes in the West, thereby exporting the Soviet crisis abroad. (For a start, these economic refugees would include the bulk of Soviet Jewry, as well as two million ethnic Germans now living in Russia.) Russia might succumb to a counter-revolution that would create a militaristic regime anxious to undo the damage done to Soviet military might. Worse still, the Soviet Union might be succeeded by rival cliques of warring states. This again would be a disaster in a world where fragmentation threatens so many other countries, and where opportunities for regional mischief keep increasing.

Frightened by such foreboding prospects, a group of Russian and US economists gathered at Harvard in 1991 to work out a "Grand Bargain" which would end the Cold War. (Gorbachev himself had proposed a similar design when, in 1991, he accepted a Nobel Peace Prize.) The US, the group said, should join in a massive new Marshall Plan. (The Harvard proponents of a Grand Bargain spoke of reform-linked assistance to the tune of $30 billion a year for an unspecified period of time.) The Marshall Plan had played a vital part in rebuilding war-torn Europe. Would not a similar plan put the Soviet Union back on its feet?

Support for a new Marshall Plan was widespread. For instance, Lech Walesa, the Polish president, told a joint session of Congress in 1991 that the US should start a new Plan to help the stricken lands east of the Elbe, to promote international cooperation, assist the reunification of Europe, and spread prosperity. The US aid lobby has also powerful support within the Clinton administration. Obviously, all business corporations like to get orders through public programs which enable them to sell their goods and services at the US taxpayer's expense. Domestic backers of aid projects also include humanitarians – clergymen, educators, media people – who consider that the US, the world's richest country, has a moral duty to help the poor throughout the globe. Better aid than arms!

The aid lobby also had powerful backing from some of the US's own allies, above all from Germany. (According to Chancellor Helmut Kohl, in the early 1990s, 40 percent of the total foreign aid to Central and Eastern Europe derived from Germany.) The Germans want more global burden-sharing, and with good reason. They have to rehabilitate East Germany; they have given to the US financial assistance for the Gulf War ($6.29 billion); they are continuing to make massive payments to the former Soviet Union. Hence the US, Britain, France, and Japan have done much less, and should, in Bonn's opinion, do much more.[57] President François Mitterrand of France shares this commitment to massive aid for the Soviet Union, as do US political leaders such as House Majority Leader Richard Gephardt and former president Richard M. Nixon.[58]

The present authors do not accept these arguments. The Marshall Plan analogue will not hold. At the end of World War II, the US was the world's leading economic power. Its per capita income was by far the highest in the world; the US was also the world's premier creditor nation. (The so-called "Dollar Gap," that is to say, the Western Europeans' unfavorable trade balance in regard to the US, was supposed to last for the foreseeable future.) The US enjoyed a decisive predominance in most scientific and technological fields. US factories, ports, and railway mar-shaling yards had never been shelled or bombed, unlike many of those installations owned by US competitors. These conditions no longer apply. The US today is a net debtor nation; the US trade balance remains unfavorable. The US remains an economic giant, but its relative position in the world is much less important than it was in 1948. Moreover, Western Europe in the late 1940s cannot be compared to the Soviet Union in the early 1990s. The US then wielded considerable political influence in Western Europe; Washington's present political influence within the former Soviet Union is much less. Above all, American aid to Western Europe provided a kind of earthquake relief only; the required political and economic institutions were already in place. In the former Soviet Union an entire society has to be recreated – a task beyond any aid-giver's scope. Private individuals and private agencies in the US can give advice, but the US government can no longer tell foreign countries how to design their respective constitutions, or how to provide for cooperation with their neighbors. Foreign aid cannot, and should not, be used as a means of nation-building abroad.

As regards Germany, the US should learn from Bonn's current predica-ment rather than imitate its mistakes. The Germans, in subsidizing the former Soviet Union, much of East-Central Europe, and the five eastern *Länder*, may have taken on more than they can manage. (The German budgetary deficit for 1991 will run at an estimated $35 billion – this in a country known in the past for its financial prudence. In fact the US – unexpectedly – has done much better in this respect than Germany.) The

US admittedly has a large budget deficit. But its *general* government deficit (including local government, state government, federal government, and social security balances) is considerably less comparatively than Germany's (2.8 percent as opposed to Germany's 5.2 percent or more).[59] Germany, as we have seen, also pays heavily for reconstructing East Germany, for equalizing East German with West German wages, for an extensive welfare state, for major changes that arise from its EC obligations, and for transferring its capital from Bonn to Berlin. No wonder German taxation has risen. The CDU has begun to do badly in public opinion polls, and Germans complain about being the world's paymasters. Germany may indeed be unable in future to go on playing its accustomed role as a locomotive that pulls the entire European economy.

There are other problems with regard to foreign aid. Aid in the past has often done more harm than good by encouraging governmental profligacy, by building up unprofitable bureaucratic lobbies both in the donor and the recipient country, and by promoting ill-considered or corrupt expenditures. It is difficult to see, for example, just how far the massive aid extended to the newly independent African countries after World War II has in fact promoted democracy or economic growth.[60] Moreover, the Soviet Union in the past has not exactly been the world's Cinderella regarding foreign aid. The Soviet Union had received massive loans; food aid; technical assistance; and a surfeit of economic advice. (During the year 1990–1, the Soviet Union obtained at least $20 billion in aid from capitalist countries.) Western markets were opened. The US prepared to grant Most Favored Nation status to the Soviet Union, and lower tariff barriers so as to encourage Soviet exports. The Soviet Union also receive other favors – none of which strike us as desirable. (For instance, the US Import-Export Bank gave certain guarantees to US investors; US grain exporters to the Soviet Union could obtain official credits – to the detriment of independent Russian farmers.) Gorbachev also sought indirect access to fund provided by Western taxpayers by seeking membership for the Soviet Union in the IMF and the World Bank. Similar favors will surely be sought by the Soviet Union's successor states. They should be rigidly scrutinized from the standpoint of the US taxpayer's interest.

Unfortunately, massive international aid does not necessarily lead to reform. Israel, for example, has been a major recipient of US generosity for many years; but Israel's economy continues to stumble along in socialist inefficiency. All too often, effective economic reform is born of financial stringency. For instance, Turkey in 1980, Mexico after 1985, Bolivia in the late 1980s succeeded because they were in financial trouble and had no alternative. Lacking money, these countries simply had to make their economies more productive by strengthening market incentives, rationalizing imports, increasing savings, and integrating themselves into the world economy more effectively than before. Similar considerations apply to General Augusto Pinochet's Chile, and to Poland in the first phase of Poland's reform effort.[61] As the London *Economist* points out, the Soviet Union is unable to absorb even the funds already received. Since 1989, Germany alone has already paid to the Soviet Union DM 56.9 billion ($33 billion). There is little to show for it. (Much assistance has already gone to building barracks for troops returning from Germany, which helps morale but does nothing to improve Russia's economy.) The Russians pleaded for foreign money to make the ruble convertible. But the Soviet Union had large gold stocks, and was also a major exporter of oil and natural gas. Why should Western taxpayers provide cash when the CIS could use its own gold hoard (said to be depleted from 2,500 tonnes in 1985 to only 240 tonnes in 1991)?

Foreign aid can of course be used productively for capital imports. Unfortunately, substituting imported machinery for Soviet machinery did not necessarily improve efficiency because of the wastefulness with which capital was used in the Soviet Union. (Over the last three decades, the net fixed capital investment rose from 17 percent of GNP to around 26 percent. Yet productivity actually fell during the 1980s.) The Soviets' low productivity derived from lack of competition and private property, poor incentives and poor organization. The *Economist* concluded that, given improvement in these two essentials, the Soviet Union would not need aid, but could finance capital imports from higher exports. Better still, the CIS could attract private investment and joint ventures from abroad, and with it, those foreign management, machinery and technological skills that come with foreign investment.[62] Foreign aid also enabled its recipients to avoid harsh choices. Russia's pace of reform has been slow by comparison with Poland and Czechoslovakia. Above all, the Soviet Union has not cut down its bloated arms sector.

Clearly, even the most extreme "cold warriors" had actually underestimated the former Soviet Union's economic militarism. It was surely unwise for the West to subsidize the Soviet military, given the Western donors' complete inability to control the use made of the aid which Western taxpayers were asked to provide. It was equally unrealistic for the West to subsidize the Soviet Union as long as the Soviets subsidized oppressive and bankrupt regimes in Cuba and Afghanistan. Even food aid, most obviously a humanitarian form of assistance, entails many problems. In part Russia's food problems today derive from it inefficient collective farms, decrepit transport and storage facilities; even when available, food may not reach the consumer. Secondly, indigenous farmers will not improve their land unless they own it. The constituent republics of the former Soviet Union will not produce enough corn, wheat, and beef until they re-introduce the private ownership of land. The former Soviet Union, moreover, could alleviate immediate shortages by making the huge Strategic Grain Reserve available to consumers now.

The US government can, however, be helpful to the Soviet successor states, including Russia, over the matter of the debts incurred by the former Soviet Union. In 1992 Yeltsin promised that Russia would pay its appropriate share of the debts. The US should not hold him to this promise – the US government is not a collection agency. Neither should the US taxpayer be obliged to guarantee loans made to unstable governments by private or public US corporations. If individuals or corporations chose to lend money to foreign governments, they should do so at their own risk. In the past, unfortunately, many corporate executives chose to ignore good advice. Those experts went unheeded who pointed out the poor security which was offered by the former Soviet Union (and also by numerous Third World governments), the tyrannical and dishonest nature of their respective regimes, and their instability. If these loans now result in losses, this should be the private investors' affair – not the US public's.

As regards the long-term task of privatizing industry and agriculture, Russia should avoid a dogmatic approach. Russia, like the other ex-communist states, can benefit from studying the experiences of many different countries, especially those which have moved away from *étatiste* (statist) economies. These include Argentina, Poland and especially the People's Republic of China, and – in a different setting – even individual cities such as Glasgow, Scotland. The Glasgow Development Authority did much to rehabilitate a once semi-derelict city; even the Bonn government thereafter consulted the Glaswegians on how to deal with East Germany. The People's Republic of China and Poland both privatized agriculture, albeit under different circumstances and by different means. (Poland had been unique in preserving its smallholders.) Poland thereafter speedily moved from food shortages to food surpluses. Russia can do the same. Reformers have made a start in Russia: in 1991 the number of privately owned farms rose from 4,433 to over 36,000. Privatization entailed the creation of smaller farms which could not use the large-sized tractors and combines employed on huge collective farms. The new, more diversified farming systems need smaller, versatile tractors, rototillers, trucks, and also grain bins, dryers, generators, small food-processing and packaging devices. These new requirements provide new opportunities for US manufacturers; in so far as the US extends aid to Russia, it should be spent on such machinery rather than food.[63]

There are other problems associated with foreign aid, technical assistance, and advice. Foreign aid cannot deal with the moral effects produced by long years of communist rule. Russian experts themselves complain that too many workers are idle, drunken, and incompetent, that all too many managers are hidebound and irresponsible. The distribution system remains primitive, the infrastructure in decay, the health care system in deep trouble. These problems are not insurmountable. There is a great deal of talent and skill in the CIS; there is a large though outmoded industrial base. Russia above all needs strong leadership; the US would therefore be ill-advised to impose some kind of democratic "loyalty test" on the Russian leadership. Even if Yeltsin were to be replaced by a military dictatorship, the US should not necessarily regard the new regime as a sworn enemy. Speculating many years ago on the downfall of communism in the Soviet Union, the present authors then argued that even an army dictatorship would be an improvement. At the time we met with considerable criticism – but we still believe that we were right.

No matter what, US public or private agencies should exercise the greatest care possible in disbursing the US taxpayer's money. Such caution is in order regarding bilateral aid, whose purpose Washington can decide, at least in theory. Even greater caution is needed with regard to multilateral aid disbursed by international agencies, bodies on whose respective directorates the US has only minority representation. These include the World Bank and the IMF. (The IMF is mostly funded through quotas imposed on its members. These quotas can be obtained politically more easily than foreign aid can be obtained by a straight vote for foreign aid in a national legislature.) Equal caution should prevail with regard to tendering advice. Advice should only be given when asked for, and on subjects requested by the petitioner. Even technical counsel can never be quite "technical" in the sense of being wholly non-political. If Western counselors propose a certain course of action to aid recipients, the advisers also take on certain political responsibilities, and justly incur blame when their plans do not work out. Private bodies are entitled to take this particular risk – but not governmental agencies.

Foreign aid also entails domestic problems within the US. Foreign aid has become unpopular in the US – in our opinion rightly so. The US now has to cope with far-reaching deficiencies within its own borders: the educational system needs to be rebuilt; public health needs to be made more accessible; the infrastructure may need to be restored. It is not obvious why the US taxpayer should spend his or her hard-earned income abroad rather than at home. Since World War II, the US taxpayer has spent astronomical sums on foreign assistance – more than all the reparations that have ever been paid by any vanquished to any victorious Western country. The private sector can make a more effective contribution both as regards investment and charity. Better to lighten the taxpayer's load than to increase it. The best service the US can render to all the formerly communist countries is to practice free trade. Indeed, Rita Klimova, a Czech professor and Czech ambassador to the US, explained at an academic symposium in Berlin in 1992 that her government wanted neither aid, nor debt relief, nor preferential treatment, merely open access to markets.[64]

Russia is now going through a "Time of Troubles," as she did during the seventeenth century and again after the 1917 revolution. Russians will have to rebuild their economic and political institutions, after a long period of social turmoil. The Russians were left with an outmoded economy and with a legacy of industrial demoralization. Ports were overcrowded, railways left in disrepair. The distribution system remained primitive, health care third rate. Old communists widely stayed in control even after the failure of the 1991 coup. Worse still was the sense of distrust inevitable in a country where colleague had suspected colleague and neighbor had spied on neighbor. (As Richard Pipes, one of the leading historians of Russia, points out, the minority nationalities have more cohesion, having for long resisted first Czarist, then Soviet oppression.) Russia will have to build new institutions from the bottom up; much responsibility will therefore fall on local authorities at a time when Moscow's word no longer counts for much in the provinces. Fortunately, the prospects for democracy are not hopeless. Ultra-chauvinist groups such as *Pamyat'* have fared badly at the polls; only a small minority wants a return of the *ancien régime*. Russia has enormous natural resources as well as an army of well-trained specialists. As always, Russia will survive.

Our cautious optimism in this regard is heightened by Yeltsin's personal ability. Though widely disparaged in the West, Yeltsin has surrounded himself with radical advisers. It was Yeltsin who, from the end of 1991 onward, embarked on radical reforms. (For instance, he opened the way to foreign investment with a right to repatriate profits; he began to free prices; he privatized most of the country's retail trade; he agreed to lease land to individual farmers, and to dissolve the state and collective farms which had brought disaster.) Yeltsin's reforms (much influenced by Poland's experience) in turn are bound to affect the other republics. It was, after all, Russia which, together with the Baltic and Caucasian republics, had made an anti-communist revolution. In Ukraine, Belarus, Kazakhstan, and the Central Asian republics, the old cadres had changed their tune, but stayed in office. It was Russia's experience, therefore, which would prove crucial for the future.

What then can the US do? Not all that much! The catastrophe produced by more than 70 years of communism is even greater than the most fanatical of Cold Warriors had predicted. There is no parallel in history for this predicament. The military-industrial complex apart, the bulk of Russia's industries are obsolescent, the infrastructure decayed; the bulk of Russia's capital investments were already below par at the time they were made. The position is made worse by environmental problems; many decades will pass until the capital stock can be rebuilt. For the time being Russia's economy can not compete on the international market, except in oil, armaments and space exploration.

Russia's most immediate economic problem hinges on currency reform. Without a stable currency neither a planned nor a market economy can work properly. (Of particular value in this regard is Germany's experience in stemming runaway inflation after World War I, and then after World War II. The US should likewise encourage Russia, indeed all the successor states, to lighten the load of government, a prescription which we also regard as suitable for our own domestic ills. According to a pre-world War I joke, which Russians will surely appreciate, "in London everything is allowed that is not forbidden; in Berlin everything is forbidden that is not allowed; in Vienna everything is allowed that is forbidden." Russians, Ukrainians, and others, having long suffered from the Berlin option, should consistently be encouraged to take up the London option instead.

As reform programs have begun to get under way, indigenous entrepreneurs have started a comeback. They include a huge army of contractors, shopkeepers, artisans, merchants, farmers – those once despised "speculators," "kulaks," and "compradores" of communist demonology. They are not a romantic lot, but it is they who must supply the bulk of the capital and enterprise on which the post-communist world must depend. Hopefully, it is this petty bourgeoisie which will constitute the rising class of the future, not just in the former Soviet Union but in all the countries of the erstwhile Warsaw Pact.

The US can give some assistance, but only on a relatively small scale. The US (and Canada) have a unique resource of a kind not available to the same extent to any other country – the presence on our side of the Atlantic of millions of Ukrainians, Russians, Balts, and other East-Central Europeans well qualified to do business with their former home countries; they should receive official encouragement. It would be a mistake to grant government-to-government loans; these are bad risks for the US government; they will saddle the recipient governments with huge debts; they encourage profligate government expenditure. As William D. Eggers, a policy analyst with the Heritage Foundation, points out, there are equally valid objections to providing US taxpayer-backed export or loan guarantees. These lead to capital distortions, and mainly benefit a small number of giant US companies (which receive the bulk of Export-Import Bank assistance). In the event of dire emergencies, the US should indeed give food aid. But this should be given on lines similar to famine relief privately provided to the Soviet Union under the auspices of Herbert Hoover after World War I. Hoover insisted on control of food distribution and payment for food; and achieved remarkable results at a small cost, thereby saving countless lives. Hoover also insisted on a training component to make Russian farmers more efficient.

The US can provide some technical aid. This should not, however, be channeled through the Agency for International Development (AID), which has incurred much criticism both from American and foreign businessmen for its bureaucratic procedures, and for its lack of familiarity with the private sector. The British have been far more successful with their "Know How Fund" (launched in 1989), and designed to fund private sector experts to assist in Eastern Europe. The US should learn from the British experience, but modify British practice. As Eggers puts it, "the US government would provide vouchers to the republic governments and some emergent private businesses, which they could use to purchase the services of American consultants and firms. This would eliminate a layer of bureaucracy and give the republic governments greater control over what kind of technical assistance they receive."[65]

Above all, the US should furnish technical assistance and financial aid to help dismantle the huge number of nuclear weapons still held by Russia, Ukraine, Belarus, and Kazakhstan.[66] This should be done through an international agency such as the International Atomic Energy Agency. There is a real danger that nuclear weapons might fall into the wrong hands. One of the financial incentives open for US use is the huge debt owed by the successor states to the West, including the US. It is unlikely that the successor states will ever pay this debt, either singly or jointly. The US might therefore, without undue risk, offer debt relief in return for at least partial nuclear disarmament. The US also has a material interest in the creation of an effective system whereby the four nuclear republics jointly control their nuclear weaponry. It is for these objectives that the US taxpayers' dollars may legitimately be spent.

For the same reason, we welcome the conclusion of the Start II Treaty, effected by Presidents Bush and Yeltsin in January 1993. We are well aware that the US has consistently erred after every major conflict in its history in cutting its defense forces to the bone. The US continues to require adequate armed forces, including an anti-missile defense, to counter possible threats from irresponsible potentates during a dangerous future when nuclear and missile technologies continues to spread. But the arms limitations required by Start II seem reasonable and deserving of political support.

By contrast, the US should not become involved in those numerous border quarrels and disputes over minorities that will continue to plague numerous successor states of the former Soviet Union. It is not within the US's power to find a just settlement in the disputes that divide, say, Georgians from Russians or Armenians from Azaris. It is risky for the US to take part in international ventures that involve the dispatch of peacekeeping forces to ethnically divided territories. Soldiers are not policemen – their respective missions are quite different. The former exist to defeat an identified enemy; the latter make their living by arresting criminals at the behest of a legally constituted authority. Peacekeeping forces cannot keep the peace, unless both contending parties agree for the peace to be kept – in which case the foreign troops are unnecessary. Nothing would be as ill-considered as to send US soldiers abroad to some remote corner of a foreign country, exposed to the attacks of ethnic guerrillas. Remember the US marincs' experience in Lebanon; remember the British Army's past inability to keep the peace between Jews and Arabs in Palestine; Hindus, Muslims and Sikhs in India during the British Empire's final years. US military power remains immense. But we should be sparing in its use – for the defense of our declared allies and our own country. Let the Western European Union, CSCE or the UN take responsibility, not the US.

Let the EC carry out a Marshall Plan for Europe. The Marshall Plan was successful, in part, because it established a European Payments Union with a fund of $350 million dollars. This allowed European currencies to become convertible with the dollar unit of account. Trade was thereby revitalized within Europe. The EC has already concluded a major reform, when it signed the European Energy Charter at the Hague in January 1992. Its purpose is to develop the vast oil and natural gas reserves of the former Soviet Union and to restructure the power industry in Europe. The Europeans will supply the capital and know-how to develop the resources and earn foreign exchange for the Russians, thus assuring the Europeans of stable supplies and prices free of dependence on volatile Middle East supplies. This cooperation may help bring economic recovery to many of the former communist-ruled states. What remains before the Europeans pour in their capital and manpower is to ensure investment protection and property rights. Siberia then could be an engine for the development of the whole of Europe. Above all, the EC and the US alike should keep tariffs to a minimum. It makes no sense to provide aid and deny trade.

The US, however, does have a major role to play as the paradigm of a constitutional, federal system of multi-ethnic cooperation based on a market economy. The states of East-Central Europe and the former Soviet Union were all built on the assumption that each country would have a dominant nationality. National minorities might be conceded group rights owed to them as members of specific ethnic minorities. The US, by contrast, insists on individual rights. Whether a person is of German, Mexican, or African descent, he or she is a US citizen, and enjoys individual rights due to any citizen. It is not impermissible for an ethnically mixed state to create group rights, or to permit individual religious or national groups to run their own schools, cultural and welfare organizations. But group rights should never override individual rights; civil rights should never depend on ethnicity – this is the great lesson that the US must teach by its example.

# 7

# The US and the New Europe
# 1985–1993

The 40 years which followed the collapse of Germany in 1945 saw greater political, economic and social change in Europe than any four-decade period in previous European history. In 1984 France's President Mitterand and West Germany's Chancellor Kohl called for a new European Union treaty. In the same year the EC and EFTA issued the Luxembourg Declaration in which they favored the creation of a single European economic area. At the end of World War II, such designs would have appeared Utopian. By the mid-1980s, however, Western Europe had become far more prosperous and united than ever before. Europeans, and also Americans, increasingly became alike in appearance and habits. It was not only superficial surface similarities – rock music, freeways and filling stations, high-rise buildings, and advertising posters; there were more deep-seated similarities.

Above all, there were great demographic changes. In Western Europe, as in the US, the proportion of women in the labor force kept rising. As more women found paid employment in industry and services, and as occupational opportunities for women widened, family values changed. At the same time, the populations of the industrialized countries grew older. The relatively well-off Northerners were the first Europeans to have fewer babies; but from the 1980s Italians, Spaniards, Greeks, and Portuguese also joined the trend. (By 1991 Italian women, strikingly, had the lowest fertility rate in Europe.)[1] Feminism became a powerful political force, transnational in character. Older people also became an increasingly powerful lobby. (In the United States, the American Association of Retired Persons, a political action group speaking for the elderly, came to be regarded by politicians in Washington as even more fearsome than the gun lobby.) The elderly became more and more important as voters. Hence their political concerns became more influential – their hostility to inflation, their demand for health care and larger pensions, sterner crime control, and more effective public transport, services needed particularly by the old. The aging process continued; so much so that from the mid-1970s onward, the EC population as a whole failed to reproduce itself. This was good news for North Africans and Middle Easterners looking for jobs in Europe, but bad news to those Europeans who wanted to maintain their respective countries' ethnic homogeneity.

The US and Western Europe also began to resemble one another in that both subcontinents attracted immigrants from the backward periphery. The newcomers comprised, among others, Mexicans and Central Americans in the US, Algerians, Moroccans, Turks in Western Europe. These newcomers looked physically different; they often performed the most menial jobs; they were, on the average, much poorer than the settled population. These minorities all contained their own underclass, a minority within a minority, nevertheless an underclass that outsiders all too often identified with the entire group. Europeans who had sneered at US racism in the past suddenly found that they had skinheads and "Paki-bashers" in their own backyards.

There was also a shift in the manner in which men and women earned their livelihood. People kept leaving the land for the city. Initially, during the nineteenth century in particular, farm workers had taken jobs in factories; thereafter people continued to depart from the land, in part because they wished to retire from work altogether. The nature of industrial employment changed; as traditional industries, such as coal mining, ship building, the manufacture of steel, declined in relative importance, science-based enterprises – computers, biotechnical industries etc. – gained.

Overall, the relative importance – though not the output – of manufacturing within the GNP of all advanced countries declined, whereas the number of jobs in service industries went up, including employment in "fast food" establishments, schools, welfare agencies, hospitals, and numerous other government jobs, or positions wholly or partly subsidized by the taxpayer. The number and influence of workers and professionals in the public services increased. Hence these men and women in turn became a major lobby calling for the further expansion of the state sector. The growth of government affected every Atlantic economy. Within the EC the state widely subsidized specific manufacturing industries as politicians and planners tried to "pick winners." (Italy stood at the top of the list, followed by Germany, with France in the third place, and Britain in the fourth among aid-givers.) The EC also heavily subsidized farming – this to a far greater extent than even the US.[2] Citizens might be reluctant to pay more taxes, but they continued to ask for more public services and entitlements. Not surprisingly, governments became more inclined than in the past to run up financial deficits. (When the total government budgets – the total of central, state and local government budgets – are added to social security balances, the US came out with a modest deficit of 2.8 percent of the GNP. By contrast, Greece had a deficit of 15.9 percent of the GNP in 1991, Italy 10 percent, Germany 5.2 percent, Ireland 2.3 percent.[3] Norway had a budget surplus, proving thereby that the creation of an extensive welfare state need not, in and of itself, lead to deficit financing.) Taxes on income, goods and services rose everywhere to pay for the welfare state.

Another shift occurred in the so-called "non-standard jobs," in what French economists call *emploi précaire*. This includes part-time work, fixed-term contract labor, self-employment – anything from consultantships to computer services and construction. (In Holland, in the early 1990s, the proportion of workers doing part-time jobs reached 33 percent, a shift which in turn entailed far-reaching changes with regard to traditional notions of work, punctuality, and leisure.) The labor force grew better educated in a formal sense. Europeans and Americans alike, on the average, spent far more time at school than their grandparents. The greatest beneficiaries were women who continued to gain all manner of professional diplomas not accessible to their grandmothers. Women became more independent in an economic sense; more and more couples lived together without marriage bonds and divorce increased, as did the number of children born out of wedlock. The impact of these changes was of course uneven. Greece and Portugal, by the early 1990s, were more traditional in their attitudes than Holland or Norway, the Deep South in the US more so than California. But cultural and consumer variations diminished as Europeans and Americans alike purchased standardized jeans, standardized sweat shirts, and relied on standardized entertainment purveyed by television, movies and music tapes. Not surprisingly, merchants, manufacturers, tourists, professional athletes, singers, actors increasingly thought in transcontinental terms and popular resistance to European unification declined. The EC obviously did well – as indicated, for example, by its rising export trade. Even during the troubled 1980s, the EC's exports substantially increased, though not in as spectacular a fashion as during the preceding decades.[4]

## THE EC: POLITICAL AND ECONOMIC BONDS

From the perspective of 1958, when the EC became operational, the new Europe was an extraordinary success. All the same, the EC's original objective – to create a common market for goods, capital, and services –

had only partially been achieved by the mid-1980s. Ideally there would be free competition within a market of nearly 300 million people – but this goal as yet remained to be reached.[5] There were also problems with regard to the enforcement of those elaborate treaties drawn up under EC auspices. This was a task for the European Court of Justice at Luxemburg. Cases might take between a year and a half and three years to decide – the law's delay alone impeded the Court's effectiveness. Some governments simply ignored court rulings, with Italy again at the top of the list. (Britain, though the least federalist of the EC member states, actually had the best enforcement record, fully justifying therefore Britain's claim to be a most law-abiding nation.)[6]

Beset by many restrictions, the European countries continued to lag behind the US and Japan in many high tech industries, including bio-technical ventures, and computers. Trade within the EC was obstructed by a host of restrictive regulations imposed by member governments under all sorts of pretexts – industrial safety, health, quality control. These barriers particularly impeded those small, innovative companies which had played such a major part in the US in pioneering new industries and creating new jobs. (Firms doing business in other EC countries had to cope, among other impediments, with vexatious border inspection of goods in transit; restrictions on the movements of peoples; differences in national product norms; problems arising from differential taxation; patents; standardization in service industries; complex issues connected with the standardization of computers, and communications and the rate of valued added taxes.)

The EC faced many other tasks. Effective unification entailed the creation of a common market for technical skills, a difficult task in a continent where the qualifications of, say, a lawyer, a physician, or an engineer varied considerably from country to country. Standardization was likewise desirable in the realm of technical specifications for products such as telephones, telex, electronic equipment, and refrigerators. (Electrolux, the world's leading appliance producer, had to alter the same item six times to meet the different electrical specification throughout the EC.) Standardization was equally needful in cross-border financial services concerned with insurance policies, mortgages, consumer credit, taxes and tariffs.

The elimination of such barriers would make a major difference. According to a report compiled under the chairmanship of Paolo Cecchini, special adviser to the EC, the resultant savings would be enormous. If all physical, technical, and fiscal barriers were eliminated within the EC, the total saving would be equal to about 5 percent of the gross domestic product of the combined EC membership; consumer prices should drop by 5 to 7 percent, and 12 million new jobs would be generated.[7] Such projections, of course, must be treated with caution; nevertheless, there would be future benefits – not merely for Europeans, but also for Americans. As Giovanni Agnelli, chairman of Fiat, put it in 1989, "forty-five percent of American capital currently invested overseas is in equity ownership within Europe."[8] The EC is quite different from Japan in that the EC does not try to cut itself off from the US. A thorough reform of the EC will therefore surely profit the US as well as Europe.

By the mid-1980s, these and other obstacles had come to appear even more objectionable than in the past. Intra-continental commerce had much increased and, say, an English lorry driver saw nothing peculiar in being asked to take a load all the way from London to Istanbul. By now great corporate and bureaucratic lobbies kept pushing for further integration. In 1985 the European Commission issued a major White Paper which provided the foundation for the Single European Act, 1986, passed by the European Parliament. (For the structure of these European organizations, see the appendix to this chapter.)

At the time, the Act seemed modest enough, "a smiling mouse" in the words of the London *Economist*.[9] In fact the Single European Act (SEA) had far-reaching consequences. The Act aimed at turning into a reality the EC's original goal of making Europe into a single market, "a Europe without frontiers." Such a design would of necessity have revolutionary consequences in politics as well as economics. The EC's political institutions and bureaucracy would gain additional power – to the intense disapproval of critics such as Britain's Margaret Thatcher. As a consequence of the SEA, members agreed to strengthen the jurisdiction of the European Court; they looked toward the elaboration of a more effective foreign policy – albeit not with much success. They made some provision for regional aid, research and development, and safeguarding the environment. The Council of Ministers could henceforth vote by a majority on most laws relating to "Project 1992" (the plan to create an EC-wide common market). The European Parliament gained additional powers to amend those laws. Having overcome bitter opposition, especially in Denmark and Ireland, the Act finally came into force in 1987.

By itself, the SEA did not bring about a total overhaul of European institutions. For instance, it did not deal adequately with monetary policy, a subject widely discussed from 1979 onward when the EMS (European Monetary System) became part of the EC's long-term agenda. Nevertheless the SEA formed a milestone on the way toward European unification, as the very term "1992" acquired symbolic as well as practical significance. EC policy-makers now spoke of a full economic and monetary union which would sweep away the remaining obstacles to free movement of people, goods, capital, and services within the Community. This was an immensely complicated process. Certainly, the entire task could not be completed by the target date. The program, to be exact, required 279 measures. By the beginning of 1990 about 60 percent had been implemented by all the nation states (except Italy). New agreements thereafter lifted border controls, created a common visa policy, dealt with questions concerning asylum, and established judicial cooperation on terrorism and crime through a computer set up in Strasbourg.[10]

In constitutional terms, the European Parliament gained a little more influence, though not much. When parliament had first begun its sittings, its proceedings had not commanded attention; membership had not carried prestige. The European Parliament contained all too many outsiders and eccentrics – beneficiaries of assorted protest votes. Henceforth the European Parliament won importance, especially as Chancellor Kohl determined to amend what was called the "democratic deficit," that is, rule through non-elected officials, within the EC. In the Council of Ministers, the individual member's ability to veto laws diminished. The greatest gain, however, was secured by the European Commission (intended by the French to have a guiding authority similar to that of the French president). The Commission alone could propose laws; the Commission therefore functioned, so to speak, as the EC's executive. Overall the Act speeded decision-making; it also imposed somewhat stricter limits on those agricultural subsidies which had consumed much of the EC's budget.

A united Europe, however, faced many more obstacles. The Founding Fathers of the EEC in 1958 had drawn on a substantial fund of idealism. United Europe would open a new chapter in world history, and end Europe's age-old hostilities. Forty years later, European civil servants and politicians had learned to get on with one another. Armed conflict within the EC had become unthinkable. But there was little idealism left – the cause of unification was discussed largely in utilitarian terms: how would it benefit or not benefit any one particular country, or any one particular lobby? These discussions were carried on in dreary legalese that bored the ordinary citizen. The EC might appeal to its supporters' heads, but not their hearts. There was a European banner (a circle of golden stars on a dark-blue background), but it was rarely displayed by private citizens. The Eurocrats never learned the art of political showmanship, of grandiose political display, practiced earlier on with so much success by tyrants such as Napoleon, Stalin, and Hitler. "Eurospeak" could not compete with ornithological-sounding names such as EMU and BERD (the former meaning European Monetary Union, the latter being the French acronym for European Bank for Reconstruction and Development).

The federalists, on the other hand, held many trump cards. They could rely on an able team of political leaders – above all Helmut Kohl of Germany, François Mitterand of France, and Jacques Delors, president of the European Commission – who held high office, knew each other well, and lobbied in concert. All were impressive. Mitterand was a man of immense culture, an organizer who had revived the somnolent French Socialist Party, and, by skillful maneuvering, had helped to ruin the French Communist Party. Having attained presidential office in 1981, Mitterand embarked on a socialist course – "Keynesianism in one country." Having failed in his endeavor, Mitterand switched to liberal capitalism and a united Europe which would benefit the most competitive firms. Kohl, the CDU leader in Germany, shared these views. Unlike Mitterand, Kohl belonged to that generation of conservatives who had gained power from the late 1970s. (Mrs Thatcher became prime minister in 1979; Ronald Reagan assumed the US presidency in 1981, the same year in which Mitterand became French president; Kohl replaced Social Democrat Helmut Schmidt in the German chancellorship in 1982.) A bear of a man in appearance, Kohl aroused amusement among the literati by speaking German with a Rhenish accent. He was renowned for his *faux pas*. Nevertheless, future historians will remember him as the man who unified both Germany, and perhaps Europe, whether by luck or good management.

Delors provided the bureaucratic know-how to the EC. An energetic visionary with long experience both in French banking and government, Delors could rely, as head of the European Commission, on a small but most effective corps of advisers, his cabinet, men of high caliber, forceful and well-trained. The same applied to the senior cadres of the Euro-bureaucracy. Jokes with regard to its size and folly were *de rigueur* in Brussels. But bureaucratic expansion in that city must be seen in perspective. By 1990 the EC's personnel numbered no more than 20,000 – compared to 50,000 employees on the payroll of the US Department of Commerce alone. (The EC does not directly deal with citizens; the national bureaucracies are responsible for enforcement. It should be possible, therefore, to keep in bounds the Euro-bureaucracy's future growth.)

On paper, Delors's powers, as president of the European Commission, were limited. In practice, he managed to centralize power in his office, and steadily worked towards its expansion. A socialist by conviction, Delors desired a new Europe that would be strong, united, and endowed with a social purpose. Delors held that unfettered competition between great conglomerates within a united Europe must be balanced by joint action for social justice. Margaret Thatcher and other free traders, by contrast, looked to a Europe where bureaucratic interference and trade union interference would be kept to a minimum; but the Thatcherites failed to prevail, given the effectiveness of Franco-German cooperation, and given also the fact that the CDU, in effect the most influential party in Europe, had never been a free enterprise party pure and simple, and West Germany had never relied on unfettered competition alone.

The federalists' greatest concern was to establish EMU. The first stone was laid in this structure with the creation of the EMS (European Monetary System) in 1979. This began as a device to manage exchange rates at a time when most EC currencies were apt to depreciate against the then all-mighty D-Mark. During the 1980s the EC countries collaborated most effectively in reducing inflation (down from 21.2 percent to 5 percent in Italy; from 13.6 percent to 2.7 percent in France; from 5.5. percent to 1.2 percent in Germany between 1980 and 1988). Following this striking success, a committee was set up in 1988 under Delors's chairmanship. This produced the *Report on Economic and Monetary Union in the European Community*, known as the Delors Report, which set out a three-stage process. A summit in Madrid in June 1989 agreed that the first stage toward EMU should start in 1990, and that an inter-governmental conference should work out the later stages. The next summit, held at Strasbourg in December of the same year, decided that the crucial conference would be held at the end of 1991, at Maastricht, eastern Holland. What was at stake, as Stanley Hoffman put it in a masterly survey, was "the future of the nation-state in Western Europe. Delors's logic is ultimately that the construction of a federal state . . . legitimacy would be provided by universal suffrage, expressed in the election of the European Parliament."[11]

EMU thus required a political as well as an economic program. Believers in a federal Europe, such as Belgian foreign minister Mark Eyskens, insisted that political reforms must be added to economic reforms in the interest of "balance" and effectiveness. In July 1989 President Bush asked the European Commission to coordinate the "rich" countries' help to Eastern Europe. The breakdown of the German Democratic Republic, and the unification of Germany thereafter, compelled the Commission to develop a complex program for further integrating East Germany, a formerly communist country, into the EC. (East Germany had already been associated with the EC in an informal fashion through special trade arrangements with West Germany.) As Delors put it, Europe would be more comfortable with a united and powerful Germany if a strong European federation could constrain Germany's ability to act alone.[12] Germany's neighbors agreed – and so did Kohl and his foreign minister Hans-Dietrich Genscher (a liberal wedded to free enterprise, in office 1974–92).

As communism collapsed in East-Central Europe, the case for a European Union seemed ever more persuasive. In December 1991 the EC countries duly met at Maastricht, where they arrived at a major new agreement, styled by Kohl "a decisive breakthrough," making the path toward European union "irreversible."[13] The agreement, to be formally signed in March 1992, and to be ratified by all states before the end of the year, embodied a transnational compromise. Generally speaking, German views prevailed with regard to the future of EMU while the French, in the main, had their way over political union. Others got consolation prizes. Britain insisted on its continued right to opt out of specific arrangements such as EC's role in labor law. Portugal, Greece, and Spain received concessions regarding subsidies payable by the "rich" to the "poor" countries within the EC.

The "General Provisions' of the treaty no longer referred to "federal objectives" because Britain objected. The aim was defined as "an ever closer union of the nations of Europe," as stated in the 1957 Treaty of Rome. The new agreement extended the EC powers in environment, education, consumer protection, health, and an all-European infrastructure, and also set up the EMU schedule. The second major element concerned a common security and foreign policy, but was not to be incorporated in the European treaties. The Treaty would set out rules to improve policy coordination through contractual arrangements among the Twelve. Such a program was to be the basis for a common defense policy to be reconciled with NATO. The WEU was to serve as the EC's military arm (9 out of the 12 EC members were in the WEU). The third element called for cooperation between member countries on immigration and political asylum, on organized crime and the narcotics trade. A Europol was to be set up, to become a European CID or FBI.

The Treaty on Monetary and Political Union gave Brussels far-reaching new powers over the nation states in the EC. The treaty would create a single European currency by January 1, 1999, with a common monetary policy and an independent Central Bank starting in 1996. States would have to meet strict economic standards (on inflation, cutting subsidies, and attaining a balanced budget) before they could substitute their respective national currencies for the ECU. According to advocates of the Mastricht treaty, all members would benefit. A genuine single market, with common standards, a single customs system, and a single currency would help to create a new prosperity. The European Parliament would gain new powers, including the right to ratify treaties, block or amend EC laws by a majority vote, and the right to be consulted on the appointment of new Euro-commissioners. A European Monetary Union would facilitate the free movement of capital within Europe – as yet divided, at the time, into separate financial markets with different rules. A common currency for the EC seemed all the more desirable, given the high cost of transferring money from one country to another in Europe.[14] In humanitarian terms, the principle of "cohesion" was to be welcomed; rich countries should indeed subsidize the poor countries, thereby expanding the Euro-market as a whole. As Delors put it with much enthusiasm – all member nations would profit from their common enterprise.[15]

Hopefully, the new arrangements would free trade, increase competition, reduce prices and widen the range of goods available throughout the region. Life insurance premiums would drop in Germany, as would banking charges; Spanish farms and industries would have to become more efficient to compete with EC products. Frontier controls in the EC would end in the beginning of 1993, creating an EC without frontiers. Other states beside EFTA wanted to join the EC – Malta, Cyprus, Turkey applied for membership. The three Baltic states, plus Poland, Czechoslovakia and Hungary, likewise planned on applying for membership.

European progress had indeed been remarkable. On January 1, 1993, the Single Market was complete – the largest and wealthiest trade association in history. All former tariffs and customs barriers had gone; customs and passport checks largely disappeared. Considerable progress had also been made in harmonizing those national and regulatory standards which national governments also used for the illegitimate purpose of keeping out foreign goods. But many questions remained unanswered. The free circulation of persons, money and merchandise would give a boost to transnational crime as well as to legitimate business. How would Europeans respond to this ever more sophisticated menace? A monetary union was to be achieved by stages, beginning in 1994. But a common EC currency policy would be vitally affected by the economic and fiscal policies pursued by all the participating countries. Germany would be the strongest partner within this union; the German currency would play a vital part in making it effective. Germany would therefore have to insist on powerful political leverage within the EC. Otherwise, Germany would be writing a blank check against its financial resources. Having experienced the trauma of a run away inflation after two successive World Wars, German citizens would be asked to substitute the untried ECU for the trusted D-Mark. In any case, said the critics, the ECU already successfully operated as an accounting and investment unit throughout the Community. Why make changes? Why abandon national currencies and a more decentralized form of financial control? Why leave enormous financial powers to a "Euro-Fed" not subject to adequate accountability?

An unforeseen factor was Germany's horrendous burden in rehabilitating East Germany. The price was far higher than anyone could have guessed. Germany's government, however, balked at raising taxes sufficiently to keep Bonn's budget in balance. Germany's inflation-weary central bank reacted by jacking up interest rates. Foreigners naturally reacted by buying up German marks and investing the proceeds in German bank deposits which paid high interest rates, far higher than those available in London, Rome, or New York. Hence the mark went up in value, whereas other currencies declined. This resulted in the near collapse of Europe's monetary market, Britain and Italy being particularly hard hit. (After unsuccessfully attempting to prop up the pound, Britain in 1992 announced its temporary withdrawal from the European Monetary System. Not surprisingly, the resulting turmoil cast a long shadow over European plans for further monetary and political unification.) Germany was supposed to be the engine driving the EC's economy. But by the end of 1992 Germany was heavily burdened; the German growth rate for 1993 was projected at only 1.2 percent (as opposed to 2.3 percent for the US and 2.5 percent for Japan).[16] Maastricht optimism had waned.

Contentious also was the principle of "cohesion." The EC's peripheral states – Ireland, Spain, Portugal, Greece – were all in favor of receiving development subsidies. The industrial core states, especially Germany, by contrast were understandably reluctant to pay hard cash to their partners. (By 1992, regional development aid was expected to reach about one-quarter of the EC's budget, as opposed to 17 percent in 1987.) The taxpayers' reluctance was all the greater as they examined Italy's record in developing its own *Mezzogiorno*. For about 40 years, astronomical sums had been spent for the purpose of bringing the South up to the standards of the North. But much of the aid had ended in the pockets of party bosses, politicians, and criminal syndicates; the gap between North and South remained, whilst discontent grew apace in the North with the Italian state as a whole.

Defenders of national sovereignty also found fault with the "European citizenship" created by Maastricht in tandem with existing national citizenships. Euro-citizens would be able to vote, not only for the European parliament, but also in local municipal elections throughout the EC if they were living and working there. Hence foreigners might obtain a key vote in frontier towns and frontier villages, as well as in resort communities – a prospect designed to anger provincials in Flanders or Bavaria, even more so in France where the Maastricht provisions concerning the franchise for foreigners in local government elections necessitated a change in the Constitution. Under the new dispensation workers and professionals would be able to move freely in Europe (from 1995 onward also citizens of EFTA states). These new opportunities were welcomed by many, but they also aroused opposition – for instance, Germans feared that Portuguese building workers would take over much of the industry because of their lower wages; the Swiss dreaded an invasion of professionals from abroad, and also of land buyers. The EC agreed in principle to a common visa policy, though asylum and immigration policies would continue to be determined by the individual member states, an important provision for European countries frightened of massive future immigration from East-Central Europe and the Third World. Citizens of EC countries, moreover, will have the right to live and work anywhere in the EC – a provision certain to displease ultra-nationalists and skinheads in every member state.

Speaking in general, the Maastricht treaty would greatly increase the power of Euro-agencies and of the Euro-bureaucracy – none of them truly accountable to the mass of Europeans. Where EFTA managed to function with a minimal public service, the Euro-bureaucracy had an inbuilt capacity for growth and an inbuilt potential for extending its functions. Under the guise of harmonization, the EC Commission created arbitrary norms for all kinds of products. The Eurocrats' critics thus never tired of pointing to resultant absurdities – apples to come in approved varieties, lawn mowers of a common pattern, with a Euro-condom, 15.2 centimeters long, as the *pièce de résistance*.[17] But the Eurocrats had a strong case. They were expected to standardize products to facilitate intra-European trade, and could therefore not be justly censured for carrying out their appointed task.

Maastricht's critics expressed equally strong reservations concerning the extension of the European Court of Justice, a body as remote from ordinary Europeans as the European commission. True enough, the Court's powers were nothing like as great as those of the Supreme Court in the US. But legal standards were unclear, with different traditions and different standards. Even the partial "judicialization" of Euro-politics was a prospect dreaded by Maastricht's opponents. There were likewise objections to the Court's insistence that the Treaty of Rome should have direct effect in national courts. Euro-directives not yet legislated into national law were regarded as EC law, once they had passed the Council of Ministers. Worse still, the Court insisted that even in cases where no directive had as yet been issued, the Treaty of Rome and the Single European Act mandated certain forms of conduct.

In their defense, advocates of a united Europe argued that bureaucratic and judicial interference was indispensable to eliminate remaining barriers on the movement of persons, merchandise, and capital. Laws and regulations concerning the environment, job protection, and consumer regulation would have to be made compatible – otherwise the new Europe would never work. There would have to be an end to covertly excluding competitors by administrative regulations. (For instance, British fork-lifts had been banned for a time in Germany because they had not been tested by German authorities.) Eurocrats also began to stress the principle of "subsidiarity," whereby each problem should be dealt with at the lowest possible level, that is, closest to the man or woman in the street. But "subsidiarity" and similar Euro-jargon meant nothing to ordinary citizens;

even experts had trouble in understanding the obscure and involved language of the Maastricht treaty. Kohl and his coadjutors, moreover, had failed to make serious inroads on the European Parliament's "democratic deficit." (The Parliament did secure a greater say in drawing up EC laws with regard to research, culture, health, and various other matters – but these concessions as yet left much to be desired.)

Maastricht also produced numerous protocols; one of the most important proposed a common social charter for all members, Britain being excluded at the Conservative government's request. Another protocol exempted Britain from the final stages of monetary union; an additional one called for higher funding for Spain, Portugal, Ireland and Greece for economic and social development. The summit also declared that national parliaments were to play a growing part in community politics. But the main purpose of the Maastricht meeting was to establish a single European currency and to give the EC more control over defense and foreign affairs in an effort to create a strong European federation. Other objects of the treaty were to provide the EC with more power to set pan-European labor laws and social policies (without Britain for the time being), and enable the EC to set up common pan-European policies on the environment, immigration, etc.[18]

The schedule for carrying out reforms of the treaty was as follows: March 1992: the treaty on economic and political union would be signed; June 1992: EC leaders were to reach agreement on community finances including cash transfers to poorer member countries. By January 1993 the treaty on European Union was expected to come into force, provided it had been ratified by member governments; by the end of 1993 agreement on a uniform political asylum policy was to take the place of cooperation between individual states; by January 1994, Stage Two of EMU was to begin. A European Monetary Institute (EMI) was to start as a precursor of a European central bank to pave the way for Stage Three. By the end of 1996 or early in 1997, states would decide whether or not to proceed to Stage Three of economic and monetary union. If they decided to go ahead, exchange rates would be fixed, and the European Central Bank would take over from EMI. Assuming a single European currency had as yet to be introduced, the heads of state and government would decide by 1998 which countries had met the EMU requirements. Those countries that had done so would enter the final stage of economic and monetary union on January 1, 1999. (Also at the end of 1998 the Western European Union treaty would come up for review.)

The three planned stages for EMU are now unlikely: with the disarray of ERM, the transition to EMU is improbable for the following reasons. First, Maastricht may never be ratified, given doubts about the treaty.

Second, Germans no longer support an EMU and the French barely approved of it. Third and most important, Britain and Italy pulled out of ERM and other currencies are under great pressure. The economic slowdown within the EC and high German interest rates have harmed the ERM and caused high unemployment rates and low economic growth. The ERM, therefore, no longer appears viable as the transition to EMU.[19]

Maastricht also promised to define and implement a common foreign and a common security policy – easier said than done in an association of 12 members with divergent interests. The Maastricht Summit did not succeed in setting up a EC foreign policy commission, but at least provision was made for a special foreign policy secretariat at Brussels, to become the embryo of an EC foreign ministry. Individual EC governments thereafter would find it harder than before to plow their own furrow without regard to the rest – as Britain had done in 1990 when she unilaterally dropped certain sanctions on South Africa, and as Germany did in 1991 by recognizing Croatia. By 1993 the EC as yet remained an economic giant and a diplomatic dwarf – as shown by the EC's relative ineffectiveness over the Yugoslav imbroglio and, previously, during the Gulf War (when only Britain had come up with a truly effective European force).

The Summit likewise had but limited success in working toward a common social policy (social charter), a subject of equal concern to Christian Democrats and Socialists. The EC countries agreed to work together on such issues as working conditions and equal treatment for women. Laws on working conditions and gender equality would be decided by 1998 by majority votes. (Laws on third-country nationals working in the EC, laws relating to the dismissal of workers, and on social security would need unanimous decisions.) Workers in future might thus expect a spate of new laws to improve their lot, and also to equalize working conditions throughout the EC. Employer federations and labor unions alike would increasingly have to operate on a transnational basis. However, "harmonization" presented many difficult problems, as workers in some industries would undoubtedly gain, whereas others stand to lose previous gains. Workers in low-wage countries such as Portugal and Greece might gain in theory, but lose in practice, as the cost of employing Greeks and Portuguese would increasingly approximate the cost of employing Germans and Frenchmen.

The only odd-man-out in the trans-European approach toward a common social policy was John Major, Margaret Thatcher's successor at Number Ten Downing Street. Major was much more conciliatory than the "Iron Lady." He got on well with Kohl, and often was content to follow the German's lead. But Major was as uncooperative over a common social policy as he was over a common monetary policy and a common foreign policy. At the end of 1991, he put the case against a social charter to the British House of Commons at Question Time, enlivened, as usual, by those boos, cheers, and catcalls beloved by parliamentarians in Westminister. The British government, he said, had broken the ability of trade unions to disorganize the British economy; he would not allow Britain to return to the bad old days. Discontent, of course, was not confined to Great Britain. In 1992 the Danish voters rejected the accord in a referendum – "the mouse that roared," according to the Maastricht opponents' approving comments. To the critics, a small elite was building a superstate without popular approval. Whether or not the treaty would pass, its makers had paid a heavy price for their long neglect of public opinion. Disillusionment was all the greater since the ratifying member states could not renegotiate the agreement. It was a matter of "take it or leave it."

The Maastricht treaty, although approved (barely) by France and Ireland, and in May 1993 by Denmark, is in deep trouble. Many Europeans have come to fear the power of Brussels, the potential controls of an EMU with a single currency and one central bank. Others are backing away from European Union, and most, in any case, want to reconsider the whole treaty later in the 1990s. Delors and company went too fast in trying to create an economic and political union with a socialist social charter. Citizens of the member states of the EC fear the loss of national sovereignty over social conditions, money matters and political independence. Some also fear the growth of a superstate ruling the EC. For them, Maastricht was illiberal, authoritarian and interventionist. While it had a redistributive policy for the poorer members, it was also restrictive of the poorer members. That is, they had to tie their interest rates, rates of inflation and deficits to the Germany Deutschmark. This hurt some states such as Britain which needed low interest rates to stimulate their economy and to reduce unemployment. Other interference by Brussels in the activities of the nation-state were also disturbing. For example, Maastricht would have given citizens of Italy working in France the right to vote in French local elections, or allowed the European Court in Luxembourg to impose high unemployment benefits on foreign workers in another state.

The EC, some economists insist, does not need an EMU with one currency, one central bank. Except for reducing transaction costs with one currency, there are mostly hardships to having an EMU. The EC is too diverse in terms of the levels of economic development among the member nations to be regulated by one central bank. National economic policy should be written by those who know the local conditions and not by Brussels following the *Bundesbank*. Rather than try to create an EMU or EU at this time, the EC should work to implement fully the reforms of the Single European Act. The free movement of people, goods, services, and capital throughout the 12 states of the community will bring economic prosperity to all 300 million people (340 million if EFTA states are added) and will make all of Europe more efficient and competitive. After the economies have converged, then implementing an EMU and EU can begin. The best future for Europe is a liberal, pragmatic, free-market customs union of the EC and EFTA and a few other states; it is not to create a superstate with heavy control and interventionist policies ruled from Brussels.

Eurospeak is being challenged in the EC. Citizens of member states want fuller use of subsidiarity, that is, that decisions should be taken at the lowest appropriate levels; they call for transparency (or openness): that is, policy-makers should debate in public important issues of policy and should consult citizens regularly. EC citizens at present do not understand what goes on at Brussels or why. They would prefer that their local governments handle legislation and regulation, with Brussels dealing only with EC-wide matters that do not infringe on national sovereignty. Member states want to scrap some existing legislation and prevent other proposals becoming law. Britain heads the list of the rejectionists, with 71 items suggested for scrapping, mostly in the realm of environmental and social affairs.

If these reforms of subsidiarity and openness are adopted, policy-makers should become more cautious in pushing excessive regulations or unnecessary rule from Brussels. But there are risks that the member nations will use subsidiarity to protect national interests, thus harming the single market and environmental controls, and that the closed doors will not be fully opened since so much EC business is done by senior diplomats in Brussels or in informal ministerial meetings away from the TV camera.[20]

Looking into the future, Europeans also have to wrestle with a more fundamental problem, that of Europe's identity.[21] As long as the Soviet empire remained in being, East and Central Europe were simply regarded as part of the communist world. But what would happen to these countries, now that the Warsaw Pact and Comecon alike had dropped into the trashbin of history? Did not Prague have as good a claim to be a European city as Bonn, Warsaw as Dublin? There was also Turkey's application to join the EC. Should Eurocrats give priority to improving cooperation between the existing Twelve (known as "deepening" in Euro-jargon)? Or should they "broaden" the union by including as many new members as possible?

These were difficult problems to resolve, especially where Germany was concerned. Chancellor Kohl had dominated the negotiations at Maastricht. Kohl, however, faced a great deal of inarticulate opposition at home. (A public opinion poll showed that 79 percent of German respondents wanted a referendum before the D-Mark would be replaced by the ECU, a currency much distrusted by the ordinary voter.) Superbly good at political maneuvering, Kohl had failed to prepare the mass of German voters for the full consequences of a full European Union.[22] By 1993 Mitterand, the other great Euro-builder, was likewise in grave political trouble within his own country. Indeed, all over Western Europe the socialist parties, essential components in the pro–Maastricht coalition, were in disarray. (The once impressive French Socialist Party almost faced electoral extinction; the Spanish socialists were divided; the Italian Socialist Party was smeared by Mafia scandals as much as the rival Christian Democratic Party; the German Social Democratic Party faced a leadership crisis.) Far from declining, nationalism was alive and well in Western as well as in East-Central Europe.

Apparently easiest to solve were the problems existing between the EC and the EFTA states (Finland, Austria, Norway, Sweden, Iceland, and Switzerland). The EFTA states, overall, had outperformed the EC. EFTA's per capita income in 1991 was nearly twice that of the EC. Between 1981 and 1990 the EFTA countries had an average unemployment rate of 2.4 percent against the EC's 10 percent. EFTA's inflation rate during that period amounted to 5.7 percent as against the EC's 7.4 percent. Economic growth was, on an average, about the same, but by 1990 EFTA's average income per head was 15 percent higher than the EC's.[23] However, Switzerland, Sweden, Finland, and Iceland had stagnated over the previous year; Sweden, and also Switzerland (once the bastion of sound money) had both suffered from inflation. Industrial enterprises in all these countries looked to the advantages of a large market; hence the EC was vital to the future of EFTA states. (The EC by 1991 took about 58 percent of EFTA's exports.) The industries of the EFTA countries would have little difficulty in complying with the EC's rules concerning mergers, public procurement policies, and state subsidies. (Government subsidies to EFTA industries amounted to only 2 percent of the manufacturing output as compared to 6 percent in the EC.) From the EC's point of view, the advantages were equally obvious. EFTA's population was small – only 10 percent of the EC's population. Nevertheless, the EFTA countries were the EC's largest foreign trading partner, more important than even the US or Japan.

Following some pretty rough negotiations, in October 1991 the EFTA and EC countries thus agreed to create a European Economic Area (EEA). Its citizens would enjoy, at least in theory, the right to move people, capital merchandise, and services throughout the 19 countries involved, and to do so without restrictions. Provided the deal were ratified by the European Parliament and the 19 countries, the EEA would become the world's largest free trade area, with a total of 380 million customers and

46 percent of the world's trade. Frontier controls will remain between the EC and EFTA and not all laws and regulations will be in effect until 1997. In order to secure membership, the EFTA countries had to make a number of concessions. The EEA, moreover, would not be a customs union with common external tariffs, only a great free trade zone. EFTA countries would be under no pressure to harmonize their taxes; they would retain such external tariffs and quotas as they chose to maintain. The EC insisted that the EFTA countries would have to accept future EC legislation, leaving the EFTA countries with the economic obligations of the EEA but without corresponding political rights. On the other hand, many EFTA countries considered joining the EEA as a first step toward becoming full members of the EC. (Austria applied in 1989, Sweden in Finland and Norway thereafter, though the Swiss in 1992 voted against the grand design, especially voters in the German-speaking cantons). But sooner or later existing difficulties were likely to be solved. With or without Swiss participation a free trade zone would extend all the way from Lisbon to Helsinki.

Once the EEA comes into existence, the new association will surely also bring about major shifts in general policy. Workers in Sweden, Norway, and Finland might have to face stiffer competition from labor in southern countries. EC social legislation will be supported by a new lobby constituted by labor-friendly Nordic countries. The EFTA countries, moreover, are environmentally conscious. They will probably insist on stricter environmental standards, thereby forcing the EC to speed its enactments of such laws. If the EFTA countries were to join the EC as full members, neutralist and pacifist sentiments would likely gain strength within the union; hence the EC might be less likely to assert its power outside its own borders. By 1993 the future was far from clear: opinion polls in Austria, Norway, and Sweden showed a majority against EC membership, whereas the Finns favored adhesion to the EC. But overall, the EC will greatly gain in economic terms from EFTA's membership. In its own interests, therefore, the US should support the EC's enlargement in this respect.

Far more difficult to resolve is the problem of the poorer countries, foremost among them Turkey. Turkey has a strong case for membership. Turkey has been linked to the EC by an association agreement signed in 1963, and in 1987 applied for full membership. Turkey provided staunch support both for NATO and for the Allied Powers in the Gulf War. Turkey is a Muslim country, but has consistently stressed its historic links to Europe; the EC would surely make a mistake if it confined membership to countries with mainly Christian (or ex-Christian) citizens, Turks argue. Turkey, moreover, has a major role to play in the Middle East; its adhesion to the EC will strengthen the EC in an area vital to its self-interest. Some argue it is both in the EC's and the US's interests to strengthen Turkey's political stability and economic well-being; hence the US should support Turkey's application.[24]

These are strong arguments. Nevertheless we side with those who would confine, for some time, membership of the EC to the countries of Western Europe; within this context the EC needs to "deepen" rather than broaden its institutions. Turkey remains a relatively backward country; the EC would be ill-advised to lengthen the list of its "poor" members (Ireland, Portugal, Greece, Spain) who make demands for transfer payments on "rich" countries in the name of fairness. Turkey has serious and unresolved problems with its Kurdish minority at home; it clashes with Greece over Cyprus. The EC has no need to shoulder these extra quarrels. Turkey's population continues to expand. If Turkey were to join the EC as a full member, Turkish immigrants could not be kept out of countries such as Germany, where their presence would only heighten skinhead xenophobia. The US, by contrast, has every reason to take a pro-Turkish stance, given Turkey's loyalty to NATO and to the US in the Gulf War. Turkey's role is all the more important to the US as Turkey and Iran both seek to extend their respective influence in the Muslim republics of the former Soviet Union. It is in the US interest, therefore, to support Turkey in every way. Washington should therefore seek to give trade concessions to Ankara, favor Turkey's membership in other transnational organizations such as CSCE and WEU, take a conciliatory line over the intractable Greco-Turkish disputes regarding Cyprus, and respond positively to Turkish efforts at increasing trade, investment, and economic cooperation.

Similarly we would advise caution to the EC in immediately admitting as full members newcomers from Eastern Europe; certainly the US should not advise the EC to take on new and onerous obligations. If the EC were quickly to admit new states from the former Warsaw Pact and the defunct Soviet Union, the new members would bring their own unsolved economic and national problems into the EC; migration would increase from the EC's new member states to the old member states – this at a time when xenophobia is on the rise. If too many newcomers were admitted, the EC's machinery of cooperation would become unworkable. The new member states, moreover, would become entitled to all those transfer payments which now go to relatively backward states such as Portugal and Greece. (The average gross domestic product of Bulgaria, Czechoslovakia, Hungary, and Poland is less than that of Portugal, the EC's poorest member.) Access to EC markets for the East-Central European state is one thing; full membership another.

It is all very well for foreigners to satirize the EC as a rich men's club. However, the EC has serious problems. Germany, by 1992, was weighed down by the burden of rehabilitating the formerly communist *Länder*; Germany shouldered a budgetary deficit; there was, moreover, a general air of pessimism expressed in numerous opinion polls. The existing EC already has its own backward areas, consisting in part of rural regions with traditional poverty of the kind found in Portugal's Alentejo and in Calabria, Italy. There are also run-down industrial areas – Belfast in Northern Ireland, Liverpool in England – whose traditional industries have decayed. The wealthier countries in the EC already bear a heavy burden through existing transfer payments. They all have assumed massive welfare obligations. By the end of 1991, only France and Luxembourg fully met the five conditions of sound economic management that European countries were expected to meet before being adjudged fit in future to join EMU (European Monetary Union).[25] Even Germany, with its traditional insistence on a sound D-Mark, would have flunked the requirement set for restraint in budget deficits, as would Belgium. Given the extent of these problems, Eurocrats have good reason for caution in adding new members to the EC.

If any East-Central European states are admitted to EC membership, the first preference should go to the Czech republic, a democratic state without minority problems. Poland stands second in line, and Hungary third. (Poland has almost no minority problem. Hungary's is small – of Hungary's population of 10.6 million people, 600,000 are Gypsies and 80,000 Jews; nevertheless Hungary has once more acquired a neo-fascist party, misnamed the Hungarian Democratic Forum, led by playwright Istvan Csurka, who blames a novel trio – Zionists, Gypsies, and the IMF – for Hungary's ills. As Timothy Garten Ash, a gifted observer, puts it, "it is foolish to construct a Europe which contains Crete but not Bohemia." To keep these countries out of the EC would be regarded by them as discriminatory. The adhesion of the Hungarian, Czech, and Polish states however should be effected gradually, to be completed perhaps by the year 2000. The first step should be to admit them to European Political Cooperation (EPC), which coordinates the foreign policy of the various EC states. Later the three states could participate in the election of the European Parliament. They should be fully represented in the 1999 Euro-election; by 2000, full membership should be granted. But even thereafter, the three states may require an extensive period of transition in which the fledgling capitalist industries may have to be protected from the full blast of competition.[26]

Not that these objectives are easy to attain. Even limited agreements are hard to conclude. (In September 1991, for example, the EC Com-

*Figure 7.1*  Economic links within Europe on 1 January 1993.

mission – attempting to negotiate treaties with Poland, Czechoslovakia, and Hungary – asked the EC foreign ministers to lower trade barriers against the Eastern Europeans' most competitive products. France, Belgium and Ireland balked at opening EC products to Eastern beef and lamb meat at a time when their own farmers were battling against higher imports. Protests from Portugal put off a proposal for phasing out quotas on textiles from these countries.)[27]

Admission of the EFTA countries, by contrast, should not raise problems of similar severity. The EFTA countries all have a higher gross domestic product per person than the EC average; the EFTA countries heavily depend for their trade on the EC; they have no minority problems; they are all working democracies. EFTA countries, however, protect their farmers even more than do the EC countries; hence even adopting the EC's Common Agricultural Policy would somewhat liberalize farm trade in the EFTA countries. The EFTA countries will also help to balance German power within the EC.

But whatever happens, the EC and the US alike will have to adjust to growing German influence in East-Central Europe. After World War II, German power in these regions broke asunder with the fall of the Third Reich. Now, however, Germany has turned into the main aid giver for the former Eastern Bloc, the chief foreign supplier of managerial and technical skill, and the principal trade partner. The German language has become the most widely taught foreign tongue, supplanting Russian and out-distancing even English. The Germans have also acquired much influence as a belated role model for hard work and entrepreneurial ambition as against the deadening egalitarianism formerly associated with Russia. (According to an Eastern European anecdote, an Englishman, a German, and a Russian free a genie from a bottle. The genie grants to each of them one wish. Says the Englishman: "my neighbor, Lord Egremont, has a fine estate. I want one like it – complete with an equally sonorous title." Insists the German: "my neighbor, Herr Müller, owns a big factory. I want one bigger still and even more modern." Complains the Russian, "My neighbor Ivan Ivanovitch Ivanov has a cow. I don't have a cow. Please kill the cow.") Fortunately, Germany today aims for profit (deutschmark nationalism), not military power. In this sense Germany's growing stake does not injure its EC partners – especially as Kohl has made every effort to associate Germany's allies with reconstruction in East-Central Europe.

European collaboration in foreign policy or EPC (European Political Cooperation, in Euro-jargon) has not been a great success. The Single European Act provided for mutual consultation so as to ensure that the combined influence of the partners be exercised as effectively as possible.[28] But Europeans have rarely managed to pull together. For example, the Falklands War of 1982 was set off by an act of aggression on the part of Argentina against a British territory. The US under President Reagan supported Britain; the EC stood aside. A few years later, in 1986, the US bombed Libya in reprisal for Libyan participation in acts of terrorism against US targets in Europe. Britain backed the US, permitting US planes to fly from British bases; the Europeans stood aloof. In the same year, a Jordanian Palestinian received a long prison sentence in Britain for plotting to blow up an Israeli passenger plane in midair. Syria was accused of masterminding this affair, and Britain broke off diplomatic relations. Again the Europeans stood aloof. In 1990 Iraq invaded Kuwait. Britain loyally backed the US by sending to Iraq a substantial part of its army. French

support was half-hearted; the units sent proved unsuited to desert conditions. The Germans provided money, and the rest excuses.

The EC record has also been unimpressive during the on-going Yugoslav
crisis since 1991; once more the EC countries have failed to see eye to
eye. A precarious truce was established in the Serb-Croat conflict under
UN auspices, but Germany forced the pace by agreeing, at the end of
1991, to recognize the independence of Croatia and Slovenia. This was
not a decision welcome to Britain, France, or Spain. There were fears of
Germany's political resurgence, and German pride in a major victory for
German foreign policy. The EC thereafter reluctantly followed suit on the
grounds that recognition was in line with the EC's new "Guidelines for
the Recognition of New States."[29] This was not an ideal solution, either
for the EC nor for the US. However, the Balkans, in our opinion, do not
form part of the US's sphere of vital interests. Bismarck, Germany's "Iron
Chancellor" in the nineteenth century, once said that the Balkans were
not worth the bones of a single Prussian grenadier. We insist his statement
equally applies to US marines.

For the immediate future, US policy-makers must assume that Germany's influence will increase within the EC's foreign policy area. Militarily, however, we believe that the EC will continue to operate only in a
defensive fashion – that is, if the EC were to be threatened by an outsider.
Dissensions concerning foreign policy are likely to grow rather than
diminish if Switzerland, Austria, and Sweden should join the EC, and
import their own neutralist and isolationist traditions. European cohesion
would be further diluted if some of the former Warsaw Pact countries
were soon to join the EC. A consequent weakening of the EC's cohesion
would not be in the US interest. Likewise there exists a special relationship
between the US and Britain, tested in past crises. Washington should
therefore do its best to safeguard this profitable relationship – without,
however, endangering the crucial US-German tie.

Such considerations should restrain the enthusiasm of US statesmen
who would wish to create the world anew. In a speech to the US Congress
on 9 September 1990, at the beginning of the Persian Gulf crisis, President
Bush spoke of a "New World Order" that might emerge from present
misery. Once the war was over, the former president reiterated his call
for a New World Order marked by international solidarity against aggression. Bush thereby repeated a theme that has appealed to American
idealism ever since the days of President Wilson and his "Fourteen Points."
Bush's argument seemed convincing at a time when the breakup of the
Soviet Union apparently left the US in the position of being the world's
only superpower. Nevertheless, we do not share such far-reaching aspirations. No matter what US Defense Department planners think, it is

unrealistic for the US to seek the position of arbiter between contending national groups in Eastern Europe or try to export parliamentary democracy to the Third World. The US is indeed a leading power; but there are other great powers to be considered – the EC, Russia, the People's Republic of China, Japan, and India – whose interests cannot simply be brushed aside. Washington must assert its influence where US vital national interests are concerned; it should not, however, be the object of US foreign policy to adjudicate between the rival claims of, say, Serbs and Croats, Russians and Ukrainians. Such interference can only lead to distrust of US motives, hopeless dispersion of effort, and high expenses, and will remain ineffective in the long run. As Molière, greatest of comic French dramatists, put it three centuries ago in his play *Le Misanthrope*:

> *C'est une folie à nulle seconde*
> *De vouloir se mêler à corriger le monde.*

(No folly is greater than to try and set the world aright.)

While we have reservations regarding a New World Order and the immediate practicability of a joint European foreign policy, we welcome the Single Market Program to achieve economic union – but only in so far as it will contribute toward the liberalization of trade and investment. Europe is a key trading partner of the US (in 1988 the EC was the largest single destination of US exports, representing 23.3 percent of the total for that year.) US exports to Europe have also been growing. Europe in the past has benefited from US investment; the US has reciprocally profited from European funds placed in America. (The National Governors Association estimated that almost three million jobs in the US – about 3 percent of the workforce – result from European investment.)[30] The US thus has a vital stake in the EC's prosperity.

Unfortunately, the EC's role in trade liberalization has been ambivalent. The greatest difficulty derives from the EC's determination through the Common Agricultural Policy (CAP) to protect German, French, Italian, and other farmers against foreign imports, including US food. (In 1991 the EC's total subsidies to its farmers amounted to 49 percent of the value of EC's production. The American farmers' support amounted to 30 percent. By contrast, the New Zealand farmers received only 4 percent of the value of their output; yet New Zealand agriculture was one of the world's most productive.) The disputes over farm subsidies unfortunately affect the inter-EC relations as well as EC-US relations; British consumers and British farmers complain as loudly as Americans. An equitable solution is not easy to find. The US farming industries themselves enjoy a broad range of subsidies which should – in our view – be diminished or eliminated. More importantly, because German and Italian farmers widely vote for Christian Democratic parties, it is unrealistic to expect Christian Democratic politicians to offend a substantial number of their voters. But these farm subsidies are expensive ($30 billion a year). The money could be spent better in other ways, especially since subsidized food always costs more than non-subsidized food. Increasing farm exports from the US to the EC would also reduce the US trade deficit.

The EC's record is also ambivalent regarding commerce in manufactured articles. The EC's movement toward unity benefited those multinational corporations which expanded their activities to Europe from the US and Japan. Firms such as AT & T, Xerox, and Sony invested heavily in Europe at a time when the EC was an under-capitalized market. Ford, General Motors, and Toyota began to produce worldwide, while Fiat and Volkswagen largely kept production at home. Not surprisingly, the "invasion" of the EC by foreign capital was resented, especially by high-technology industry. Many EC states therefore subsidized their own "national champion" industries. (Between 1986 and 1989 average annual subsidies amounted to $90 billion.)[31] Numerous EC companies are protected monopolies; others survive on subsidies only; government contracts are loaded against foreign firms.

Nevertheless, US trade negotiators hold strong cards of their own, because the US is a major European market. Even at its most forbidding, the EC was never as exclusionist as Japan, which built its industrial might on the backs of Japanese consumers. The EC values US trade; the EC has accordingly made some concessions in fields such as industrial standards, banking regulations, and other contentious matters. American firms operating in Europe will enjoy the self-same operating efficiencies and economies of scale that the integration of the European market will bring to European firms. The trend towards industrial cooperation through major consortia has likewise benefited US entrepreneurs. European affiliates of American companies have participated in European research and manufacturing consortia; American companies with a substantial European presence have taken part in European collaborative programs. For instance, Pratt and Whitney worked with Rolls-Royce (Britain) and Turbomeca (France) on the RTM 322 engine's development. Business in the US – just as business worldwise – must respond to the new trend toward internationalization. Fortunately, the US, by its continued inventiveness and foreign contacts, is better suited to do well in the race than critics assume. The US, accustomed to a continental, free trade system, is actually better qualified to take advantage of an EC-wide free trade area than are individual nations in the EC.

To strike a note of economic optimism at a time of recession (at the end of 1992) seems either light-hearted or irresponsible. The US is heavily indebted, with a large federal deficit, and large private obligations incurred by private companies. Germany and Japan save far more than does the US; American companies have been bested in many fields in which they once ruled supreme, such as the consumer electronics industry. A good deal of US physical capital is obsolete; the US share of intellectual capital may also be on the decline. (The percentage of US patents granted to US corporations and citizens has fallen from 62 percent in 1980 to 53 percent in 1990.)[32] A nation that snickers at "nerds," but worships grown-up men who excel at throwing a ball into a basket, may well end with a shortage of much-needed "nerds." Americans are concerned about loss of jobs, decaying industries, falling living standards, rising costs of health, tuition, and taxes. Citizens are disturbed by the plight of the cities – with race riots, crime, drugs, the homeless and the panhandlers. The loss of international competitiveness in some industries, decaying infrastructures, the decline in achievements at various levels in schools further erodes US confidence. Although Americans spend one and a half times as much as on students as Japan, the US school system produces all too many functionally illiterate people and scores low among developed nations on math and science tests.[33]

Nevertheless, the US is not destined for an inevitable downward slide – a point to which we shall return. The US can rectify existing weaknesses by reducing the burden borne by US business through over-regulation; the US can encourage domestic saving by changing its tax policies. The US is not on the way to becoming merely a country of burger flippers and motel maids. In 1938 Europe as a whole had a higher percentage of the world's manufacturing than the US. Thereafter, the US gained the lead and has maintained it ever since – albeit not at the level attained in the decade after World War II, when much of Europe was ruined. According to the Council of Competitiveness, the US only gets a "B average" on the "Technology Report Card." Even so, the US continues to do extremely well in numerous endeavors that may be crucial for the economy of the future. (These include database systems, genetic engineering, aircraft, jet and rocket propulsion, pollution reduction and recycling, software, medical technology, voice recognition and vision in computers, and computers.) Contrary to widespread misconceptions, the US is not a nation of dropouts. (By age 24, something like 85 percent of US adults have completed high school.)[34] Contrary to mistaken forecasts, the US competes successfully in a broad range of services, agriculture, and numerous other pursuits. In short, the US can and will be able to compete with the new Europe; indeed, the economies of North America and Europe are complementary. It is not a question of "dog eat dog" but of "work together – prosper together."

## THE EC: MILITARY AND POLITICAL COOPERATION

Whatever the flaws in Western Europe's political arrangements, militarily the West has performed amazingly well. In 1990 the Warsaw Pact broke asunder; in 1991 the Soviet Union disintegrated, to be replaced by an as yet ill-defined Commonwealth of Independent States (CIS). In retrospect, it is easy to forget how enormous the armed might of the now defunct Soviet Union was. As late as 1990, by which time a number of major reductions had been made, the Soviet Union had in uniform a total of about 4,258,000 men, with another 5,560,000 in reserve.)[35] The Soviet Union land forces were by far the largest in Europe; the Soviet navy ranked as the world's second; the Soviet ballistic missile forces and strategic aviation were formidable – between them they formed the most awesome aggregation of military forces ever assembled in peacetime. Even the German *Wehrmacht* as assembled by the Third Reich before World War II looked puny by comparison.

The Gorbachev revolution after 1985 at first made no difference in this respect. As Ambassador Richard F. Staar has pointed out, Soviet arms spending continued to rise – at disastrous cost to the Soviet civilian economy, the Soviet consumer, and, ultimately, to the Soviet system as a whole. (According to Sergei M. Rogov of the USSR Institute of the US and Canada, military expenditure was expected to go up from 26 percent of the Soviet budget to 36 percent in 1991.) The Soviets continued to deploy advanced versions of intercontinental ballistic missiles, but also silo-based and mobile ones. (The US had no weapons in that category.) The Soviets reportedly worked on new Delta ballistic missile submarines. The START treaty, signed between the US and the Soviet Union in July 1991, also permitted the Soviets to maintain a great array of defensive weapons against ballistic missiles, aircraft, and Cruise missiles.[36] Again, the US had no comparable counter-force. Given such massive armaments, given also the difficulties in verifying compliance with treaty obligations, caution was in order for the Western powers.

Would the Soviet Union have ever used this force against Western Europe? The secret intentions of Soviet policy-makers will only be uncovered when the archives of the former Soviet Union become available to researchers – perhaps not even then. But the declared doctrines of the Soviet armed forces had stressed the importance of surprise, deception, and the strategic initiative. Theirs was not a defensive doctrine; they believed in the merits of a sustained offensive. Would the Soviets have confined their military interests to safeguarding the Warsaw Pact from aggression? According to the Soviets' own statements, the answer to this question was "no." Soviet theoreticians had elaborated a doctrine of "proletarian internationalism" whereby the working class of one country might legitimately give support to revolutions in other countries – it was on these grounds that the Soviets had sent arms to Cuba and Vietnam, Cuban proxy forces had fought in Angola and Ethiopia, and Soviet troops had intervened in Afghanistan.

Would Soviet troops have intervened in Western Europe, had there been no NATO. alliance? We cannot be sure. We do know, however, that during the Portuguese revolution of 1974, the pro-Moscow-oriented Portuguese Communist Party briefly hoped to seize power in Lisbon, intending to install a communist dictatorship on the Eastern European model. There was nothing in Soviet doctrine or Soviet experience which would have prevented Soviet forces from supporting their communist comrades in Portugal – or for that matter in Italy or France, which also had large communist parties – without NATO's preventive armaments.

NATO, however, had built an impressive deterrent force designed to contain any Soviet advance, and to prevent military blackmail at the conference table.[37] In the end, NATO won without firing a shot. NATO's bloodless victory was unique in history – as complete as it was unforeseen. For all its weaknesses, NATO effectively protected Western Europe from Soviet threats; the pessimists' fears were confounded; the optimists' hopes were bettered. In 1989, during its last year, the Warsaw Pact powers, for the first time, announced a defensive doctrine; they enunciated a somewhat ill-defined doctrine of "reasonable sufficiency." Thereafter the Soviet forces withdrew, or prepared to withdraw, from Eastern Europe, thus completely altering the strategic balance. At the end of 1991, the former Soviet Union, by then reconstituted as the CIS, agreed that the member states would form their own separate armies. The former Soviet armed forces would therefore be divided. (Ukraine proceeded to form its own army immediately.) The four "nuclear" states (Belarus, Russia, Ukraine, and Kazakhstan) resolved to maintain a unified command, with the dominant voice going to Russia. Belarus, Ukraine, and Kazakhstan publicly announced their intention of becoming nuclear-free states, but as Graham Allison, an American expert, put it, "do not count on today's preferences lasting as circumstances change or less responsible people become more influential."[38] At the time of writing, the position as yet remained uncertain, with tensions between Russia and Ukraine over the future of the Black Sea fleet and the Crimea, and nuclear weaponry remaining in Ukraine.

Both former President Bush and President Gorbachev made proposals for massive reductions in arms, each set of suggestions being designed to preserve existing strategic advantages for the respective proponent's country. Early in 1992 a key military advisory panel urged on the Bush administration to reduce further the US arsenal of strategic military weapons, and by radically changing the secret plans for targeting those arms. The remaining arsenal would still exceed the combined number of French, British, and Chinese nuclear arms. US policy thereafter would place greater emphasis on using the nuclear deterrent to prevent the destruction of allies in NATO, or Israel and Taiwan, to prevent interference with access to critical raw materials such as oil, and to discourage the spread of "ABC" (atomic, bacteriological, chemical) weapons in the Third World.[39]

All this was good news. Nevertheless, even though the Cold War is over, the US will continue to face an uncertain future in a world where ethnic quarrels abound, and ballistic missiles continue to proliferate. By 1991 countries as varied as Israel, South Africa, Syria, Iraq, Egypt, Iran, Libya, Saudi Arabia, India, and Pakistan had either developed missile forces, had acquired missiles from abroad, or were carrying on research. (India alone was developing the Aqni, with a range of 1,500 miles, and was also said to be working on an intercontinental ballistic missile.)[40] Under these circumstances it was particularly important for the US to proceed with its anti-ballistic missile defense. The US's lack of adequate preparations constitute its most obvious strategic weakness. In this regard the US has done even worse than the British before World War II; the British had mistakenly argued that the bomber would always get through, neglected their fighter plane defense, and thereby nearly incurred defeat in the Battle of Britain in 1940. It is an error that the US dare not repeat.

At the time of writing, the CIS's future was far from clear. Westerners feared that the CIS's projected central command might not work as intended, and that even the individual "nuclear" republics might suffer from an erosion of authority. There was new concern about the proliferation of nuclear arms. Proliferation might take place on an official level, through cooperation between established governments. Existing non-proliferation treaties and the work of the International Atomic Energy Agency (IAEA) were designed to prevent such contingencies.[41] The Iraqui example, however, showed how difficult enforcement could turn out in practice.

Equally scary was the thought that some of the former Soviet Union's 30,000 nuclear weapons might find their way into the international arms bazaar – a real possibility regarding tactical nuclear weapons of small bulk and weight. Linked to these fears was the dread of a new brain drain, as unemployed Soviet arms experts might be hired by Third World countries and thereby contribute to the indirect proliferation of nuclear weaponry. The US therefore has a direct stake in planned and orderly destruction of nuclear weaponry. By the end of 1991, the US Congress had appropriated

$400 million for this purpose, to be used at presidential discretion. This was money well spent. We also agree with Professor Allison's suggestion to set up an international agency with money, technology, and a mandate to assist in disabling and destroying such weapons. Other G7 governments, which choose to participate, would make matching contributions. Western favors such as recognition, food, trade, concessions, loans should be given as rewards. NATO, early in 1992, offered to help dismantle CIS nuclear weapons in return for food and medical supplies.

How should NATO respond to changing circumstances?[42] The central front was "thinned out"; Germany ceased to contain the greatest military forces ever assembled in peacetime. Tactical nuclear weapons were withdrawn at a time when a massive assault from the Warsaw Pact on Western Europe was no longer to be feared. Strategists therefore stood to answer several key questions. Should the US presence continue in Europe at a time when the Soviet Union has disintegrated, and when its successor states are too much concerned with their own problems to consider aggression abroad? Assuming that NATO will continue, how great should be the US's commitment of military forces in Europe? Above all, how should NATO relate in years to come to WEU (Western European Union)?[43] Answers to these questions differ greatly.

Some Americans argue for a complete US withdrawal from NATO. Their desire reflects a revival of isolationism, evidenced by the preoccupation with domestic affairs during the 1992 presidential campaign. According to the neo-isolationists, NATO has served its purpose. Let Europeans build their own security system – linked, however, to the US in order to reassure Germany's neighbors.[44] Yeltsin is a responsible statesman; the last thing on earth Russia wants is a war with the West. The successor states of the Soviet Union face troublesome problems in their relations with one another. Nevertheless, the outlook is hopeful. (A protocol to the CIS agreement concluded at Alma Ata, 1991, recognized the current borders of all Commonwealth members.) At last, the argument continues, the US deals with thoroughly responsible people who have no quarrel with the US. The US should thus aim for constructive interaction with the successor states of the Soviet Union in whose well-being Americans have a direct stake, as they did in the now defunct Soviet Union.[45] Hence the US needs to spend less on defense, and benefit domestically from the resultant "peace dividend." Planned troop reductions should be extended, and these withdrawals will require structural as well as quantitative changes in the US defense forces. US troops should mainly be deployed at home, capable of acting quickly and supported by a ready reserve force.

European opponents of NATO, like their American counterparts, also derive from several parts of the political spectrum. Some of them hold –

as do numerous American intellectuals – that the US is on a downward slope, and that Europe must therefore break with US entanglements. NATO's opponents include the heirs of De Gaulle, who hope that Europe will one day include Russia; Europe will then stretch from the Atlantic to the Pacific – the one and only superpower of the twenty-first century. Others are more modest in their expectations; they stress the merits of full Franco-German integration; France should resign itself to becoming part of the D-Mark block, station its nuclear *Force de frappe* on the Oder River in East Germany, and make sure that it does not end as a *Québec européen*.[46] Militarily, Franco-German cooperation has already found expression in the creation of a Franco-German brigade of 5,000 men, to be expanded into a corps of 40,000 men. These troops will be outside NATO's command; they could form the core of a new European defense force wholly independent of NATO, with its foremost object to serve WEU. Such an arrangement could presage a future clash of interests; moreover, Germany and France between them would dominate European defense. Both Britain and smaller countries such as Holland thus expressed reservations. From the US standpoint, the best option would be one favored by Britain, whereby all WEU members would provide contigents from their own national forces; these would jointly deal with challenges affecting EC interests in cases not involving NATO. If the EC were to intervene, say, in trouble spots such as Bosnia-Hercegovina, US troops would not be involved. But apart from such organizational problems, ordinary citizens in Europe have been impressed by the immediate inconveniences of any military alliance – the ear-shattering noise of low-flying military aircraft, and the massive environmental damage, with ground and water pollution, brought about by foreign troops. (The Soviet army's record in this respect was by far the worst, but the Americans was bad enough.)

We ourselves hope that NATO will continue, at least for the time being. (At the time of writing discussions were under way for the creation of two joint US-German corps, as well as a German-Dutch corps.) At present no European country wants all US troops to leave – not even France, which, after all, requires a transatlantic counterweight to the might of united Germany. Neither do we believe that there will ever be a "European House" embracing all the lands between the Atlantic and Pacific. The disagreements *within* the EC and CIS, as they presently exist, are bad enough. A "European House" would surely be a house even more divided against itself. Culturally, the US has at least as good a claim to be considered a part of Europe as Russia; countries such as Poland, Czechoslovakia, and Hungary would rather join NATO than form a new alliance with Russia. Militarily, it is unrealistic to assume that Germany would ever depend on France for a nuclear deterrent. The Germans will either rely on the US or build their own deterrent. NATO's defense framework is workable and long-established; the various national units have performed well. By contrast, the mixed Franco-German units still face many problems. Their respective military bands make a magnificent ensemble; but operationally, the new units suffer from differences regarding language, command structure, operational doctrine, and weaponry. In a world where minor powers increasingly acquire rocketry and the skills required to manufacture nuclear weapons, Europe cannot become an independent superpower without its own strategic capability. Most Europeans would not desire such an expensive expedient.

The world remains a dangerous place. In the past, the Soviet Army, for all its weaknesses, was not merely by far the most powerful military force, but also the most widely trusted of Soviet institutions among its own citizens. (A poll taken in May 1991 indicated that the Soviet Army was the institution in which respondents had the most confidence[47] – a result that paralleled similar opinion surveys in the US.) The present Russian army is beset by many weaknesses; but in future it might once more astound the world. The globe may also become more perilous as the Soviet Union's successor states might sell high-tech equipment at bargain prices to Third World countries such as Iraq and Iran. NATO is not merely a military but also a political alliance with a long-established machinery for transnational cooperation. NATO up to now has benefited the US by deterring the Soviets, keeping the peace among European states and giving the US leadership within the Atlantic alliance. There remain, moreover, many informal links A major US base such as Kaiserslautern in West Germany ("K-Town" in US military lingo) depended heavily on American jobs and business; there were numerous ties of friendship and marriage between Americans and Germans. Even the limited withdrawals under way in 1992 occasioned a good deal of disruption. A complete US withdrawal would occasion even more trouble.

NATO, moreover, has shown a great deal of flexibility in adapting to the demise of its *raison d'être*. Militarily, NATO has adjusted to the breakup of the Soviet Empire by substantial troop reductions. The classic doctrine of "forward defense" has given way to a new concept that relies on smaller, more flexible forces. Battlefield nuclear weapons will disappear, medium-range nuclear weapons will remain in NATO arsenals, but they will no longer be in constant deployment on warships and submarines. A much larger proportion of NATO forces than hitherto will consist of reserves. NATO will still be unable to operate "out of area"; but at least it will continue as a Euro-American enterprise.[48]

In the civilian sphere NATO in 1991 created a new institution called the North Atlantic Cooperation Council (NACC). This will comprise the

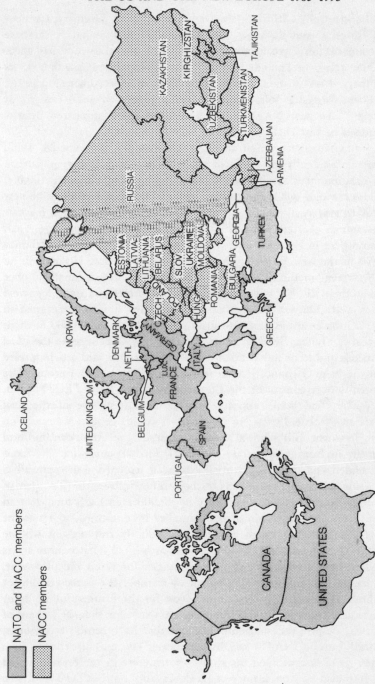

*Figure 7.2* The North Atlantic Cooperation Council (NACC), created in 1991. NACC includes NATO countries; Georgia's formal membership is still pending.

NATO countries, the CIS, the Baltic republics, Poland, Hungary, Czechoslovakia, Bulgaria, and Rumania. NATO officials will consult with these
various countries on a great variety of issues; by doing so they will meet
halfway the desire of Poland, Hungary, and Romania to join NATO as
full members. (NACC met for the first time on December 20, 1991.)
British Prime Minister John Major tactfully described such designs as
"unsettling."[49] To push NATO to the borders of the Ukraine and Belarus
would indeed be just that.

NATO adopted a new crisis management strategy on May 28, 1992.
The new strategy calls for a cut of two-thirds of US forces in Europe
and the creation of a multinational rapid deployment corps of 100,000
men able to respond quickly to threats to the alliance in Europe. The new
strategy is to replace the old Cold War strategy – warding off a massive
Soviet assault in central Germany – so as to be able to respond to small
attacks anywhere in Europe. This would provide NATO with "maximum
flexibility" in the new Europe. The Rapid Reaction Force (RRF) will be
the main element in the new system. The US may have a small number
of troops in the RRF, but will provide a reserve force and air and logistical
support as well. The US will make large cuts in their forces assigned to
NATO. (US forces are expected to drop from 300,000 to 100,000 in three
or four years.) France, Belgium and Italy want the RRF to serve the EC's
security needs and to be independent of NATO. Britain, and others, prefer
to retain the NATO connection in order to link the US to Europe. The
debate then is over control of the Euro-force. Will it be the EC, NATO,
or the WEU? The WEU appears likely to be in charge of the new
Euro-force in the late 1990s.

Under President Bill Clinton's administration the American military
commitment in Europe is certain to shrink further, now that the Cold
War has ended and the Soviet threat has been lessened. European allies
have all made substantial reductions in their military strength. (The British
in 1991 thus decided to cut their army by 40,000 men.) US total ground
forces in future may be diminished in number by one-third, to a total of
about 500,000 men.[50] A much larger proportion than at present will be
stationed in the US and only 100,000 or less in NATO. Hence more stress
will need to be placed on logistic arrangements for rapid redeployment,
and on pre-positioning heavy equipment in Europe. We ourselves do not
feel qualified to prescribe precise force levels for the future. But we agree
with Fernando Nogueira, the Portuguese minister for defense, when he
stresses that, despite the enormous changes that have come over Eastern
and Central Europe, NATO has by no means become superfluous at a
time when there is continued instability, not merely in the former Soviet
empire, but also in the former Yugoslavia and on NATO's southern

boundary from the Maghreb to the Middle East. "In a world going through intense and accelerated change, our transatlantic dimension, our military structure and our collective experience will continue to provide the indispensable foundation for a stable security environment in Europe."[51] NATO may not last for ever; the alliance may perhaps have become obsolete by 1999, when NATO will have reached its fiftieth birthday. But in the meantime, it behooves the US to support the alliance, share power in NATO, and abstain from the conventional American error of largely dismantling US land forces at the end of an emergency. This mistake cost the US dearly after World War I and World War II – it is not an experience to be repeated.

For the next decade or so, NATO should continue in some form, and the US should back it. Europeans may rail at American leadership – but they still prefer to be led by the US to being headed by another European power. The NATO connection is particularly valuable to Germany, which finds that NATO enhances the legitimacy of German foreign policy while reassuring France. The US can improve its own position by proposing a number of reforms that would please the Germans without harming any other power. The German language should be raised to a position of equality with English and French. German troops should be put under national command within NATO, on a par with British, French, and American troops; NATO's supreme European command should be headed by a European.

Whatever NATO's ultimate scope, policy-makers will have to remodel the alliance so as to take account of the Europeans' enhanced role. Inter-European cooperation has many aspects – political (through the EC), military (through WEU), and also in the field of arms production (a field in which European manufacturers bitterly compete both with one another and with the US). As early as 1976 the Independent European Program Group (IEPG) came into being to promote cooperation in the production of conventional weapons. IEPG endeavored to coordinate research and development, facilitate the standardization of equipment and its interoperability – a major consideration in an alliance where there was an embarrassing abundance of weapon models. In more general terms IEPG aims at maintaining an adequate technological and industrial base in Europe, while strengthening the European factor in transatlantic relations. At the same time IEPG has repeatedly stressed its commitment to Atlantic solidarity and rejected any kind of protectionism designed to create a "Fortress Europe."[52] The US has a direct interest in strengthening its European allies; IEPG's efforts should therefore be welcomed rather than deplored.

Within the NATO alliance, the future role of the Western European Union (WEU) is of major importance to US geo-political concerns. WEU originated in the Brussels Treaty concluded in 1948 between Britain,

*Figure 7.3* The Western European Union (WEU).

France, and the Benelux countries, and at the time, Britain was by far
the strongest power within this grouping. Its original object was to provide
security against the resurgence of a vengeful and defeated Germany, as
much as against Soviet ambitions. In 1954 the Brussels Treaty Organization admitted West Germany, as well as Italy, and the Brussels Treaty
Organization was transformed into a WEU. WEU has its own Parliamentary Assembly, and its own secretariat. But all real work regarding defense
was, however, done by NATO, and WEU's role in successive confronta-
tions with the Soviet Union resembled that of the British House of Lords,
as defined in Gilbert and Sullivan's *Mikado:*

> The House of Peers, throughout the war,
> Did nothing in particular
> And did it very well.

It was only from the mid-1980s onward that WEU's members decided to reactivate the organization, part of Europe's search for a new political and military identity. (It now includes all EC states except Ireland, Greece, and Denmark.) In 1987 an agreement was reached on a "Platform of European Security Interests," and the WEU thereafter sought to extend its membership in accordance with the Single European Act. WEU will surely become that "European pillar" of the transatlantic alliance for which President John F. Kennedy once called with verve and prescience. WEU seems more suitable for this task than the IEPG, narrowly centered on armaments, or the so-called Euro-group within NATO which excludes France.

During the Gulf War, Europe's record was admittedly far from brilliant. (The only major contribution came from Britain, which sent 45,000 men – but even this sizeable body constituted no more than 8 percent of the total Allied forces involved.) Nevertheless, the WEU did some useful work in the Gulf, a region outside the direct defense area of Europe or NATO. WEU coordinated British, French, Dutch, and Italian naval forces in the Gulf. A precedent was thus set for joint European action in "out of area" conflicts. However, WEU's future role was as yet far from clear at the time of writing. France favored an independent European force to support an independent EC foreign policy. Germany wanted the best of both worlds. WEU would form the future defense arm of the EC, but work in association with NATO. To Germany, this would be a way of drawing France (militarily a full member of WEU) closer to NATO, while preserving close links to the US. Britain, Italy, the Netherlands, Portugal, and Denmark put more emphasis on NATO; they want the WEU to remain subordinate to NATO rather than constituting the core of the EC's defense. From the US standpoint, the British view is preferable, since the NATO alliance maximizes US influence in Europe. It is also in the US interest that WEU should become capable in future of operations outside NATO's designated areas in Europe. But whatever happens, WEU will become a major force in its own right. "It is now inconceivable to consider the defense of Europe outside the essential Alliance [WEU]."[53] The WEU's council of foreign and defense ministers will meet biannually; the WEU has acquired organizational framework, with its own secretariat. This body in turn coordinates the work of five "working parties." (A special working party deals with all-European development, NATO, and the EC. A standing defense ministries group is concerned with operational military issues. The verification group specializes on arms control. A Mediterranean group copes with regional affairs, and a Space group with plans to build joint reconnaissance and verification satellites.) At present, the WEU is in no position to replace NATO. Only NATO has the military muscle and the organizational resources to defend its members. In future, however, the WEU will play a much more important part. The WEU would be well advised to move from Paris to Brussels so as to facilitate cooperation with NATO during a ten-year transitional period. The WEU might ultimately be linked to wider regional security unions, set up within the former Warsaw Pact states and the former Soviet Union. Between them these would form a European Security Union. The WEU might then take over from NATO some time in the 21st century. The US should, however, preposition material in Europe and maintain its airlift capacity while cooperating with the WEU and the CSCE (Conference on Security and Cooperation in Europe).[54]

In discussions concerning NATO's future, the CSCE and the CCMS (Committee on the Challenges of Modern Society, a body as yet little known to the public) deserve mention. NATO – like the Warsaw Pact – was founded by men to whom a clear, smokeless sky over a factory town signified misery and unemployment, whereas black clouds pouring from factory chimneys meant work was once more returning to a city stricken by either an air raid or a disastrous slump. The growing ecological concerns of the 1960s also affected NATO. As early as 1969, the North Atlantic Council, then meeting in Washington, decided to give a new "social and environmental dimension" to NATO and set up the CCMS for the purpose. In 1990 the NATO Summit in Brussels agreed to expand the CCMS's scope, and to invite experts from Central and Eastern Europe as well as from the Soviet Union to participate in the CCMS's work. The CCMS carries out studies on environmental problems, particularly on the ecological effects of military activities. In addition, the CCMS has concerned itself with major questions such as protection against marine biological fouling, the reduction of air pollution from marine engines, pollution prevention strategies for sustainable development, remedial action for contaminated land and groundwater, and such like.[55]

More ambitious still in scope is the CSCE. The CSCE had its origins in 1975 when the Helsinki Final Act endorsed fundamental principles concerning peaceful coexistence, human rights, and constitutional government. The CSCE therefore held periodic meetings to consider progress regarding particular aspects of the agenda ("Baskets") as defined in the Helsinki Final Act. Between major review meetings, there were formal discussions on matters such as economic cooperation, human rights, cultural cooperation, the reduction of conventional weapons, etc. The CSCE's organization was at first loose and informal. Yet the CSCE exerted considerable indirect influence as Soviet and other Eastern European dissidents began to appeal to the principles laid down in Helsinki – much to the Soviet authorities' annoyance.

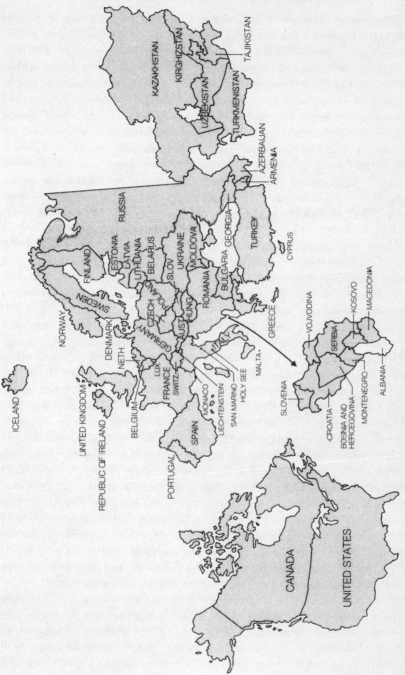

*Figure 7.4* The Conference on Security and Cooperation in Europe (CSCE) area.

In November 1990 the CSCE summit, held in Paris for the first time, adopted a Charter for a United Europe providing for permanent CSCE institutions. In June 1991 the Council of Foreign Ministers met in Berlin; the Council will form the central forum for political consultation within the CSCE. For the present, the Council's powers do not amount to much. It can pass resolutions, and prepares for summit follow-up conferences that are held every other year. But there will be a Committee of Senior Officials to implement resolutions, while a permanent secretariat will be responsible for administrative and public relations work. A Conflict Prevention Center in Vienna is designed to help the Council of Foreign Ministers in reducing risks of conflict. Military information is to be exchanged through a specially installed communications network. A hot-line will link all CSCE capitals to handle emergencies.[56] The CSCE spans the US, Canada, the EC, the former Yugoslavia, the former Warsaw Pact countries, and the successor states of the Soviet Union; it is potentially a powerful association. It provides not merely an international forum, but also a possible instrument for influencing public opinion. (For instance, in 1990, the CSCE at a meeting in Bonn recognized the link between a pluralistic democracy and a market economy.)

From the US standpoint, the CSCE is worth backing. No matter what may be the preferences of spokesmen for a US *realpolitik*, US foreign policy cannot work effectively without strong support from public opinion. The CSCE does not have the UN's large bureaucracy (with its 23,000 full-time employees scattered over the globe); the CSCE does not run up the UN's big budget ($1.56 billion for the year 1990–1). The US does not have any direct quarrel with any of the CSCE's members either in Western, Central, or Eastern Europe, or the CIS states. The CSCE members do not promote terrorism abroad, as do UN members in good standing such as Iran and Syria. The CSCE lacks those disruptive Third World lobbies which have traditionally looked askance at the US on the grounds that the US is selfish, rich, "white," insensitive – and generally fails to provide enough aid. Neither does the CSCE suffer from that double standard of morality which for so long has beset the UN's General Assembly in dealing with the US and its NATO allies on the one hand, and the Third World on the other. Spanning the continent of Europe and the Atlantic, the CSCE may well make a genuine contribution to European peace.

The CSCE was a Cold War product. Once the war ended, CSCE sought a wider purpose. During 1991, the CSCE could not get Yugoslavia to move to peaceful negotiations. The group of 51 states had become, in President Havel's words, "a mere debating club." Havel wanted CSCE decisions to be put in treaty form and sanctions taken against those who break the treaties. He also desired the group to have a UN-like security council and to put together peacekeeping forces. The US and Britain opposed Havel's reforms and fear the CSCE trying to do things other European institutions already do. The British felt the CSCE should remain basically a political institution concerned with rule of law, human rights, and peace, and should work by morally pressuring member governments. For that reason, the CSCE decided to accept the Central Asian states of the CIS into membership in order to embed them in European democracy and exercise some influence over those who have nuclear weapons. As a result, at the meeting in Prague in February of 1992, the ten new states of the former Soviet Union and the original members signed a nuclear non-proliferation resolution and promised to supply information on conventional weapons also. The Prague meeting also moved away from decisions only by unanimity in order to be able to pass resolutions against gross violators of CSCE principles. The US and Britain opposed an interventionist role, arguing that the WEU, NATO, and the UN were better equipped to do so. The CSCE hopefully, therefore, will continue to do what it has done best: monitor human rights and help restore democracy in the new states.[57]

Equally worthy of US support is the recently formed NACC (North Atlantic Cooperation Council), located in Brussels. According to former German foreign minister Hans-Dietrich Genscher, the council has four primary tasks: to put into effect the Treaty on Conventional Armed Forces in Europe; to ensure the security and speedy destruction of tactical nuclear weapons on the CIS's territory; to secure agreement for the Treaty on Non-Proliferation of Nuclear Arms from those countries which have not as yet signed; and to furnish civilian opportunities for scientists formerly engaged in research on weapons of mass destruction. The NACC decided to discuss the Nagorno-Karabakh dispute to try to get a peace accord. Violence continues, however, between Armenian and Azeri.

There is yet another organization that also has been concerned with human rights in non-communist Europe. The Council of Europe (CE) was set up in 1949 in Strasbourg to work for European integration through strengthening pluralist democracy, to protect human rights, and to promote European cultural identity. The original members (10) were Belgium, Denmark, France, Britain, Ireland, Italy, the Netherlands, Luxembourg, Norway and Sweden. The Council was expanded to include all 12 EC members and EFTA's 6, plus Cyprus, Liechtenstein, Malta, San Marino and Turkey. The Council has remained a consultative body concerned with protecting human rights, that could make no binding decisions unless ratified by member states. Nevertheless, the Council was not a mere talking shop; it favored European integration, it sponsored human rights and issued over 120 instruments such as the Convention for the Protection of

*Figure 7.5* The Council of Europe, 1992.

Human Rights. A Court of Human Rights developed out of the 1950 convention.[58]

With the collapse of the Warsaw Pact and the Soviet Union, membership in the Council of Europe is expected to increase. In 1990 Hungary secured admission; in 1991 Poland, Romania, Czechoslovakia and the Baltic states joined. Membership is expected to extend to all European states, and the Council has called for an all-European parliamentary assembly. The Council of Europe wants a role in the new Europe and has offered to help coordinate human rights issues in the CSCE.

In spite of CSCE and the Council of Europe, NATO and WEU the US cannot afford to neglect the UN. It is true that, in the past, the UN has laid itself open to serious criticisms. For instance, the UN forms by itself a global lobby for international aid – given for the most part at Western expense, and to little effect for the purpose in raising living standards in the recipient countries. Nevertheless, the UN has proved useful to the US in a variety of ways. It was under UN auspices that the

US resisted communist aggression in Korea; it was under UN auspices that the US waged the Gulf War; UN backing played a major part in gaining both domestic and international support for US policy-makers. The UN has recently become involved in peacekeeping operations in the former Yugoslavia; again UN intervention may prove of some utility in the future to allow humanitarian intervention to save populations from genocide or bad governments.

As regards the US's own future stance toward the UN, Washington can gain a good deal of goodwill both in Tokyo and Berlin by proposing both Germany and Japan for permanent membership in the Security Council. Given their economic power, both states have a perfectly good claim to membership. To support Japan and Germany will prove an advantage to US diplomacy at small cost. To see Russia, Germany, Japan, Britain, France, and the US all represented in the Security Council will also symbolize that, at long last, both World War II and the Cold War have passed into history.

Once the Cold War had ended, President Bush called for a "New World Order" in which the US would play a predominant part. The American public, however, decisively rejected such an activist role for the US; the 1992 presidential election was largely fought on domestic issues. The American public does not want to pay for a New World Order at a time when the US has so many unsolved problems at home. Isolationism has become respectable even with impeccable establishment members such as Richard Hyland, editor of *Foreign Affairs*. We ourselves prefer to side with a scholar such as Alexander George, an American political scientist, who offers more prudent advice. The US needs, George says, to limit its concerns and encourage free markets and trade, foster human rights, peacefully settle disputes, embargo the spread of nuclear weapons, restrict terrorists, promote democracy, strengthen mediation and peacekeeping in regional and world organizations – not withdraw from the world arena. This is a full enough agenda for the nation. Let the US share responsibility with other regional powers and organizations – but not try to act as democracy's policeman throughout the world.

## POLICY RECOMMENDATIONS

The object of US policy should be, above all, to safeguard American national interests. The US cannot, and should not, act as the world's policeman, or aspire to the creation of an ill-defined "New World Order." It is beyond the US's capacity to export democracy all over the world, settle the quarrels of contending national groups throughout the globe, or assure world-wide prosperity. The US should confine its efforts to helping its declared friends and harming its avowed enemies.

The US will indirectly benefit from a strengthening of the EC. The EC will in turn benefit by the adhesion of EFTA countries. The EC, in our opinion, will also be able within a reasonable period to grant membership to the Czech Republic, as well as Hungary and Poland. The EC will, however, be rendered unmanageable if it should extend full membership beyond this point until democracy and free enterprise advance in former communist states.

A common security and foreign policy for the EC can be worked out through the WEU, NACC, and CSCE, and with NATO's cooperation.

The US should support the deepening of the EC before widening it until the states of Central and Eastern Europe adopt market economies and democratic governance. Associate membership and freer trade should be offered during the period of reconstruction aided by the West, much like the Marshall Plan that restored Western Europe.

The US should support all efforts to strengthen the EC by the removal of all internal barriers, direct and indirect, on the movement of persons, merchandise, and capital within the EC. It should at the same time use such diplomatic influence as it has to commit the EC to low external tariffs and to low export subsidies. Such endeavors of course require reciprocity on the part of the US and, in future, on the part of the projected North American Free Trade area.

Within the EC, the US should maintain a special relationship with the United Kingdom, historically its closest ally. The US should equally look to a close relationship with Germany. Germany will not turn into a Fourth Reich; German and US interests largely coincide. The US can strengthen its ties with Germany by advocating the equality of the German language within the EC and NATO, on a par with English and French; by putting German troops under a national command within NATO; and by advocating for Germany a seat on the UN Security Council.

NATO has proved a magnificent success in the past, but now requires restructuring. Given widespread unrest and instability on NATO's southern and eastern circumference, the US should continue its NATO membership for at least another decade while gradually transferring power to the

WEU. Thereafter the WEU can become the security pillar of the EC, acting in collaboration with the US through the NACC and the Atlantic Alliance.

The Balkans, indeed South-Eastern and Central Europe as a whole, form part of the EC's natural hinterland. US troops should not therefore be deployed anywhere in the formerly communist states, whether in the former Yugoslavia or some other disturbed area formerly included in the Warsaw Pact. Outside NATO's operation area, the US should confine military intervention – if ever required – to the Middle East.

As long as the US remains a part of NATO, the US should encourage the WEU, but should strive to keep it subordinate to, not independent of, the NATO structure. In the long run, it is in the US interest that WEU should become capable of conducting operations outside the present NATO structure and of replacing NATO.

The spread of nuclear weapons and nuclear technology constitutes a clear and present danger to the US. While we are sceptical of foreign aid, we regard as justifiable technical and financial assistance to the nuclear members of the CIS for the destruction of nuclear weapons.

It has been a constant practice in US history rapidly to dismantle its defense forces after every major conflict. The US should not repeat this dangerous error in the pursuit of a dubious "peace dividend." Defense industries and defense forces, once dismantled, are hard to reconstitute. The US should therefore not reduce its future defense expenditure beyond the outlay projected by the Bush administration for 1993-4.

Special priority should be given within this context to the development of anti-missile defense against such possible future enemies as a missile-armed Middle Eastern state or the People's Republic of China.

Do not dismantle NATO, which was formed to keep the Germans down, the Russians out, and the US in Europe. The Cold War is over and the Soviets no longer threaten NATO, but the other two reasons for NATO persist, i.e. to keep control of the Germans and to keep the US involved in Europe so as to prevent any future European conflicts.

The US must remain in Europe and in NATO for at least another decade. The US forces should be reduced to around 100,000 men with material prepositioned for reinforcements in time of war.

NATO needs a new strategy now that the Soviet threat has receded. What is needed is a Rapid Reaction Force of 100,000 to respond quickly to small wars and to keep the peace.

Through the NACC a smaller NATO should cooperate with the EC and CSCE as a conciliation and peacemaking group to monitor human rights and to help restore democracy.

The US need not turn isolationist nor adopt a New World Order; instead the US should limit its concerns to its vital national interests and encourage free markets and trade, foster human rights, embargo the spread of ABC weapons, promote democracy and strengthen mediation and peacekeeping in regional and world organizations. The US should share all these responsibilities with other powers and not try to play the policeman of the world.

## APPENDIX: THE EUROPEAN COMMUNITY'S MAIN INSTITUTIONS AS OF 1993

### The European Commission

The European Commission members are appointed by the 12 governments. The Commission has a president and 5–6 vice-presidents who are appointed for two years. There are currently 17 Commissioners (2 each from the larger EC states – Germany, France, Britain, Italy, Spain – and 1 each from the rest). All are nominated by their national governments and appointed for a four-year term by the Council. Decisions within the Commission are, when necessary, taken by a simple majority. The Commission initiates legislation proposals, implements decisions taken by the Council, and also has the power to enforce EC treaties and derivative legislation. No nation's decisions could interfere with EC policies. The Commission has a large staff (15,055 officials), and they are divided into 31 departments or directorates. The Commission has been likened to a Cabinet which institutes policies and studies that are then sent along to the Council of Ministers, which makes policy. A Commission proposal could only be amended by unanimous vote. The successive presidents of the Commission were: Walter Hallstein (1958); Jean Rey (1967); Franco-Maria Maffatti (1970); Sicco Mansholt (1972); François Xavier Ortoli (1973); Roy Jenkins (1977); Gaston Thorn (1981); Jacques Delors (1985).

Over time the EC has developed into a kind of federal system. The Commission's proposals, if accepted by the Council, are binding on the member states. Voting in the Council has shifted from unanimity to qualified majority in most matters.

## The Council of Ministers

The Council of Ministers is the principal legislative body of the EC. Its members are ministers from the member states who represent their country at the Council. Most meetings of the Council are in Brussels, where the General Secretariat (with 1,900 officials) is situated. Council meetings are also held in Luxembourg and in the nation holding the rotating six-month presidency.

The Council holds periodic meetings with member ministers depending on the subject under discussion. Foreign ministers attended more meetings than, say, agricultural ministers or environment ministers because they discuss political and institutional matters of the EC and need to meet more often. The Council is helped in its deliberations by a Committee of Permanent Representatives (COREPER). Senior officials of COREPER come from the member states and play a major role in the effective operation of the Council. But in recent years COREPER officials have had to take a back seat to member state ministers, and national representation has somewhat damaged the community spirit. COREPER is better able to coordinate negotiations on a community basis on policy matters between the Council, the Commission and other community institutions.

Decisions are not reached on a one vote, one state basis, and major decisions have to be unanimous, others can be by qualified majority. The more powerful states have more votes than do the smaller states: Germany, France, Italy and the United Kingdom ten votes; Spain eight; Belgium, the Netherlands, Portugal and Greece five each; Denmark and Ireland three and Luxembourg two. Voting procedures were changed by the Single European Act to a qualified majority instead of unanimity on most issues. The European Council (Summit) developed after 1974 at the suggestion of French president Giscard d'Estaing and German chancellor Helmut Schmidt; the leaders (heads of states, foreign ministers and the president of the European Commission) of member states started to meet directly two or three times a year. These Summit meetings have become a regular part of the system since 1986 and provide guidelines from the heads of states to the Council of Ministers and Commission for action by them. Summits are useful for their informality, which allows flexibility in setting guidelines, making important decisions and in resolving disagreements. It is a quicker, more flexible device for decision-making than the Council of Ministers, and the Council is useful for exchanging views. The Summit leaders feared that the EP, once it was elected by popular vote, would become a supranational assembly. The European Council then is a means of protecting the sovereignty of the nation-state. All of its decisions must be unanimous.

### The European Parliament

The European Parliament is the EC's only directly elected body. It has been called the democratic conscience of the EC – the Parliament must be consulted by the Commission and the Council of Ministers; and the Parliament questions their activities. (In the Single European Act, the European Assembly was called the European Parliament.) The first elected EP was in 1979, and since then it has tried to increase its legislative and supervisory powers. The Single European Act won the EP the power of veto over agreements between the EC and other nations; and the EP now has control over enlarging the EC. According to some critics, the EC should develop along the lines of the American system of three branches of government, with the Court of Justice becoming the Community's Supreme Court, the Council of Ministers becoming the executive branch of the EC, and the EP serving as the legislative branch.

The EP's structure is complex. The Secretariat, about 2,900 officials organized into seven divisions, is in Luxembourg. But monthly meetings of parliament are held in Strasbourg and committee meetings in Brussels. Some foresee all these activities being centralized in Brussels. For the moment, the EP's effectiveness is impaired by constant moves, and even more, by lack of strong legislative power. The EP has genuine functions concerning the budget, but in legislative matters the EP is only consulted and can be ignored. The Treaty of Maastricht, if ratified, and if effectively enforced, may give the EP a little more power.

The EP has 518 members, elected every 5 years. (The allocation of seats is as follows: Belgium 25; Denmark 16; Federal Republic of Germany 99; France 87; Greece 25; Ireland 15; Italy 87; Luxembourg 6; Netherlands 31; Portugal 25; Spain 64; United Kingdom 87. Members are not, however, grouped as representatives of nations but by political affiliation. The main groups are the Socialists (the largest body), the European Democratic Alliance (mainly Gaullists); European Democratic Group (Conservatives); European People's Party (Christian Democrats); European Right; French and Italian Communists respectively, each with their allies; Greens, Liberal and Democratic Group; Rainbow Group (mainly regionalist parties). Before 1979, members of the EP were appointed by national governments apt to use the EP as a place of exile for discarded politicians. But once members were directly elected, work in the EP became increasingly attractive, and the EP turned into a much more dynamic institution than hitherto. The EP further gained from the vigor of its president, Enrique Barón Crespo, a Spanish scholar, a moderate socialist who believes in the creation of a European federal state along the model of the United States. The EP meets once a month for a week in plenary session. Debates concern commission reports, major current issues, statements of other EC bodies. Since 1986 the EP has had more power – for example, it can vet international agreements and amend EC laws related to the Single Market program. The EP also approves applications for new EC membership.

## Court of Justice

The Court of Justice (13 members) deals mostly with cases brought by the Commission or member states and interprets community law to national courts. It sees itself as the interpreter of the community's treaties and legislation. In addition to the Court of Justice for hearing cases, there are also four chambers of 3–6 judges for less important matters. Then in 1986 a Court of First Instance was set up to relieve the main court of some routine cases.

The Court of Justice, like the American Supreme Court, has become very important in interpreting community legislation and, by its decisions, promoting EC policy and integration. The court now has the power to cut off community funds to nations which ignore the Court's rulings. The Court is located in Luxembourg. Six advocates-general comment on the main points of each case in relation to EC law and how to interpret the law.

# 8

# The US: A Hopeful Future

From the very beginnings of European settlement in North America, the new country was to Puritans a City built upon a Hill, a light shining to heaven. This splendid image, however, always went with profound self-questioning. Woe betide the City if she were ever to forget the Lord's commandments; she would be laid low by insensate pride. This strain has continued in American thought to the present day. Today's variants of Puritan forebodings see the US hurtling to destruction through the cult of pleasure and flagrant immorality. Christians believe that homosexuality, AIDS, crime, drugs, lesbianism, and general godlessness will assuredly destroy us – as Sodom and Gomorrah had been in antiquity. A mirror-image of perdition exists in the minds of many self-described progressives – the US has strayed from the path of virtue and seems destined to sink in a morass of racism and sexual oppression. America, especially white middle-class America, has surrendered its soul to insensitivity and greed. Race riots, such as the 1992 outbursts in Los Angeles, are but the external symptom of internal decay.

## THE PESSIMIST'S CASE

Forecasts concerning the US's impending doom have increasingly derived from secular assumptions, with the extreme right and the extreme left projecting mirror-images of a gloom-laden future. Native-born pessimism merged with an all-embracing sense of cultural decline voiced by intellectuals such as Oswald Spengler after World War I and Arnold Toynbee after World War II about Western civilization in general. Today many intellectuals and media pundits think we are in economic decline as well.

The average American who reads the morning newspaper might well assume that the country is in a desperate state. As Cynthia Tucker, a well-known and respected journalist, puts it in a syndicated column: "the economy is in shambles. The recession is a deeply rooted economic slump . . . the legacy of the Reagan Revolution is sending the economy on a steady downward spiral."[1] Unless the US can reverse its present course, put an end to the biggest military spending binge in its history, and recover compassion for the poor, the country will face its inevitable demise.

The campus left is also much concerned with the decline of Western civilization and the need for multiculturalism, but arrives at very different conclusions. To them, the US is the new Egypt, the new House of Bondage, where women, ethnic minorities, and sexual deviants are demeaned and exploited. This is the message of many "multicultural" or ethnic studies courses in prestigious universities. But the day of vengeance will come, they claim. Having degraded its own citizenry, exploited the Third World, wrecked the earth's ecological balance, the American establishment will get its deserts. Such millenarian visions, with the US cast as the world's chief villain, achieved global acclaim during the Vietnam War. Then European intellectuals learned from US leftists, with the US serving both as an admired model and a hated counter-model for young Europeans, especially young Germans. (Prominent Germans such as Oskar Lafontaine, an influential left-winger within the German SPD (Social Democratic Party), had studied at US universities, while the late Petra Kelly, a militant leftist, was half-American.)

Other grim forebodings center specifically on the fate of US capitalism. Marxists used to argue that the US workers were bound to get steadily poorer; the scale of enterprise would constantly increase; US monopoly capitalism would suffer from ever-growing crises, and its internal contradictions would become irresolvable; thereafter, the system, having ravaged the Third World, would ultimately collapse in a horrendous upheaval. Marxist forecasts once made with an air of certainty by professors such as Paul A. Baran and Paul M. Sweezy, are not often heard on US campuses nowadays. Marxism-Leninism has collapsed in the Soviet Union, and former proponents of the Marxist-Leninist creed do not like to be reminded of their former adherence to the faith. In a more diffuse form, however, the legacy of Marxism persists, in what traditional Marxists regard as adulterated versions. Since the Vietnam War and thereafter, Marxist critiques of US capitalism have blended with other strains, especially romantic notions derived from the nineteenth century. According to the "New Left" and its heirs, US capitalism is to be censured – not so much for impoverishing Americans, but for spoiling the masses with worthless merchandise, degrading the people through consumerism, foisting a "false consciousness" on Americans, and debauching the Third World.

The right also has apprehensions: "We are losing our country to aliens" – a cry heard since this country began. The "new immigrants" who flood the US will not assimilate. White Americans will be overborne by a tide of Hispanics, Asians, and Africans who will turn the US into a Third World country characterized by poverty, crime, and corruption. The impact of immigration over the last 20 years has indeed been startling. In 1926, to give just one example, the city of Los Angeles had a population of no more than 1.3 million. Of these 90 percent were white. The rest comprised 45,000 Hispanics, 33,000 blacks, and 30,000 Asians. Today the city of Los Angeles has 3.4 million, with 8.9 million living in the metropolitan area and the surrounding county. Forty percent of the city's population are Hispanics, according to the preliminary census of 1990; 37 percent are "Anglos" (that is, whites descended from Europe), 13 percent black, and 10 percent Asian/Pacific, or "other." Los Angeles has become the country's new Ellis Island; its people speak Spanish, Tagalog, Cambodian, Korean, Swahili, Farsi, and a great host of other tongues. Los Angeles is also ridden by gangs (with an estimated total membership of 90,000 or more). Gang members take pride in their respective affiliation to the "Crips," the "Bloods," the "Dukes," the "Mob Crew," whose bloody fights over territory and "honor" seem more suited to the age of the Montagues and Capulets than to a modern city. No wonder that pessimists predict the impending dissolution of US society, as crime, drugs and gangs terrorize many American cities, bringing death and destruction to Los Angeles in May 1992.

Many moderates even agree that the US is now on the wrong track. As the new pessimists see it, the US is becoming less and less able to cope with a competitor such as Japan, a competitor supposedly whose managers are supremely efficient, whose workers are dedicated and loyal, and whose products often outperform those of the US. Then there are other Asian countries such as South Korea and Taiwan who have adopted the Japanese way. Admittedly, the US still holds a commanding lead in science and technology. But its future leadership stands imperilled. The scientific enterprise has become, in many respects, enormously costly; bureaucracy, all too often, is stifling creative endeavor. Public confidence in science has declined in part as a response to scientific scandals, in part as a reaction to misdirected expenditure and technologically flawed projects.

A new anti-scientific spirit is part of the pessimistic strain abroad in America. This has many components: a romantic desire on the part of town-bred intellectuals to return to a natural existence in harmony with the earth; fear of the scientist as a new Sorcerer's Apprentice, unable to control the creations of science; dislike of a self-appointed scientific vanguard; declining respect for the expert in every field; and a deterioration in scientific and technical education on every level. Faced with these problems, the pessimists argue, the US will end up as an obsolescent giant.

To make matters worse, the pessimists also believe, the US is also on the road to becoming increasingly ungovernable. Unless the present process of slow disintegration is checked, American might will wane – not through some sudden cataclysm, but through gradual erosion. While the US supposedly gives employment to about 70 percent of the world's lawyers, it also has one of the world's highest crime rates; the prevalence of crime only reflects wider social disparities in a country ridden by corruption and violence. America's critics say there is assuredly something wrong with a land where less than one-fifth of the people have high confidence in the honesty and ethical standards of senators, congressmen, local politicians, and trade unionists.[2] The US crime rate is paralleled by a high rate of drug addiction. The ethnic minorities are supposedly hardest hit – but it is not they alone who suffer. Something has obviously gone awry, says the liberal-left, with a US that sustains periodic riots, permits many of its inner cities to become "no-go" areas at night for respectable people of any race, fails to educate a substantial minority of its young men and women, and allows – if not encourages – the feminization of poverty (through woman-headed households).

Far from being solved, our problems are getting worse: as the rich get richer, the poor get poorer – according to all Democratic candidates for the US presidency in 1992. This assertion finds support not merely among campus radicals, but from sources such as the London *Economist*. Since 1970 the average family income of the richest fifth of the US population moved up substantially; the poorest two-fifths barely held their own. Moreover, of Americans who live in census tracts where more than 40 percent of the people are poor, about two-thirds are black. "The gap between rich and poor is not just a matter of economic stratification. It is poisoned by racial differences."[3]

Not surprisingly, the charges continue, owing to the cult of multi-culturalism the US is also losing its former sense of cohesion; we are witness to the disuniting of America, bemoans historian Arthur Schlesinger. Destined for ethnic Balkanization, beset by insoluble economic and social problems, the US cannot continue to exercise global leadership. Or, as a German critic puts it with relish, the 12,000 violent incidents that take place every year in the New York subway system represent but petty triumphs of violence in a country whose establishment has made it impossible for the perpetrators of such deeds to succeed in any other way. How can a country so corrupted aspire to lead the world?[4] US history, the argument continues, is a sad story of Robber Barons followed by junk bond dealers; the tale will assuredly come to a sorry end.

Other scenarios of decline draw on the experience of great empires that have perished in the past – especially the British. By the end of the last century, Britain's power had already begun to diminish. The British could not keep up with their industrial competitors – Germany and the US. British imperial resources were becoming overstretched in relation to the country's declining economic capacity. Britain's fate may become that of the US, which is being overtaken by its rivals, especially Japan and the smaller industrial countries of the Pacific Rim, as well as Germany. The US will end as an over-armed and under-brained dinosaur, fit for extinction. On the face of it, US power as yet remains immense, with thousands of nuclear weapons and with hundreds of thousands of men deployed overseas as far afield as Germany, Kuwait, and South Korea. But the US's real strength is ebbing away, as did Britain's after the heyday of the Victorian empire.[5]

One of the most knowledgeable proponents of the "Imperial overstretch" thesis is Paul Kennedy, a historian of distinction at Yale University, whose book *The Rise and Fall of the Great Powers* (1987) made him a celebrity. He surveys many great empires whose eventual demise poses a grim lesson to the US, which has likewise taken on excessive responsibilities incommensurate with its economic strength and social efficiency. As Kennedy puts it with much eloquence, conservatives widely welcome the new "knowledge explosion" and the ongoing metamorphosis from "materials-based" to "knowledge-based" industries, as if the US were inevitably going to be the chief beneficiary of such a transformation:

> But if knowledge is to be the basis of the nation's wealth and strength, is it not alarming that America's seventeen year olds consistently score below those of other advanced societies on international tests of mathematics, natural sciences, foreign languages, and the like? That their knowledge of history is abysmal, and of geography even worse; (three quarters of them not even knowing where the Persian Gulf is). Can one be as confident about the future . . . when American illiteracy rates are much higher than those of every other advanced industrial democracy?[6]

There is much additional evidence of decline, say the pessimists. In 1945 the US accounted for something like half the world's economic production, admittedly not a reasonable base period for a time series. By 1991 the US only had about 23 percent, less than half of what it possessed at the end of World War II. The US, once proud of being the world's richest country, has ceased, according to some critics, to have the world's highest per capita income. (In fact by 1990, the US gross domestic product per head of the population exceeded everyone's, with Canada, Switzerland, Japan, Sweden, West Germany, France, the UK, and Italy following in that order.)

According to the pessimists, the US has also experienced a relative decline in its manufacturing industries; once well-remunerated industrial workers now have to seek employment in lower-paid service industries. The parallel with Great Britain is obvious – its once-famed Morris Minor cars, and ocean liners built by Harland and Wolff, have disappeared from the world market. The US has experienced relative decline in other vital economic sectors, so the argument continues. During the early 1950s, the US accounted for nearly three-quarters of the world's oil output. Twenty years later, the US share had fallen to less than one-seventh, and the US, the world's largest oil consumer, had also turned into the world's largest importer. Unexpectedly, the US also has problems with regard to its steel, electronics, car, and agriculture production. US farmers now face heavy competition from the EC, a major producer of food surpluses, and also from a number of Third World countries that have successfully improved their farming methods. Once Eastern Europe and the successor states of the former Soviet Union recover from the dead hand of communism, US growers will also have to reckon with competition from the CIS and its former Warsaw Pact allies – hence many more US farmers will be driven out of business.

But the real causes of America's economic stagnation are none of the above, according to Henry Rowen of the Hoover Institution. They are low savings and investment; a decline in the quality of the workforce; poor performance by managers; growing regulatory and legal burdens which raise the costs of doing business in the US; weaknesses in technology exploitation, and a large and growing health care burden (now 13 percent of GNP, which may increase to 20 percent by 2000 unless reforms are made). In the US the cost of capital is higher than in Japan, and R & D by industry is lower in the US than in other industrial nations, Rowen observes, further weakening our growth performance.

These and other related problems, the charge sheet continues, have produced severe financial instability. When World War II ended, Europeans complained of the "Dollar Gap" created by the imbalance between massive US exports to Europe, and scanty US imports from Europe. Now the position is reversed. The US imports more than it exports. Compounding this problem is the growing US budgetary deficit; as Kennedy puts it, "the only historical examples that comes to mind of Great Powers increasing their indebtedness *in peacetime* are France in the 1780s, where the fiscal crisis finally led to revolution, and Russia early in this century."[7] (But as Thomas Sowell, Hoover Senior Fellow, has noted, the United States became a great nation by being a debtor nation into which Britain and other countries poured vast amounts of capital needed to develop the country. The US was a debtor nation until World War I, when it started lending money to its allies in Europe. Perhaps "great nation" may not be the appropriate category in the first place, because prosperous nations like Switzerland may be more relevant. (Much of American indebtedness may only reflect this country's declining savings rate, with the resulting import of capital from abroad because the US is perceived as a safe haven for foreign capital.)

The US nowadays only manages to pay its way by importing vast amounts of foreign capital; this may entail a creeping foreign takeover of the US economy, pessimists claim. (Despite widespread US apprehensions concerning the Japanese capital influx in particular, European purchases of US assets far outweigh the Japanese. In 1990, British, French, and German firms bought $21 billions worth of US companies. Having worried greatly during the 1960s and the 1970s over *le défi américain*, the American challenge, the French in 1990 actually took the lead, spending $12 billion on acquiring US firms in that year alone. The French thereby capped three years of British activity, in which the British had been the leading foreign investors.)[8]

The US – to summarize the charges – faces a decaying infrastructure, an inadequate education system that leaves all too many Americans, especially black and brown Americans, functional illiterates, helpless in a society in which intellectual capital steadily gains in importance over physical capital. All these problems are made infinitely worse by the excessive amount spent by the US on defense: US military expenditure forms a much larger proportion of our GNP than that of Germany and Japan (2.9 percent and 1.0 percent respectively, as against 6.3 percent for the US in 1988). (In fact, neither of these countries with their post-World War II restrictions on the military are a reasonable comparison. Furthermore, Germany and Japan can spend so little on military defense because the US spends so much.) The US also disburses a much larger portion of its GNP to research and development in defense-related industries, whereas Germany and Japan concentrate on commercial production. This siphons off too many of the best US scientists and engineers from the design and production of civilian goods for the world market into wasteful arms production: hence we have trouble in competing on the world market and our relative position continues to deteriorate.

Altogether, pessimists lament, our values are wrong; our country has gone astray. We maintain mighty forces overseas, yet we cannot solve our problems at home. Not surprisingly, there is now in the US a profound sense of discouragement. Even a popular publication such as *Time* now lambastes the US as a land of whiners and complainers.[9]

## THE OPTIMIST'S CASE: RACE, CULTURE, AND POLITICS

We do not share these pessimistic assumptions, though we recognize that the US faces numerous and difficult problems. These do not spring from American greed, but in part from social conditions that have parallels in the highly industrialized countries of Western Europe as well. The US accepts massive numbers of immigrants, both legal and illegal; the US frontiers are indeed much more porous than those of any European country; no one knows for sure how many undocumented aliens are living in the country at any one time. Moreover, the composition of the US population has continued to change. Between 1980 and 1990, the proportion of Hispanic peoples went up by 53 percent; the share of Asians increased by 107.8 percent. There were also major changes within these distinct groups. (Central Americans provided the largest percentage of Hispanic new-comers, Vietnamese and East Indians of Asians.) Some are highly skilled. Many others, however, lack any formal education, industrial training, or knowledge of English needed for well-paid employment. As long as poor young people keep coming to the US, the proportion of poor people will necessarily go up – no matter what governments choose to do. Moreover, this immigration occurs at a time when the gap between unskilled and high-skilled workers is tending to widen all over the industrial world. The poorly paid get the rough end of the stick, now that computer literacy has become an indispensable qualification for many jobs. The US must contend also with serious educational problems, high costs of health care, and rising transport costs, because its educators and government bureau-crats are performing badly and because our infrastructure has deteriorated.

Above all, the US faces crime. In dollar terms, the biggest thieves by far are white-collar criminals. But in social terms the most destructive offenders are those who perpetrate violence. The great metropolitan areas in the US are indeed much more unsafe than any great European city; this insecurity has led to the decline of many great US cities. Urban crime in turn is linked to the civic breakdown that characterizes so many US cities: homelessness, the partial collapse of the inner city family, the resultant feminization of poverty, the sale and consumption of drugs and alcohol. None of the afflictions are confined to one race; but black people suffer in particular. (In 1950 17.2 percent of black families were headed by single women, as against 5.3 percent of white families. By 1990 the respective figures stood at 56.2 percent and 17.3 percent. White family disorganization, in other words, has reached the black level of the post-war era. Black disorganization had increased to such an extent that more than half of black families no longer had a father in the home.) Moreover, at no previous period in US history was hedonism preached by so substantial a part of the opinion-making classes as a new gospel alike for the upper and the underclass. There is no consensus on how to deal, say, with a pregnant teenage girl who is herself the daughter of an unwed mother, and the grandchild of an unwed grandmother, all successively on welfare. Drugs are also a growing cancer in American society.

It is worth knowing, however, that the problems of crime are not new in the US, either on the ill-policed frontiers or the ill-policed cities of the past. With its huge territory, vast numbers of immigrants, mobile, youthful population, ethnic diversity, and easy availability of firearms, the US has always had to contend with crime on a much larger scale than, say, Great Britain, a small island with a relatively homogeneous and stable population. (Incredibly, nearly half of the British population in 1991 had not moved house at all during the last ten years. Of those who did move, only 6 percent had moved more than 30 miles.) The US crime problem horrifies Europeans; the violence in Belfast, Northern Ireland, pales before the violence of New York or Los Angeles. Crime has been on the increase, especially in inner city ethnic enclaves and, by the 1990s, had spread to the heartland of America. Enclaves such as New York, Detroit, Philadelphia, Los Angeles, Oakland, face ever-increasing problems, as middle-class people (including middle-class blacks and Hispanics) have moved to the suburbs, leaving behind an impoverished residual population. The vast majority of inner city people – the point bears stressing – are not criminals. On the contrary, they are most likely to become crime victims. Their problems are made worse by minimum wage laws which make it expensive to hire unskilled youths, by the exodus of industries from city cores, by the difficulties experienced by single-parent households and job seekers who do not own an automobile, by the slum dwellers' high dropout rates from high schools, and by a street culture that despises the "nerd" and glorifies the pimp and the drug dealer. Society gives them the choice of whether to work or not. Owing in part to a declining work ethic, most of the black underclass do not work full-time or indeed at all. (This underclass may be as large as 25 to 30 percent of the black population; the black middle class numbers about 30 percent.)

The problems of US inner cities received world-wide notoriety as a result of the Los Angeles riots of 1992. All over Western Europe, journalists and television commentators delighted in portraying the US as a hapless, gun-toting giant, intolerant, racist, yet addicted to preaching his own virtues to foreigners. American self-criticism was even harsher. The riots were represented in apocalyptic terms – a giant catastrophe born of black hopelessness and despair. Ultimate responsibility reputedly lay with the greed and selfishness of America's white middle class, replete with race prejudice, indifferent to the plight of the poor. As things stand, it is claimed, the US cities keep rotting away, and as they decay, so will the nation.

From the standpoint of the US as a whole, urban riots such as those which shook Los Angeles, while shocking, are not catastrophic. The majority of Americans no longer live in cities, but in suburbs (in fact new cities) and in smaller towns. The overwhelming majority of Angelenos themselves watched the riots on their television sets, not in the streets. The riots left South-Central Los Angeles with its large Latino population largely untouched; citizens lined up to protect their shops rather than torch them. The worst hit Latino areas were those where most immigrants (many of them illegal) were recent arrivals from Central America, people without jobs or cash. To describe the rioters as unhappy people pervaded by existential *Angst* and anger does them an injustice. The Rodney King incident (in which Los Angeles police officers brutally beat a black motorist whom they had caught after a high-speed chase, and after resisting arrest) served as a trigger for the riots. But King's case was not the underlying cause. For uprooted urban people, rioting is fun for the participants, providing drama and excitement as well as loot. Riots may provide substantial gain for confirmed criminals, as well as a grand carnival for ordinary folk caught in what San Francisco District Attorney George Beckwith correctly called a "feeding frenzy."[10] The Los Angeles riots were not some apocalyptic *Götterdämmerung* occasioned by black rage. (By one preliminary estimate, more than half the people arrested were Hispanics and 10 percent were white.)[11] The majority of the shops looted were owned by Hispanics and Koreans; in addition many black-owned stores went up in flames. The riots burst out in a city whose police force was under-manned, ill-led, ill-organized and demoralized. Above all, the police were afraid of using force early on lest they be denigrated thereafter by that host of sensitive and compassionate folk who preach from the relative safety of TV studios and who have little understanding of a police officer's lot in a tough, crime-ridden neighborhood.

To blame white racism for the ills of black America entails other difficulties. Variables cannot be accounted for by a constant. White racism, according to its critics, is an immutable force. Yet during the last half century, black average incomes have gone up, the percentage of black poor has diminished; blacks by 1992 occupied positions once closed to them. A black soldier, Colin Powell, served as chairman of the Joint Chiefs of Staff; Douglas Wilder, a black politician, gained distinction as governor of Virginia; black mayors headed the greatest cities and over 6,600 elected black officials serve at various levels of government. This social shift could not have occurred if white racism were an unchanging element in the

American political economy. Neither does the "white racism" explanation account for many other variables, i.e. the striking disparities between established institutions in their ability to integrate the races. The armed services and professional athletics do far better in this respect than high schools in racially mixed neighborhoods; yet white soldiers and white athletes are not noticeably more tolerant than white school teachers. Similarly, analyses of US society that hinge on white racism do not account for the way in which, say, black West Indians, on the average, have done consistently better than native-born black Americans. Both groups have had to face the same degree of white racism; yet their response has been quite different, for complex historical reasons.[12]

White racism certainly exists in the US. But one should not attribute to it the same importance in the creation of social disorder as do most native and foreign critics of the US. Instead we stress more general factors, especially crime. "High" culture and "popular" culture alike in the US have always had a love affair with the loser, the teller of hard luck stories, and the criminal – be it the bandit in the Old West, the bootlegger in an old-style "ethnic" neighborhood, or the "gang-banger" in today's inner city. These people have been widely romanticized as Robin Hoods in modern dress or ethnic rebels, whereas they are "robbing hoods." Throughout history it has always been the poor who have been the main victims of crime – not the rich, who have better means for self-protection. Crime inevitably worsens poverty. Store owners will not open businesses in neighborhoods where customers get mugged, merchandise is stolen, or shops are burned in a riot. When shops close down, the poor will suffer because they cannot conveniently buy necessities. Landlords will not make repairs in buildings where tenants cannot be made to pay rent – hence housing stock deteriorates. Fear of crime is pervasive and poisons the lives of the poor. Police officers all too often fear assignments in crime-ridden districts, as do school teachers, pharmacists, and other professionals who are essential to the community.

What is the cause? Expert opinion differs widely; but there is little dispute that the black poor face special problems which, in part, differentiate them from the old-style European immigrants to the US. Unlike European or, for that matter, Asian and Hispanic newcomers, the bulk of black Americans did not come voluntarily to this country. Black people arrived as slaves, and the Southern plantations, from the start, created a culture of black dependency. There were indeed "free people of color," even black plantation owners, but slavery initially shaped black culture in the US. Slavery was smashed with the Civil War, but the freedmen did not receive land of their own – unlike the white serfs liberated from a similarly harsh condition in Russia. For long the great majority of Southern blacks made a scanty living as farm laborers and sharecroppers, still in a state of partial dependence. From the 1930s, Southern agriculture became increasingly mechanized; a great black trek began from the Southern countryside to the cities, especially the Northern industrial towns. Some blacks did very well. Blacks increasingly made their way into the ranks of skilled labor, even into the professions. But opportunities for semi-skilled and unskilled workers rapidly declined after World War II, as industrial processes grew increasingly complex, and as factories, mines and workshops required far fewer hands than in the olden days. Blacks, moreover, had to compete with immigrants, especially Asians and Hispanics who developed their own kinship networks whereby workers secured jobs for relatives and friends, and in the case of Asians provided funds for investment from savings.

To cope with these and related problems, Presidents Johnson and Nixon vastly expanded the existing welfare state. Contrary to a widespread misconception, poverty programs during the Reagan and Bush administrations continued to grow. (In 1990 dollars, expenditure on the total "safety net programs" went up from $54.9 billion to $70.5 billion between 1981 and 1991.) Yet by 1992, public opinion polls revealed widespread discontent among both white and black voters with these programs. There was widespread agreement that the poverty programs themselves encouraged a culture of dependency, that too much money went to a huge welfare *nomenklatura*, and that the welfare bureaucrats were far more out of touch with the poor than the old-style Tammany Hall "ward-heelers" (petty political fixers) had ever been. The inner city problems moreover worsened in many other ways. As segregation ended, successful middle-class blacks moved into the suburbs, as did whites, leaving the inner city poor to their own devices. Affirmative action programs may or may not have helped middle-class blacks; but affirmative action programs did little for the poor; on the contrary, they heightened white hostility to growing social expenditure and an increased tax burden.

By the early 1990s, the optimism that had once inspired the "War against Poverty" had gone. Presidents Reagan and Bush attempted to reform some existing programs, and employed a different rhetoric. But they did not offer an alternative system. President Bush later weakly came forward in support of Housing Secretary Jack Kemp's plan for encouraging "enterprise zones" in the inner cities, where entrepreneurs would receive tax concessions. Public housing tenants would be encouraged to manage and ultimately own their own homes. Welfare rules would be changed to encourage families to stay together. Inner city schools would be improved by allowing parental choice in the selection of schools through a new system of vouchers.

As we see it, the root cause of inner city poverty is not merely a dysfunctional welfare system; nor is it merely material deprivation. (Third World people look with astonishment at a country where many so-called poor people own cars, radios, television sets, and guns, and where the availability of food stamps to obtain free food is taken for granted.) Poverty transcends race; in absolute numbers there are more white poor than black or Latino poor. Poverty is not limited to inner cities; there are rural poor, even suburban poor, in the US whose problems receive much less publicity than their compatriots' in big cities. But for whatever reasons blacks, and to a lesser extent Hispanics, contain a much higher proportion of poor people, and a large number of them live in inner cities. The cause of black inner city poverty remains bitterly disputed. But no one doubts that poverty is linked to crime, as is the breakup of the family, especially the black inner city family. (By the beginnings of the 1990s, 66 percent of black families had a female head; 66 percent of black children were born out of wedlock, without a father figure, or financial support from the father.) Dysfunctional in a more intangible sense was also the false consciousness developed by rap singers and chic intellectuals who despised those boring virtues which had traditionally made for upward social mobility – hard work, punctuality, frugality, courtesy, and obedience to lawful orders. Equally dysfunctional was the cultural legacy derived from the olden-time slave-owning white South, with its peculiar blend of macho exhibitionism and collective self-pity.

What is the answer? Lawrence Mead, a political economist, argues in *The New Politics of Poverty* (1992) that the major cause of poverty has been the reluctance of the poor to work or to take responsibility for their lives. There have been plenty of job opportunities – look at how new immigrants go to work. Black unemployment has been high for years; yet 1 million or so illegal immigrants find work each year, as do millions of legal ones.

The 1988 Family Support Act encouraged "workfare," but covered too few people. The entire welfare system should be abolished to make people go to work, many conservatives claim, as do some scholars on the liberal-left. Mickey Kaus, in *The End of Inequality* (1992), insists that welfare sustains the underclass and keeps it idle, poor, illegitimate and criminal – so, cut off the lifeline of welfare. No welfare should be given to those who do not go to work. The work ethic increases self-respect and self-reliance. Such a program, however, will be expensive – training schools, day care for children, support while training – perhaps as high as $60 billion. But this will decline as people start to work and will be paid for by tax revenue produced by new workers. Intensive skills training is essential to make the urban underclass employable, as are day care centers so black mothers can return to school and acquire literacy and job skills. The global economy has cost the US jobs; hence black and whites have to upgrade their skills in order to be able to get jobs in the new service, information-based economy.

The 25–30 percent of the black and brown population in the underclass are poor, have low educational scores, and little work experience. Bad schools and family deterioration often produce unemployable people, criminals and drug addicts. What is needed, according to Nobel laureate Gary S. Becker, is a GI Bill for young blacks and Hispanics to give them a sound education. Vouchers for schooling would provide competition for schools to do a good job. Trade schools, private schools, on-the-job training could much improve the skills of the young underclass.

People from the black underclass also have to change their value system and acquire attitudes and skills for this new era. For reasons unknown to us, many inner city blacks despise entrepreneurial drive, the work ethic, family-oriented values; too many drop out of high school and are functionally illiterate, too many turn to drugs and crime. Black inner city people can learn from Asians who stay together in families, work hard, encourage learning and create their own opportunities – helped not by the state, but by fellow Asians. While many inner- city black youths have learned to despise menial jobs, Asian and Latinos take them. Blacks, too often, refuse to take jobs at pay rates suitable to their low skills. To solve these problems self-help groups need to expand in the black community; churches should play a bigger role, and black volunteerism needs to be developed among the black middle class.

We ourselves do not profess to know all the answers, We do, however, place special stress on the role of adequate police protection. The US has failed its poor by failing to give to them the citizen's first entitlement – security of life and property. Crime diminishes social mobility – for the shopkeeper whose store is looted, for the school child prevented from learning, for all and sundry. Police protection must always be based on the principle that prevention is better than cure, that steady patrolling in a neighborhood is preferable to benign neglect followed by bouts of energetic repression. During the eighteenth century, English Redcoats and their Scottish allies successfully subdued the feud-and war-torn Scottish Highlands, once impassable to strangers. During the nineteenth century Victorians successfully pacified London, previously the most crime-prone and riot-ridden city in the world. Well-policed and supplied with adequate transport, London turned from the violent city of Dickens's days to one of the safest in Europe. Late twentieth-century Americans should do just as much. The restoration of order in the city works best when police officers walk the beat on foot and get to know their neighborhoods.

Police action must go with wider social reforms. Policing works best when linked to civic action: the proper removal of litter and of graffiti, the setting up of crime-watch organizations. Such reforms should include a well-thought-out program of turning public housing projects into privately owned condominiums whose owners have every reason in the world to defend their property against decay and crime. (During the 1992 Los Angeles riots, the residents of Nickerson Gardens, a huge public housing project in the middle of Watts, successfully banded together to keep out rioters and looters. The residents did so because the project was in the process of being transformed into private property.)

In achieving such a transformation, we place special stress on the development of human capital, the role of religious commitment and civic values in general. Education of course must play its part. But it is unrealistic to assume that educational programs alone can do the trick, no matter how well they are financed. A gang leader in, say, a tough area does not in the least want to be retrained as a bank clerk, welder, or insurance salesman. Why submit to a boring routine and an exacting boss when a criminal career offers an immediate prospect of wealth, power, and prestige – beautiful women, a fast car, a high-powered gun, admiration among followers and fear among strangers? Such men only understand force. But even within city gangs, the confirmed criminals form only a relatively small cadre – the professional officers and noncoms of crime. Once the cadres are smashed, the rank and file, so to speak, will disperse.

Whatever their race or socio-economic status, church-going families, be they Buddhists, Muslims, Catholics, Pentecostals, Old Amish, Scientologists, Mormons, Jews, and so forth, have a low crime rate. Families that pray together do not always stay together. (A great many Chicano gang members come from intact families.) But on the average, families headed by both a father and a mother have far fewer problem children, a higher living standard, a lower crime rate, and a better school attendance and graduation rate for their offspring than single-parent families.

The US crime problem is serious, but the US does not stand anywhere near the top of the list. The leading places are filled by Third World nations which, nevertheless, escape that academic censure which is so freely made available to the US.[13] Above all, US crime is overwhelmingly non-political; very few acts of terrorism are committed for political reasons. However inefficient some municipal police forces may be in preventing crime, not one has ever lost control of the streets in any city to a dissident political movement. As regards unintended homicide, fatal traffic accidents have become a major source of mortality in the industrialized world. Americans can take some pride in being, on the average, more civic-spirited and competent drivers than Germans, French, or

Italians; measured in terms of miles driven, these Europeans cause even more slaughter on the roads than do Americans. (It is not for nothing that the German word for a motorist is *Kraftfahrer*, a power driver.) The American achievement is all the greater, given the ethnic heterogeneity of the US, a diversity matched by no other great industrialized country. For better or worse, the US is also a youthful country (the young – ages 12–21 – commit far more crimes) than their elders. American society is distinguished by great mobility. Americans think nothing of pulling up stakes, driving for two thousand miles, and starting life afresh somewhere else. (There is no compulsory residential registration in the US, as there is, say, in Germany, where each move must be reported to the *Einwohnermeldeamt*.) The US is also unusual in that the mass of the population own firearms. (Lenin once urged "arm the workers." The Americans followed his advice. Americans own an estimated 70,000,000 firearms.) The surprise, therefore is not that there is so much crime in the US, but that there is not more.

We likewise need to take a comparative approach toward US education. There is indeed a great deal wrong with it. We have failed over the last 40 years to educate many blacks, many Hispanics and some whites; test scores of our secondary school students limp behind those of our main competitors because students are not well taught in mathematics, sciences and literature and language. The US public schools are apt to be over-bureaucratized and do not stress hard subjects; in the inner cities students are often unruly and underachievers. Too many pedagogues believe that schools should provide psychological therapy, entertainment, ethnic cheer-leading, rather than intellectual discipline and a command of hard subjects. By and large, parochial and private schools do better than public schools, and should be officially encouraged by vouchers. Overall, parochial and private schools are also more disciplined, more academic, and accomplish more with less money. All too commonly, public schools are undemanding and unsafe; they over-value athletic skills; they under-value intellectual pursuits. They also have to baby-sit the dumb, the uninterested and the delinquent, while shortchanging the brightest and the best.

These failings derive primarily from the anti-intellectual and egalitarian biases commonly found within the educational bureaucracy; hence inadequate attention is given to the gifted and expulsion for bad behavior is too often not enforced. School systems are over-administered; the size and complexity of the educational *nomenklatura*, with their teach-speak jargon, mirrors the problems of over-government in so many other aspects of American life.

The first target of reform should be the teachers' unions, who have won for teachers the shortest work day and school year in the industrialized world. Unions oppose merit raises and fitness-for-the-job tests, and have made it almost impossible to fire the incompetent. Pressure for reform should come primarily from local school boards, but tying federal grants to reforms could help force changes. Competition will pressure public schools to reform; thus privatizing, vouchers, a new GI Bill for school dropouts will improve the schools.

The United States needs to establish an effective apprenticeship system for those who tend to drop out and for those who do not want to go on to college. (Germany trains about 70 percent of its workers in a work and classroom apprentice system. Training on the job is supplemented by 1,500 vocational schools for general education and specialized training.) For the economy of the future we shall need highly skilled workers; and since business and industry do not spend much on training, this must be largely a job for the schools. A voucher system, as espoused by Gary Becker, would stimulate students to go on for further training and might capture some dropouts as well.

The US spends much more on those who plan to go to university, so offering help to those who do not will improve the workforce greatly. Companies should be pressured to provide more training by gaining government tax credits or by a "pay or play" tax for mid-size companies and up. (Becker's GI Bill would help blacks and Hispanics who drop out of school at such a high rate and workers' children who cannot afford the relatively high costs of university education.) To improve the schools through competition, vouchers and benefits must go to private as well as public schools. But local authorities must better control costs and force reforms. A well-educated youth is a national necessity, not just for economic growth, but for a peaceful civic culture. Ignorance is more costly in the long run than education.[14]

The debate over multicultural education has become part of an American *Kulturkampf*, a cultural war, that arrayed adherents of traditional Western cultural values and traditional family values against militant feminists, militant gays and lesbians, militant Chicanos and African-Americans, and advocates of "politically correct" views. During the 1980s, something like six million new immigrants came to the US; counting the illegal immigrants, the total must have been even higher – possibly as many as nine million newcomers. In New York, Chicago, Miami, El Paso, Los Angeles and San Francisco, schools were flooded by children unable to speak English. Overburdened teachers thus faced problems on a scale that hardly existed anywhere else. (Most Commonwealth immigrants to Britain, for example, knew at least some English; West Indians in particular spoke English as their native tongue.) The diversification of the student body led to all kinds of experimental solutions. High among them ranked bilingual or "multicultural" education, which itself took many different forms. According to ethnic and feminist militants, Third World people and women in the US had been subject to educational oppression; the remedy was to break the predominance of the regnant establishment, and the spiritual hegemony of Dead European White Males (DEWM's).

We stand opposed to multiculturalism as practiced on liberal campuses or in public schools. We should like to emphasize once again that except for black Americans, the immigrants have come to the US by choice; they emphatically do *not* wish to live in a Third World country or to be made backward by absorbing Third World cultures instead of Western culture. When a naturalized citizen swears the oath of allegiance, the new American vows to uphold the constitution and adopt the American creed. We welcome the teaching of foreign cultures and languages in secondary schools and college; we note with regret, however, that foreign language training has dropped to a new low in American schools and that Western civilization courses have widely given way to largely irrelevant "world civ" courses. We note with regret that multiculturalism falsifies history, and avoids hard options. Real language training commonly ends where the irregular verbs begin. We disagree with the implicit assumption that the liberal American professoriate constitutes or should constitute the moral role model and moral reference group for the country at large. We particularly object to the anti-historical, the anti-Western culture biases that infuse so much of contemporary American education.

Instead we call for the primacy of Western culture and of "hard" subjects in education. At a time when employment in traditional manufacturing industries is declining, when educational requirements increase in service industries, we cannot afford an under-skilled underclass. Neither can we afford a huge welfare establishment and a huge welfare clientele at a time when the US economy is increasingly becoming locked into a highly competitive global economy. (To give specific figures, in 1955, imports and exports of goods and services respectively accounted for only 5 percent of the US gross national product. By 1988, the respective figures stood at 13.1 percent and 15 percent.) Americans therefore need to adopt better skill training programs such as the German apprenticeship system which turns out well educated, highly skilled workers.

However, when we criticize our educational systems, it is easy to forget that foreigners also have their problems, and that US education has specific strengths. These include flexibility and diversity (with private as well as public schools and universities). Overall, something like two-thirds of the world's best universities for research and postgraduate training are to be found in the US. Ever since Hitler wrecked German academia and exiled or murdered many of Germany's best scientists, the US has consistently headed the global list of Nobel Prize winners, (with Britain in second place). The US is clearly doing some things right.

We are also moderately optimistic with regard to the US race problem – especially future relations between blacks and their non-African-descended neighbors. Blacks are widely identified with the underclass. Most blacks are not members of the underclass and the great majority of the underclass are not criminals. Moreover, the US's present problems are in no wise new. An underclass has existed in American cities ever since the eighteenth century. (In Philadelphia, the largest American city before the Revolution, one out of every four adult white males was poverty-stricken by the standards of the time.) Widespread misconceptions to the contrary notwithstanding, inequality may in fact have substantially declined in the US over the last two centuries.[15]

Neither is there anything new about an underclass that is at least partially defined in ethnic terms. During the mid-nineteenth century, the underclass in New York and London alike contained a large Irish component. Contemporary accounts are full of complaints about Irish slum dwellers "living in the midst of us, but estranged from our religion, our laws, our manners, and our government," paupers always prone to crime, violence, and insurrections.[16] The problems connected with this underclass were supposedly insoluble. Nevertheless, the Irish underclass has since disappeared both in Britain and the US; indeed, Irish Americans as a group enjoy among the highest average family incomes in the US – a shift that would have seemed inconceivable to mid-Victorian observers.

A similar shift has begun in the condition of black Americans. Whereas the great majority of blacks 60 years ago lived below the poverty level as then defined, there is now a substantial black middle class, estimated as about one-third of the black population. Admittedly, the parallels between mid-nineteenth-century Irish and late twentieth-century blacks should not be over-stressed. The Irish were indistinguishable by their skin color from their neighbors. However poverty stricken, the Irish had a Catholic legacy, and – as observers noticed both in New York and the London East End – a deep respect for the family and the priest; and then had to work, for there was no welfare system. Nevertheless, blacks have made major advances; few would have anticipated them during Roosevelt's days.

Since World War II, the US has undergone a whole series of further socio-demographic shifts. Before World War II, the great majority of leading Americans in business, government, the armed forces, and academia were Protestants of Northern European descent (WASPS). There was widespread discrimination against Catholics and Jews – not to speak of Chinese, Japanese, African-Americans, Mexicans, and others. In World War II there were already major changes, as wartime manpower shortages opened up new job opportunities to Americans of every skin color and every faith. At the same time racism ceased to be tolerable. (For example, in 1943 the US repealed existing exclusion laws directed against the Chinese.) When the war ended, GIs of whatever ancestry benefited from the GI Bill and from postwar prosperity. During the 1950s and the 1960s there was an end to legal discrimination against blacks. Unofficial discrimination against Jews and Catholics was largely terminated. Americans ceased to regard their nation as mainly Northern European and Protestant. Indeed, there was a remarkable change in that, contrary to then prevailing stereotypes, Irish, Italian, and Polish Catholics acquired, on the average, higher family incomes than white Protestants. "Catholics earn more money than any other Christian denomination."[17] At the same time certain non-European groups radically improved their position against whites in terms of average family incomes, especially Americans of Japanese, Chinese, and Filipino descent. And educated hyphenated Americans have dropped the hyphen, moved into the professions and became part of the establishment.

In addition, there has been a striking shift in the make-up of immigration, with huge numbers of newcomers from Asia and Latin America. These immigrants were themselves extraordinarily varied in their composition, with Vietnamese, Indians, and Koreans among the Asians, as well as Chinese and Japanese, and San Salvadorians, Guatemalans, Argentinians among the Latin Americans, as well as Mexicans, Cubans, and Puerto Ricans. Overall, the proportion of whites within the population somewhat diminished, though nothing like as quickly as legend would have it. (Between 1980 and 1990 the proportion of whites within the population declined from 83.1 percent to just over 80 percent. The Hispanics in the country comprise a substantial proportion of persons who describe themselves as "white." The term "Hispanic" is a cultural, not a racial designation.) Moreover, there may be a new shift toward white immigration, as disappointed citizens from the former Warsaw Pact countries and the former Soviet Union will seek new places for themselves overseas.

Certainly the US's ethnic mosaic has become ever more complex. Not only were the newcomers even more mixed in their ethnic composition than their predecessors, they also had, on the average, more children. The immigrants' high birth rate contributed to white fears of being overrun by aliens who competed with Americans for jobs, welfare services, and schooling – this at the indigenous taxpayer's expense. There were also widespread concerns that the US would be Latinized, or end as a Third World nation. Hispanics, goes the argument, are unlike European immigrants of earlier generations; the Hispanics' respective homelands are geographically near to the US; immigration for Hispanics does not entail a traumatic journey across the Atlantic, as it did for Italians, Germans and Irish. Whatever its declared policy, the US is therefore already becoming a bilingual country by force of circumstance. Hispanics, the argument continues, often stay poor for generation after generation; hence the traditional melting pot will not work for them. We disagree. According to our findings, the "new" immigrants do not differ all that much from "old" immigrants; the newcomers have similar aspirations. In time Hispanics also learn English – the only tongue that readily serves Hispanics, Chinese, Turks, Norwegians as an instrument for communication, a tongue essential for advancement in the new country (a point readily made by advertisers on Hispanic TV in the US). The "new" immigrants moreover differ enormously in their educational[18] and occupational makeup; they include numerous entrepreneurs and professionals, as well as those unskilled and semi-skilled workers whom Americans traditionally associated with immigrants. English will certainly prevail.

For all its ethnic troubles, the US shines by comparison with multi-ethnic countries all over the world – the former Soviet Union, Romania, the former Yugoslavia, the Lebanon, Cyprus, Ethiopia, India, Iraq, Iran, Burma, Burundi – the list is long. No other country in the world has done as well in integrating immigrants from many different backgrounds. The US is also unusual in another way: it is a huge country, yet untroubled by local or regional independence movements – unlike, say, the former Soviet Union, former Yugoslavia, Spain, Canada, Sudan, or even Great Britain. Our optimistic assessment will offend many of our academic colleagues in ethnic studies, African-American studies, area studies and related disciplines whose practitioners are apt to magnify domestic ills. Their unfavorable perception of the US is not surprising. Few or no conservatives teach such disciplines. On the contrary, teachers in the humanities and social studies at major US universities overwhelmingly stand left of center in politics. (Only 2 percent of college teachers in area and ethnic studies describe themselves as conservative – this in a country where abut 33 percent or so of the general population chooses this designation.)[19] Such academic and clerical critics are apt to forget that foreigners fled their own countries and chose to come to the US – the world's greatest magnet for immigrants. By contrast, few US citizens of any race choose to leave their country permanently: African-Americans rarely go to Africa; few Jewish-Americans now settle in Israel; US citizens of Hispanic origin do not commonly emigrate to Mexico, Cuba, or other Spanish-speaking countries. In this sense, the US passes the true litmus test of acceptability and is perceived as a land of opportunity by millions of immigrants who have fled their own countries because of bad political or economic conditions. People keep coming and they seldom leave.

The US has other enormous strengths. Political discontent there is aplenty; but very few Americans challenge the US constitution, or wish to alter the political system. Whereas Hitler and Stalin alike worried with good reason concerning plots by generals, no US president has ever done so – in the US such conspiracies belong in the realm of political thrillers or conspiratorial movies such as *JFK*. Ethnically divided the US may be, but no ethnic minority in the US has ever sided with an enemy in wartime. (The mass of German-Americans proved as loyal in World War I as the bulk of Japanese-Americans were devoted to the US cause in World War II.)

The US is indeed unique in its ability to assimilate huge numbers of newcomers. From its beginnings, the US has fluctuated in its ethnic composition. Over the last decade, the number of Asians has vastly increased; so have the Hispanic people, who are likely to replace blacks as the largest ethnic minority by the beginning of the next century.[20] The processes by which immigrants adjust to their new country are not uniquely American. Other countries have also experienced the challenge posed by successive newcomers and ethnic shifts. To take just one example, the experience of London's East End, successively the home of Flemings, French Huguenots, Irish, Jews, and Pakistanis, parallels that of many American cities. London's East End also experienced inner city violence, poverty, the out-migration of successful people, and the kind of ethnic succession which turned L'Eglise Neuve, built in 1743 in Brick Lane as a French Huguenot church, first into a Methodist chapel, later a synagogue, and eventually into a mosque.[21]

But the US, unlike any European country, was built from the start by immigrants. And whatever his or her origins or religion, an immigrant becomes an American, and is accepted as such by taking the oath of allegiance. Fellow-Americans may like or dislike the new citizen's ethnic group; but they do not generally assume that a naturalized citizen remains somehow an alien. In this respect, the US is very different even from Western European democracies. A foreigner naturalized in Britain becomes a British subject, a subject of the Queen. In this capacity, he or she may aspire to the highest honors (in 1992 four foreign-born peers sat in the House of Lords – all economists). But a naturalized foreigner can never become an Englishman, a Scotsman, or a Welshman – not because British people are more xenophobic than their neighbors, but because Britons define their nationality in a manner very different from Americans. Similarly, few Germans regard a naturalized Turk as a fellow German; few Frenchmen accept a naturalized Arab as a fellow Frenchman, unless he or she can speak French without a trace of an accent and never makes a grammatical mistake!

Widespread misconceptions to the contrary, the bulk of the newcomers wish to learn English, wish to stay in the US, and work, they want to fit into a capitalist consumer society; and relatively few are on welfare.[22] According to a widespread fear, the Hispanics will one day "Latinize" the US, or they will turn California into a Spanish-speaking Quebec. But in fact, the Hispanic newcomers – like their Italian, German, and other predecessors – do not form a single, cohesive bloc; they are divided by nationality, education, occupation, and social class. In this respect, as in so many others, the "new immigrants" correspond to "old immigrants" such as the Germans. Thus two leading US scholars, writing on the German American past, have criticized the "misguided notion" that Germans, the largest group besides the British contingent during the eighteenth century, formed a unified group self-confident and wholly committed to the German language.[23] Germans, however, did cling to their language and culture somewhat more than did Italians or Hispanics. The Hispanics of today share with the German-speaking immigrants of yesterday a legacy of divisiveness, regionalism and dissension. Immigrants of whatever nationality, moreover, came, and continue to come, in penny-packets; Asians jostle Hispanics; Hispanics jostle Europeans; neighborhoods change, as wealthy people of any ethnic origins sell their existing residences and buy superior accommodations in some wealthier suburb. Our society is too mobile to permit the creation of a Quebec; our ethnic composition will change, but we shall all be Americans and the new immigrants will integrate into the old American way just as the old immigrants did – unless biculturalism or multiculturalism succeeds in disuniting America.

What of that host of discontented and alienated people who are supposed to make up a large portion of the ethnic minorities in the US? Such discontented men and women exist – but they are not nearly as numerous as experts in multicultural studies claim. Indeed, the great majority of Americans are reasonably satisfied with the lives that they lead and their financial condition. This generalization goes counter to those literary and sociological critiques that see the majority of blacks and Hispanics as alienated and unhappy. Such pessimistic interpretations are not borne out by public opinion polls.[24] As a nation we do better than our critics believe.

## THE OPTIMIST'S CASE: ECONOMIC ASPECTS

The 1992 presidential election brought out hordes of nay-sayers and Cassandras. According to Clinton and his academic advisers, we had a stagnant economy, massive unemployment, and were rapidly losing manufacturing jobs. News organizations reported that American business and industry lost 167,000 jobs in August, 1992, when in fact 85,000 jobs in manufacturing and 25,000 in services were created. Economic reporting was too pessimistic; even though there was slow growth (2 percent) in the first half of 1992, from 1988 to 1992 the US averaged GDP growth of 4 percent. The US completed the longest peacetime expansion in its history in 1990. Unemployment at 7.5 percent was not high by previous periods of recession, nor as high as many nations in the EC. The recession in the 1980s was worse (10.8 percent) and in the depression of the 1930s, it was 25 percent. By the end of 1992, the economy was slowly growing again – too late for Bush, but enough to make President Clinton cautious about implementing his campaign promises. For example, Clinton spoke of jump-starting the economy by massive public investment – bad idea and bad Keynes! Better to give entrepreneurs some help by indexing the capital gains tax to inflation. Other "bad promises" were taxing foreigners, and soaking the rich.

The US remains by far the world's most productive country. The American worker, overall, is still the world's most productive laborer. In fact, the US has been undergoing an industrial resurgence in some fields. Exports are up; imports are down. Statistics concerning comparative gross domestic product (GDP) of different nations are apt to be deceptive; it is hard to get accurate comparable data. (Published statistics always undervalue those sectors of any economy that do not rely on monetary transactions. Above all, official statistics take little or no account of the "Second Economy," which functions underground, and escapes the tax-gatherer's and the census-taker's notice.) Table 8.1 therefore only has illustrative value; but it does give a clear indication of the US's over-whelming economic might. (In 1988 the US's GDP exceeded that of the main four EC partners, the Soviet Union, the People's Republic of China, and India combined.)

Table 8.1 US GDP in billion dollars, 1988

| US | 4,881.00 |
|---|---|
| Japan | 2,859.93 |
| West Germany | 1,208.29 |
| France | 949.99 |
| Italy | 828.98 |
| Britain | 826.32 |
| USSR | 583.10 |
| People's Republic of China | 332.79 |
| India | 267.24 |

Source: The Economist Book of Vital World
Statistics, London, The Economist, 1990, p. 32.

True enough, the US's share in the world's total economic production, in terms of published figures, declined from about 50 percent in 1945 to roughly 23 percent in 1991. But 1945 is not a good point of departure for making international comparisons. When World War II ended, much of Europe lay in ruins; Japan and China had suffered enormous devastation; so had the Soviet Union. The US was the only major power than had escaped war damage within its own borders. Indeed, the demands of war had caused a sudden and unprecedented expansion in US economic production. Thereafter the rest of the world recovered – in part as a result of US aid to Western Europe and Japan. The US achieved precisely what its policy-makers desired: freer trade, the economic renaissance of its allies and enemies. Naturally, the US's *relative* economic standing in the world declined thereafter; the US proportion of global production went back nearer to what it had been before the war, roughly 23 percent by 1973 as compared to 25 percent in 1938. But the US gross national product enormously increased in absolute terms – the US was and remains the world's premier economic power: the place whose life-style is the world's envy (leftist intellectuals excepted).[25]

Will the economic giant collapse because Americans spend too much and save too little? Collapse is unlikely, asserts economist Henry Rowen, but the danger is near-stagnation of real incomes because of continued low productivity growth (1.9%) during the 1980s in comparison to the EEC (2.9%) and Japan (3%). But Richard B. McKenzie argues the opposite: the 1980s saw renewed competitiveness, modest growth and modest economic gains. Many observers assume that the US savings rate is too low, and hence will impede future prosperity. Economists, however, cannot define an ideal rate of investment or agree on such terms as savings. (Indeed, during the Great Depression Keynesians insisted that the Slump derived from excessive saving and under-consumption.) It is certainly accepted that, in nominal terms, gross investment fell from about 18 percent of the GNP in 1978 to just about 14 percent in 1990. But, according to the late Warren Brookes, these figures may be deceptive. They ignore the revolution in information technology over that period. The real cost of "computing power" has greatly fallen since 1980 and continues to fall. This revolution, in turn has depressed the real price of producing capital goods. The result may have been that private investment rates – adjusted for inflation – were every bit as good during the 1980s as they had been during previous decades. US tax laws unfortunately favor debt over equity financing; double taxation of dividends discourages equity financing. But if the system were to be reformed, if taxes were kept low and official expenditure kept in bounds, savings would take care of themselves.[26]

Will the US go to pieces because Americans buy too much from foreigners, and too little from fellow-Americans? Are US manufacturing industries in a state of decay and will this be fatal? According to the pessimists, the well-paid car worker is being replaced by a poorly paid assistant in a fast food joint, a young man or woman who supposedly performs meaningless labor in a dead-end job. In the US, as in all other advanced countries, the service sector has indeed grown. But it is an immensely varied sector; many service jobs are highly remunerated, many more require high educational qualifications. (Contrary to a widely accepted stereotype, something like nine-tenths of the new jobs created during the 1980s did not go to hamburger flippers but to white-collar workers.)[27] And while it is true that the number of farmers and industrial workers has declined, farm and industrial productivity has increased. Fewer workers were thus required because of productivity advances. American workers in manufacturing are once again the world's most productive workforce. America did not "disindustrialize" itself during the 1980s. Real manufacturing output rose by 38 percent between 1980 and 1989; manufacturing input as a percentage of GNP rose by 1.3 percent by 1989, and not just as consumer goods (capital goods production went from 28 percent to 38 percent.) Exports of manufactured goods grew by 90 percent between 1986 and 1992. Workers' wages slowed down after 1970, but there was a shift from money wages to non-wage compensation such as social security contributions, health and life insurance, vacation and sick leave days, and other fringe benefits. Non-wage benefits are now 21 percent of wage salaries. Total compensation – that is, wages plus benefits – rose from $9.61 per hour in 1959 to $26.25 in 1990.[28]

Intellectuals should stop deriding low-paying entry-level jobs, said George McGovern, once the Democratic Party's leading liberal. He changed his mind about low-paying jobs after a stint in the hotel business. McGovern recently explained (in the *Los Angeles Times*) that low-wage, entry-level jobs are beneficial to the economy and to the individuals who hold them. Liberals see them as a blight on the economy to be eradicated by federal regulation. But McGovern rightly explained that such jobs provide lifetime benefits, for any job may train for a better job, and keeps people off welfare. Young people especially need this workplace experience to gain work skills such as punctuality, taking directions, becoming a self-starter and a decision-maker. Many inner city black youths especially do not seem to have learned these basic skills at home or in school. Role models are often absent in single-parent black households, wrote McGovern. Yet the government keeps raising the minimum wage, thus denying jobs to unskilled youths whose productivity is so poor they were not worth hiring at say $4.50 an hour. And the Bush administration waged a bizarre campaign against legitimate businessmen who employed young people for working them too many hours![29] If the federal government were to stop raising the minimum wage and worrying about how many hours young people work, American business could hire many of the now unemployed.

In any case, the percentage of the GNP accounted for by manufacturing amounts to about one fifth, roughly the same as a generation ago. Indeed, America's record as a manufacturing country remains stupendous. Between 1987 and 1991 the US's volume of manufactured exports nearly doubled; over the same period the volume of exports from other industrialized countries went up, on the average, by only a quarter. Between 1991 and 1992, industrial production in fact rose by 2.1 percent in the US, whereas industrial production actually declined in Germany and Japan, two chosen role models for the US according to its critics. There was indeed serious unemployment in the US – but nothing like as severe as in the EC.

US industry still has many star performers. Contrary to widespread misconceptions, these include the iron and steel industry; its exports quadrupled between 1987 and 1991. Exports of aircraft, electrical machinery, pharmaceuticals, telecommunication equipment, and clothing all nearly doubled during the same period. Americans lead in numerous technology-based firms such as computer software and hardware of all types, microprocessor chips, aerospace, biotechnology, new materials, energy and environmental control. When the Japanese government's Economic Planning Agency surveyed in 1991 some 110 critical technologies, it found that American firms dominated 43 of them, Japanese firms 35, European and others 34. The US also dominates the world's entertainment industries and reigns supreme in service industries (including pursuits as different as the fast food and construction industries). This is not then a story of inevitable decline.[30]

Robert Hall of the Hoover Institution insists the US is not as badly off as the pessimists claim, because the US is the leading creative, innovative economy in the world. Structural changes have moved the US to employ fewer in manufacture and more in service and information industries and in software. US firms export some of their semi-skilled and skilled work to low-wage countries and production to Japan and South Korea, for example. (Hoover economist Thomas Sowell rejects the popular notion that competition is a zero-sum game and that whether we are "winning" or "losing" can be measured by shares of the market and the like. As long as consumers around the world get better and cheaper products through international trade, we are all winning.) The US dominates in the most creative aspects of the world economy and profits accordingly. Those who work with their hands are less well paid in the US than those who work with their brains. The problems of growing wage inequality could be solved by retraining workers in higher skills. Although US primary and secondary schools do badly in international tests, American universities are among the finest in the world and will guarantee that the US will probably continue to dominate the new information and software industries in the future.

Will the US be outperformed in future by Japan? Japan is a formidable competitor. Japan invests a great deal more in manufacturing than does the US – a fault that should be corrected by reforming US tax policies and lessening the weight of regulation. The Japanese do indeed turn out excellent cars, high quality electronic goods, and many other highly specialized products. Japanese banks now occupy a leading position in worldwide finance, as does the yen. The Japanese still save more and work longer hours than any other industrial society; and business and government work in unison. But in many other fields, Japan remains much less efficient than the US. These include agriculture, the distributional trades, and a variety of service industries such as publishing. Above all, the US is a huge continental power with great natural resources; Japan, by contrast, is a small island country without much natural wealth. Moreover, argues Taichi Sakaiya, a Japanese economist much concerned with the future, Japan's real problems are much deeper. Japan is well placed to turn out mass-produced manufactures of high quality. But because of its tradition of individualism and creativity, the US is much better positioned than Japan to meet the future challenges of an evolving "knowledge value" society. Oddly enough, while US and European firms have for years tried to imitate Japanese management techniques, the Japanese have now begun to copy Western models.[31] Japan also has other unsuspected problems; for instance during the 1980s, US productivity actually rose faster than Japan's while, in absolute terms, US productivity remains the highest in the world.

What of foreign investments? Will savers abroad take over the US by buying its chief assets? Fears of alien investors are deeply felt; they reflect perhaps in part the relative inadequacy of domestic saving in the US: 27.9 percent of the Japanese GDP goes to investments; 21.4 percent of Italy's; 20.9 percent of France's; 20.3 percent respectively of East Germany's and South Africa's; but only 15.8 percent of the US's. (In part our relatively low rate of savings derives from our tax code which, in certain respects, rewards borrowers and penalizes the saver.) From 1982 onward, foreign lending in the US thus greatly expanded. As an official report puts it:

Though total US holdings of foreign assets have continued to increase on average during the 1980s, foreign ownership of US assets has increased at an even faster pace. As a consequence, the postwar role of the United States as net lender to and investor in the rest of the world diminished during the 1980s. According to official estimates, since 1985 the United States has acquired a position of net indebtedness toward the rest of the world, a position last assumed by the United States in World War I. At the end of

1987, total US assets abroad were recorded at $1.17 trillion, $368 billion less than recorded foreign assets in the United States. Although these official estimates may substantially underestimate the true US net asset position, the trend implied a change in the traditional role of the United States as a net lender.[32]

The consequences of this shift are supposedly deplorable. Not only do aliens now own a much larger slice of the US than they did a generation ago, the composition of foreign investments has also changed. In 1982 the share proportion of foreign funds invested in setting up new enterprises in the US nearly equalled the proportion of funds from abroad used to take over existing businesses. By 1990 six times as much alien money was spent on takeovers than on setting up new firms. This change in the composition of foreign lending contributed to further suspicions concerning foreign investment. Few people mind when foreigners set up a new factory in a town where unemployment is rife, and new jobs are at a premium. By contrast, far more Americans object when foreigners take over existing US firms, thereby acquiring control over US technical know-how. Foreigners are also resented when they acquire US land, US minerals, or other "national assets." In this respect the US public differs little from the public in Third World countries.

We do not, however, share these popular suspicions. We do not regard international trade and investment as a zero-sum game where one country's gain is necessarily another country's loss. On the contrary, prosperity knows no border lines. The US, for example in the nineteenth century owned much of its success to the inflow of foreign (especially British, but also German and French) capital. Critics of foreign investments moreover err when they make a distinction between the beneficent effects of investments in new enterprises, as against the allegedly ill consequences entailed in takeovers of existing firms. No one should object when foreigners save US jobs by rescuing failing firms. In fact, New Yorkers cheered when the late Robert Maxwell, the British press tycoon, acquired the *Daily News*, a money-losing tabloid. Nobody minded when Germany's Engelmann group restored to prosperity the Great Atlantic and Pacific Tea Company, the owner of the A. and P. grocery chain. There is indeed an element of racism in our distrust of foreign investors. Despite competition from the Japanese and French, the British remain the largest foreign investors overall. Yet no one objects to US subsidiaries of British firms such as Grand Metropolitan's Burger King junk food emporiums, Marks and Spencer's Brooks Brothers men's clothing stores, or Bass's Holiday Inns.[33] All these seem as American as apple pie. It is the Japanese, by contrast, who arouse resentment.

This resentment is mistaken, for the role of foreign capital, in economic terms, has nothing to do with the investor's nationality, language, or skin color. No matter whether they operate in the US or in Burundi or Bangladesh, foreign investors bring in not only capital, but certain assets, be they management skills, or a new technology, knowledge of foreign markets, or whatever. If the foreign investors have no such advantages, they won't survive in business. Above all, foreign investments are an involuntary tribute to US economic and political stability; foreigners put their funds here because they regard them as safe. When foreigners invest money in the US we should thank them – we could hope for no better compliment.

As regards the future outlook for our economy, a good deal of pessimism was engendered by the recession which began in 1990 and continued thereafter. Ours is widely supposed to be a recession-prone country, judging by those setbacks which we have experienced since the end of World War II. However, as economist Herbert Stein points out, none of the postwar recessions in the US can compare with those that hit the US in the first third of the present century. Overall, US production continued to expand; the GNP steadily went up; the increase in wealth is startling. The US performance looks even better when US progress is measured in terms of consumption per capita. As Stein argues, the true object of economic activity is – or should be – to make people better off. In material terms, this object is achieved by providing for greater personal consumption. (Investment, from this perspective, may be regarded as a provision to assure future consumption.) In this respect the US has done remarkably well. Pessimistic forecasts notwithstanding, the US has experienced only three postwar dips in overall personal consumption (1973–4; 1979–80; 1989–92). The largest of these dips amounted to only 1.8 percent, in 1973–74 – at a time when gasoline was misallocated and car sales plummeted. Overall, personal consumption per capita has continued to go up; the percentage of people in poverty has greatly diminished since World War II. US economic history therefore has been a tale of progress, not of decline.[34]

Stein has more good news. Our real GNP per capita remains the world's highest. The government sector in the United States has enormously expanded during the last 60 years, but it is still moderate by international standards. (Relative to the GNP, government expenditures and receipts are about the same level as they are in Japan, and lower than in any other industrial country.) Americans justly complain about excessive government taxation and regulation of business and environmental laws. It is impossible to calculate the total cost of compliance with government regulations to industry and to the environment; the costs are clearly increasing, but they are not overwhelming. (According to a study cited by Stein, they account for 3 percent of the GNP, about one year's normal growth.) Government expenditure for goods and services has considerably increased over the last 60 years – but nothing like as fast as private expenditure. Neither is the US about to be dominated by a few giant monopolies. Such fears used to be widespread in the past; they are hardly heard anymore nowadays, given the diversity of American business enterprise in general.

Excessive pessimism is also inadvisable with regard to the US budgetary deficit, a major issue in recent years. Like many other governments, the US spends too much in relation to its income. (At the time of writing, Japan was exceptional in possessing a surplus.) The US deficit keeps growing; so does the share of the revenue used for the payment of interest. This is indeed bad news, especially as the deficit will keep growing – at least in the short run. However, the problem should be seen in perspective. The US remains the world's biggest borrower in absolute terms. But in relative terms, reckoning the deficit as a percentage of the gross domestic product, the situation is not nearly as bad as the pessimists assert. In 1992 the US deficit amounted to 3.6 percent of the GDP, therefore less (in that order) than that of Australia, Sweden, Britain, Canada, and Belgium, not to speak of Italy and Greece, the latter with a hefty 14.5 percent of GDP.[35] Yet economists and politicians who predict disaster for the US on account of its spendthrift habits never make equally gloomy forecasts about Sweden or Canada, which indeed are often described as possible role models for the US.

Clearly, budget deficits must be reduced if economic growth is to increase. The interest on the debt takes much of the meager savings of Americans and crowds out funds for private investment. Long-term interests rate are high (7–8 percent), so new investment is frightened off to long-term government bonds instead of to investment in business and industry. Yet the problem is easily solved: $50 billion a year can be cut off the deficit by a $0.50 tax on gasoline and by taxing 85 percent of social security benefits.

## THE ROAD AHEAD

For the foreseeable future, the US will remain the world's leading military and economic power. The US has a positive role to play in continuing to promote the cause of global free trade. Not that the future will be free of trouble. Paul Kennedy's theory concerning "imperial overstretch" should be taken seriously. In all probability, the Soviet empire faltered in part because the Soviet Union could not forever maintain its existing level of military spending in peacetime. Ian Smith's UDI (Unilateral Declaration of Independence, issued in Rhodesia in 1965, ended in 1980) could not be permanently sustained – not because the Rhodesian army was defeated, but because the Rhodesian state could not keep up the expenditure required to resist both African guerrilla warfare and an international economic embargo.

Kennedy's generalization, however, has certain weaknesses. He is apt to measure power in a somewhat mechanical manner. Power cannot be counted in units like eggs. Power can only be defined within specific historical contexts. In 1921 the Irish forced Britain to withdraw from Southern Ireland. In 1962 France agreed to withdraw from Algeria. But no one, least of all Irish or Algerians, ever argued that Eire was more powerful than the United Kingdom, or that Algeria was mightier than the French Republic. As regards military expenditure, Britain, at the height of its power before World War I, spent less on its military than any of its major European rivals. Far from contracting, British economic production massively expanded at the zenith of British imperial might.[36] The US today disburses a larger share of its GNP on defense than Britain did before World War I. However, this percentage has dropped over the last 30 years. Widespread misconceptions on the subject notwithstanding, the US spent a larger proportion of GNP on defense under the presidency of John F. Kennedy than of Ronald Reagan. Yet in terms of assumed crisis indicators such as inflation, budgetary deficits, international trade deficits, and such like, the US was better off in the early 1960s than in the late 1980s. In any case, the hostility to President Reagan's assumedly excessive rate of defense spending derived more from political than from economic considerations. In 1988, for example, the US under Ronald Reagan devoted exactly the same proportion of its GNP to defense as did Zimbabwe under Robert Mugabe – 6.3 percent to be exact.[37] Yet no American critic ever attributed Zimbabwe's economic problems to military over-spending, or censured Mugabe for devoting too many resources to the Zimbabwean military.

Most professors dislike military spending, not merely because they prefer peace to war, and spending on welfare to arms, but because professors compete with the military for public acclaim and public funds. Since the ending of the draft, moreover, young college teachers have rarely served in the military; indeed, they mostly have few or no acqaintances who have ever worn a uniform. Nevertheless, even those who dislike military spending should regard it as a national insurance premium well within the ability of the US to pay. This expenditure strikes us as needful, given the uncertainties created by the Soviet hard-liners' unsuccessful coup in 1991, the past military buildup within the Soviet Union which kept outproducing the US in military hardware, and the instability that continues to prevail in various Soviet republics, the former Yugoslavia, the Middle East and elsewhere. Post-Cold War Europe is still a dangerous place. And recent Russian-Chinese trade accords for military sales do not give promise of arms control.

As regards military expenditure in general, we do not believe that armaments wreck the US economy. In fact, both critics and opponents of defense spending in peacetime have overestimated its relative importance. During the 1930s, Marxists took for granted that capitalist states could not solve the internal contradictions of their social system and would be forced to compete in imperial rivalries, to spend money on arms and to war against each other. At present, advocates of enlarging the military budget optimistically refer to the many "spin-offs" from military programs that supposedly benefit civilian industries. But in truth, as Murray Weidenbaum puts it, "both critics and supporters of defense programs have overstated their case about the impact – positive or negative – of military spending on the US economy. The US economy is both complex and massive. It is not readily propelled or retarded by the relatively small share of the GNP devoted to military outlays."[38]

Weidenbaum's argument is worth examining in detail. First of all, the relative importance of defense to the US economy has sharply declined since the end of World War II. The share dropped from a high of 39 percent in the fiscal years 1944 and 1945 to 14 percent during the Korean War, 10 percent at the peak of the Vietnam War, and 6.5 percent at the height of the Reagan defense buildup (1986–7). Defense spending as a share of the federal budget had amounted to more than 90 percent during World War II, 70 percent during the Korean War; it was 28 percent in 1987, and declined again thereafter. At the same time there was a striking increase in civilian spending; the recent budgetary deficits derived not from military disbursements but from the rapid expansion of transfer payments for civilian expenditure, coupled with reductions in income tax rates.

Widespread assumptions to the contrary, statistical analysis does not support the contention that civilian society is being depleted by military demands. By 1988, for example, the military accounted for only 1.7 percent of the total US labor force (down from 18.3 percent in 1945, and 2.7 percent in 1965). Research and Development (R & D) in 1987 accounted for 30.3 percent of the total R & D expenditure in the US, down from 46.2 percent in 1965. The overall pattern is clear. Whatever problems the US economy confronted in the 1980s, these did not derive from an excessive growth of the military sector. On the contrary, the economic impact of defense has declined – albeit irregularly – over the last three decades.

Far from declining as a result of excessive military expenditure, the US economy has continued to expand its output. As Fernand Rau, managing director of *Crédit Européen* put it, after a decade of relative decline, the US clearly regained during the 1980s its rank as the leading economic and political superpower. Neither the erratic movements in the dollar exchange rate, nor the huge balance of payments deficit, nor the massive US national debt interfered with the US's dominant position.[39]

Neither is the US likely to go the way of the British Empire. Even at the heyday of the British Empire, at the end of the last century, Britain never remotely enjoyed the economic and military primacy that the US commands in the world today. Britain faced several other powers of formidable strength; by 1880 the US and Germany posed powerful economic challenges. France and Russia, while economically more backward, outspent Britain in terms of military expenditure.[40] Austro-Hungary and Italy also ranked as great powers in a world in which Britain was at best *primus inter pares*, first among equals.

By contrast, the US stands out today as the mightiest country in a world where the former Soviet Union has politically disintegrated (but retains formidable military and nuclear forces), while Japan and Germany, though strong economically, do not form a military threat to the US. The same consideration applies in the cultural sphere. No other country – neither Russia, Germany, Britain, France, nor China – exercises comparable influence on the rest of the world as does the US today. Half a century ago, many intellectuals in the West (and also numerous French, Italian, and Spanish workers) had looked on the Soviet Union as the land of the future. Later there were successive love affairs between Western left-wingers and assorted Marxist-Leninist dictatorships in other parts of the world. In the late 1940s, idealistic youngsters from the West worked on the Yugoslav Youth Railway, and came back with marvelous tales of socialist reconstruction. During the 1960s young men and women worked in the Cuban cane fields to bring a brighter future to Castro's island. Tyrants such as Mao Zedong and Ho Chi Minh used to arouse enthusiasm among left-wing professors and their students. Even "bush-Marxism" of the kind practiced in Angola and Mozambique found admirers in the West. None of these regimes evoke approbation in retrospect. Communism has broken down in the Soviet Union, once the "workers' fatherland"; the once-powerful Italian and French parties have been reduced to left-wing sects. Sociologists and political scientists all over the world are asked to explain why most of them had no inkling of this great cataclysm before it happened. The left has failed; capitalism or the market system has triumphed, and the US is the prime example of capitalist success.

The US now forms the main world model. This is not to say that it is the only country that commands global interest. Japan and Germany have plenty of admirers who prize economic and technological efficiency. There are many francophiles and anglophiles – and with good reason. But it is the US which stands out as the main international paradigm for democratic government and military and economic strength, whether as an example to be criticized or lauded. No other country can compare with the US in its military and economic power and global influence. No other country occupies as important a position in the sciences as does the US. (Between 1957 and 1989, the US won 53 percent of the world's Nobel Prizes in the sciences and 60 percent in economics; comparable figures for the entire EEC were 30 and 23, for Japan 2 and 0.)

The US ascendancy will not last forever; nothing does. The ending of the Cold War may in fact have the odd effect of lessening a national sense of purpose. The US will surely face new challenges from Europe as the EC becomes more effective through integration. But growing EC prosperity will reciprocally benefit the US. Militarily, it is unlikely that any foreign country will gain that superiority now held by the US as long as it keeps modernizing its forces and disarming Russian nuclear weapons. The US should, however, take pride in more than its wealth or armed might. Its true strength lies in its ability to uphold its dedication to the rule of law and constitutional government. During the 1960s these were widely decried by the campus left as "formal democracy" that stood in the way of true revolutionary endeavor. But it is precisely the rule of law that appeals to the former subjects of dictatorships. Nothing was more moving than to listen to telecasts of debates in the Russian Parliament during the 1991 coup when speaker after speaker spoke in favor of constitutionalism and legality.

The US also should take pride in running the world's most successful experiment in multi-ethnic integration. Whereas other multinational countries such as the former Yugoslavia and the former Soviet Union disintegrated, and perhaps even Belgium, Canada, and India face a possible breakup, the US has retained its cohesion, despite the many efforts made inside and outside academia at cultural deconstruction. Still, this battle has just started and no one can prejudge its outcome. Speaking in general, the US has largely managed to resist "hyphenization," – not in the sense that Americans despise their ancestors, but in the sense that the majority of second-generation hyphenated Americans do not derive their personal identity from their ethnic heritage. Ethnicity forms only one of several components of an American's legacy – not necessarily even the most important one. Whereas the former Yugoslavia and the former Soviet Union had come to stress group rights, the great majority of Americans continue to stand on individual rights – those rights due them, not as Irish-Americans, African-Americans, Jews, Scandinavians, or whatever, but as American citizens.

The US is certainly divided by innumerable cleavages, social, racial, ethnic, political, ideological. Yet the country is too diverse, the political kaleidoscope too changeable, for polarization of the kind familiar in countries such as Nigeria, Cyprus, or the Lebanon. In many ways foreigners envy us – and not merely for our wealth. The Thomas hearings may serve as an example. In 1991 the US Senate Judiciary Committee held hearings on the confirmation of Judge Clarence Thomas to the Supreme Court. From the Atlantic to the Pacific, US viewers stayed glued to their TV sets. Had Thomas used obscene language to Anita Hill ten years ago? Or had he not? The nation was divided, with bitter disagreement, not only on Thomas's personal fitness for the post, but also on the extent of sexual harassment in the US. Many Americans considered the hearing a national mudbath, given the nature of the evidence presented. Foreigners looked on with incomprehension or amusement as they searched for a new vocabulary to translate the American experience (*harcèlement sexuel*, the French neologism for sexual harassment, is not found in the standard *Larousse* dictionary.) Yet Americans did not realize how lucky they were. A highly controversial issue was debated in public instead of being relegated to a secret committee. American congressional manners may be open to criticism; but they shine by comparison with those displayed in the British Parliament, where jeering and booing is part of the accepted order. Bosnia, Lebanon, Northern Ireland would have thanked God with all their heart had their respective fellow citizens turned from bloody conflict to a televised scandal enlivened by filthy speech.

How should the US employ its enormous strength in the world at large? A new brand of isolationism has found an array of advocates. These include revisionist scholars who still blame the US for the Cold War. The isolationists also comprise men and women on the "hard right," such as journalist Patrick Buchanan, and liberal populists such as Tom Harkin, a presidential candidate in 1992. William Hyland, editor of *Foreign Affairs* and formerly a "Cold Warrior," has called for more concern for our domestic problems, and he would downgrade our foreign policy commitments. Hyland believes the American people will not accept a $300 billion defense budget when the communist threat has been defeated. The US, he suggests, should start disengaging in order to save resources so we can treat domestic crime, drugs, homelessness and health and education problems. The US doesn't have to defend Western Europe or Japan; they can defend themselves. The new isolationism may well gain strength, especially within the Democratic Party where fear of foreign entanglements, dread of war, and commitment to massive social expenditure fuse with economic nationalism. But the US cannot, and should not, retreat into a "Fortress America."

Interventionists, by contrast, divide into three schools of thought. Advocates of democratic activism believe that the US should find a new national purpose, now that the Cold War is over. So-called realists like Henry Kissinger want the US to be the policeman of the world. Others say the US's mission should be to export democracy all over the globe. Advocates of democratic activism include American scholars such as Larry Diamond and Joshua Muravchik; they believe that the US can only fulfill its national destiny by assuring self-government to the oppressed all over the world.[41] For its adherents, democratic interventionism combines morality with *realpolitik*; democratic nations make much better allies than tyrannies. It is therefore in the US's interest to support the former, and wipe out the latter. If the US wants a peaceful world, it must export democracy. A third view stresses internationalism, but with greater use of the UN and regional organizations with a greater stress on human rights and democracy.[42]

Unfortunately, these prescriptions are not as easy to carry out as it sounds. Even if the US were all-powerful, it is not always certain how US strength should be used. In 1992, to give just one example, the Algerian military regime took steps to prevent Islamic fundamentalists from gaining power by lawful elections. The military defended its action on very reasonable grounds. Only a small percentage of the electorate had voted. Western-style democracy would not work in a backward country riddled by ethnic and clan divisions. Above all, the Fundamentalists, once in power, would abolish democracy and institute an ideological dictatorship, as the Nazis had done in Germany in 1933. What should the US have done under such circumstances?

In any case, US usable power remains limited and the world a risky place. We ourselves believe in intervening abroad – but only where US vital interests are directly threatened. When foreign statesmen describe themselves as enemies of the US, they should be taken at their word: they are sure not to lie. The US should take suitable counter action. But the US cannot eradicate evil regimes or impose its own institutions on the world at large. Such a foreign policy would make excessive demands even on the strength of the US; such a foreign policy would moreover never gain essential domestic backing. Like it or not, the world continues to be made up of sovereign states. Between them they command a great degree of trust. US politicians cannot afford to ride roughshod abroad over such loyalties. Indeed scholar-politicians as distinguished and varied in outlook as Hans Morgenthau, Henry Kissinger, and George F. Kennan have all shown in the past that it is either perilous or impossible for the US to base its foreign policy on the higher morality alone. It is beyond the power of the US and the inclination of its people to enforce democracy from the Ukraine to Syria, the People's Republic of China to Burundi. Where necessary the US should intervene only in coalition with the UN or regional groups; it should not be the policeman of the globe, but should cooperate with others to keep the peace.

The US should not over-extend itself, either militarily, or as a supplier of foreign aid. We have explained elsewhere why foreign assistance has so widely failed in its purpose. The US, having been in the foreign aid business for nearly a half a century, should now reconsider its priorities, and provide aid only for purposes immediately beneficial to the US. (It is, for instance, in the interest of the US that former Soviet scientists should be subsidized by US dollars instead of selling their respective skills to aggressive Third World governments.) The US should maintain reduced military commitments in Western Europe as long as Western Europeans desire a US presence for the purpose of continuing to stabilize the continent.

# Conclusion and Recommendations

During the early 1990s there was in the US a widespread sense of gloom. This sprang from two concerns: short-term fears concerning the budget deficit, the recession, and long-term apprehensions over the US's future ability to compete internationally. In relative terms, however, the recent recession has not been unduly severe. There was neither a decline in output nor heavy unemployment by international standards. (The EC had higher unemployment rates – 10 percent – during the 1980s.) Americans, first of all, need to regain a sense of optimism. (In the last five years, the United States has almost doubled the volume of its exports while foreign exports increased by 25 percent. The OECD statistics record that the US portion of manufactured exports went up from 14 percent in 1987 to 18 percent in 1991.) This rise is largely due to the fact that the US economy is the world's "most efficient user of manpower" – almost twice as productive as Japan's. Even in manufacturing, supposedly a declining sector in the US, Americans are not only about as productive as Japan, but also lead in pharmaceuticals, biotechnology, aerospace, computers and new materials. It is not inevitable that Japan or the "Little Tigers" will catch up. But if they do, the US would not necessarily suffer. Competition from Japan and others means better, cheaper products to consumers. It is also a spur to production, because competition promotes innovation and efficiency and shifts resources to better use. Americans, among other things, spend too much on health care, yet often get poor care. They have a cumbersome, expensive legal system that costs business and citizens a lot; they over-regulate business and over-protect the environment; their excessive concerns costs jobs for workers and raises the costs of doing business for owners. The US has in part an outmoded educational system that fails to educate all too many youths through high school for a knowledge-based economy. These problems are not easy to solve – but they are not insurmountable.

Clearly, Americans should not be complacent, especially when we look at Germany or Japan. Japan's impressive economic growth rate is attributed in part to its high proportion of GDP saved and invested rather than consumed. Investment in new machines provided the engine for a high growth rate. There is accordingly widespread consensus among economists that the US must increase its savings, and improve the training of its workers. US companies should learn how to think in long-term prospects; means must be found for reining in health care spending on the part of US firms and the government; health care spending places a heavy burden on US industries and accounts for 13 percent of US gross domestic spending (twice that of Japan); the US must spend more on R & D, and perhaps invest more in public structures such as highways, bridges, railways, and airports. There is also widespread agreement that much of the "peace dividend" should go into education, not into health care.

How is this to be done? Michael T. Jacobs, in his book *Short-Term America* (1991), argues that corporate America would become less short-term oriented if banks were allowed to become major stockholders in industry, as they are in Germany. Clyde Prestowitz proposes giving shares owned by long-term stockholders more voting power. Martin Anderson, Senior Fellow at the Hoover Institution, believes that up to $50 billion a year could be saved if federal spending were to be prevented from rising 4 percent to 5 percent per annum. His would seem to us an attainable object. It is equally feasible to save in other ways, for instance by reducing the enormous subsidies paid by the public to US farmers and industry, overall a wealthy section of the community. Above all, policy-makers should keep in mind that one of the most important social service any government can render to its people is to maintain a stable currency, and protect hard-working and hard-saving citizens from being robbed by inflation.

Economists agree America has to increase its competitiveness, but disagree on how to do it. American workers are no longer the world's highest paid. American productivity (GDP per worker) is still the highest in the world, although Germany and Japan are catching up. This is easily explained; lower productivity nations imitate US technology and can improve more rapidly than the US, which has to invent or improve its technology. Hence Japan's productivity went up 341 percent between 1967 and 1989, whereas the US's improved by only 83 percent.

The US has to augment its productivity without depressing wages further. Devaluation has been tried, but this has impoverished some workers and made imports more expensive. And opening up new markets has had only modest results. Alan S. Blinder in *Maintaining Competitiveness with High Wages* (1992) argues that we can improve productivity by investment and reallocation of labor. Investment is needed in plant, machinery, and public infrastructure. Reallocation of labor increases productivity by ending protection for uncompetitive industries. The Japanese switched from textiles, steel and ships to autos, electronics and banking. The US should permit routine, low-skilled industries to go offshore, and concentrate on high-skill complex tasks. This will require better education and retraining.

But the best strategy, according to Blinder, is to improve labor relations. Labor and management must learn to get on better and to cooperate more. Profit sharing, for example, has raised productivity over 90 percent of the time. Encourage worker participating on the production line, tie pay to performance so as to lesson the need for cyclical layoffs. The US can learn from Japan on how to treat employees: job security, joint consultation on changes in the workplace, fair sharing of profits so as to keep wage differentials narrow, benefits and perks widely available. Japanese managers have impressed both American and British workers by a lack of class consciousness; by a willingness to explain rather than dictate; and by their team spirit. They have managed to create reciprocal loyalties; they have created incentives to improve products; they have allowed workers to modify their equipment and work rules to produce more productive, flexible work teams.

Education is also a major key to economic growth. The rate of return on education is the same as returns on investment in physical capital in developed countries. General education has a higher rate of return than vocational education, claims economist George Psachacapoulos, because vocational education costs more and general education produces more flexible students who can fit into more jobs. But the US probably needs both, with good vocational education as in Germany replacing the shameless racket it has often become in America.

As regards US foreign policy, isolationism and the fear of imperial overstretch should be rejected. We have stressed the cultural and political links that tie the US to Europe. The great majority (some 80–85 percent) of Americans derive wholly or partially from European ancestry. The US has played a vital role in the defense of Europe, and should continue to play a part in the new Europe. The US and its democratic allies won a stunning victory over communism, fascism and other authoritarian systems. Triumphalism is justified, according to *Foreign Affairs* editor William Hyland. The transition to democracy from communism, however, is likely to be long, hard and not everywhere successful. Military dictatorships may possibly succeed some of the former communist tyrannies. Economic recovery is bound to be slow, deprivation could lead to "unfulfilled expectations" and "disenchantment."[1]

The old Europe was chock full of ethnic and national rivalries. World Wars I and II changed borders, but left numerous minorities on the wrong side. Irredentism has again burst into flame – Croat versus Serb, Hungarian versus Romanian, Moldovian versus Russian, Armenian versus Azeri. The old Comecon system of barter has broken down and there is no market for the shoddy goods of Eastern Europe and the old Soviet Union. Raw materials, where they exist, can be sold for hard currency, but little or nothing else. The communist economies have fallen almost to a near subsistence level, and foreign bankers are hesitant to invest, as long as property rights and commercial law remains uncertain and the ruble is not convertible.

US private capital has a role to play, both within the EC and in the formerly communist countries.[2] The US can give some aid – but should only do so on a highly selective basis. But as we see it, the main responsibility for Eastern Europe must be the EC's. The US can no longer afford to be either the world's chief aid giver or the world's policeman. The US needs to remain aware of the threats of nationalism in Eastern Europe and the Balkans. In cooperation with our European allies, we can help to contain conflict, if not stop it. The EC should become the engine for growth and integration for the whole of Europe. The US helped restore West Europe; now the EC has the experience, manpower and resources to do it for Eastern Europe as well. The US also should use the CSCE as conciliator and mediator of Europe. Within NATO, the WEU may well play a much more important part in future. Within ten years, the WEU might even replace NATO. But for the time being there is no effective substitute for NATO; the US has done well for NATO and NATO has done well for the US; we should remain a member of the alliance, but give an increasing degree of responsibility and authority to Europeans. American foreign policy, therefore should return to its roots and traditional goals: protect the country's borders, keep foreign powers out of North America, ensure American commerce access to markets and resources worldwide. The US should protect only its vital national interests in Latin America, West Europe and East Asia (Japan, Korea and Taiwan). It is not the US's mission, however, to act as an arbiter of global morality.

For the US, the new Europe poses many questions. What should America's role be in the new Europe? After all, US policies had been based on "double containment" (of Germany and the USSR) of a divided Germany and a divided Europe. Now both divisions have collapsed. How should the US organize a German-American partnership with the ending of the Cold War, the collapse of the Communist bloc and German unification? What role will the Europeans want the US to play in the new Europe, in the EC, in NATO, in Eastern Europe? Do the Americans and the Europeans still need each other? Are new institutions needed or can old ones be modified? Clearly with the ending of the Cold War, security is no longer the preeminent issue, but how the US should act in the changing European house is uncertain. What role, if any, should the US play in the WEU, or in the CSCE? Clearly, the US and the EC must sustain, contain, and integrate Germany into the Atlantic Community and into Europe while rebuilding the economies of former communist states.

As we see it, the US should be a partner and cooperate with a new, broader EC combining regional associations with all the states of Europe through NATO, the North Atlantic Cooperation Council (NACC), the WEU, the CSCE and the Council of Europe. As regards NATO, the US should be reducing its presence in Europe while cooperating with a European-wide defense force in the WEU and a mediating body in the CSCE. The US should keep some troops and material in Europe to guard against any revival of a Russian threat or regional conflicts in Central and Eastern Europe. Cooperation with the Atlantic Alliance is essential to ensure that the Europeans will not again go to war among themselves. The US should not make the mistake made after every major conflict in which the US engaged during its history, that is, cut its defense forces to the bone. The world remains a dangerous place, and the US must act accordingly. The US does have an overriding interest in preventing the proliferation of conventional arms, as well as the proliferation of so-called "ABC" (atomic, bacteriological, and chemical) weapons. This policy entails appropriate restrictions on its own arms exports: we cannot tell the world to do as we say, not do as we do.

The CSCE, not the EC, should become the major political forum for pan-European cooperation. Old border disputes and ethnic and religious rivalries threaten most of the states of Europe except for the EC and EFTA members. The shattered Soviet Union is deeply threatened by ethnic nationalism inside and outside of the CIS. Quarrels are likely to break out among Russians, Georgians, Ukrainians, and between them and the various Asian communities in side and outside the new republics. Remember, pre-1914 and pre-1939 Europe were cockpits of national and ethnic hatreds. European institutions, not American ones, are better able to cope with these historic quarrels.

To sum up, the US is in much better shape than pessimists assume. The US will continue to play a dominant role in world affairs. It should not exaggerate its own capability for doing good, however, and should intervene abroad only where major US interests are at stake or under the direction of the UN. Americans cannot retreat from the world, and seek safety in a new "Fortress America." As the British *Economist* put it in an article addressed to the US: "You Can't Go Home Again."[3]

# Notes

## 1 Introduction

1 Page Smith, *Trial by Fire: A People's History of the Civil War and Reconstruction*, New York, Penguin Books, 1990, p. 29.
2 See Peter Duignan and L. H. Gann, *The Rebirth of the West: The Americanization of the Democratic World, 1945–1958*, Oxford, Blackwell, 1992, *passim*.
3 Mark P. Lagon and Michel Lind, "American Way: The Enduring Interests of US Foreign Policy," *Policy Review*, Summer, 1991, pp. 38–44. See also Peter Duignan and L. H. Gann, *The United States and Africa: A History*, New York, Cambridge University Press, 1984, ch. 5.
4 Alexis de Tocqueville, *Democracy in America*, ed. J. P. Mayer, Garden City, NY, Doubleday and Co., 1969, p. 33. See also Daniel J. Boorstin, *America and the Image of Europe*, New York, World Publishing Co., 1964, *passim*.
5 "An American," *Collected Verse of Rudyard Kipling*, New York, Doubleday, 1910, pp. 97–9.
6 Nathan Glazer, "The Structure of Ethnicity," *Public Opinion*, October–November 1984, pp. 2–5.
7 Cited respectively from Pierre Berton, *The Invasion of Canada, 1812–1813*, Ontario, Penguin Books, 1988 edn, p. 42, and Arthur Hertzberg, *The Jews in America: Four Centuries of an Uneasy Encounter*, New York, Simon and Schuster, 1989, p. 157.
8 Leo Schelbert and Hedwing Rappold (eds), *Alles ist ganz anders hier: Auswanderer-Schicksale in Briefen aus zwei Jahrhunderten*, Walter-Verlag, Olten and Freiburg, 1977, pp. 42, 67, 100, 115.
9 Charles Wentworth Dilke, *Greater Britain: A Record of Travel in English-speaking Countries During 1866–67*, Philadelphia, J. B. Lippincott, 1869, p. 219.
10 James M. McPherson, *Battle Cry of Freedom: The Civil War Era*, New York, Oxford University Press, 1988, p. 549.
11 Cartoon reprinted in Thomas A. Bailey, *A Diplomatic History of the American People*. Englewood Cliffs, NJ, Prentice-Hall, 1974, p. 467.

12  Marx to Engels, 8 October 1858, in *On Colonialism: Articles from the New York Tribune and other Writings by Karl Marx and Frederick Engels*, New York, International Publishers, 1972, p. 322.

13  Cited in David Dimbleby and David Reynolds, *An Ocean Apart: The Relationship Between Britain and America in the Twentieth Century*, New York, Random House, 1988, p. 25.

14  A. J. P. Taylor, *The Struggle for the Mastery of Europe 1848–1918*, Oxford, Clarendon Press, 1954, pp. xxlx–xxx for detailed figures.

15  Cited by Dimbleby and Reynolds, *An Ocean Apart*, p. 44.

16  Quoted by Frank Costiglolia, *Awkward Dominion: American Political, Economic, and Cultural Relations with Europe, 1919–1933*, Ithaca, Cornell University Press, 1984, p. 178.

17  Dimbleby and Reynolds, *An Ocean Apart*, pp. 335–6.

18  David Ellwood, "The American Challenge and the Origins of the Politics of Growth," in M. L. Smith and Peter M. R. Stirk (eds), *Making the New Europe: European Unity and the Second World War*, London, Pinter 1990, pp. 184–200. See also Duignan and Gann, *The Rebirth of the West*, chs 1 and 2.

19  Richard Grenier, "Around the World in American Ways," *Public Opinion*, March 1986, pp. 3–5.

20  Paul Hollander, *Anti-Americanism: Critiques at Home and Abroad: 1965–1990*, New York, Oxford University Press, 1991. Stephen Haseler, *Anti-Americanism: Steps in a Dangerous Path*, London, Institute for European Defense and Strategic Studies, 1986, *passim*.

21  Steve Dryden, "Europe in America," *Europe*, June 1991, pp. 6–8. Peter S. Rashid, "Made in Europe," *ibid.*, pp. 11–12.

22  Haseler, *Anti-Americanism*, pp. 17–18.

23  *Ibid.*, pp. 24–5.

24  *Ibid.*, pp. 58.

25  Sidney Blumenthal, "Short-Termers: Bush and the CEO's," *The New Republic*, 27 January 1992, pp. 15–16.

26  Paul Fussell, *BAD: Or the Dumbing of America*, New York, Summit Books, 1991.

27  "Europe's Open Future," *The Economist*, 22 February 1992, p. 47. "European Immigration," *The Christian Science Monitor*, 11 August 1991, p. 22.

28  Richard Bernstein, *Fragile Glory: A Portrait of France and the French*, New York, Alfred A. Knopf, 1990, p. 144.

2  An Expanding Alliance 1945–1987

1  Theodore H. White, *The Making of the President 1960: A Narrative History of American Politics in Action*, New York, Atheneum, 1961, pp. 215–22.

2  For the original, with a commentary, see "Scribifax las für Sie," *Criticon*, no. 108, July–August 1988, p. 203.

3  Ralf Dahrendorf, *Society and Democracy in Germany*, Garden City, NY, Doubleday and Co., 1969, pp. 400–11. Arnold Beichman, "Be All Their Quotes Remembered," *The Washington Times*, 14 December 1989, p. 52.

4   Anatoli Sobchak, cited in Donald H. Fanger, "Homo Sovieticus," *Times Literary Supplement*, 15 March 1991, p. 6.

5   William James Adams, *Restructuring the French Economy: Government and the Rise of Market Competition Since World War II*, Washington, DC, The Brookings Institute, 1989, p. 107. On Marshall Plan see Peter Duignan and L. H. Gann *The Rebirth of the West: The Americanization of the Democratic World, 1945–1958*, Oxford, Blackwell, 1992, ch. 5.

6   William Park, *Defending the West: A History of NATO*, Boulder, CO, Westview Press, 1986.

7   The Soviet Union, on paper, possessed 175 divisions, augmented by approximately 60 satellite divisions, by 1959. It was estimated that the Soviet Union could provide another 125 divisions within 30 days of mobilization. But as regards actual frontline divisions, the Soviet force was less impressive; there were 8 tank divisions stationed in East Germany, with another 7 divisions in Hungary and Poland. NATO's forces in Western Europe comprised just under 22 divisions in the Central Area (including 3 from Britain, 5 from the US, 2 from France, 7 from West Germany, 2 from Belgium, 2 from the Netherlands, and including some Canadian forces in addition. The northern flank comprised 1 Danish and 1 Norwegian division. The southern flank included 12 divisions from Turkey, 5 from Greece, and 7 from Italy. NATO had a decisive maritime superiority. For details see the Institute for Strategic Studies, *The Soviet Union and the NATO Powers: The Military Balance*, London, ISSS, 1959.

8   Thomas Hirschfeld, "Tactical Nuclear Weapons in Europe," *Washington Quarterly*, Winter, 1987, pp. 101–21.

9   F. Kober, "Strategic Defense, Deterrence, and Arms Control," *Washington Quarterly*, Winter 1987, pp. 123–52.

10  See Daniel J. Nelson, *Defenders or Intruders? The Dilemmas of US Forces in Germany*, Boulder, CO, Westview, Press, 1987, *passim*.

11  John Keegan, "Western Europe and its Armies, 1945–1985," in L. H. Gann (ed.), *The Defense of Western Europe*, London, Croom Helm, 1987, p. 23.

12  Summarized from the "Well-Heeled Dwarf Beside the Giant," *The Economist*, 6 December 1986, p. 62.

13  Stanley Kober, "Strategic Defense, Deterrence, and Arms Control," *Washington Quarterly*, Winter 1987, pp. 123–52.

14  See Nelson, *Defenders or Intruders?, passim*.

15  The literature on European unification is immense. See, for instance, Peter Duignan and L. H. Gann, *The Rebirth of the West: The Americanization of the Democratic World 1945–1958*, Oxford, Blackwell, 1991; Gerald Dorfman and Peter Duignan, *Politics in Western Europe*, Stanford, CA, Hoover Institution Press, 1991, especially the chapter on European Unification efforts; Ian Thomson, *The Documentation of the European Communities: A Guide*, London, Mansell, 1989, *passim*; Stanley A. Budd and Alun Jones, *The European Economic Community: A Guide to the Maze*, London, Kogan Page, 1989; Richard Mayne (ed.), *Handbook to the Modern World: Western Europe*, New York, Facts on File Publications, 1986, p. 643. Also see, by the same author,

*The Recovery of Europe*, London, Harper and Row, 1970, and Stanley Hoffmann, "The European Community and 1992," *Foreign Affairs, Fall 1989*, pp. 27–47.


3   The US and its Main Partners: Informal and Formal Links 1949–1985

1   Donald C. McKay, *The United States and France*, Cambridge, MA, Harvard University Press, 1951, p. 271.
2   Quoted in Ted Morgan, *FDR: A Biography*, New York, Simon and Schuster, 1985, pp. 666–7.
3   Anthony Sampson, *Anatomy of Europe*, New York, Harper and Row, 1968, pp. 180–1.
4   See Paul Hollander, "Alienation and Adversary Culture," *Society*, May–June 1988, pp. 41–8.
5   For the part played by Britain and the remaining countries of Western Europe within NATO, see L. H. Gann (ed.), *The Defense of Western Europe*, London, Croom Helm, 1987, *passim*.
6   David Dimbleby and David Reynolds, *An Ocean Apart, The Relationship Between Britain and America in the Twentieth Century*, New York, Random House, 1988, p. 297.
7   Katherine Stephen, "An American's Complaint about the Great Snooty Britons," *International Herald Tribune*, 14 May 1992, p. 7. For a general analysis, see William Roger Louis and Hedley Bull (eds), *The Special Relationship: Anglo-American Relations Since 1945*, Oxford, Clarendon Press, 1986.
8   US exports, in 1988, stood as follows (in million dollars): total: 320,385; Canada: 113,155; EEC: 75,926; Asia: 99,750; Africa: 7,431. Within the EEC, the most important customers were the following: Britain: 18,404; Germany: 14,331; France: 10,086; Italy: 6,782. See *World Almanac and Book of Facts*, New York, 1990, p. 133. For the ranking of foreign countries, see *Gallup Poll* no. 306, March 1991, p. 41.
9   Seymour Martin Lipset, *Continental Divide: the Values and Institutions of the United States and Canada*, New York, Routledge, Chapman and Hall Inc., 1990, *passim*.
10  Andrei Markovits, "Anti-Americanism and the Struggle for a West German Identity," in Peter H. Merkl, ed., *The Federal Republic of Germany at Forty*, New York, New York University Press, 1989, p. 37.
11  James Clyde Sperling, "The Federal Republic of Germany, the United States, and the Atlantic Economy," in Merkl, *The Federal Republic of Germany at Forty*, p. 381. On German political culture, see also Peter Duignan and L. H. Gann, *The Rebirth of the West: The Americanization of the Democratic World, 1945–1958*, Oxford, Blackwell, 1991, pp. 199–210.
12  Werner J. Feld (ed.), "The Role of the Federal Republic of Germany in NATO," in Merkl, *The Federal Republic of Germany at Forty*, p. 405.
13  Cited by James Chace and Elisabeth Malkin, "The Mischief Makers: The American Media and De Gaulle, 1964–1968," paper presented at the Centennial

Conference on De Gaulle and the Construction of Europe, New York, October, 1990.

14   D. L. Hanley, A. P. Kerr, and H. H. Waites, *Contemporary France: Politics and Society Since 1945*, London, Routledge and Kegan Paul, 1979, p. 219.

15   Crane Brinton, *The Americans and the French*, Cambridge, MA, Harvard University Press, 1968, pp. 256–7.

16   Quoted in Martin Anderson, *Revolution*, San Diego, CA, Harcourt Brace Janovich, 1988, p. 19.

17   For a general appraisal of the Low Countries, see Galen Irwin, "Belgium and the Netherlands," in Gerald A. Dorfman and Peter J. Duignan (eds), *Politics in Western Europe*, Stanford, CA, Hoover Institution Press, 1991, 2nd edn, pp. 87–121.

18   John H. Skinner, The Defense Forces of the Low Countries," in Gann, *The Defense of Western Europe*, p. 270.

19   Nigel de Lee, "The Danish and Norwegian Armed Forces," in Gann, *The Defense of Western Europe*, p. 87.

20   Stephan Thernstrom (ed.), *Harvard Encyclopedia of American Ethnic Groups*, Cambridge, MA, Harvard University Press, 1980, table 13, p. 1066.

21   John Lamberton Harper, *America and the Reconstruction of Italy: 1945–1948*, Cambridge, MA, Cambridge University Press, 1986, p. 160.

22   Norman Kogan, *A Political History of Italy: The Postwar Years*, New York, Praeger, 1983, pp. 78, 304.

23   Stanley G. Payne, *The Franco Regime 1936–1975*, Madison, WI, The University of Wisconsin Press, 1987, p. 339.

24   John Gunther, "Spain and Portugal," in Dorfman and Duignan, *Politics in Western Europe*, p. 252.

## 4   Germany: Key to a Continent

1   Werner Weidenfeld, "Kontinuität and Wandel in den deutsch-amerikanischen Beziehungen," in James A. Cooney, Wolfgang-Uwe Friedrich, and Gerald R. Kleinfeld (eds), *Deutsch-Amerikanische Beziehungen*, Frankfurt, Campus Verlag, 1989, pp. 21–36.

2   The German Democratic Republic's population in 1989 amounted to 16,736,000. Its size stood at 41,768 square miles. The addition of East Germany to the Federal Republic of Germany gave united Germany a population of about 78.7 million. The combined territory of united Germany amounted to just under 138,000 square miles. For all aspects of West German history, see Dennis L. Bark and David R. Gress, *A History of West Germany*, 2 vols, Oxford, Blackwell, 1992.

3   Tom Peters, "German Management, the Unsung Economic Miracle," *German Brief*, 8 February 1991, p. 17.

4   William Wallace, *The Transformation of Western Europe*, New York, Council on Foreign Relations Press, 1990, pp. 25–8, 50.

5 *Frankfurter Allgemeine Zeitung*, Information Services; *German Brief* 3, no. 91 (11 January 1991), 25. It should be noted that the statistics refer to book value. In terms of market values (which of course fluctuate) the US position was better. Also the US trade deficit with the world at large was declining.

6 "Capital Punishment," *The Economist*, 18 May 1991, p. 72.

7 "Schools Brief: West Germany Pauses to Fret," *The Economist*, 26 December 1988, pp. 82–3.

8 Norman M. Naimark, "Is It True What They're Saying about East Germany?" *Orbis*, Fall 1979, pp. 549–77. For a more general appraisal, see Naimark, "Revolution and Counterrevolution in Eastern Europe," in Christiane Lemke and Gary Marks (eds), *The Crisis of Socialism in Europe*, Durham, NC, Duke University Press, 1992, pp. 61–83; Michael J. Sodaro, *Moscow, Germany and the West from Kruschev to Gorbachev*, Ithaca, NY, Cornell University Press, 1990.

9 *Statistical Abstract of the United States 1989: 109th Edition*, Washington, DC, U.S. Department of Commerce and Bureau of Statistics, 1989, p. 822. The per capital figures given (in current and constant [1984] dollars were $10,330 for East Germany and $10,320 for West Germany for 1985 and $8,309 as against $8,115 for 1975. In real terms, East Germany's per capital income was nearer to one-third of West Germany's.

10 For the condition of youth, see Barbara Hille, *Nicht nur Blauhemden: Die Situation der Jugenlichen in der ehemaligen DDR*, Melle, Verlag Ernst Noth, Konrad Adenauer-Stiftung, *Deutschland Report*, no. 13, 1991; Wolf Oschliess, *Vierzig zu Null im Klassenkampf: Sprachliche Bilanz von vier Jahrzenten DDR*, Konrad Adenauer-Stiftung, no. 6, 1990.

11 "Viewpoint: The Commerzbank Report on German Business and Finance," *The Economist*, 3 March 1991, p. 70. See also issues of *German Brief*, 1989 and 1990.

12 Francis S. Kiefer, "Eastern German Jobless Rate Soars," *Christian Science Monitor*, 7 May 1991. "Schock mit schlimmen Folgen," *Der Spiegel*, no. 44, 26 October 1992, pp. 102–15.

13 Johannes Rogalla von Bieberstein, "Die Linke und die deutsche Einheit," *Criticon*, March-April 1991, p. 78.

14 German Information Center, *This Week in Germany*, 11 January 1991, pp. 4–5. George Akerlof, Andrew Rose, Janet Yellen, and Helga Hessenius, "Brookings Papers on Economic Activity, 1991," cited in *The Economist*, 11 May 1991, p. 65.

15 "Don't Mention the Wall," *The Economist*, 6 April 1991, p. 67. See also *German Brief*, April 1991.

16 Arthur Hanhardt, "*Die DDR-Politik der USA; Möglichkeiten und Grenzen*," in Cooney *et al.*, *Deutsch-Amerikanische Beziehungen*, pp. 271–80.

17 See "Reunification Blues for East German Scientists," *Science*, August 1991, p. 691; Girard C. Streichen, "Dismantling the East German State," *Christian Science Monitor*, 3 October 1991, p. 4.

18  For the work of the *Treuhandanstalt*, see *German Briefs*, 1990–1.

19  *German Brief*, 3 (10 May 1991), 2.

20  "Carl Zeiss: Cold War," *The Economist*, 18 May 1991, p. 81.

21  Cited by Timothy Garton Ash, "Poland after Solidarity," *New York Review of Books*, 27, no. 11 (13 June 1991), 51.

22  See *German Brief*, 8 November 1991, p. 7.

23  "Landflucht im blauen Dunst," *Der Spiegel*, 27 April 1992, pp. 76–9.

24  *German Tribune*, February 1992, p. 41.

25  For a general discussion, see Irwin L. Collier, "On the First Year of the German Monetary, Economic and Social Union," *Journal of Economic Perspectives 5*, no. 4 (Fall 1991), 179–86.

26  *German Tribune*, February 1992, p. 15.

27  See *German Brief*, September–November 1991, and *Christian Science Monitor*, 19 November 1991, p. 19.

28  Amy Kaslow, "Visiting Experts Describe European Scene," *Christian Science Monitor*, 30 May 1991, p. 9; *Wall Street Journal*, 22 October 1991, p. 8.

29  "The Drifting D-Mark," *The Economist*, June 1991, p. 11.

30  M. Koch-Hillebrecht, *Das Deutschenbild: Gegenwart, Geschichte, Psychologie*, Munich, C. H. Beck, 1977, pp. 64–75. For a full-scale history of US–West German relations, see Wolfram F. Hanrieder, *Germany, America, Europe: Forty Years of German Foreign Policy*, New Haven, CONN, Yale University Press, 1989. The standard history in English on the West German state is Bark and Gress, *A History of West Germany*. For our own interpretation of Germany's political culture see Peter Duignan and L. H. Gann, *The Rebirth of the West: The Americanization of the Democratic World, 1945–1958*, Oxford, Blackwell, 1991, pp. 133–48, 199–209.

31  David White, "When Johnny Goes Marching Home Again," *Financial Times* (London) 31 December 1991, p. 122.

32  Kurt Sontheimer, "How Real is German Anti-Americanism? An Assessment," in Frank Trommler and Joseph McVeigh (eds), *America and the Germans, an Assessment of a Three-Hundred Year History*, vol. 2, Philadelphia, University of Pennsylvania Press, 1985, p. 118.

33  "Of State and Industry," *The Economist*, June 8, 1991, p. 15.

34  "Less Work + More Pay = Higher Costs," *German Brief* (10 May 1991, 1.

35  See *The United States and a United Germany: A Symposium, September 27–30, 1990*, Tempe, Consortium for Atlantic Studies, Arizona State University, 1990; James A. Cooney, Gordon A. Craig, Hans Peter Schwarz, and Fritz Stern (eds), *The Federal Republic and the United States: Changing Political, Social and Economic Relations*, Boulder, CO, Westview Press, 1984; Hanrieder, *Germany, America, Europe*.

36  Peter W. Schroeder, *Stuttgarter Nachrichten*, November 26, 1990.

37  See Edwina S. Campbell in *United States and a United Germany*, pp. 206–18.

38  See *United States and a United Germany*, pp. 233–9.

39  See Andrei S. Markovits and Simon Reich, "Should Europe Fear the Germans?" *German Politics and Society*, no. 23 (Summer 1991), pp. 11–21.

5   East-Central Europe: The Great Transformation 1985–1992

1   The standard reference book is the *Yearbook on International Communist Affairs*, edited by Richard F. Staar, published as an annual from 1966 up to and including 1991, by the Hoover Institution Press, Stanford, CA. The series was introduced by a general survey, *World Communism: A Handbook 1918–1965*, Stanford, Hoover Institution Press, 1973. Also see Richard F. Staar, *The Communist Regimes in Eastern Europe*, Stanford, Hoover Institution Press, 1988; *East-Central Europe and the USSR*, New York, St Martin's Press, 1991; *Foreign Policies of the Soviet Union*, Stanford, Hoover Institution Press, 1991.
2   Ralf Dahrendorf, *Reflections on the Revolution in Europe*, New York, Time Books, 1990, p. 24.
3   Alexander Shtromas and Morton A. Kaplan (eds), *The Soviet Union and the Challenge of the Future*, 4 vols, New York, Paragon House, 1988–9.
4   Clifford A. Rich, "Politics and Government in Italy," in Clifford A. Rich (ed.), *European Politics and Government: A Comparative Approach*, p. 299.
5   Tony Judt, *Marxism and the French Left: Studies on Labour and Politics in France, 1830–1981*. Oxford, Clarendon Press, 1986.
6   Between 1973 and 1986, the US ratio of debt grew by 40.8 percent, that of West Germany by 121 percent, and of Japan by 194.2 percent. See Craig Roberts, "What Everyone 'Knows' About Reaganomics," *Commentary*, vol. 91, no 2 (February 1991).
7   Between 1980 and 1987, the gross national product (in 1982 dollars) went from 3,187 to 3,847. Manufacturing increased from 665 to 839. See table B.11, on p. 321 of *Economic Report of the President Transmitted to the Congress January 1989*, Washington, DC, US Government Printing Office, 1989.
8   Ole R. Hosti, "American Reactions to the USSR: Public Opinion," in Robert Jervis and Seweryn Bialer (eds), *Soviet-American Relations After the Cold War*, Durham, NC, Duke University Press, 1991, pp. 23–47.
9   See Peter Duignan and L. H. Gann, "European Unification, 1944–1992," in Gerald A. Dorfman and Peter J. Duignan, *Politics in Western Europe*, Stanford, CA, Hoover Institution Press, 1991, pp. 378–424.
10  Stanley Hoffmann, "The European Community and 1992," *Foreign Affairs*, Fall, 1989, pp. 27–47.
11  For Soviet relations with the West, see for instance, Walter C. Clemens, *Can Russia Change? The USSR Confronts Global Interdependence*, Boston, Unwin Hyman, 1989; Robbin F. Laird and Susan L. Clark, *The USSR and the Western Alliance*, Boston, Unwin Hyman, 1990.
12  Eli Abel, *The Shattered Bloc: Behind the Upheavel in Eastern Europe*, Boston, Houghton Mifflin Co., 1990, p. 253. For Gorbachev's record, see for instance Stephen White, *Gorbachev in Power*, Cambridge, Cambridge University Press, 1990; Leigh Sarty, *The Soviet Union Under Gorbachev 1985–1990*, Ottawa, Center for Canadian Soviet Studies, Carleton University, 1990; Richard Sakwa, *Gorbachev and his Reforms 1985–1990*, New York, Philip Allan, 1990;

Barukh Hazan, *Gorbachev and His Enemies*, Boulder, CO, Westview Press, 1990. Vilho Harle and Jyrki Iivonen (eds), *Gorbachev and Europe*, London, Pinter, 1990; Françoise Thom, *The Gorbachev Phenomenon*, London, Pinter, 1990; Tsuyoshi Hasegawa and Alex Pravda (eds), *Perestroika: Soviet Domestic and Foreign Policy*, London, Sage Publishers, 1990.

13  Sabrina Petra Ramet, "Priests and Rebels: The Contribution of the Christian Churches to the Revolutions in Eastern Europe," *Mediterranean Quarterly*, vol. 2, no. 4, Fall 1991, pp. 96–110.

14  Johanna Neumann, *The Media: Partners in the Revolution of 1989*, Washington, DC, the Atlantic Council of the United States, 1991.

15  See Anders Aslund, *Gorbachev's Struggle for Economic Reform*, Ithaca, Cornell University Press, 1989. See also Robert D. Kaiser, *Why Gorbachev Happened: His Triumph and His Failure*, New York, Sinon and Schuster, 1991; Ernest Mandel, *Beyond Perestroika: The Future of Gorbachev's Russia*, New York, Routledge, 1989.

16  See for instance Alvin Z. Rubinstein, "Client States: From Empire to Commonwealth," *Orbis*, Winter 1989, pp. 67–8; Clemens, *Can Russia Change?*, *passim*; Laird and Clark, *The USSR and the Western Alliance*. The best surveys of East-Central Europe and the USSR are Keith Sword (ed.), *The Times Guide to Eastern Europe*, London, Times Books, 1990; William E. Griffith (ed.), *Central and Eastern Europe; The Opening Curtain?*, Boulder, CO, Westview Press, 1989; Richard F. Staar, *Foreign Policies of the Soviet Union*, Stanford, CA, Hoover Institution Press, 1991.

17  Timothy Garton Ash, *The Magic Lantern: The Revolution of '89 Witnessed in Warsaw, Budapest, Berlin and Prague*, New York, Random House, 1990, p. 133. See also Timothy Garton Ash, *The Uses of Adversity: Essays on the Fate of Central Europe*, New York, Random House, 1989. Other general works include Stephen R. Graubard (ed.), *Eastern Europe . . . Central Europe . . . Europe*, Boulder, CO, Westview Press, 1991; Gale Stokes (ed.), *From Stalinism to Pluralism: A Documentary History of Eastern Europe Since 1945*, New York, Oxford University Press, 1991; Reiner Weichardt (ed.), *The Central and East European Economies in the 1990s: Prospects and Constraints*, Brussels, NATO Economic Directorate, 1991; Paul M. Johnson, *Redesigning the Communist Economy: The Politics of Economic Reform in Eastern Europe*, Boulder, CO, East European Monographs, 1989; Richard F. Staar (ed.), *East-Central Europe and the USSR*, New York, St Martin's Press, 1991; Charles Gati, *The Bloc That Failed: Soviet-East European Relations in Transition*, Bloomington, IN, Indiana University Press, 1990.

18  For an explanation on how revolutions came to the Soviet bloc, see Gati, *The Bloc That Failed*, and also J. F. Braun, *Surge to Freedom: The End of Communist Rule in Eastern Europe*, Durham, NC, Duke Universities Press, 1991, which describes the collapse of communism in the Warsaw Bloc; Arthur R. Rachwald, "Poland," in Staar, *Yearbook on International Communist Affairs*, 1991, pp. 316–28. For the historical background see, for instance, Michael D. Kennedy, *Professionals, Power and Solidarity in Poland: A Critical Sociology of Soviet-type Society*, New York, Cambridge University Press, 1990; Andre

W. M. Gerrits, *Failure of Authoritarian Change*: *Reform*, *Opposition and Geo-politics in Poland in the 1980s*, Aldershot, Hants, Dartmouth Publishing Co., 1990; Roman Laba, *The Roots of Solidarity, 1982–1985*, Princeton, NJ, Princeton University Press, 1991; Arthur R. Rachwald, *In Search of Poland*: *The Superpowers" Response to Solidarity, 1982–1985*, Stanford, Hoover Institution, 1990; Bártlomiej Kamiński, *The Collapse of State Socialism*: *The Case of Poland*, Princeton, NJ, Princeton University Press, 1991; Adam B. Ulam, *The Communists*: *The Story of Power and Lost Illusions, 1938–1991*, New York, Scribner's, 1992.

19 Elemer Hankis, "What the Hungarians Saw First," in Gwyn Prins (ed.,) *Spring in Winter: The 1989 Revolutions*, Manchester, Manchester University Press, 1990, p. 18.

20 Bennett Kovrig, *Communism in Hungary: From Kun to Kádár*. Stanford, CA, Hoover Institution Press, 1979, p. 431. See also Ash, *The Magic Lantern*, *passim*; János Kornai, *The Road to A Free Economy: Shifting from a Socialist System, The Example of Hungary*, New York, W. W. Norton, 1991; Györgi Csepeli, *Structures and Content of Hungarian National Identity*, Frankfurt-am-Main, Verlag Peter Lang, 1989.

21 Abel, *The Shattered Bloc*, p. 46.

22 Philip Windsor, "German Disunity," in Richard Mayne (ed.), *Handbooks to the Modern World: Western Europe*, New York, Facts on File Publications, 1986, p. 313.

23 F. Stephen Larrabee, "From Reunification to Reassociation: New Dimensions of the German Question," in F. Stephen Larrabee (ed.), *The Two German States and European Security*, New York, St Martin's Press, 1989, p. 29. For US published statistics on the respective per capita incomes of the two German states, see US Department of Commerce, Bureau of Statistics, *Statistical Abstract of the United States, 1989*, Washington, DC, 1989, p. 822, table 1411.

24 For accounts written by senior officials of the former GDR, see, for instance, Günter Schabowski, *Der Absturz*, Berlin, Rowohlt Verlag, 1991, and Carl-Heinz Janson, *Totengräber der GDR*, Düsseldorf, Econ-Verlag, 1991.

25 Zdenek Suda, "Czechoslovakia," in Staar, *Yearbook on International Communist Affairs*, 1990, pp. 319–39; Sharon L. Wolchik, *Czechoslovakia*, New York, Columbia University Press, 1989.

26 For his views see Václav Havel, *Disturbing the Peace: A Conversation with Karel Hvizddala*, New York, A. Knopf, 1990.

27 Trond Gilbert, *Nationalism and Communism in Romania: The Rise and Fall of Ceauşescu's Personal Dictatorship*, Boulder, CO, Westview Press, 1990; Daniel M. Nelson, *Romanian Politics in the Ceauşescu Era*, New York, Gordon and Breach, 1988.

28 Cited in Robert R. King, "Romania," in Staar, *Yearbook on International Communist Affairs*, 1990, p. 347.

29 For the general background, see David A. Dyker, *Yugoslavia: Socialism, Development and Debt*, New York, Routledge, 1990; Monika Beckman-Petey, *Der Yugoslavische Föderalismus*, Munich, Oldenbourg, 1990; Harold Lydall,

*Yugoslavia in Crisis*, New York, Oxford University Press, 1989; Misha Glenny, *The Full of Yugoslavia: The Third Balkan War*, London, Penguin, 1992.

30  Nicholas C. Pano, *Albania*, New York, Columbia University Press, 1989.

31  See Aimee Breslow, "Monitoring Eastern Europe's Transition," *Washington Quarterly*, Autumn 1991, pp. 203–18, for an excellent survey of the literature on the revolution in Eastern Europe.

32  Daniel N. Nelson, "Europe's Unstable East," *Foreign Policy*, no. 82, Spring 1991, pp. 137–58.

33  Cited by Daniel Chirot, "After Socialism What? The Global Implications of the Revolutions of 1989 in Eastern Europe," *Contentions*, Fall 1991, pp. 29–48.

34  Stephen Sestanovitch, "Fiddler on the Roof: Gorbachev's Balancing Act," *The New Republic*, 27 May 1991, p. 20.

35  John B. Dunlop, "Will the Soviet Union Survive Until the Year 2000?" *The National Interest*, no. 18, Winter 1989–90, pp. 65–75; Andrei Amalrik, *Will the Soviet Union Survive Until 1984?*, New York, Harper and Row, 1970.

36  Janice Brown and Grazyna Sikorska, *Conscience and Captivity: Religion in Eastern Europe*, Washington, DC, Ethics and Public Policy Center, 1988.

37  Paper given by Roman Leszczyński, "Financial Markets and Capitalization," Conference on the Economic Transition in Central and Eastern Europe, Hoover Institution, May 1991.

38  For work on this subject, see, for instance, Susan M. Collins and Dani Rodrick, *Eastern Europe and the Soviet Union in the World Economy*, Washington, DC, Policy Analyses in International Economics Series, Institute for International Economics, 1991.

39  Thomas Moore, *Privatization Now or Else: The Impending Failure of Democracy and Freedom*, Stanford, CA, Hoover Institution Press, 1991.

40  *Ibid.*, pp. 3–4.

41  *Ibid.*, p. 6

42  Eric Bourne, "New Western Aid Hints Shift of View of Romania as Outsider," *Christian Science Monitor*, 22 May 1991, p. 6.

43  Ash, *The Magic Lantern*, p. 136.

44  In the 1991 elections, only 42.5 percent of the electorate went to the polls. The legatees of the Solidarity movement contained a majority. But they were badly splintered, in part as a result of an electoral law that provided even the "Friends of Beer Party" with a few representatives in parliament. The two communist successor parties scored a respectable vote (12.1 percent of the vote for the Democratic Left Alliance, and 8.9 percent for the Peasant Party). By contrast, the Democratic Union, headed by former Solidarity prime minister Tadeusz Mazowiecki, received 12.2 percent. Prime minister Jan Krzystof Bielecki's Liberal Democratic Congress received 7.2 percent. Other groups comprised Catholic Action, 8.8 percent; Central Alliance, 8.7; Confederation for an Independent Poland, 8.6; and numerous additional bodies. *The Economist*, 2 November, 1991, p. 43.

45  See Nelson, "Europe's Unstable East," *passim*.

46  See Steven L. Burg, "Yugoslavia in Crisis," *Washington Quarterly*, Autumn 1991, pp. 5–19.

47 Howard LaFranchi, "EC Plans Migrant Policy," *Christian Science Monitor*, 7 August 1991.
48 Klaus Hornung, "Sturm auf Europa," *Criticon*, no. 118, March–April 1990, pp. 85–7.
49 Reported in the *San Francisco Chronicle*, 21 June 1991, p. 2.
50 Czechoslovak forces in 1991 were expected to fall from 200,000 to 130,000. Hungarian force levels declined from 100,000 to 70,000 men. Polish forces diminished from 300,000 men in 1988 to about 250,000 men thereafter. The Bulgarian army retained about 100,000 men, the Romanian army 180,000 or thereabouts; the Bundeswehr was scheduled to number 370,000 men. See Nelson, "Europe's Unstable East," pp. 137–58.

6 Embattled Empire: From Soviet Union to CIS

1 "Independent Ukraine," *The Economist*, 7 December 1991, pp. 54–7.
2 Richard F. Staar, *The New Russian Armed Forces: Preparing for War or Peace?* Stanford, CA, Hoover Institution Press, 1992, *passim*; an important source.
3 The literature on the Soviet empire is vast. For the individual nationalities within the Soviet Union, see the various books in the *Studies of Nationalities in the USSR* series, General Editor Wayne S. Vucinich, published by the Hoover Institution Press, Stanford, CA. For an interpretative study, see Robert Conquest, *The Last Empire: Nationality and the Soviet Future*, Stanford, CA, Hoover Institution Press, 1986. See also Lubomyr Hajda and Mark Beissinger (eds), *The Nationalities Factor in Soviet Politics and Society*, Boulder, CO, Westview Press, 1990; Henry S. Rowen and Charles Wolf, Jr (eds), The *Future of the Soviet Empire*, New York, St Martin's Press, 1987; Rachel Denber, *The Soviet Nationality Reader: The Disintegration in Context*, Boulder, CO, Westview Press, 1992.
4 See for instance the following: Mervyn Matthews, *Poverty in the Soviet Union: The Lifestyles of the Underprivileged in Recent Years*, Cambridge, Cambridge University Press, 1986, and *Patterns of Deprivation in the Soviet Union Under Brezhnev and Gorbachev*, Stanford, CA, Hoover Institution Press, 1989; Anthony Jones, Walter D. Connor, and David E. Powell (eds), *Soviet Social Problems*, Boulder, CO, Westview Press, 1991; Rowen and Wolf, *The Future of the Soviet Empire*; Brad Roberts and Nina Belayeva (eds), *After Perestroika: Democracy in the Soviet Union*, Washington, DC, Center for Strategic and International Studies, 1991.
5 R. J. Rummel, *Lethal Politics: Soviet Genocide and Mass Murders Since 1917*, Brunswick NJ, Transaction Publishing, 1990.
6 Stephen Kotkin, *Steeltown, USSR: Soviet Society in the Gorbachev Era*, Berkeley, CA, University of California Press, 1991.
7 For a perceptive analysis, see Daniel Chirot, (ed.), *The Crisis of Leninism and the Decline of the Left*, Seattle, WA, University of Washington Press, 1991.
8 Ellen Mickiewicz, "Ethnic Differentiation and Political Communication," in Jones et al., *Soviet Social Problems*, pp. 24–38.

9  Walter C. Clemens, Jr, *Baltic Independence and the Russian Empire*, New York, St Martin's Press, 1991.

10 Bohdan Kravchenko, *Social Change and National Consciousness in Twentieth Century Ukraine*, London, Macmillan, 1985, p. 171.

11 For the structure of communist rule and its crisis see, for instance, Richard F. Staar (ed.), *East-Central Europe and the USSR*, New York, St Martin's Press, 1991; Richard F. Staar, *The Communist Regimes in Eastern Europe*, 5th edn, Stanford, CA, Hoover Institution Press, 1988; Vladimir Tismaneu, *The Crisis of Marxist Ideology in Eastern Europe; The Poverty of Utopia*, London, Routledge, 1988; Jacek Kuron, Janos Kis, Vladimir Bukovsky, Vilem Precan, "The Crumbling of the Soviet Bloc," *Journal of Democracy*, Winter 1990, pp. 71–90; Roy Medvedev, "After the Communist Collapse: New Political Tendencies in Russia," *Dissent*, Fall 1992, pp. 489–95. Adam B. Ulam, *The Communists: The Story of Power and Lost Illusions: 1948–1991*, New York, Scribner's 1992.

12 Charles Gati, "The Unsettled Condition of Eastern Europe," in Rowen and Wolf, *The Future of the Soviet Empire*. A more recent appraisal is Charles Gati, "East Central Europe: The Morning After," *Foreign Affairs*, 1990–91, pp. 129–45.

13 Richard F. Staar, "East-Central Europe: The End of the Beginning," in Staar, *East-Central Europe and the USSR*, pp. 1–2.

14 Robert Conquest, "I Told You So," *Encounter*, September 1990, p. 24.

15 David Remnick, "Dead Souls," *The New York Review of Books*, 19, December 1991, vol. 38, no. 21, p. 79.

16 For his own background, see Eduard Shevardnadze, *The Future Belongs to Freedom*, New York, Free Press 1991.

17 Between 1979 and 1987, US exports to Eastern Europe diminished (in million dollars) from 5,913 (out of a total of 184,473) to 2,238 (out of a total of 249,570). By contrast, the US exported more than four times that amount to the OPEC countries alone. *Economic Report to the President Transmitted to Congress, January, 1989*, Washington, DC, Government Printing Office, 1989, p. 427.

18 Ludmilla Alekseeva, *Soviet Dissent: Contemporary Movements for National, Religious, and Human Rights*, Middletown, CONN, Wesleyan University Press, 1987.

19 Ronald I. McKinnon, "Macroeconomic Control in Liberalizing Socialist Economies: Asian and European Parallels," paper presented to the CEPR Conference "Finance and Development in Europe," Santiago de Compostela, Spain, December 1991.

20 Leslie W. Bowden, *Perestroika in the Soviet Union and Western Involvement*, Washington, DC, The Atlantic Council, 1989, p. 44, cited from *Trud*.

21 Gabriel Schoenfeld, "Bedtime Story: Lights Out for the Soviet CP," *The New Republic*, 8 July 1991, pp. 15–17.

22 For its history, see Christopher Andrew and Oleg Gordievsky, *KGB: The Inside Story of Its Foreign Operations from Lenin to Gorbachev*, New York, Harper-Collins, 1990.

23　Abraham Brumberg, "Russia After Perestroika," *New York Review of Books*, 27 June 1991, pp. 53–60.

24　"Indicators of Change in Soviet Security Policies, August 1–October 1990," The Atlantic Council of the United States, *Bulletin*, vol. 1, no. 21, 5 October 1990, pp. 1–2. For a wider survey see *Orbis*, "The Soviet Military Today," Spring issue, 1991.

25　The Atlantic Council of the United States, *Bulletin*, vol. 1, no. 12, 30 May 1990, p. 199.

26　*Ibid.*, vol. 11, no. 2, February 1991, p. 1.

27　Richard F. Staar, "Soviets Fail to Follow Spirit and Letter of CFE Treaty," *San Francisco Chronicle*, 16 July 1991, p. 19. See also Richard F. Staar, *USSR Foreign Policy: A New Era?* Stanford, CA, Hoover Institution Press, Working Papers Series 1–89–15, 1989.

28　Stephan Sestanovitch, "Fiddler on the Roof: Gorbachev's Balancing Act," *The New Republic*, 27 May 1991, p. 22.

29　"Power to the Republics," *Financial Times*, 27 June 1991, p. 18.

30　Daniel Sneider, "Draft Program for Communist Plenum . . .," and "Gorbachev Squares off with Party Hard-Liners," *Christian Science Monitor*, 25 July 1991, pp. 1–3.

31　Daniel Sneider, "Gorbachev Bids for Investment and G-7 Backing," *Christian Science Monitor*, 15 July 1991, p. 2.

32　John B. Dunlop, *Christian Democracy Antidote to Extreme Russian Nationalism*, Stanford, CA, Hoover Institution Press, Working Papers in International Studies, 1991; Medvedev, "After the Communist Collapse," pp. 489–95.

33　Interview in *Der Spiegel*, "Gespräch mit Vizepräsident Alexander Ruzkoi," no. 44, 26 October 1992, pp. 202–16.

34　Richard F. Staar, "The Next Coup Attempt in Russia," *Chicago Tribune*, 12 November 1992, pp. 11–12.

35　"Russia: Anniversary Blues," *The Economist*, August 15, 1992, p. 42.

36　Maxim Kniazov, "Death of a Mastodon," *Christian Science Monitor*, 16 July 1991, p. 7.

37　Cited in "The Big Picture: Resolving the Leadership Crisis," *New Dimensions*, vol. 5, no. 8, August 1991, p. 50.

38　For a discussion, see for instance, Michael McGwire, *Perestroika and Soviet National Security*, Washington, DC, The Brookings Institution, 1991.

39　Quoted in *Christian Science Monitor*, 8 July 1991, p. 1.

40　For a detailed discussion, see John B. Dunlop, *Ethnic Russians Confront a Loss of Empire*, Stanford, CA, Hoover Institution Studies Working Paper 1–91–9, 1991.

41　Marshall I. Goldman, "Three Days that Shook My World," *World Monitor*, October 1991, pp. 30–4. For Gorbachev's own views, see Mikhail Gorbachev, *The August Coup: The Truth and the Lessons*, New York, Harper-Collins, 1991.

42　For the first biography in English see John Morrison, *Boris Yeltsin, from Bolshevik to Democrat*, New York, Dutton, 1991. See also Boris Yeltsin, *Against the Grain: An Autobiography*, New York, Summit, 1991; Leon Aron, "Boris Yeltsin's First 100 Days," *Backgrounder Paper no. 869*, Washington,

DC, The Heritage Foundation, 1991; Vladimir Solovyov and Elena Klepikova, *Boris Yeltsin: A Political Biography*, New York, Putnam and Sons, 1992.

43  Dale Hersping, "The Soviet Military Reshapes in Response to Malaise," *Orbis*, Spring 1991.

44  *Der Spiegel* interview with President of the Officers Stanislaw Terechov, "Alles wird verschachert," and "Erhebe dich, du grosses Land," in *Der Spiegel*, no. 45, 2 November 1992, pp. 194–6.

45  Vitali Vitaliev, "For System Read Mafia," a review of Arkady Vaksberg, *The Soviet Mafia*, London, Weidenfeld and Nicolson, 1991, in the *Times Literary Supplement*, 4 October 1991, p. 12.

46  For a general discussion see Annelise Anderson, *The Ruble Problem: A Competitive Solution*, Stanford, CA, Hoover Institution Press, 1992.

47  "The Lords of Misrule," *The Economist*, 6 April 1991, p. 20.

48  Elisabeth Rubinfien, "Russia Offers Privatization Plan Amid Turmoil, Currency Crisis," *Wall Street Journal*, 2 October 1992, p. A11.

49  Caroll Boger, "How Much Hunger?," *Newsweek*, 2 December 1991, pp. 32–4.

50  Richard F. Staar, "Russia Has Lots of Grain – Just Ask the Army," *Wall Street Journal*, January 21, 1992, p. 20A, translated into Russian by *Izvestia* (Moscow), 22 January 1992.

51  Cited by Michael Ignatieff, "The New Republics," *The New York Review of Books*, 21 November 1991, pp. 30–2.

52  Cited in Robert Wright, "The Experiment that Failed: Why Soviet Science Collapsed," *The New Republic*, 28 October 1991, pp. 20–3.

53  Elisabeth Rubinstein, "Soviets Term Foreign Debt Very Grave," *Wall Street Journal*, 12 November 1991, p. k2.

54  In 1992 the majority of the CIS members – Russia, Kazakhstan, Uzbekistan, Tajikistan, and Armenia – concluded a collective security pact which committed them to come to one another's aid in case of attack, and which secured to Russia a controlling military role. This pact, concluded at Tashkent, excluded Belarus, Azerbaijan, Moldova, and Kirghizstan.

55  "Mere Shock or Therapy Too," *The Economist*, 22 February 1992, p. 63.

56  Graham Allison and Robert Blackwell, "America's Stake in the Soviet Future," *Foreign Affairs*, Summer 1991, pp. 778–91. For wider problems of Soviet relations with the West, see Richard F. Staar (ed.), *United States-East European Relations in the 1990s*, New York, Crane Russak, 1989, and his *Foreign Policies of the Soviet Union*, Stanford, CA, Hoover Institution Press, 1991.

57  Amy Kaslow, "Germany Pushes Western Aid to the Soviet Union," *Christian Science Monitor*, 16 July 1991, and "The World From Bonn," *Christian Science Monitor*, 23 July 1991, p. 6.

58  William D. Eggers, "Guidelines for Aid to the Soviet Union," *Backgrounder Paper* no. 856, Washington, DC, The Heritage Foundation, 1991.

59  See "Economic and Financial Indicators," *The Economist*, 20 July 1991, p. 118.

60  See for instance our own assessment in Peter Duignan and L. H. Gann, *The United States and Africa: A History*, Cambridge, Cambridge University Press, 1984, pp. 314–24. For a general critique written at a time when foreign aid

was still in fashion, see P. T. Bauer, *Dissent on Development: Studies and Debates in Development Economics*, Cambridge, MA, Harvard University Press, 1972.

61 Ala Stoga, "West's Summit Could be Diverted by 'Grand Bargain,'" *Christian Science Monitor*, 2 July 1991, p. 8.

62 "The Shaky Economics of Soviet Aid," *The Economist*, 20 July 1991, p. 81.

63 Dimitry Mikheyev and Alan Reynolds, "Do the Russians Need Food Aid?" *Hudson Opinion*, January 1992, p. 1.

64 Horst Tomann, *The Transition Problem in Eastern Europe: Some Lessons for Germany*, Berlin, Institute für Wirtschaftspolitik-und Wirtschaftsgeschichte, 1992, p. 7.

65 Eggers, "Guidelines for Aid to the Soviet Union," p. 13.

66 In 1992 the Russian parliament approved a treaty to eliminate a third of US and ex-Soviet strategic weapons. This was the START treaty, the last major arms limitations agreement between the US and the former Soviet Union, signed in 1991. A more radical "framework" agreement, signed between former President Bush and Boris Yeltsin in 1992, provided for additional reductions to about 3,000 to 4,000 warheads in each arsenal. The Russian military acknowledged that the government, at the time of writing, had found only a small part of the funds needed to dismantle weapons.

7 The US and the New Europe 1985–1993

1 "The New Europeans," *The Economist*, 16 November 1991.

2 For statistical details see "Aid Addicts," *The Economist*, 8 August 1992, p. 61, and "Featherbedded Farmers," *The Economist*, 23 May 1992. In terms of direct payments, cheap loans, and price support (known as the producer subsidy equivalent, PSE), the EC's was not the highest in dollar terms. As a proportion of its production it was 49 percent in 1991, as opposed to Japan's 66 percent, or Switzerland's 80 percent. American farmers got much less support, with a PSE of 30 percent. New Zealand, one of the world's most efficient agricultural producers, stood at the bottom of the list with only 4 percent of its farm output subsidized.

3 "Economic and Financial Indicators," *The Economist*, 20 July 1991, p. 118.

4 The EC's exports (in million dollars) went up as follows: 1960: 43,539; 1970: 116,664; 1980: 691,208; 1989: 1,133,259. Corresponding US figures were as follows: 1960: 20,601; 1970: 43,241; 1980: 220,786; 1989: 363,985. Particularly impressive was the performance of Germany, whose exports in 1989 nearly equalled the US's, whereas in 1960, they had been only half of the US's. See Directorate of Intelligence, *Handbook of Economic Statistics, 1990: A Reference Aid*, Washington, DC, US Government Printing Office, 1990, p. 144.

5 "How Europe has Failed," *The Economist*, 24 November 1984, p. 13.

6 "Policing Europe's Single Market," *The Economist*, 20 January 1990, pp. 69–70.

7 Michael Silva and Bertil Sjögren, *Europe 1992 and the New World Power Game*, New York, John Wiley, 1990, p. 126.

8 *Ibid.*

9   "The History of the Maastricht Summit," *The Economist*, 30 November 1991, p. 47; Derek W. Urwin, *The Community of Europe: A History of European Integration Since 1945*, London, Longman, 1991, esp. pp. 234–7; Michael Burgess, *Federalism and European Union: Political Ideas, Influences and Strategies in the European Community, 1972–1987*, London, Routledge, 1989; Roger Morgan, *West European Politics Since 1945: The Shaping of the European Community*, London, B. T. Batsford, 1972.

10  *Financial Times*, 19 June 1991, p. 11. "Policing Europe's Single Market," *The Economist*, 20 January 1990, pp. 69–70. The texts of the Commission's proposals are published as COM documents by the Commission. Proposed legislation appears in the "C" Series of the Official Journal of the European Community. General works on European unification include Peter Duignan and L. H. Gann, "European Unification, 1944–1992: An Overview," in Gerald A. Dorfman and Peter J. Duignan (eds), *Politics in Western Europe*, Stanford, CA, Hoover Institution Press, 1991, pp. 378–424; European Community Study Group, *Making It Work: The Future of the European Community*, London, Centre for Policy Studies, 1984; Kim R. Holmes and Jay P. Kosminsky, *Reshaping Europe: Strategies for a Post-Cold War Europe*, Washington, DC, The Heritage Foundation, 1990; Silva and Sjögren, *Europe 1992 and the New Power Game*; Gregory F. Treverton (ed.), *The Shape of the New Europe*, New York, Council of Foreign Relations, 1991.

11  Stanley Hoffmann, "The European Community and 1992," *Foreign Affairs*, Fall 1989, p. 41.

12  "The History of the Maastricht Summit," *The Economist*, 30 November 1991, pp. 46–7.

13  *This Week in Germany*, 13 December 1991, p. 1.

14  "Tangled Transfers," *The Economist*, 7 November 1992, p. 102.

15  Jacques Delors, *Le Nouveau Concert Européen*, Paris, Editions Odile Jacob, 1992.

16  "Recession or Doom," *The Economist*, 24 October 1992, p. 13.

17  Angelo Codevilla, "The Coming Euromess," *National Review*, 8 June 1992, p. 42.

18  *Wall Street Journal*, 11 December 1991, pp. 3 and 10.

19  Martin Wolf on paradoxes of Maastricht, *Financial Times*, 10 December 1992.

20  See Andrew Hill, "The S word . . .," *Financial Times*, December, 1992.

21  For a recent appraisal, see Derek W. Unwin, *The Community of Europe: A History of European Integration Since 1945*, New York, Longman, 1991; John Palmer, *1992 and Beyond*, Luxembourg, European Communities Publication, 1989.

22  Tony Allen-Mills, "Kohl's Triumph Stokes Fires of Neo-Nazi Hate," *The Sunday Times*, 15 December 1991, p. 19.

23  "Lest a Fortress Arise," *The Economist*, 26 October 1991, pp. 81–2; Mark M. Nelson, "Pact Expands Europe's Common Market," *Wall Street Journal*, 23 October 1991, p. A12.

24  "Turkey, Europe, and the United States," The Atlantic Council, *Bulletin*, vol. 11, no. 5, 28 May 1991.

25  The criteria set were as follows: Low inflation (the inflation rate should be no more than 1.5 percent above the average of the three EC countries with the lowest price rises); satisfactory interest rates (long-term interest rates should be within two percentage points of the average of the three members with the lowest rates); low deficits (national budget deficits must be less than 3 percent of the GDP); low debts (the public debt ration was not to exceed 60 percent of GDP; currency stability (a national currency must not have been devalued in the two previous years and must have remained with the normal 2.25 percent fluctuation margins of the exchange rate mechanism (ERM). See *The Economist*, 14 December 1991, p. 52.

26  Timothy Garton Ash, Michael Mertes, and Dominique Moisi, "Let the East Europeans In," *The New York Review of Books*, 24 October 1991, no. 17, pp. 19–22.

27  Howard LaFranchi, "EC is Likely to be Larger, Sooner," *Christian Science Monitor*, 11 September 1991, p. 3.

28  For the text, see Jean De Ruyt, *European Political Cooperation: Toward a Unified European Foreign Policy*, Washington DC, The Atlantic Council of the United States, Occasional Paper, 1989.

29  *This Week in Germany*, 20 December 1992, p. 1. The European Community adopted the following guidelines for the recognition of new states in Eastern Europe and the Soviet Union: the EC declares that it will be willing to recognize those states that have constituted themselves on a democratic basis, accepted the appropriate international obligations and have committed themselves in good faith to a peaceful process and to negotiations; it will not recognize entities that are the result of aggression.

30  James D. Bell, *Catching the Boat: The 1992 Opportunity: An Atlantic Business Perspective*, Washington, DC, The Atlantic Council of the United States, Occasional Paper, 1990, p. 11.

31  Walter Goldstein, "EC-Euro-Stalling," *Foreign Policy*, no. 85, Winter 1991–92, pp. 129–47.

32  Thomas A. Stewart, "The New American Century," *Fortune*, Special Issue, Spring-Summer, 1991, pp. 12–23.

33  *The Economist*, 7 September 1991, pp. 16–17.

34  Nancy J. Perry, "The Workers of the Future," *Fortune*, Special Issue, Spring-Summer, 1991, p. 69.

35  International Institute for Strategic Studies, *The Military Balance: 1989–1990*, London, ISS, 1989, pp. 32–42.

36  Richard F. Staar, "Soviet Arms Out of Control," *New York Times*, 19 August 1991, p. 11.

37  See L. H. Gann (ed.), *The Defense of Western Europe*, London, Croom Helm, 1987, for details. See Peter Duignan and L. H. Gann, *The Rebirth of the West: The Americanization of the Democratic World, 1945–1958*, Oxford, Blackwell, 1991, pp. 365–408, for NATO's origins and history. See also Colin McInnes, *Nato's Changing Strategic Agenda: The Conventional Defense of Central Europe*, London, Unwin Hyman, 1991.

38  Graham Allison, "Nuclear Objectives," *Financial Times*, 3 January 1992, p. 8.

39  *Washington Post*, 6 January 1991.

40  Robert F. Ellsworth, "European Security in a New and Different World," *The Atlantic Council Special Report*, Washington, DC, vol. 11, no. 13, 5 November 1991.

41  Laurence Scheinman, *Non-Proliferation and the IAEA: A US Soviet Agenda: Report of the Atlantic Council's Program on Nuclear Non-Proliferation*, Washington, DC, The Atlantic Council of the United States, June 1990.

42  For recent publications that attempt to see into the future see Andrew J. Goodpaster and Ian O. Lesser, *NATO To the Year 2,000: Challenges for Coalition, Deterrence and Defense: A Report of the Atlantic Council's Working Group on the Future of NATO*, Washington, DC, The Atlantic Council of the United States, 1988; S. J. Deitchman, *After the Cold War: US Security for the Future*, Washington, DC, The Atlantic Council of the United States, 1990; Willem F. van Eekelen, *The Changing Environment of Transatlantic Relations*, Paris, European Strategy Group, 1991; National Defense University, *The Alliance at Forty: Strategic Perspectives for the 1990s, and Beyond*, Washington, DC, 1991; Lawrence S. Kaplan, *NATO and the United States: The Enduring Alliance*, Boston, MA, Twayne, 1988.

43  Alfred Cahen [formerly Secretary-General of WEU], *The Western European Union and NATO: Building a European Defence Identity Within the Context of Atlantic Solidarity*, London, Brassey's, 1989; and *The Western European Union (WEU) and NATO: Strengthening the Second Pillar of the Alliance*, Washington, DC, The Atlantic Council of the United States, 1990.

44  Ted Galen Carpenter, "US Must Shake Its NATO Habit," *Christian Science Monitor*, 19 June 1991, p. 18.

45  For earlier projections, see, for instance, G. Jonathan Greenwald and Leonard Sullivan, Jr, *The Western Stake in the Future of the Soviet Economy*, Washington, DC; Andrew J. Goodpaster, Walter J. Stoessel and Robert Kennedy, *U.S. Policy Toward the Soviet Union: A Long-Term Western Perspective 1987–2000*, Lanham, MD, University Press of America, 1988.

46  Alain Minc, *La Vengeance des nations*, Paris, Grasset, 1991, *passim*.

47  Catherine Bacarrère-Bécane, *The Soviet Army in Search of a New Identity*, Arlington, VA, US-CREST, European Viewpoints Series, no. 1, August 1991, p. 50.

48  For detailed suggestions, see van Eekelen, *The Changing Environment of Transatlantic Relations*, p. 51ff.

49  Cited by Scott Sullivan, Ann McDaniel, and Pia Hinckle, "The Birth of a New NATO," *Newsweek*, 18 November 1991, p. 32.

50  For details see International Institute for Strategic Studies, *The Military Balance 1990–1991*, pp. 12–27; Lambert W. Veenendaal, "Conventional Stability in Europe in 1991: Problems and Solutions," *NATO Review*, vol. 39 no. 4, August 1991, pp. 21–6. For the case against US involvement see, for instance, Earl C. Ravenal, *Designing Defense for a New World Order: The Military Budget in 1992 and Beyond*, Washington, The Cato Institute, 1991; David P. Calleo, *NATO: Reconstruction or Dissolution*, Washington, DC, Johns Hopkins Foreign Policy Institute, 1992; Center for Strategic and International

Studies, *The Atlantic Partnership: An Industrial Perspective on Transatlantic Defense Cooperation*, Washington, DC, CSIS, 1991; The Atlantic Council of the United States and the Institute of World Economy and the International Relations of the Soviet Academy of Sciences, *The Future of the Soviet Academy of Sciences in a Pluralistic World*, Washington, DC, 1991.

51 Fernando Nogueira, "The European Security Architecture: The Role of the Eurogroup," *NATO Review*, vol. 39 no. 4, August 1991, p. 5; Elizabeth Pond, *After the Wall: American Policy Toward Germany*, New York, Twentieth Century Fund, 1990, p. 75ff.

52 Guy Coeme, "The Role of IEPG," *NATO Review*, vol. 39 no. 4, August 1991, pp. 15–20.

53 Cahen, *The Western European Union (WEU) and NATO*, p. 33.

54 "WEU Set To Take on Bridging Role...," *The German Tribune*, 14 July 1991, p. 11.

55 Deniz Yuksel-Beten, "CCMS: NATO's Environmental Programme..." *NATO Review*, vol. 39 no. 4, 1991, pp. 27–31.

56 "Helsinki Accords," *The German Tribune*, 29 September 1991, p. 9.

57 See Francine Kiefer, in *Christian Science Monitor*, 3 February 1992, p. 4.

58 See *Political Handbook of the World: 1992–1993*, New York, McGraw-Hill, 1992, *passim*, for all groups in Europe.

8   The US: A Hopeful Future

1 Cynthia Tucker, "Democrats Ignore '92 Campaign Fodder," *San Francisco Chronicle*, 15 August 1991, p. A25. For an opposing journalistic assessment see op-ed. page, *New York Times*, 16 October 1992.

2 According to a survey published in *American Enterprise*, July–August 1991, p. 76, the precise percentages were 19 for senators, and local office holders respectively, 17 for congressmen, 13 for trade unionists.

3 "American Survey," *The Economist*, 26 October 1991, p. 23. In fact, though wages slowed down in their growth, there was however a shift from money to more non-wage compensation, i.e. health insurance, vacations, and the fringe benefits. If these are factored in total, compensation almost doubled.

4 Rolf Winter, *Ami go home, Plädoyer für den Abschied von einem gewalttätigen Land*, Munich, Goldmann Verlag, 1990, especially pp. 128, 132.

5 For the British experience, see, for instance, Aaron L. Friedberg, *The Weary Titan: Britain and the Experience of Relative Decline 1895–1905*, Princeton, NJ, Princeton University Press, 1988.

6 See a major review essay by Paul Kennedy, "Can the US Remain Number One?," *New York Review of Books*, 16 March 1989, pp. 9–16, in which he discusses four books: Friedberg, *The Weary Titan*; David C. Hendrickson, *The Future of American Strategy*, New York, Holmes and Meier, 1987; Annelise Anderson and Dennis L. Bark (eds), *Thinking About America: The United States in the 1990s*, Stanford, CA, Hoover Institution Press, 1988; and

David M. Abshire, *Preventing World War II: A Realistic Grand Strategy*, New York, Harper and Row, 1988.

7 For a brief summary of his views, see Paul Kennedy, "The (Relative) Decline of America," *Atlantic Monthly*, August 1987, pp. 29–38.

8 Steve Dryden, "Europe in America," *Europe*, June 1991, pp. 6–8.

9 Jesse Birnbaum, "Crybabies: Eternal Victims: Hypersensitivy and Special Pleading . . .," *Time*, 12 August 1991, pp. 16–18. For a detailed refutation of the declinists see Richard B. McKenzie, *America: What Went Right*, Washington, DC, Cato Institute, 1992.

10 Marsha Tonsured and Craig Marine, "Many S. F. Looters Caught in Feeding Frenzy," *San Francisco Examiner*, 10 May 1992, p. A14.

11 Walter Shapiro, "Lessons of Los Angeles," *Time*, 18 May 1992, pp. 38–9.

12 For a brilliant discussion see Thomas Sowell, *Ethnic America: A History*, New York, Basic Books, 1981, especially p. 216ff.

13 According to *The Economist Pocket World In Figures*, London, Economist Books, 1990, p. 76, the following was the number of murders per 100,000 population in 1986: Philippines 38.7; Lesotho 36.4; Sri Lanka 18.9; Jamaica 17.96; Guyana 15.6; Lebanon 13.17; Zimbabwe 12.6; Thailand 12.36; Bahamas 12.2; Botswana 11.0; Rwanda 9.7; Honduras 9.4; Tanzania 8.77; USA 8.60; Mexico, 7.42; Luxembourg 7.0.

14 *The Economist*, 5 December 1992, p. 36.

15 Robert Middlekauff, *The Glorious Cause: The American Revolution 1763–1780*, New York, Oxford University Press, 1982, p. 36. In Boston and Philadelphia at the same time the lower half of the population owned only 5 percent of the taxable wealth: Lee Soltow, *Distribution of Wealth and Income in the United States in 1798*, Pittsburgh, Pittsburgh University Press, 1990.

16 Cited in Chaim Berman, *London's East End: Point of Arrival*, New York, Macmillan, 1975, pp. 54–5. For a similar description of the Irish in New York, see Charles Wentworth Dilke, *Greater Britain: A Record of Travel in English-Speaking Countries during 1866–1867*, Philadelphia, J. B. Lippincott, 1869, vol. 1, p. 252.

17 Andrew M. Greeley, *The American Catholic: A Social Portrait*, New York, Basic Books, 1977, especially p. 57.

18 See for instance L. H. Gann and Peter Duignan, *The Hispanics in the United States: A History*, Boulder, CO, Westview Press, 1986. See also Earl Shorris, *Latinos: A Biography of the People*, New York, W. W. Norton and Co., 1992.

19 According to the most recent figures published in *The American Enterprise*, July–August 1991, p. 97, 2 percent of faculty in area and ethnic studies describe themselves as conservative; 14 percent in the political and social sciences, anthropology, and social work; 15 percent in the humanities; 20 percent in economics; as against 52 percent in business management and 68 percent in industrial arts.

20 According to 1990 census figures there are some 20.1 million Hispanics in the US. Of these, 63 percent are Mexican-Americans, 11 percent are Puerto Ricans, 5 percent Cuban-Americans, 12 percent are Central or South American, and 8 percent are classified as other. African-Americans now number

about 12 percent of the population; by the year 2010 the blacks are supposed to rise into second place. All such forecasts are, however, speculative.

21 Berman, *London's East End*, p. 39.

22 We have written on this subject at length with regard to the Hispanic immigrants in Gann and Duignan, *The Hispanics in the United States: A History*.

23 Frank Trommler and Joseph McVeigh (eds), *America and the Germans: An Assessment of a Three-Hundred Year History*, Philadelphia, University of Pennsylvania Press, 1985, paperback edition, 1990, p. xl.

24 For a detailed breakdown that compares significant different ethnic groups see *Public Opinion*, October–November 1984, especially p. 23. 87 percent nation-wide professed to be "very happy" or "pretty happy"; 87 percent of blacks and 80 percent of Hispanics did so. (The happiest lot, according to this reckoning, were the Scandinavians with 94 percent.) Corresponding figures for being happy or reasonably happy in their marriage were: 97 percent nationwide, 94 percent for blacks, 98 percent for Hispanics. For their financial situation: 71 percent nationwide, 55 percent for blacks, 71 percent for Hispanics.

25 For the optimist's case, see Joseph Nye, *Bound to Lead: The Changing Nature of American Power*, New York, Basic Books, 1990. See also interview with Joseph Nye by Frederic Smoler, " "Are We Really Going the Way of the British Empire," *American Heritage*, May–June 1991, pp. 45–56.

26 "Discreditable," *The Economist*, 4 January 1992, p. 20.

27 "White Collar Workers: Too Many Computers Spoil the Broth," *The Economist*, 24 August 1991, p. 30.

28 For a thoughtful analysis see Edward P. Lazear, "The Labor Market and International Competitiveness," in Anderson and Bark, *Thinking About America*, pp. 367–82.

29 See editorial in the *Wall Street Journal*, 19 November 1992.

30 "Can America Compete," and editorial, *The Economist*, 18 January 1993, pp. 13–14, 65–6.

31 Takashi Oka, "Interview with Takashi Sakayia: Japan Needs Creative Work Force," *Christian Science Monitor*, 14 August 1991, p. 7; "Japan Encourages Its Young: Management Focus," *The Economist*, 10 August 1991, p. 55.

32 *Economic Report of the President Transmitted to the Congress January 1989*, Washington, DC, Government Printing Office, 1989, p. 129.

33 "American Survey: Fear of Foreigners," *The Economist*, 10 August 1991, pp. 15–16.

34 Herbert Stein, "Reflections on Recession," *The American Enterprise*, July–August 1991, p. 6–9. See also Nye, *American Heritage*, and McKenzie, *America: What Went Right*.

35 "Economic and Financial Indicators," *The Economist*, 15 August 1992, p. 90.

36 Just before World War I, the proportion of GNP devoted to defense stood as follows: 3.4 for Britain, 4.6 for Germany, 4.8 for France, 6.3 for Russia. British industrial production went up from 54 in 1880 to 100 in 1913 (1913 equalling 100). The output of key raw materials during the same period went

up as follows (in million tons): coal, 149 to 268; steel, 1.3 to 6.5; pig iron 7.8 to 11. See A. J. P. Taylor, *The Struggle for Mastery in Europe 1848–1918*, Oxford, Clarendon Press, 1954, p. xxix–xxxiii; Murray Weidenbaum, *Military Spending and the Myth of Global Overstretch*, Washington, DC, Center for Strategic and International Studies, 1991, Significant Issues Series, vol. xl, no. 4, p. lx, 3.

37 United States Arms Control and Disarmament Agency, *World Military Expenditures and Arms Transfers*, Washington, DC, Government Printing Office, 1989, pp. 69, 71.

38 Other works that criticize the assumption that America is in decline include Murray Weidenbaum, *Rendezvous With Reality: The American Economy After Reagan*, New York, Basic Books, 1988; C. Michael Aho and Marc Levinson, *After Reagan: Confronting the Changed World Economy*, New York, Council on Foreign Relations, 1988.

39 Weidenbaum, *Military Spending and the Myth of Global Overstretch*, p. lx, 3.

40 Defense expenditure, in million pounds, stood as follows in Europe in 1880: France, 31.4; Russia, 29.6; Britain, 25.2; Germany, 20.4. See Taylor, *The Struggle for Mastery in Europe*, p. xxviii.

41 See for example, Joshua Muravchik, *Exporting Democracy: Fulfilling America's Destiny*, Washington, DC, American Enterprise Institute, 1991.

42 See *New York Review of Books*, 5 November 1992, p. 59.


Conclusion and Recommendations

1 James Schlesinger, "New Instabilities, New Priorities," *Foreign Policy*, no. 85, Winter 1991–2, p. 7.

2 See McKenzie, *America: What Went Right, passim.*

3 "You Can't Go Home Again," *The Economist*, 28 September 1991, p. 15.

# Bibliography

Eli Abel, *The Shattered Bloc: Behind the Upheaval in Eastern Europe*. Boston, Houghton Mifflin Co. 1990.

David M. Abshire, *Preventing World War II: A Realistic Grand Strategy*. New York, Harper and Row, 1988.

William James Adams, *Restructuring the French Economy: Government and the Rise of Market Competition Since World War II*. Washington, DC, The Brookings Institute, 1989.

C. Michael Aho and Marc Levinson, *After Reagan: Confronting the Changed World Economy*. New York, Council on Foreign Relations, 1988.

Annelise Anderson, *The Ruble Problem: A Competitive Solution*. Stanford, CA, Hoover Institution Press, 1992.

——, and Dennis L. Bark (eds), *Thinking About America: The United States in the 1990s*. Stanford, CA, Hoover Institution Press, 1988.

Timothy Garton Ash, *The Magic Lantern: The Revolution of '89 Witnessed in Warsaw, Budapest, Berlin and Prague*. New York, Random House, 1990.

Dennis L. Bark and David R. Gress, *A History of West Germany*, 2 vols, Oxford, Blackwell, 1992.

Richard J. Barnett, *The Alliance: America-Europe-Japan: Makers of the Postwar World*. New York, Simon and Schuster, 1983.

Monika Beckman-Petey, *Der Yugoslavische Föderalismus*. Munich, Oldenbourg, 1990.

James D. Bell, *Catching the Boat: The 1992 Opportunity: An Atlantic Business Perspective*. Washington, DC, The Atlantic Council of the United States, Occasional Paper.

Cyril E. Black, Jonathan E. Helmreich, Paul C. Helmreich, Charles P. Issawi, and A. James McAdams, *Rebirth: A History of Europe Since World War II*. Boulder, CO, Westview Press, 1992.

Daniel J. Boorstin, *America and the Image of Europe*. New York, World Publishing Co., 1964.

J. F. Braun, *Surge to Freedom: The End of Communist Rule in Eastern Europe*. Durham, NC, Duke University Press, 1991.

Janice Brown and Grazyna Sikorska, *Conscience and Captivity: Religion in Eastern Europe*. Washington, DC, Ethics and Public Policy Center, 1988.

Stanley A. Budd and Alun Jones, *The European Economic Community: A Guide to the Maze*. London, Kogan Page, 1989.

Michael Burgess, *Federalism and European Union: Political Ideas, Influences and Strategies in the European Community, 1972–1987*. London, Routledge, 1989.

Alfred Cahen, *The Western European Union and NATO: Building a European Defense Identity Within the Context of Atlantic Solidarity*. London, Brassey's, 1989.

Center for Strategic and International Studies, *The Atlantic Partnership: An Industrial Perspective on Transatlantic Defense Cooperation*. Washington, DC, CSIS, 1991.

Daniel Chirot (ed.), *The Crisis of Leninism and the Decline of the Left*. Seattle, WA, University of Washington Press, 1991.

Walter C. Clemens, *Can Russia Change? The USSR Confronts Global Interdependence*. Boston, Unwin Hyman, 1989.

——, *Baltic Independence and the Russian Empire*. New York, St Martin's Press, 1991.

Nicholas Colchester and David Buchan, *Europe Relaunched: Truths and Illusions on the Way for 1992*. London, The Economist Books, 1990.

Susan M. Collins and Dani Rodrik, *Eastern Europe and the Soviet Union in the World Economy*. Washington, DC, Institute for International Economics, 1991.

James A. Cooney, Gordon A. Craig, Hans Peter Schwarz, and Fritz Stern (eds), *The Federal Republic and the United States: Changing Political, Social and Economic Relations*. Boulder, CO, Westview Press, 1984.

——, Wolfgang-Uwe Friedrich, and Gerald R. Kleinfeld (eds), *Deutsch-Amerikanische Beziehungen*. Frankfurt, Campus Verlag, 1980.

Robert Conquest (ed.), *The Last Empire: Nationality and the Soviet Future*. Stanford, CA, Hoover Institution Press, 1986.

David P. Conradt, *The German Polity*. New York, Longman, 1989.

Ralf Dahrendorf, *Society and Democracy in Germany*. Garden City, NY, Doubleday and Co., 1969.

——, *Reflections on the Revolution in Europe*. New York, Time Books, 1990.

S. J. Deitchman, *After the Cold War: US Security for the Future*. Washington, DC, The Atlantic Council of the United States, 1990.

David Dimbleby and David Reynolds, *An Ocean Apart: The Relationship Between Britain and America in the Twentieth Century*. New York, Random House, 1988.

Robert A. Divine, *Since 1945: Politics and Diplomacy in Recent American History*. New York, Alfred A. Knopf, 1985.

Jacques Delors, *Le Nouveau Concert Européen*. Paris, Editions Odile Jacob, 1992.

Rachel Denber, *The Soviet Nationality Reader: The Disintegration in Context*. Boulder, CO, Westview Press, 1992.

Gerald A. Dorfman and Peter J. Duignan, *Politics in Western Europe*. Stanford, CA, Hoover Institution Press, 1991.

Alex N. Dragnich, *Serbs and Croats: The Struggle in Yugoslavia*. New York, Harcourt Brace Jovanovich, 1992.

Peter Duignan and L. H. Gann, *The Rebirth of the West: The Americanization of the Democratic World, 1945–1958*. Oxford, UK, and Cambridge, MA, Blackwell, 1991.

David A. Dyker, *Yugoslavia: Socialism, Development and Debt*. New York, Routledge, 1990.

L. H. Gann (ed.), *The Defense of Western Europe*. London, Croom Helm, 1987.

Charles Gati, *The Bloc That Failed: Soviet-East European Relations in Transition*. Bloomington, IN, Indiana University Press, 1990.

Andre W. M. Gerrits, *The Failure of Authoritarian Change: Reform, Opposition and Geo-politics in Poland in the 1980s*. Aldershot, Hants, Dartmouth Publishing Co., 1990.

Paul Ginsborg, *A History of Contemporary Italy: Society and Politics: 1943–1988*. London, Penguin Books, 1990.

Misha Glenny, *The Fall of Yugoslavia*. London, Penguin, 1992.

Andrew J. Goodpaster, Walter J. Stoessel, and Robert Kennedy, *U.S. Policy Toward the Soviet Union: A Long-Term Western Perspective 1987–2000*. Lanham, MD, University Press of America, 1988.

Mikhail Gorbachev, *The August Coup: The Truth and the Lessons*. New York, Harper-Collins, 1991.

Stephen R. Graubard (ed.), *Eastern Europe . . . Central Europe . . . Europe*. Boulder, CO, Westview Press, 1991.

William E. Griffith (ed.), *Central and Eastern Europe: The Opening Curtain?* Boulder, CO, Westview Press, 1989.

Györgi Gsepeli, *Structures and Content of Hungarian National Identity*. Frankfurt-am-Main, Verlag Peter Lang, 1989.

Lubomyr Hajda and Mark Beissinger (eds), *The Nationalities Factor in Soviet Politics and Society*. Boulder, CO, Westview Press, 1990.

D. L. Hanley, A. P. Kerr, and H. H. Waites, *Contemporary France: Politics and Society Since 1945*. London, Routledge and Kegan Paul, 1979.

Wolfram F. Hanrieder, *Germany, America, Europe: Forty Years of German Foreign Policy*. New Haven, CONN, Yale University Press, 1989.

Vilho Harle and Jyrki Iivonen (eds), *Gorbachev and Europe*. London, Pinter, 1990.

Stephen Haseler, *Anti-Americanism; Steps in a Dangerous Path*. London, Institute for European Defense and Strategic Studies, 1986.

Paul Hollander, *Anti-Americanism: Critiques at Home and Abroad: 1965–1990*. New York, Oxford University Press, 1991.

Francis Jacobs and Richard Corbett, *The European Parliament*. Boulder, CO, Westview Press, 1990.

Carl-Heinz Janson, *Totengräber der GDR*. Düsseldorf, Econ-Verlag, 1991.

Robert Jervis and Seweryn Bialer (eds), *Soviet-American Relations After the Cold War*. Durham, NC, Duke University Press, 1991.

Anthony Jones, Walter D. Conor, and David E. Powell (eds), *Soviet Social Problems*. Boulder, CO, Westview Press, 1991.

Tony Judt, *Marxism and the French Left: Studies on Labour and Politics in France, 1830–1981*. Oxford, Clarendon Press, 1986.

——, *Past Imperfect*. Berkeley, CA, University of California Press, 1992.

Robert D. Kaiser, *Why Gorbachev Happened: Making Sense of the Man and His Revolution*. New York, S. and S. Trade, 1991.

Bártlomiej Kamiński, *The Collapse of State Socialism: The Case of Poland*. Princeton, NJ, Princeton University Press, 1991.

Lawrence S. Kaplan, *NATO and the United States: The Enduring Alliance*. Boston, MA, Twayne, 1988.

Paul Kennedy, *The Rise and Fall of the Great Powers . . . .* New York, Random House, 1987.

Robert O. Keohane and Stanley Hoffmann (eds), *The New European Community: Decision-making and Institutional Change*. Boulder, CO, Westview Press, 1991.

Norman Kogan, *A Political History of Italy: The Postwar Years*. New York, Praeger, 1983.

János Kornai, *The Road to A Free Economy: Shifting from a Socialist System, The Example of Hungary*. New York, W. W. Norton, 1991.

Stephen Kotkin, *Steeltown, U.S.S.R.: Soviet Society in the Gorbachev Era*. Berkeley, CA, University of California Press, 1991.

Roman Laba, *The Roots of Solidarity, 1982–1985*. Princeton, NJ, Princeton University Press, 1991.

Robbin F. Laird and Susan L. Clark, *The USSR and the Western Alliance*. Boston, Unwin Hyman, 1990.

Walter Laqueur, *Europe in Our Time: A History 1945–1992*. New York, Viking, 1992.

F. Stephen Larrabee (ed.), *The Two German States and European Security*. New York, St Martin's Press, 1989.

Finn Laursen, *EFTA and the EC: Implications of 1992*. Maastricht, Netherlands, European Institute of Public Administration, 1990.

Christiane Lemke and Gary Marks (eds), *The Crisis of Socialism in Europe*. Durham, NC, Duke University Press, 1992.

Juliet Lodge, *The European Community and the Challenge of the Future*. London, Pinter, 1989.

William Roger Louis and Hedley Bull (eds), *The Special Relationship: Anglo-American Relations Since 1945*. Oxford, Clarendon Press, 1986.

Harold Lydall, *Yugoslavia in Crisis*. New York, Oxford University Press, 1989.

Ernest Mandel, *Beyond Perestroika: The Future of Gorbachev's Russia*. New York, Routledge, 1989.

Richard Mayne (ed.), *Handbook to the Modern World: Western Europe*. New York, Facts on File Publications, 1986.

——, *The Recovery of Europe*. London, Harper and Row, 1970.

Michael K. MccGwire, *Perestroika and Soviet National Security*. Washington, DC, The Brookings Institution, 1991.

Colin McInnes, *Nato's Changing Strategic Agenda: The Conventional Defense of Central Europe*. London, Unwin Hyman, 1991.

Peter H. Merkl (ed.), *The Federal Republic of Germany at Forty*. New York, New York University Press, 1989.

Thomas Moore, *Privatization Now or Else: The Impending Failure of Democracy and Freedom*. Stanford, CA, Hoover Institution Press, 1991.

Kenneth O. Morgan, *The People's Peace: British History 1945–1989*. Oxford, Oxford University Press, 1990.

Roger Morgan, *West European Politics Since 1945: The Shaping of the European Community*. London, B. T. Batsford, 1972.

John Morrison, *Boris Yeltsin, from Bolshevik to Democrat*. New York, Dutton, 1991.

Joshua Muravchik, *Exporting Democracy: Fulfilling America's Destiny*. Washington, DC, American Enterprise Institute, 1991.

National Defense University, *The Alliance at Forty: Strategic Perspectives for the 1990s, and Beyond*. Washington, DC, 1991.

Daniel M. Nelson, *Romanian Politics in the Ceauşescu Era*. New York, Gordon and Breach, 1988.

Neill Nugent, *The Government and Politics of the European Community*. Houndsmill, Hants, Macmillan Education, 1991.

Joseph Nye, *Bound to Lead: The Changing Nature of American Power*. New York, Basic Books, 1990.

William Park, *Defending the West: A History of NATO*. Boulder, CO, Westview Press, 1986.

Stanley G. Payne, *The Franco Regime 1936–1975*. Madison, WI, The University of Wisconsin Press, 1987.

Elizabeth Pond, *After the Wall: American Policy Toward Germany*. New York, Twentieth Century Fund, 1990.

Gwyn Prins (ed.), *Spring in Winter: The 1989 Revolutions*. Manchester, Manchester University Press, 1990.

Henry S. Rowen and Charles Wolf, Jr. (eds), *The Future of the Soviet Empire*. New York, St Martin's Press, 1987.

R. J. Rummel, *Lethal Politics: Soviet Genocide and Mass Murders Since 1917*. Brunswick, NJ, Transaction Publishing, 1990.

Jean De Ruyt, *European Political Cooperation: Toward a Unified European Foreign Policy*. Washington, DC, Atlantic Council of the United States, Occasional Paper, 1989.

Anthony Sampson, *Anatomy of Europe*. New York, Harper and Row, 1968.

——, *The Changing Anatomy of Britain*. New York, Vintage Books, 1984.

Leigh Sarty, *The Soviet Union Under Gorbachev 1985–1990*. Ottawa, Center for Canadian-Soviet Studies, Carleton University, 1990.

Sbagia, Alberta (ed.), *Euro-politics: Institutions and Policy Making in the "New" European Community*. Washington, DC, Brookings Institution, 1992.

René Schwok, *US-EC Relations in the Post-Cold War Era: Conflict or Partnership?* Boulder, CO, Westview Press, 1991.

Robert Sharlet, *Soviet Constitutional Crisis from De-Stalinization to Disintegration*. New York, Armonk, 1992.

Alexander Shtromas and Morton A. Kaplan (eds), *The Soviet Union and the Challenge of the Future*. 4 vols, New York, Paragon House, 1988-9.

Michael Silva and Bertil Sjögren, *Europe 1992 and the New World Power Game*. New York, John Wiley, 1990.

Stanley R. Sloan (ed.), *NATO in the 1990s*. Washington, DC, Pergamon-Brassey's, 1989.

Michael Smith, *Western Europe and the United States: The Uncertain Alliance*. London, George Allen & Unwin, 1984.

Michael J. Sodaro, *Moscow, Germany and the West from Krushchev to Gorbachev*. Ithaca, NY, Cornell University Press, 1990.

Vladimir Solovyov and Elena Klepikova, *Boris Yeltsin: A Political Biography*. New York, Putnam and Sons, 1992.

Richard F. Staar, *The Communist Regimes in Eastern Europe*. 5th edn, Stanford, CA, Hoover Institution Press, 1988.

——, *East-Central Europe and the USSR*. New York, St Martin's Press, 1991.

——, *Foreign Policies of the Soviet Union*. Stanford, CA, Hoover Institution Press, 1991.

——, *The New Russian Armed Forces: Preparing for War or Peace?* Stanford, CA, Hoover Institution Press, 1991.

Gale Stokes (ed.), *From Stalinism to Pluralism: A Documentary History of Eastern Europe Since 1945*. New York, Oxford University Press, 1991.

Keith Sword (ed.), *The Times Guide to Eastern Europe*. London, Time Books, 1990.

Ian Thomson, *The Documentation of the European Communities: A Guide*. London, Mansell, 1989.

Vladimir Tismaneu, *The Crisis of Marxist Ideology in Eastern Europe: The Poverty of Utopia*. London, Routledge, 1988.

Horst Tomann, *The Transition Problem in Eastern Europe: Some Lessons for Germany*. Berlin, Institute für Wirtschaftspolitik- und Wirtschaftsgeschichte, 1992.

Gregory F. Treverton (ed.), *The Shape of the New Europe*. New York, Council of Foreign Relations, 1991.

Frank Trommler and Joseph McVeigh (eds), *America and the Germans, an Assessment of a Three-Hundred Year History*, vol. 2., Philadelphia, PA, University of Pennsylvania Press, 1985.

Adam B. Ulam, *The Communists: The Story of Power and Lost Illusions: 1948–1991*. New York, Scribner's, 1992.

——, *The Rivals: America and Russia Since World War II*. New York, Viking, 1971.

Derek W. Urwin, *The Community of Europe: A History of European Integration Since 1945*. London, Longman, 1991.

Willem F. van Eekelen, *The Changing Environment of Transatlantic Relations*. Paris, European Strategy Group, 1991.

William Wallace, *The Transformation of Western Europe*. New York, Council on Foreign Relations Press, 1990.

Murray Weidenbaum, *Rendezvous with Reality: The American Economy After Reagan*. New York, Basic Books, 1988.

Stephen White, *Gorbachev in Power*. Cambridge, Cambridge University Press, 1990.

——, Alex Pravda, and Zvi Gitelman (eds), *Developments in Soviet and Post-Soviet Politics*. Durham, NC, Duke University Press, 1992.

Rolf Winter, *Ami go home, Plädoyer für den Abschied von einem gewalttätigen Land*. Munich, Goldmann Verlag, 1990.

Vincent Wright, *The Government and Politics of France*. New York, Holmes and Meier, 1989.
Boris Yeltsin, *Against the Grain: An Autobiography*. New York, Summit, 1991.

# Index

# INDEX